DATE					

The Mexican University and the State

The Mexican University and the State

Student Conflicts, 1910–1971

By Donald J. Mabry

 Texas A&M University Press, College Station

Library of Congress Cataloging in Publication Data

Mabry, Donald J., 1941–
    The Mexican University and the state.

        Bibliography: p.
        Includes index.
        1.   Universidad Nacional Autónoma de México—
Students—History—20th Century.   2.   Student
movements—Mexico.   I.   Title.
LE7.M62M25   378′.1981   81-48377
ISBN 0-89096-128-X   AACR2

Manufactured in the United States of America
FIRST EDITION

To Mark and Scott

Contents

Preface

THE National Autonomous University of Mexico (UNAM) is not only the principal educational and cultural institution of that nation, but also one of the chief oppositionist centers to the national government. It is one of the few national institutions to escape the tutelage of the state. This autonomy was won in 1929 and has been maintained since principally by UNAM students, who have been quick to defend their institution against governmental attempts to control it. Ironically, perhaps, UNAM is also the principal training ground for those who govern Mexico. The university and the state coexist, as they have for decades, in a state of tension.

This study is a history of the university-state conflict since the reopening of the university and the beginning of the Mexican Revolution in 1910. It is not a history of the university; that task belongs to someone else. Instead, this work traces the history of major student conflicts to illuminate the issues that brought confrontation between the national government and the national university. Contrary to popular mythology, there have not been many great conflicts but many small ones instead, usually confined to a single school and limited to local issues.

The major conflicts involved the role of the Mexican university in the society at large. Government officials tended to demand that the university value economic development most highly, whereas universitarios put academic freedom as their first priority. Intermingled with this issue has been the university demand that the government provide funds but no control. Because such student-oriented issues as class attendance or examination systems often provided the immediate impetus for a strike, one can easily misread the fundamental issues at play. Students played the role of "shock troops" through petitions, demonstrations, acts of violence, and tumults. They were excitable, idealistic, and, as children of the elite, relatively immune from harm. That student leaders did not always understand the role of their strikes in the larger conflict attests to their innocence.

Some student leaders did become successful politicians in their post-university lives, for the university and its internal politics taught them more than academic subjects. Thus, student politics are part of national politics. In my research, I made efforts to trace the careers of student politicians as one means of understanding Mexican national politics.

Although student politics have interested me for the past quarter-century, my interest in this topic is part of my general interest in the origins and operations of oppositionist political movements. Research into the origins of the Partido Acción Nacional uncovered the possibility of a systematic study of university student politics in the 1920s and 1930s. As is often the case, further investigation led to an expansion of the topic and a change of focus in order to encompass the broad sweep of student upheavals in UNAM since 1910.

Researching this history proved to be more involved than I had imagined it would be when I began the project some years ago. Many files of student organizations were destroyed in conflicts or were not available. I accepted the advice of Mexican friends not to interview participants in recent events, because the participants were still concerned about the consequences of sharing their perceptions. Instead, the story was pieced together from many different and scattered sources. Periodicals, especially newspapers, provided the skeleton. Memoirs, ephemeral literature, archival data, and studies provided most of the flesh. The result, however, is a comprehensive account. There is little reason to believe that anything significant was missed.

The trail of sources led to many people and institutions. During four trips to Mexico, materials were located in the Biblioteca Nacional, Hemeroteca Nacional, Biblioteca del Instituto Nacional de Antropología e Historia, Biblioteca del Colegio de México, Biblioteca Central de UNAM, Biblioteca de México, Biblioteca de la Universidad de las Américas, Biblioteca Miguel Lerdo de Tejada, the Archivo Histórico de UNAM, and the Archivo Ezequiel A. Chávez of UNAM, among others. Larissa Lomnitz, Ana Ma. Rosa Carrión, and María Carmén Ruiz Castañeda were especially helpful in locating materials. In the

United States, I was fortunate to have access to the resources of Mitchell Memorial Library of Mississippi State University, the Television Archives of Vanderbilt University, Watson Memorial Library of the University of Kansas, the Latin American Collection of Tulane University, and the Library of the Center for Inter-American Relations in New York. Peter H. Smith generously allowed me to use his massive machine-readable biographical archive.

Many people in the United States played a role in the progress of this study. I appreciate the help of John C. Henry, Jim Scally, John Britton, Jack Corbett, Libby Nybakken, and Earl B. Brand, Jr.; each contributed something unique. Bob and Estela Shafer gave me hospitality and food for thought more than once during my forays into Mexico. Rod Camp performed yeoman duty in reading the manuscript, sharing his data and his thoughts, and encouraging me throughout the process; his support is an unpayable debt.

Financial support for the research and writing of the book came from several different sources, all of which deserve recognition. At Mississippi State University, Chester McKee and the Office of Research and Graduate Studies, Lyell Behr and Charles Lowery of the College of Arts and Sciences, and the MSU Development Foundation aided the work. The American Philosophical Society awarded me a small grant at a critical juncture. Sue, my wife, and Mark and Scott, our sons, provided the vast majority of the funding by yielding claims on the family's fiscal resources just as they gave me the necessary time.

The responsibility for the finished product is mine.

DONALD J. MABRY

Abbreviations of Student Organizations

ACJM. Asociación Católica de la Juventud Mexicana (Mexican Catholic Youth Association)—traditional Catholic youth group founded in the 1910s.

CESM. Confederación Estudiantil Socialista de México (Socialist Student Federation of Mexico)—left-wing group founded in 1934 and later reorganized into the CESUM.

CESUM. Confederación de Estudiantes Socialistas Unificados de México (Confederation of Unified Socialist Students of Mexico)—leftist group formed in 1938 to replace the CESM.

CEU. Consejo Estudiantil Universitario (University Student Council)—created in April, 1966, to oust Ignacio Chávez from the rectorship and re-create student governance of UNAM; left-wing.

CIDEC. Confederación Iberoamericana de Estudiantes Católicos (Iberoamerican Catholic Student Federation)—right-wing hemispheric Catholic group created in Mexico in 1938.

CJM. Confederación de Jóvenes Mexicanos (Federation of Mexican Young People)—government-backed political arm of the Partido de la Revolución Mexicana / Partido Institucional Revolucionario.

CNE. Confederación Nacional de Estudiantes (National Student Federation)—the principal student organization until it split into left and right wings in the 1930s; after 1935 the CNE was right-wing.

CNECM. Confederación Nacional de Estudiantes Católicos de México (National Federation of Mexican Catholic Students)—created in 1926 to insure that preparatory students would receive Catholic indoctrination and to resist the anticlerical state; in 1931, it became UNEC.

CNED. Central Nacional de Estudiantes Democráticos (National Central of Democratic Students)—communist youth group active in the 1968 conflict.

CNER. Confederación Nacional de Estudiantes Revolucionarios (National Federation of Revolutionary Students)—left-wing group created in 1928 and active into the mid-1930s.

CNH. Consejo Nacional de Huelga (National Strike Committee)—the student strike organization in 1968.

CoCo. Coordinador de Comités de Lucha (Fight Committees Coordinator)—left-wing student group organized in 1971.

FEM. Federación Estudiantil Mexicana (Mexican Student Federation)—the UNAM student group created in 1916 and also known by the acronyms FEU and FEUM. The group split several times, and its separate groups have held various ideological positions.

FER. Federación de Estudiantes Revolucionarios (Revolutionary Student Federation)—leftist group of the 1930s.

FET. Federación de Estudiantes Técnicos (Technical Students Federation)—created in the 1930s by technical school students, by the 1940s it was the FNET and was supported by the government.

FEU. Federación Estudiantil Universitaria (University Student Federation)—also known as the FEM and FEUM.

FNET. Federación Nacional de Estudiantes Técnicos (National Federation of Technical Students)—government-backed technical school students' organization.

FUER. Frente Único Estudiantil Revolucionario (Only Revolutionary Student Front)—left-wing group created in the 1930s.

FUSA. Federación Universitaria de Sociedades de Alumnos (University Federation of Student Societies)—short-lived (1961–1966) organization of some UNAM student societies.

MURO. Movimiento Universitario de Renovadora Orientación (University Movement of Renovational Orientation)—ultrareactionary PRI student group, often seen as clerical.

UNEC. Unión Nacional de Estudiantes Católicos (National Catholic Students Union)—Jesuit-sponsored university student organization of the 1930s and early 1940s; center-right in politics.

The Mexican University and the State

1. Introduction

THE re-creation of the National University of Mexico in 1910 symbolized Mexico's entrance into the world of modern nations, for the university was to be living proof that the nation had escaped the barbarism that many thought was characteristic of the nation's public life in the nineteenth century. The university, with its National Preparatory School (Escuela Nacional Preparatoria, ENP), its professional schools, and the new School of Graduate Studies, was to be the place where the finest minds, young and old, would gather to deliberate in peace and tranquility on the mysteries of the universe and the best means of advancing material and scientific progress. It was to be the central cultural and educational institution, one that would guide generations to come. The child of Justo Sierra, leading intellectual and secretary of public education, it was the gift of Porfirio Díaz, president and dictator (1876–1880, 1884–1911), on the centennial of the founding of the nation. Scholars and administrators from around the world were invited to the inaugural ceremonies to witness the progress that had been made. Little did anyone know that the university would not only serve these functions but would also become one of the principal centers of opposition to Mexican governments.[1]

Porfirio Díaz was unlikely to realize the implications of the founding of the university, for he was unaccustomed to serious opposition.

[1] Justo Sierra first proposed the re-creation of the university in 1881; see his "La Universidad Nacional (proyecto de creación)," *El Centinela Español*, February 10, 1881. Daniel C. Levy, *University and Government in Mexico: Autonomy in an Authoritarian System*, p. 138, asserts that the re-creation was an act of the positivists, but see Juan Hernández Luna, "Sobre la fundación de la Universidad Nacional: Antonio Caso *vs.* Agustín Aragón," *Historia Mexicana* 16 (1967): 368–381, for the argument that positivists resisted Sierra. There is little question that positivism was the dominant philosophical mode within the new university, however.

The strongman of the nation since his successful revolt in 1876, he had suborned, repressed, and outfoxed the opposition for years. If tough generals dared not threaten him, how could intellectuals and students pose a serious threat? The faculty were supporters of the system, the students those who benefited from it. More dangerous rivals, such as General Bernardo Reyes and former treasury minister José Yves Limantour, had been unofficially exiled. The most recent aspirant to the presidency, Francisco I. Madero, had been safely ensconced in jail. He would be allowed to escape to the United States in October 1910 after Díaz and the university were inaugurated.

Politicians should have known better, for the university had a long history of political controversy. Founded originally by royal cédula in 1551 as the Royal and Pontifical University, it had trained much of the social elite of Spain's most valuable colony. By 1775, some 29,882 *bachillerato* degrees, as well as 1,162 degrees of *maestro* and *doctor*, had been granted. Staffed primarily by ecclesiastics, the university had imparted Spanish scholastic values to generations of colonials, thus serving as one bulwark of the social order. In 1833, when the Liberals finally took power and sought to destroy the colonial past, the university was attacked for its conservative, traditional, and ecclesiastical character. Vice-President Valentín Gómez Farías issued orders to suppress the university. Outraged at these and other Liberal measures, Conservatives demanded the ouster of the Liberals; Antonio Santa Anna, the president who had been safely on leave in 1833, rallied to the cause and established a Conservative government. The university was reopened in 1834, only to be suppressed again in 1857 when the Liberals came back to power. The next year the Conservative party regained control of Mexico City and reopened the university. Battered in the storms of the Liberal-Conservative conflicts of the ensuing years, the university was definitively closed in 1865 by Maximilian, Emperor of Mexico. Its constituent parts survived the waves of fortune and misfortune, being shifted in and out of different legal statuses, but preserving some continuity with the past.[2]

[2] Arturo González Cosío, *Historia estadística de la Universidad, 1910–1967*, p. 17; Lucio Mendieta y Núñez, *La reforma universitaria integral*, pp. 17–22; Raúl Carrancá, *La universidad mexicana*; Julio Jiménez Rueda, *Historia jurídica de la Universidad*, pp. 65, 73.

The Liberals, led by President Benito Júarez and Secretary of Public Education Gabino Barreda, founded a new institution, the Escuela Nacional Preparatoria, to lead Mexican higher education. The Prepa, as its alumni affectionately called it, was to give a common cultural experience to all those who eventually pursued professional studies. Part secondary school, part college, the Prepa was exclusive and all-encompassing. To complete its curriculum and to graduate was to guarantee oneself entrance into one of the professional schools: law, medicine, engineering, plastic arts, or philosophy. Unlike that of the old university, the Prepa curriculum of five years was designed and taught by the most modern thinkers Mexico could produce—positivists, men who sought to use scientific methodology to modernize the nation. The reformers sought to override whatever conservative and obscurantist teachings might survive in the professional faculties. In their view, graduates of the Prepa, few in number, would be a cadre that would modernize Mexico.

The dream of Juárez and Barreda evolved differently, however, for the conquest of power by Díaz in 1876 changed the direction of the nation. Positivism continued to dominate the teaching and curriculum of the Prepa and the professional faculties, but freedom of inquiry was eroded by the demands of the dictatorship. Educators were expected to acquiesce, at least, to the national government. Rather than leading the nation onto the path of systematic, critical inquiry, the Prepa and the professional schools tended to produce persons allied with the dictatorship. Foreign ideas and books predominated in the classrooms and libraries. The system produced imitative rather than original thinkers.[3]

Sierra's goal was to stimulate debate and learning while giving coherence to higher education by creating a single institution with an arts and sciences graduate school as its capstone. Administratively, the new university was the Prepa, the professional schools, and the new Escuela de Altos Estudios, governed by a rector and a University Council. A director headed each school and, with two faculty representatives, sat on the University Council with the rector and his key aides. Sierra failed to obtain autonomy for the university, for the president of

<hr>

[3] Michael E. Burke, "The University of Mexico and the Revolution, 1910–1940," *The Americas* 34 (1977): 252–254.

the nation appointed the rector, but he had gotten students the right to sit on the council without a vote.[4]

This organizational scheme evolved slowly as different governments or different rectors came to power. Until the creation of secundarias (secondary schools, roughly equivalent to grades seven through nine in the United States), post-elementary students entered the National University through the ENP (or a comparable institution). Students who successfully completed this five-year curriculum then directly entered a facultad or escuela of the university. The preparatory system provided the general education commonly provided in the first two years of college in the United States system. The distinction between a facultad and an escuela is not absolutely clear except that the former are the traditional disciplines and the latter tend to be more professionally oriented. For this study the distinction is not important. As the need arose, the university subdivided existing schools (from law came the schools of economics and social and political sciences) or created new ones. The rector would retain most of his powers, but the council would be modified in membership with the addition of voting students and, in 1945, put under the control of a governing board (junta gubernativa). These changes and the other conflicts in governance are part of the subject of this study and will be treated later.

The National University has dominated twentieth-century Mexican education and culture, as Sierra had hoped. As the prestigious institution, its curricula and organization would be emulated by other universities. Between 1910 and 1971, the period of this study, it granted more degrees than any other Mexican university and enrolled more than half of the nation's university students. By 1920, there were only five state universities; in 1940, that number had grown to seven and the private Universidad Autónoma de Guadalajara had been created. UNAM's preparatory school was *the* preparatory school. One indication of the importance of the National University was that 70 percent of the national political elite attended it. Dominating Mexican education more than even this suggests, the university "incorporates" the degrees of other institutions into its system; that is, it recognizes such degrees as equivalent to its own after it certifies the quality of the curricula and instruction. Through its vast cultural programs, institutes,

[4]"Ley constitutiva de la Universidad Nacional de Mexico," *Boletín de Instrucción Pública* 14 (1910): 638–646.

publishing efforts, and electronic media, it nurtures and arbitrates Mexican culture.[5]

The dream of such an institution almost died aborning, for the Mexican Revolution began only a few months after the university's official inauguration in September 1910. The Revolution (always capitalized in Mexico to identify the revolution that began in 1910 and still continues, according to Mexican officials) is dated from November 20, 1910, the day Francisco I. Madero called for it to begin. In fact, however, the Revolution began in different places at different times for different reasons. Madero and the Anti–Re-electionist party, which drew members from the middle and upper strata of society, primarily wanted political democracy ("Effective Suffrage, No Re-election") to replace the aging dictatorship of Díaz. Workers revolted against years of exploitation. Peasants were most interested in "Land and Liberty," the battle cry of the followers of Emiliano Zapata, for they had been squeezed off their lands, forced into debt peonage, and discriminated against in favor of foreigners. Zapata (and others like him) fought to restore the rights of the peasantry; he became one of the symbols of the Revolution. From Chihuahua state, far to the north of Zapata's central Mexico, came Pancho Villa leading cowboys and other members of the rural masses in the fight for a more just social order. Industrial workers and miners rose against the conditions nurtured by the Porfirian regime. Nationalists from all classes demanded an end to foreign penetration. Between November 1910 and May 1911, many groups revolted against the established order.

The Revolution developed from events and the desires of people, not from a coherent ideology, and those like Madero who could not understand the revolutionary dynamic were swept aside by violence. Irregular armies so bloodied the national army that Díaz resigned and went into exile in May 1911, to be replaced by interim president Francisco de la Barra, who was to hold office until his successor could be inaugurated in November after the October elections. Madero easily won that election, because he had become a national hero for his op-

[5] On the importance of UNAM in political recruitment, see Roderic Camp, *Mexico's Leaders: Their Education and Recruitment;* see Peter H. Smith, *The Labyrinths of Power: Political Recruitment in Twentieth-Century Mexico,* pp. 46–47, 84–86, 103, for data on university enrollments, the role of UNAM, and political recruitment. Richard King, *The Provincial Universities of Mexico,* places these institutions in perspective.

position to Díaz, but he failed to secure control of the nation. The Por-firist factions remained armed and free to plot a counterrevolution, while the Zapatista and Villista demands for redress of grievances were sent to committee for study. Zapata revolted against Madero during the latter's first month in office; others soon followed. Madero also alien-ated laborers by using government troops to break strikes. Seeing the weakness of the Madero government, ambitious men began to plot or to lead revolts. Some led government troops; others massed irregular armies recruited during the anti-Díaz revolt. General Victoriano Huerta, who had served Díaz as well, overthrew the Madero govern-ment in February 1913 with the aid of Porfirio Díaz's nephew Félix and the compliance of U.S. Ambassador Henry Lane Wilson. Three days later, Madero and Vice-President José María Pino Suárez were "shot while trying to escape." Huerta was thereafter seen as a murderer and counterrevolutionary, even though he instituted social reforms while president.

The murder of Madero and the usurpation by Huerta kindled the flames into a raging fire for the next four years as rival leaders threw armies against each other in hope of gaining control of the nation. Ve-nustiano Carranza of Coahuila proclaimed himself First Chief of the Constitutionalist Armies, vowed to avenge Madero's death, and prom-ised to restore constitutional government. A political moderate with ties to the Porfiriato, which he had served as a senator, Carranza began promising land and labor reforms, as the struggle continued, in order to gain support from the masses. Joining him were Álvaro Obregón and Plutarco Calles of Sonora. Obregón, a farmer, emerged as the most effective general of the Revolution, a sympathizer of the plight of workers and peasants, and a shrewd politician. Villa, who revered Madero as a somewhat mystical figure, cooperated with Carranza, whom he disliked, in the effort to oust Huerta. Zapata continued his fight against any government that would not meet the demands of his people. When Huerta left in July 1914, the victorious generals began to fight each other for supremacy. The leading factions met in the Con-vention of Aguascalientes (1914–1915) and elected Eulalio Gutiérrez as president, but control would be established by bullets, not ballots. By late 1916, Carranza, with the decisive help of Obregón, had won con-trol of enough of the country to call a constitutional convention.

Even the United States, though uninvited, joined the fray, for

President Woodrow Wilson decided to teach Mexicans how to be democratic, and used force to do it. To protect the oil fields of Tampico from the nearby armies of Huerta and revolutionaries and to try to interdict the flow of arms to Huerta's government through the port of Veracruz, the Wilson administration invaded Veracruz in April 1914 and took control of the two cities. This intervention hastened the resignation of Huerta but raised the ire of Mexican nationalists. In 1916, the United States invaded again, sending General John Pershing into Chihuahua and south in hot pursuit of Villa, who had raided New Mexico in a desperate attempt to rally nationalists to support his political ambitions. Mexicans came through the Revolution with strong xenophobic sentiments, directed primarily against the United States.

Neither Wilson nor Carranza understood the Revolutionary dynamic, for the Mexico envisioned by the Constitution of 1917 was dramatically different from the 1857 document treated so cavalierly by Huerta in 1913. The armed struggles had clarified the goals of the Revolution, especially for the many generals who served as delegates to the constitutional convention. The new constitution forbade foreigners from owning land near the national borders or engaging in politics and gave the president the right to eject them summarily from the country. Subsoil mineral rights were returned to ownership by the nation, a provision that mining and petroleum companies (primarily foreign in ownership) would resist. Property ownership was declared to be a social right subject to definition by the state. Large landed estates (haciendas) were forbidden in favor of small property holdings and ejidos (communal or collective farms). Laborers were guaranteed not only the right to organize and strike but also such rights as minimum wages, profit sharing, and owner-supplied educational facilities. Article 3 of the new constitution guaranteed that primary education would be free, obligatory, and *secular*. Radical anticlericals were determined to limit the access of the Roman Catholic church and other religious groups to young minds. Many Revolutionaries saw the church as the embodiment of reactionary politics and obscurantism, usually allied with their recent opponents. The constitution sought more than the separation of church and state; it sought to weaken, if not destroy, the church as an institution. The church could own no real property; its clergy lost all political rights. Religion was to be an entirely private matter; clergy were forbidden to wear clerical garb in public, and religious symbols could not be used by political parties. The Constitution of 1917 was redefining Mexico as a secular nation in which the interests of the workers and peasants were paramount.

People, not constitutions, determine policy. Carranza and subsequent presidents would choose which parts of this constitution to follow in the name of the Mexican Revolution. Carranza was no radical, but he proclaimed the constitution in February 1917 rather than invite another civil war. He enforced those provisions with which he agreed, an easy task because the document contained a number of contradictory ideas. Arguing that the non-re-election stipulation did not apply in his case since he was only First Chief, he had himself elected president. Rather than enforce national ownership of subsoil minerals and provoke dangerous opposition from domestic and foreign interests, he temporized while taking a nationalistic stance. Not until Cárdenas in 1938 would any president dare to fully enforce this provision, although Calles began enforcing some of it in late 1925. A similar fate befell many of the other "radical" constitutional provisions: only when a president agreed with them and thought enforcement possible would they be implemented.

Governments between 1917 and 1934 had to contend with strong oppositionist forces, often willing to resort to violence. Carranza had won control, but army generals and regional strongmen (caudillos) remained powerful. When Carranza tried to impose a successor in 1920, Obregón and others successfully revolted. Carranza was murdered while fleeing to Veracruz, possibly in hopes of going into exile. Sonorans took control of the nation. Adolfo de la Huerta served as interim president until Obregón was elected for 1920–1924. The third Sonoran, Calles, served the 1924–1928 term. Obregón had to put down a serious rebellion led by de la Huerta in 1923 when Calles was chosen as the government candidate for the presidency. Calles had to fight the very serious Cristero rebellion of 1926–1929. Although never as serious as these, other revolts or threats of violence by strongmen harried presidents in these years. Equally serious was the attitude of the United States toward Mexico, for the government in Washington had the power to influence Mexican conditions.

Washington had three principal concerns about Mexican developments. The fighting created claims by U.S. citizens against the Mexican government. Land redistribution also affected U.S. citizens. The issue of petroleum ownership was constantly raised, for powerful men in the United States were deeply disturbed by the Mexican constitutional provisions. Until some of these issues could be resolved, Washington refused to recognize the Obregón government.

Obregón, a political realist, made the moves necessary to pacify the United States and strengthen his own hold on the nation. His government renegotiated public indebtedness with U.S. bankers, thus recognizing the validity of the Revolutionary debt. Mexico also recognized U.S. claims. Through the Bucareli Agreements of 1923, Obregón made a "gentlemen's agreement" not to expropriate oil holdings if the companies had performed "positive acts," that is, had actually begun to exploit the property. The U.S. recognized the Obregón government shortly thereafter and helped it quash the de la Huerta rebellion. Workers and peasants also helped the government defeat the rebels, for Obregón redistributed land, supported the labor movement, fostered education for the masses, and pacified generals.

Calles expanded his predecessor's land and labor programs in addition to instigating his own social reform movement, but much of his attention was devoted to the church-state conflict and petroleum policy. When Calles began enforcing the anticlerical provisions of the constitution, resistance quickly grew into the Cristero rebellion. Catholics in the United States took a keen interest in these events, and some tried to pressure Washington into intervening in Mexico. The U.S. government had previously been pressuring Calles to guarantee oil rights, an issue that Calles tried to compromise without seeming to sell out to the powerful northern neighbor. In 1928, before either issue was settled, Obregón was assassinated by a Catholic fanatic before the Revolutionary hero could take the presidency to which he had just been re-elected. Calles left office as scheduled in 1928, but he had taken the steps necessary to settle differences with the United States, pave the way for a truce in the church-state conflict, and create a political system that would guarantee that people like himself would control politics for generations.

Calles continued to dominate Mexican politics as jefe máximo through 1934. Interim president Emilio Portes Gil (1928–1929) was no stooge, but he could not ignore Calles. Pascual Ortiz Rubio (1929–1932), even though an elected president, found Calles's influence so strong and the problems of the economic depression so great that he resigned. Abelardo Rodríguez (1932–1934), who was as conservative as Calles had become, understood his role and carried it out. Because of Calles's domination, Mexican historians refer to the period as the Maximato.

Lázaro Cárdenas (1934–1940) ended Calles's influence and re-kindled the Revolutionary spirit with massive social reform and a reorganization of politics. Cárdenas sought to extend the power of the state into almost every important sphere, creating what Mexican historian Arnaldo Córdoba calls a corporatist state. Peasants were organized into the National Peasant Confederation; workers were encouraged to join the Mexican Workers Confederation; and even business and industry were required to join national confederations. In 1938, Cárdenas created the Partido de la Revolución Mexicana, organized into four sectors—peasants, workers, military, and popular. Cárdenas and the left had begun their move in 1933 by getting the presidential nomination from the government party for the young general and governor, and continued it by implementing pro-labor and pro-peasant policies after Cárdenas took office in December 1934. When Calles objected too strenuously to this leftward shift, he was exiled in 1935. In his six-year term, Cárdenas changed Mexico. He redistributed more land (usually into ejidos) than did all of his predecessors combined. Workers were given control of the nationalized railroads. Foreign oil properties were nationalized in 1938. Socialists were not only heard and given government posts but their ideas were sometimes implemented. Cárdenas became the spokesman of the Revolution, and conservatives feared him. [6]

The Cárdenas administration represented the peak of Revolutionary fervor, for subsequent presidents have usually been less controversial and more conservative. Manuel Ávila Camacho (1940–1946) was chosen because he represented order, stability, and moderation, which many wanted after the drama of Cardenismo. Ávila Camacho was also the last of the Revolutionary generals to become president; the demilitarization program in which he participated was achieving success. Cognizant of the discord created by social reform and the anticlericalism of the 1930s and of the dangers and opportunities presented by

[6] Arnoldo Córdoba, *La política de masas de Cardenismo* and *La formación del poder político en México*.

U.S. participation in World War II, Ávila Camacho sought national unity. The reorganization of Cárdenas's PRM into the Partido Revolucionario Institucional (PRI) in 1946 perhaps best symbolized this change in tone. Henceforth, the Revolution was institutionalized and only needed people to administer it. Subsequent presidents have come from the bureaucracy of the PRI.

In the years since 1946, Mexico has continued to have controversy, but nothing approaching that which surrounded Cárdenas. President Miguel Alemán (1946–1952), the first graduate of the national university to hold that office, pursued pro-business, pro-industry, and pro-U.S. policies at the expense of the masses. Rapid economic growth, generated by the war and post-war conditions, eased the burden, however. Adolfo Ruiz Cortines (1952–1958) continued the industrialization policies of his predecessor but tempered them with public works and other programs that helped the average citizen. His reputation for honesty in contrast to the reputation for corruption of the Alemán administration helped him defeat his three opponents in the 1952 presidential elections. Adolfo López Mateos (1958–1964), former secretary of labor, adopted a moderate reformist strategy by such measures as land redistribution and increasing education budgets, but quickly crushed railroad and teacher strikes in 1959. Gustavo Díaz Ordaz (1964–1970) was a hardline conservative who tolerated little dissent. He defeated the doctors' strike of 1964–1965 by outmaneuvering them and crushed the 1968 student movement with soldiers; he left office a much-despised man. Luis Echeverría (1970–1976), the minister of gobernación (government) under Díaz Ordaz, shared some of the culpability for the deaths of 1968 and sought to placate his opposition by pouring money into education, advocating a "democratic opening," and using leftist rhetoric in domestic and international arenas. Economic problems, exacerbated by international inflation, quantum jumps in energy prices, government deficit spending, and declines in investor confidence, made Echeverría one of the least popular presidents in recent Mexican history.

Throughout the twentieth century, Mexicans have debated and fought over what kind of society the nation should be. Few would assert that they want to recreate the capitalistic, exploitative, and neocolonial society of Porfirio Díaz, although some have wanted to do so and others assert that it has happened. Most demand social justice for the general population while disagreeing as to what the term means. The constitution and other political documents promise fair elections, equality of opportunity, equality before the law, profit sharing, fair wages, land redistribution, and other measures designed to guarantee a decent livelihood, together with the elimination of monopoly and privilege. Governments claim to be the embodiment of the Mexican Revolution, and thus manipulate its symbols in public rituals. In practice, however, Mexican governments have sacrificed some or all of these promises, depending on the circumstances, in favor of rapid capitalistic development. Different groups in society have tried to lever the government to adopt policies they advocate. The levers used have included lobbying, personal friendship, demonstrations, riots, rebellion, and control of key organizations. The National University has been one of these key organizations and a battleground for persons trying to influence national policy or seek personal gain. Some of the conflict within the National University outlined in this book is part of a larger national struggle.

The National University has a life of its own aside from its role in Mexican history. It is a self-perpetuating organization with a support network independent of the national government from which it receives its funding. Only the Catholic church surpasses its historical continuity from the early colonial days to the present, but the church must operate in an officially anticlerical state. The university represents a more modern religion, the belief in the efficacy of education. It defines its mission as the search for truth and as the enabling of Mexicans to improve their physical and cultural condition. The words of venerated politicians, educators, and intellectuals are cited to bolster this self-definition. Publicly committed to pluralism in ideas, it can and does resist efforts to teach an official ideology. The acceptance of this role by most decision-makers is aided by the fact that so many have been students of the university or teach there. Loyalty to the institution is strong, even though most students never graduate and professors teach only a course or two. The national government, with the exception of a period in the 1930s, has funded the university in spite of differences between the two.

It is this independence of the university and its self-definition that have brought it into conflict with the state. The latter has sought to control society, to centralize authority. The growth of an activist, centralizing state is one of the major themes of twentieth-century Mexican history. The state reaches down into labor unions, peasant cooperatives, and neighborhood associations through official agencies or the official party. In the Mexican system, the personification of the state is the national president, who wields enormous power. University leaders, however, argue that the university must be an exception because their institution must be able to examine any idea and must be a place where criticism, even of the state, can take place. The university must be privileged not for its own sake but for the good of society. Political leaders, either because of ideological differences or political ambition, have often refused to accept the university's self-definition. Instead, some have sought to control and direct the university.

This book is about the role of UNAM students in the confrontations between the university and the state and the efforts of the university to achieve and maintain its autonomy. It is not a history of the university, of Mexican politics, or even of student political activism, although elements of all three form part of the study. The book focuses on student politics and student strikes against the university, because the students obtained and then preserved university autonomy. Through their general strikes, they forced the state to intervene in the university. Moreover, many of the student leaders later assumed major political posts in the state and, in turn, had to deal with a new generation of striking students, demonstrating that the university and the state are interlocked in spite of the differences in their missions.

The history of the conflict between the state and the university further illuminates the political socialization of those who govern Mexico. Many politicians cut their political teeth by engaging in university student politics. Others occupied no student leadership posts but did spend formative years in this politicized environment, where they established lifelong relationships with activist students and professors. This complex socialization process is only beginning to become clear as scholars study the phenomenon in Mexico. Those familiar with Mexican history and politics will recognize most of the names mentioned in the text or accompanying notes, however. Roderic Camp's forthcoming book on the socialization of Mexican political elites, to be published by the Fondo de Cultura Económica in Mexico, examines the issue in detail.

The focus on student political activity is important for another reason. The students argued for university autonomy and co-government (cogobierno), the two principal goals of the Latin American University Reform Movement. This movement, usually dated from the student upheaval at the University of Córdoba in Argentina in 1918, demanded an autonomous university, democratic university governance through elected administrators and student parity with faculty members on governing councils, modern curricula and instruction, and no required class attendance. The Reform Movement saw the university and its students as the agents of social change and criticism of the government. These ideas spread rapidly to other Latin American countries after 1918 and formed the ideological basis for university struggles in a number of countries. Through international student congresses, held first in Mexico in 1921, students exchanged ideas and built networks. Even in Mexico, the Reform Movement was cited as a goal and as a justification for student actions, even though most of the ideas were advocated in Mexico prior to 1918.[7]

Students of the National University of Mexico have consistently expressed interest in social reform and criticism of the state, regardless of their or the state's ideological bent. In part, this represents the idealism of youth, the belief that a better world is possible if only older adults were not so blind or corrupt. Perhaps equally important, these expressions represent a rebellion against established authority as a younger generation tests its muscles against those in power. The strikes developed a ritualistic character, with all participants understanding the unspoken rules. Further, the social-reform content of the Mexican Revolution encouraged students to advocate social justice as an act of patriotism. This book traces these events and suggests how seriously one should take such activities.

[7] On the origins of the University Reform movement see such works as Joseph Tulchin, "Origins of Student Reform in Latin America: Córdoba, 1918," *Yale Review* 61 (1971): 575–590; David Spencer, ed., *The Latin American Student Movement*; Richard J. Walter, *Student Politics in Argentina*. See also *The Latin American University*, edited by Joseph Maier and Richard W. Weatherhead, particularly José Luis Romero, "University Reform," pp. 135–146, and Alistair Hennessy, "Students in the Latin American University," pp. 147–184. The Córdoba Manifesto is reprinted in Spencer, pp. 21–25. In that same volume, see also David Spencer, "Latin American Student Politics and University Reform," pp. 9–13; Chris Hamilton, "Origins of the University Reform Movement: Student Politics in Argentina between 1918 and 1922," pp. 14–20; and Luigi Einardi, "University Autonomy and Academic Freedom in Latin America," pp. 39–50. *Daedalus* (Winter 1968) devotes the entire issue to students and politics.

Faculty members play an important role in the story but not to the same extent as do students. Until the late 1940s, virtually all UNAM faculty members practiced a profession full-time outside the university and only taught an occasional course; even after the creation of full-time professorships, the number of part-time faculty members remained high. The influence of these part-timers is hard to determine, but in terms of intellectual formation it has been higher than most scholars have suspected. Nevertheless, it cannot compare with that of a student leader who entered the university as a prep student and stayed on a daily basis for seven to ten years. When possible, this study will note which faculty members were influential in student politics.[8]

The study is divided into chronological parts to demonstrate the dynamics of the subject. Chapter 2 starts with the founding of the National University in 1910 and stops just before the general strike of 1929. Because the 1929 strike is pivotal, all of chapter 3 is devoted to it. Chapter 4 examines student politics under the first autonomy law and ends with the passage of the second autonomy law in 1933. Chapter 5 is the story of UNAM's attempt to survive without government financial support. Chapter 6 covers the 1935–1944 period, during which the rapprochement between the university and state took place. Chapter 7 describes that long period (1945–1961) during which the third autonomy law and the accession of pro-government rectors brought relative peace to the university. Student activism increased in the 1960s, and chapter 8 sketches this development until the incident in July 1968 that led to the bloodiest student-state conflict in Mexican history. Chapter 9 briefly examines the 1968 movement and its aftermath through June 10, 1971. More has been written on this period than any other, so the account in this study is not detailed. Chapter 10, the last, puts the history of the university-state conflict into perspective.

[8] Donald J. Mabry and Roderic Camp, "Mexican Political Elites, 1935–1973: A Comparative Study," *The Americas* 31 (1975): 452–469; Roderic Camp, *Mexican Political Elites: 1935–1975*; Peter H. Smith, Codebook Transformed Dataset on Political Elites in Mexico, 1900–1971, and companion data file on computer tape (on file at The University of Wisconsin, Madison); and the Roderic Camp collection of letters from Mexican public persons form the basis for biographical data on students who later became important politicians.

2. The First Phase of the Conflict, 1910–1928

THE state changed dramatically during the first eighteen years of the national university's existence. Founded in 1910 during what proved to be the last year of the Porfiriato, the university had not completed its first year before the old dictator was replaced by an interim president in May 1911. The election of Francisco I. Madero that year seemed to promise the advent of a democratic state in which a university could flourish, but Madero's opposition, from the left and the right, conspired and undermined the new president. Madero's murder and Huerta's coup in 1913 marked the beginning of a period of civil war, rebellion, changing governments, scarce resources, and uncertainty that would last until Venustiano Carranza finally emerged the victor in 1916. Even though Carranza himself was ousted in 1920, he brought some order and stability to the nation and had been shrewd enough to minimize efforts of the United States to determine national policies and to accept the (then) radical Constitution of 1917. Presidents Obregón (1920–1924) and Calles (1924–1928) would further strengthen the state by building political coalitions, implementing social reform measures, expanding state activity, neutralizing opponents, and maintaining the United States at a comfortable distance. By 1928, this bigger, interventionist state with a publicly stated social reform mission would have been unrecognizable to the people of the Porfiriato.

The clashes of ideas and people during this redefinition of the state were epic. Many of the victorious ideas were expressed in the constitution (such as nationalism, social justice, and opposition to monopoly and privilege); others, such as socialism, became part of the ordinary conversation of the politically minded. Opponents of the Revolution muttered in private or cloaked themselves in Revolutionary rhetoric. Caudillos stalked the land. A few, such as Carranza,

Obregón, and Calles, commanded national attention. Some were only able to dominate their state or region. Younger men, such as Vicente Lombardo Toledano and Manuel Gómez Morín, were initiating public careers that led to national political and intellectual prominence after 1928. These last two cut their political teeth in the National University. University students have often opposed the administration of their universities and, by extension at least, the state of which the university is an agency.

Students began opposing the state even before the National University was founded in 1910. Most students supported the Díaz regime and the positivist philosophy prevailing in the university, but a few expressed opposition to either or both. Others protested the lack of funding for their schools.[1] Rather than being the beginning of a university-led campaign against the dictatorship, these conflicts were local, however. Nevertheless, the incidents suggest some of the common reasons why students and other university people have consistently opposed the government.

The Díaz government had little difficulty in handling these isolated student protests, which lacked the organizational clout necessary to mobilize the general university-level population. Law students, in 1896, demonstrated against Díaz in front of a government building, but rurales quickly intervened and dispersed the demonstrators. No immediate repercussions were apparent, although two of the student leaders, Querido Moheno and José Ferrel, later played an active part in opposing Díaz. Moheno eventually rose to a cabinet post in the Huerta government (1913–1914), and Ferrel ran against Diego Redo, the Díaz candidate, for governor of Sinaloa. Medical students began opposing the government as early as June 1907, as a result of a seemingly insignificant incident. Although there was latent hostility toward the director of the school, Dr. José Terres, a Díaz appointee, left a June 6 meeting of the medical school in a huff when he misinterpreted hissing at a late student arrival as an insult directed toward himself. Stu-

[1] Ciriaco Pacheco Calvo, "La organización estudiantil," *El Universal*, March 20, 1934; Jorge Prieto Laurens, *Cincuenta años de la política mexicana*, p. 17; and Prieto Laurens, "El verdadero proceso histórico estudiantil," *El Universal*, March 28, 1934. Pacheco Calvo also published *La organización estudiantil en Mexico*, but, because I saw the newspaper articles first, I will usually cite them. They appeared in *El Universal* on March 20, 22, 27, and April 4, 6, 1934. There is little, if any, difference.

dents protested the director's behavior and his high-handed treatment of students. After some students were expelled, those who remained organized a Sociedad de Alumnos de la Escuela Nacional de Medicina, an organization that would play an important role in university politics in the summer of 1910.[2]

Only a few cases of isolated anti-Díaz activity occurred in 1910. The first real student strike against Díaz apparently occurred in the Instituto Científico y Literario of San Luis Potosí; it was led by Juan Barragán, later a Revolutionary general, federal deputy, and president of the Partido Auténtico de la Revolución Mexicana. Barragán, a law student at the time, asserted that the students, led by the Maderist Student Club (of which he was secretary), declared a strike on March 21, 1910, in opposition to the seventh re-election of Díaz. Significantly, the Maderist Club contained a number of students who would later play prominent roles in Mexican politics. With the death of Madero in 1913, most of these students joined the Constitutionalist cause to fight either with arms or with pen against Victoriano Huerta, the man who many thought responsible for Madero's death. Barragán himself left the university to begin a lifelong career as a soldier-politician. Jorge Prieto Laurens, prominent in early student movements and the first phase of the Revolution, remembered that he and a few other students supported General Bernardo Reyes as the opposition to Díaz, wearing red carnations to symbolize their discontent with the old dictator, but later became partisans of Madero.[3] No doubt other isolated cases of anti-Díaz sentiment could be catalogued, but there was no sustained anti-Díaz student movement until the Primer Congreso Nacional de Estudiantes of September 6–18, 1910, a few days before the official inauguration of the new National University. Yet even this Primer Congreso emerged from particularistic concerns rather than from a more generalized sentiment.

[2] Alfredo Ibarra, Jr., "El contenido transcendente de nuestra Revolución," *El Nacional*, November 20, 1944; "Oposición estudiantil al General Díaz," *Excelsior*, November 28, 1937. The June 1907 student leaders were Alfonso Cabrera, José Prado Romana, Manuel Escontría, and José Siurob.

[3] Agustín Arriaga Rivera, "El movimiento juvenil," in *México: Cincuenta años de revolución*, p. 220; Juan Barragán, "La primera huelga de estudiantes," *El Universal*, May 19, 1967, and Juan Barragán letter to Roderic Camp, April 3, 1974. Some of the Maderist club students who rose to prominence were Manuel Aguirre Berlanga, Constitutionalist deputy and secretary of gobernación, Gonzalo Santos, governor of San Luis Potosí and regional strongman, and Gabriel García Rojas, Supreme Court justice.

Students from the National School of Medicine butted heads with the government in the summer of 1910. They sent an open letter to Justo Sierra, minister of public instruction, to complain of filthy, unhygienic conditions in the school, the lack of financial support for the school, and the deception practiced by the medical school administration in showing Sierra only the best parts of the school during his June 15 visit. Medical student protests mounted when they found the government unresponsive to their petitions. By June 25, they were complaining that the government shut them out of practical experience and income by appointing regular physicians instead of interns to the General Hospital. A student commission visited Díaz to argue their case. The wage reduction for interns passed by the Senate particularly stuck in their craw; Díaz promised to overturn the Senate law if necessary, a promise that seemed to shock the students by its demonstration of the irrelevance of the Congress. Adding fuel to student discontent was an incident in Puebla on July 7 wherein two students, Luis Sánchez Pontón and Alfonso G. Alarcón, were jailed for agitation. To the students, their legitimate right to protest had been violated by the police. Alarcón was one of the principal organizers of the Primer Congreso. Aided by other students, Alarcón and Sánchez Pontón were released, but the casualness with which the Díaz dictatorship treated elite students engendered resentment.[4]

This rising student resentment burst forth during the Primer Congreso, called by medical students to discuss issues facing all students in higher education. On July 24, 1910, *El País*, the daily newspaper with the largest circulation in the nation, published the call for the congress and its agenda. On September 6, delegates from each higher education institution were to meet in Mexico City to discuss a laundry list of student concerns: the best means of appointing professors to teaching posts, the necessity of student participation in the formulation of rules and regulations in the schools (the new university would allow students to have a voice in the University Council, but no vote), the relationship of non-official schools with the government, relations between schools in Mexico City and the states, examination systems, disciplinary measures, the problems of casual or irregular students, and the necessity of developing solidarity among students.

[4] *El País*, June 15, 21, 26, 1910. This newspaper was Catholic in its editorial policy.

Cabrera, Escontría, and Alarcón, all of the medical school, organized the congress with the aid of representatives of every major school in the Federal District. The fourteen-person organizing committee included two women as well as Gustavo P. Serrano (later secretary of industry and commerce under Ávila Camacho) and Luis L. León (later secretary of agriculture under Calles). The students of each school were to elect delegates; the state schools were allowed three delegates each but only one vote. Porfirio Díaz was invited to preside over the opening and closing ceremonies; the congress was not planned as an anti-Díaz meeting.[5]

Initially, the congress proceeded as planned. The day before it opened on the sixth, officers were elected. Only Atilano Guerra and Serrano of the organizing committee repeated as officers, serving as president and vice-president, respectively. Sánchez Pontón and Alarcón, semi-martyrs at this point, became second vice-president and second secretary, respectively. Women were not ignored, for among the officers was Isabel Díaz González of Toluca, who later became a national political leader. Although the Federal District students represented a majority of the one hundred delegates, state students were given ample representation to preserve the congress's claim to national scope. Some of the delegates became important political or intellectual figures: Aarón Sáenz, Alfonso Reyes, Rafael Heliodoro Valle (a Honduran who later taught in the university and then represented his country in Washington), and León. Emilio Portes Gil of the Tamaulipas Normal School had been elected a delegate but his state governor refused to allow him to attend.

The opening speeches praised the nation and stressed the importance of students to the future of the nation. U.S. imperialism was attacked and the Díaz government criticized for detaining Rubén Darío, a critic of U.S. foreign policy, in Jalapa so he could not attend the ceremony. During the following days, the students debated examination policy, finally deciding that there should be two reconocimientos (written exams) during the year and that professional exams ought to be both practical and theoretical. The congress agreed that irregular students could revalidate their courses after removing their incompletes by taking the same exams as regular students. The delegates also agreed that Anti-Reelectionists (who opposed Díaz) could be professors.[6] All of these issues would reappear more than once in the history of the university, although in somewhat different guises.

What appeared to be an inconsequential student meeting days before the September 16 centennial celebration of Mexican independence quickly took an anti-government turn. Francisco Castillo Nájera and others began demanding democracy in Mexico and the resignation of Díaz. On the thirteenth, mounted police were sent into the Alameda to break up a student political rally called to protest the arbitrary nature of the Díaz regime, using the Rubén Darío case as a rallying cry. The arrested students were soon released and the incident was closed, but many of the congress delegates joined the anti-Díaz revolution in the ensuing months.[7]

Independently of this stillborn student movement, Catholic students were seeking an alternative to the official ideology, positivism. The state, officially anticlerical, had in fact allowed the Catholic church some latitude in building churches and holding social congresses. In the university, however, Catholic ideas were virtually ignored by positivist professors except to denigrate them. Because of this hostility, a small group of Catholic students from the Escuela Nacional Preparatoria (ENP), the commerce school, and the national normal school formed, in 1910, the Sociedad Filosófica-Católica de Estudiantes under the leadership of Father Vicente Zaragoza. The group met only on Sunday mornings, but it included Prieto Laurens, Montes de Oca, and René Capistrán Garza, who formed the Liga de Estudiantes Católicos, which became the youth wing of the National Catholic Party in 1911. Eventually, these and other students formed the Asociación Católica de la Juventud Mexicana in 1913 under Father Bernardo Bergoend and would participate in the state-church conflict of the 1920s. In their student

[6] *El País*, September 6–10, 1910; Pacheco Calvo, "La organización estudiantil," *Reforma Universitaria*, August 25, 1957; Emilio Portes Gil, *Autobiografía de la Revolución Mexicana*, pp. 99–100; Alfonso G. Alarcón, *Burla, burlando: Anales epigramáticas del grupo de delegados al Primer Congreso Nacional de Estudiantes, reunido en la ciudad de México en 1910*, pp. 9–17 ff.; and Rafael Heliodoro Valle, et al., *Añoranza del Primer Congreso de Estudiantes* (1910).

[7] Portes Gil, pp. 99–100; Alarcón, pp. 12–14. All became cabinet officers or senators, or both; they were: Aarón Sáenz, Jorge Prieto Laurens, Martín Luis Guzmán, Luis Montes de Oca, Marte R. Gómez, and Froylán C. Manjarrez.

days, however, they sought to keep Catholic thought alive in the university.[8]

The initial student protest movement of September 1910 against the Mexican government neither forestalled the university's inaugural ceremonies on September 22 nor led to a permanent national university student movement. The National University of Mexico formally opened amidst speeches praising the role of universities in society and of the National University in Mexican history (for the orators counted the Royal and Pontifical University and the new university as one), and predicting a brilliant future for students and professors alike in shaping the national destiny. Representatives of major universities in the world paraded in academic regalia, attesting to the prestige of the Mexican institution. For Justo Sierra, it was the culmination of years of effort; he had first suggested the idea in 1881. As he spoke to those gathered for the inaugural ceremonies he would dream that his university would become one of the great universities of the world and lead Mexico to higher levels of achievement. He had failed to separate the university from the state—necessary, he thought, for free inquiry—but he had gotten students a voice on the University Council.[9]

As a state dependency with students who had demonstrated an interest in determining policy, the university was not placid its first year. The rector, appointed for a three-year term by the national president, was a creature of the government, responsible to the Secretary of Public Instruction. Although most students settled into the academic routine after September, a few joined the Madero cause. Secretary of Public Instruction Francisco Vázquez Gómez issued a call to students and professors to avoid forming political groups, which perhaps indicated that political agitation was increasing. Students were more likely to argue about grades and exams than national politics, however. Med-

[8] Prieto Laurens, Cincuenta años, p. 14. The literature on the Mexican Catholic youth movement is extensive; see Antonio Rius Facius, La juventud católica y la Revolución Mexicana, 1910–1925, and the bibliographic essay in Donald J. Mabry, Mexico's Acción Nacional: A Catholic Alternative to Revolution.

[9] Vlademar Rodríguez, "National University of Mexico: Rebirth and Role of the Universitarios (1910–1957)," pp. 19–22; Antonio Carrillo Flores, "El problema universitario de Mexico," Así (February 3, 1945): 20; Justo Sierra, "La Universidad Nacional (proyecto de creación)," El Centinela Español, February 10, 1881, in Jorge Pinto Mazal, La autonomía universitaria: Antología, pp. 23–27, "El gobierno y la Universidad Nacional," La Libertad, March 25, 1881, in Pinto Mazal, pp. 29–35, and "Inciativa para crear la Universidad," in Pinto Mazal, pp. 37–49.

ical students rebelled at exams in 1911, arguing that abandoning the reconocimientos (written exams) was unfair. Some were expelled until the new medical school director investigated the incident and reinstated them. Obtaining high grades was important but also expected. Law student grades ranged from 73 percent to 100 percent, with most being above 95 percent. Of the 114 students examined in 1909–1911, 112 or 98.2 percent passed. Rector Joaquín Eguía Lis faced a strike by students in the school of fine arts that same year. Students in the painting department declared a strike against the director of the school because they wanted painting raised to equal stature with architecture, the primary curriculum. The strike failed after several months. Eguía Lis was interested in separating architecture from fine arts, but such an action apparently needed congressional action, unlikely in the midst of a revolution with its changing governments.[10] The fall of Díaz in May 1911, the subsequent provisional presidency of Francisco de la Barra, and the presidential election of Madero in 1911 left little energy to be devoted to university problems.

The Revolution entered the university precincts in 1912 disguised as a student-versus-administration dispute over examination policy. Eguía Lis, who doubled as head of the Oficina del Registro Público de la Propiedad, was tied to Díaz. Although he managed to stay in power after Díaz fell, for Madero removed few of Díaz's henchmen from office, the arrival of Luis Cabrera, assistant law school director and a Madero supporter, to the directorship on April 20, 1912, signaled a change of direction. Cabrera was a moderate in the Revolution and was concerned with legalism and order. As he surveyed the law school, he saw enormous grade inflation resulting from the use of a final oral ex-

[10]"Ley Constitutiva de la Universidad Nacional de Mexico," *Boletín de Instrucción Pública*, 14 (1910): 638–646. On students in the Revolution, see Prieto Laurens, *Cincuenta años*, pp. 18–20. Francisco Vázquez Gómez, "Acuerdo por el que se recomienda a los profesores y alumnos de las escuelas dependientes de la Secretaría de Instrucción Pública y Bellas Artes que se abstengan de formar agrupaciones de caracter político," *Boletín de Instrucción Pública*, 18 (1911): 177–178. On the medical school conflict, see Joaquín Eguía Lis, *Informe del rector de la Universidad Nacional de México*, p. 53, and F. Zarraga, "Informe correspondiente a la marcha de la Escuela N. de Medicina del 1 de junio de 1910 al 8 de enero de 1912," *Boletín de Instrucción Pública* 19 (1912): 77–78. On law school grades, see "Informe que rinde la Secretaría de la Escuela Nacional de Jurisprudencia acerca de los trabajos hechos en la misma Escuela en el año de 1909–1910," *Boletín de Instrucción Pública* 15 (1911): 268–272. On the Bellas Artes strike, see Eguía Lis, *Informe*, p. 57.

amination instead of written exams twice a year as required by university statutes. Inevitably, the pass rate climbed to 95 percent (for fifth-year students in 1911–1912 it reached 100 percent) from its previous 85 percent rate. At the beginning of the academic year in 1912, Cabrera announced that the law school would return to written exams every four months. Students, aware that the secretary of public instruction would probably again exempt them, paid little attention at that point. Cabrera himself suggested that a mixed system might be used. The students and administration badly misjudged the situation.[11]

Lurking behind the examination question were other factors that prompted the student strike against Cabrera in June–July 1912. Most of the students and faculty had been supporters of the Porfiriato; Cabrera was the only Madero supporter who had an official position. President Madero and Vice-President José M. Pino Suárez were unpopular in the conservative school. Besides his ties to these two, Cabrera wanted to run a tight ship without interference from students or faculty members, was more apt to give orders and expect blind obedience than to negotiate and avoid confrontations. As a federal deputy candidate in Coayacán in the Federal District while director of the law school, he forced the issue of his political allegiances. The students, of course, wanted the easiest exam system possible and knew that going to the written trimesterly exams would mean that more would not pass. The exam issue was sufficient to make Cabrera unpopular, but resentment was deeper. Many thought Cabrera had misled them by not making his intentions clearer. Some thought he was hostile to students, for, during the first months of 1912, he had ended the practice of loaning library books overnight because, he said, students did not return them, and had closed the school's gymnasium and baths because they were left in filthy conditions. His firing of popular Porfirist politician Miguel S. Macedo, Mexico's greatest penalist and a leading con-

---

[11]This account is pieced together from the sources listed below; no subsequent citations will be made. "El 32 aniversario de la Universidad," *La Nación*, September 26, 1942, p. 26; Rodolfo Martínez Suárez, "La fundación de la Escuela Libre de Derecho," *Excélsior*, October 7, 1955; Eguís Lis, *Informe*, pp. 45–49; "Minutero histórico. Se funda la Escuela Libre de Derecho," *El Universal Gráfico*, July 24, 1944; Lucio Mendieta y Núñez, *Historia de la Facultad de Derecho*, pp. 169–178; Octavio González Cárdenas, *Los cien años de la Escuela Nacional Preparatoria*, pp. 226–228; Emilio Portes Gil letter to Roderic Camp, October 20, 1972; and Jesús Silva Herzog, *Una historia de la Universidad de México y sus problemas*, pp. 30–31.

servative, solidified the anti-Madero forces against him. It was the exam controversy, however, that served as the immediate cause of the strike.

Students quickly protested the bulletin-board notice, posted during the third week of June, stating that written exams would be given during the first week of July. That classes were to be suspended so that students could study brought little solace. Although the students complained that Cabrera had no right to introduce a new system (he responded by saying that the system had been approved in 1908) and that the written system was unfair because some classes had started in March and others in May, Cabrera held firm: the students were to obey the administration or leave the school. In a student meeting presided over by Alfonso Reyes, the students named a commission made up of Ezequiel Padilla, Guillermo Valenzuela, Enrique Domínguez, and Oscar Mendéndez to ask Vice-President and Minister of Public Instruction José Pino Suárez to intervene in their behalf. Pino Suárez agreed to see only one person. Padilla, the representative, explained the students' position and received the minister's request that their demands be put in writing. When Padilla reported back to the law students on the twenty-seventh, Cabrera, who was there, minimized the causes of the strike. To the students, Cabrera was demonstrating his contempt for them and his dictatorial nature. On June 29 they formed a strike committee led by Padilla, Leopoldo Ortiz, José María Gurría Urgell, and two students from each year of the school. Outside the committee but influential in the strike were Emilio Portes Gil, the MacGregor brothers, Luis and Vicente, and Manuel Herrera Lasso. The students decided to strike until Pino Suárez rendered a verdict on their petition. The strike action spread to demonstrations against Cabrera in Coayacán, an assault on a Japanese salesman, and altercations with the police. When Cabrera displayed increased hostility to the students during their July 1 meeting, they decided to send a commission back to Pino Suárez. When he refused to meet them, they got a meeting with President Madero. Madero, faced with the conservative-backed Pascual Orozco rebellion in the north, asked them to return to classes, pointing out that the strike was damaging to his administration during these tense days. Yielding to a few hundred students would seriously undermine his already tenuous authority.

At this point, what had been essentially an internal crisis became a test of the ability of Madero to govern. The president had little choice but to back Cabrera, since the strikers were receiving support from anti-Maderists. When the strike committee demanded Cabrera's resignation, the director lambasted the strikers, asserting that their demands were ridiculous, the director lambasted the strikers, asserting that their student support, that he intended to use his right to govern, and that Pino Suárez had authorized the use of police in the dispute. Cabrera closed the school for fifteen days, suspended the strikers, and expelled the leaders. Led by Padilla, who dramatically tore up his student credential, the strikers marched out of the meeting. At a subsequent meeting on July 4, the strikers issued a public statement that their complaint and actions were against Cabrera, not the government, and that they had named a committee to bring specific charges against Cabrera to Madero. If Madero would fire Cabrera, they promised to return to classes.

Had it not been for the substantial aid of conservative and wealthy lawyers, some of whom were former supporters of Díaz who were using the strike to embarrass Madero, the students would have had little choice but to capitulate within a few weeks. The expelled leaders would probably have been reinstated after a decent interval. The risks were high, however, and few students would have wanted to risk their professional careers by continuing the strike. Encouraged by the opposition to Madero, the students turned to the Colegio de Abogados de México and to wealthy law firms for aid in creating a new law school, one outside the jurisdiction of politicians. Those who responded were an honor roll of politicians and intellectuals of the old regime: Jorge Vera Estañol, Emilio Rabasa (who employed the brother of Gurría Urgell), Miguel Macedo, David Bernard, Alberto Palacios, Emilio Raz Guzmán, and others. By July 8, when enrollment began, 130 students had signed up for the new school, the Escuela Libre de Derecho.

At first, it looked as if the national law school was doomed. By July 24, the Escuela Libre, equipped with a building, an administration, a competent faculty (some of whom also taught in the national law school), and 178 students, opened for classes. The national law school, still under Cabrera's leadership, had reopened on July 15 in an effort to regain students but only 20 went to class that day. By the twenty-seventh, the students totaled 53 instead of the 239 before the strike. Congressmen

Nemesio García Naranjo, Francisco M. de Olaguíbel, and José María Lozano introduced a bill to grant the Escuela Libre a 50,000 peso subsidy. Its defeat may have saved the national law school. Within a few years, the national school regained its enrollment and surpassed its rival, whose anti-Madero role became anachronistic with his overthrow and death in 1913. In the months between the Escuela Libre's founding and Madero's demise, it served as an opposition center within a few blocks of the national palace.

The significance of the 1912 law strike, however, was in its longterm implications. Two of the strike leaders, Portes Gil and Padilla, later served Mexico at the highest governmental levels. Portes Gil was interim president, 1928–1930, during which time he had to face the first general university strike, and later served as one of the grand old men of Mexican politics. Padilla was secretary of education in 1929, Mexican ambassador to the United States during World War II, and the chief opposition presidential candidate in 1946. Other strike leaders served as prominent politicians, intellectuals, and university professors after they left the Escuela Libre. The Escuela Libre has survived to the present day by producing alumni who distinguished themselves.

The strike established a pattern for future student strikes. Students demanded high grades, easy exams, and a role in making educational policy. If rudely rebuffed by the administration, they would close the school and appeal to higher (usually presidential) authority. Outsiders with non-academic motives would surreptitiously intervene in the affair, using the students to attack the government in power or some other opponent. Even the creation of a rival institution would recur.

The university was inevitably caught up in the turmoil of the Mexican Revolution because it was an arm of the state and an elitist, conservative institution with Porfirian origins as well as with ties to the colonial past. The constitutive law of 1910[12] creating the university gave the president of the republic the right to name the university rector for a three-year term; the rector reported to the minister of public instruction and fine arts. The president or the minister had the power to hire

[12] "Ley Constitutiva" is the text. The legal structure is explained in Eguía Lis, *Informe*, pp. 8–9.

and fire professors and control the budget. Congress could not only use its budget-making power to control the university, but was also the original source of university authority; a power it would freely exercise during the Revolution. Each of the schools of the university was headed by a director who sat on the University Council, which governed the institution. The rector presided over the council as one of his administrative duties. The minister of education appointed four representatives to the council, and students and faculty members elected representatives from their schools. Students could only attend meetings dealing with academic matters and could not vote. Thus, although the university administration nominally controlled the institution, ultimate power rested in the hands of the president. The law students in 1912 knew this and went to the president to resolve the crisis rather than confining the dispute to the university itself.

In a nation with an 80-percent illiteracy rate, crushing poverty, and scarce fiscal resources, the National University, with its several thousand students and budget of 1,174,501 pesos, had little claim on the public purse. The exact number of students is unknown, but scattered data indicate that most were in the ENP, which had 1,345 students in 1910–1911. The law school, one of the larger professional schools, never had more than 388 in the first three years. The medical school, the largest, had only 557 students in 1918. Only 143 professional degrees of any kind were granted in 1911. The need for public education in the Federal District and the nation was at the primary-school level. Those who reached the ENP were mostly children of the well-to-do or the ambitious middle classes; few others could afford it even with scholarships. Thus the students tended to be the socially prominent, which, in the early days of the Revolution, meant that they were children of the Porfirian elite. That few of them actively supported the Revolution and many were openly hostile did not endear them to any government, be it Madero's, Huerta's, or Carranza's. Similarly, the professors also came from the same strata and held anti-Revolutionary views.[13] More serious, Mexican governments were strapped

[13]The budget figure for 1911–1912 is from Arturo González Cosío, *Historia estadística de la Universidad, 1910–1967*, p. 51, and represents approximately one percent of the total federal budget. On the ENP see Rodríguez, "National University," pp. 35–36. On law, see Eguía Lis, *Informe*, 45, but "informe . . . Jurisprudencia . . . 1909–1910," p. 272, says median annual attendance was 388. On medicine, see "Labores del Departamento Universitario, 1918–1919," *Boletín de la Universidad* 2 (1919): 9. Public school

for money as they sought to defend themselves from their armed opponents. Unfortunate, perhaps, for the university was the accident that it was born on the eve of a revolution.

The attacks on the university came quickly. As a result of the 1912 strike, an effort was made to omit the university from the national budget as well as to fund the Escuela Libre instead of the national law school. Both Porfirist and liberal congressmen thought the institution worthless. Ezquiel A. Chávez, one of the founders of the university, a politician who served both the Porfirian and early Revolutionary regimes, and twice rector after 1910, joined with Félix Palavicini, a liberal, to persuade Congress to fund the university, thus saving it. Rector Eguía Lis, in his annual report published in 1913, advocated all but financial separation of the university and state, an effort to get the university out of the political arena. Congress cut the budget of the Escuela de Altos Estudios by over 50 percent in 1912 and 1913 because they believed an arts and letters graduate school to be superfluous. Some congressmen criticized the school for using foreign intellectuals as professors. Chávez, named director of Altos Estudios, discovered that the school had only one paid professor, a German botanist whose contract was let during the Porfiriato, and Antonio Caso and Joaquín Palomo Rincón, who taught for free. The secretary of the school, Alfonso Reyes, resigned because his father Bernardo was involved in a plot to overthrow the Madero government; the son hoped to keep the school out of this political controversy. Chávez expanded the faculty by creating more non-salaried professorships, thus circumventing congressional hostility. That year Nemesio García Naranjo, an ultraconservative, made an effort to change the ENP curriculum, leading to its separation from the university and thus out of the liberals' hands, but the rector was able to block the move. In 1913–1914, a strike closed the Bellas Artes school with a posted notice that the school was closed "by order of the Revolution," that is, Diego Rivera, David Alfaro Siqueiros, and José Clemente Orozco led the students in what became a lengthy strike, lasting until 1916, in protest of traditionalism in the

---

(federal, state, and municipal) enrollment in 1905 was 575,972; private, clerical, and association schools had 152,917; the 68 professional schools and colleges taught 9,327; see *New York Times*, April 25, 1914. The Mexican population in 1910 was 15.16 million. Prieto Laurens, *Cincuenta años*, p. 13, says the ENP had little more than a thousand students in 1909; he asserts (p. 17) that most students and professors supported Díaz.

academy of art and in favor of incorporating it into the university (which they achieved). President Victoriano Huerta, who had overthrown Madero in 1913 and was implicated in his murder, issued a university statute to control the university, but it had little effect because he had to concentrate on repelling attacks from Carranza's Constitutionalist armies and President Woodrow Wilson of the United States.[14]

The year 1914 was little better. In March, President Huerta closed the medical school for two months because of riotous student behavior. Venustiano Carranza, as First Chief of the Constitutionalist armies, issued a decree removing the university from the president's authority, but it was irrelevant because he did not control the Federal District. When the United States invaded Veracruz in 1914, some students tried to link up with Obregón, Villa, Cándido Aguilar, and Zapata to resist Yankee imperialism, and Huerta militarized the university, ordering students to wear uniforms and to drill.[15] The national political situation was so confusing that university administrators were never sure who was in charge. Huerta went into exile in August. The Convention of Aguascalientes, called to find a compromise president, named Eulalio Gutiérrez, but Villa and Carranza began fighting for control of the country.

University administrators tried to escape the buffeting winds of the Revolution by asking for university autonomy. Minister of Education Félix Palavicini spoke for university autonomy in September 1914. A group of professors, led by Chávez, Julio García, and Jesús Galindo y Villa, proposed an autonomy law in December 1914. The proposed law would have allowed the faculty to elect the rector, a provision that probably would have doomed it, but the national political circumstance meant that nothing came of the proposal. Carranza began talking of creating a technical school that would be a people's university, an

[14] "32 aniversario," *La Nacional*, September 26, 1942, p. 26; Eguía Lis, *Informe*, p. 9; Eugenio Hurtado Márquez, *La universidad autónoma 1929–1944: Documentos y textos legislativos*, p. 8; Michael E. Burke, "The University of Mexico and the Revolution, 1910–1940," *The Americas* 34 (1977): 255; Alberto Bremauntz, *Autonomía universitaria y planeación educativa en México*, pp. 34–35.

[15] Ezequiel A. Chávez, letter, "Al Sr. Director de la Escuela Nacional de Medicina," March 9, 1914, in Archivo Ezequiel A. Chávez, UNAM, Caja I; Hurtado Márquez, *Universidad autónoma*, p. 8; Prieto Laurens, *Cincuenta años*, pp. 49–51; Miguel Castro Ruiz, "Altibajos de la Universidad desde su reaperatura hasta el movimiento de 1929," *La Nación*, July 2, 1951, p. 12.

obvious threat to the university. President Gutiérrez signed a decree in 1915 giving the university autonomy, but the victory of the Constitutionalist forces that year invalidated the decree. Rectors came and went as different armies occupied Mexico City. Chávez, elected on December 1, 1913, would not swear loyalty to Carranza, so he turned the rectorship over to Valentín Gama on September 2, 1914. Gama lasted until July 1, 1915, when José Natividad Macías took the post. Autonomy might have avoided this turnover, as its proponents argued, but no government stayed in power long enough to act.[16]

The Macías rectorship bore the brunt of government hostility during the first decade of the university. Revolutionary generals made an effort to raid the university budget to pay war costs; some wanted the university to award them degrees. Some politicians advocated abandoning higher education to private enterprise. The transitory Article 14 of the Constitution of 1917 eliminated the Secretariat of Public Education and Fine Arts, thus technically eliminating the university. A decree in April, however, created the Departamento Universitario y de Bellas Artes, but in July Carranza considered eliminating this department and putting the university back into the Secretariat of Education without a separate identity. In response, Macías proposed university autonomy in July 1917, a proposal he had made in 1914 and had failed to get incorporated into the 1917 constitution. His proposal would allow the president to name the rector to a one-year term and the council to nominate candidates. The rector would not be allowed to hold any other public office.

On July 14, Palavicini also made a serious proposal to remove the university from politics, as did others, all to no avail. In his view, professorships were being awarded as payoffs to friends of the government and the students had become a reactionary class. His proposed autonomy law would have the council elect the rector by a majority of votes; the directors of the schools could remove the rector. The council would include two professors from each school and one last-year student from each school. Students would be limited to a voice on curricula, teach-

[16]Bremauntz, *Autonomía universitaria*, p. 35; Ezequiel A. Chávez, "Proyecto de Ley de Independencia de la Universidad Nacional de Mexico," December 2–7, 1914, Archivo Chávez, Caja IV; this box also contains the decree of Gutiérrez. Chávez annotated his documents. On Carranza and the technical school, see Narciso Hernández Soto, "El Instituto Politécnico Nacional, fruta de la Revolución Mexicana," *El Legionario* (August 1954): 23–25.

ing methodology, and disciplinary issues. A group of professors and students presented an autonomy proposal that same month to Congress. All these efforts failed, however, and the university was shifted into the Departamento Universitario y de Bellas Artes in December. The rectorship became a cabinet post. The ENP was given to the Federal District government. Having lost its largest and most important school, the university tried to circumvent the government's intention by creating a preparatory curriculum in Altos Estudios.[17]

The autonomy issue receded from public view for the next five years, for both the Carranza (1917–1920) and Álvaro Obregón (1920–1924) governments concentrated their efforts on other domestic issues and on Mexico's relations with the United States. The latter was pressing Mexico over land and damage claims arising from the Revolution and the question of retroactivity of constitutional provisions giving ownership of subsoil minerals to the Mexican nation, provisions that threatened U.S. investors.

The university community did not perceive the Obregón government as a threat, even though it did intervene in the internal affairs of the institution. In part, this lack of fear was explained by the election of José Vasconcelos, a prominent university-trained professor, as rector on June 9 to replace Balbino Dávila, who had been elected on May 11. Vasconcelos moved to the newly created secretary of public education position in 1921 and delegated much of his authority over the university to Antonio Caso, the ENP director. In 1920, however, he and Obregón had intervened in the election of school directors, but in favor of the students, the potentially most explosive group in the university. Obregón ordered that the directors be elected by a special system in which the professors and students of each school would choose three candidates from among whom the head of the university depart-

[17]Hurtado Márquez, *Universidad autónoma*, p. 8; "32 aniversario"; José Natividad Macías, "La suspensión del Departamento Universitario," a press interview with *El Universal*, July 11, 1912, reprinted in Pinto Mazal, *Autonomía universitaria*, pp. 51–54; Félix F. Palavicini, "Proyecto de ley para dar autonomía a la Universidad," *El Universal*, July 14, 1917, in Pinto Mazal, pp. 55–62; "Memorial que los profesores y estudiantes de la Universidad llevan a la H. Camara de Diputados," *El Universal*, July 28, 1917, in Pinto Mazal, pp. 75–82; Jiménez Rueda, *Historia jurídica*, p. 193; Antonio Carrillo Flores, "El problema universitario de Mexico," *Así* (February 10, 1945): p. 36. The students were Manuel Gómez Morín, Alfonso Caso, Antonio Castro Leal, Teófilo Olea y Leyva, Vicente Lombardo Toledano, Jorge Prieto Laurens, Miguel Torner, Luis Enrique Erro, and Alberto Vázquez Mercado.

ment would appoint the candidate with the most votes. Since the students outnumbered the professors, control of elections passed to them for the first time in university history. The first use of the new system was in the facultad of chemical sciences in June, resulting in the election of Roberto Medellín by the students; Vasconcelos had wanted someone else but abided by the student decision. The only exception to the system was in Bellas Artes, where artists outside the school were allowed to vote. Vasconcelos allowed more student power and, on October 12, incited a student assembly to demonstrate against the Venezuelan dictator Juan Vicente Gómez. Vasconcelos continued to be a power in the university for some time. Mariano Silva y Aceves, elected on October 12 to replace Vasconcelos, lasted only until the election of Antonio Caso on December 12. Vasconcelos expected to control Caso.[18]

Political activity in the prep school, however, brought Vasconcelos and Caso into a direct confrontation, which the former won. By August 1923, Plutarco Elías Calles had announced his presidential candidacy for the elections the following year. Supporters quickly jumped on the bandwagon of this sure winner, who had the support of the incumbent administration. Vasconcelos tried to stay neutral, a posture that would eventually cost him his cabinet post and put him into the opposition camp. Vicente Lombardo Toledano, the ENP director, had his own political interests as one of the principal leaders of the Confederación Regional de Obreros Mexicanos. Lombardo had used his director's position to build a student political group within the school, thus using the school as a power base for national politics. Pro-worker demonstrations and political slogans became commonplace. Vasconcelos, who held more conservative views, got Lombardo Toledano's resignation.[19]

The director put his minions to work to create a crisis. On the morning of August 17, a group of students began to protest the resigna-

[18] Rodríguez, "National University," p. 61; "Nombramiento de profesores de escuelas y facultades universitarias hechos por elección," *Boletín de la Universidad* 1 (1920): 69–74. See also Burke, "University of Mexico," pp. 257–259, on Vasconcelos as rector. The shortage of trained faculty encouraged the use of recent graduates as professors. The interim government of Adolfo de la Huerta had little effect on the university.

[19] "Interesante carta dirigida al señor Ezequiel A. Chávez, por el Secretario de Educación Pública [Vasconcelos]," *El Demócrata*, September 20, 1923, reprinted in *Boletín de la Secretaría de Educación Pública* 2 (1924): 283–285; Fernando Pérez Correa, "La universidad: Contradicciones y perspectivas," *Foro Internacional*, 14 (1974): 388; "32 aniversario"; John W. F. Dulles, *Yesterday in Mexico*, pp. 122–123.

tion and denounce Vasconcelos. Committees were named to plead with Vasconcelos to reinstate Lombardo Toledano, to urge the director to withdraw his resignation, and to ask newspapers to support the student cause. Students threw stones and other projectiles at the policemen and firemen ordered into the school's patio to break up the demonstrations. The police officer in charge fired warning shots, but the students beat him so badly that he died within a few days. Vasconcelos, in a public statement, asserted that Lombardo Toledano had not preserved order in the school and that the educational function had been neglected. The director countered that the education secretary had constantly interfered with the university.[20]

The Obregón government backed Vasconcelos. Twelve students were expelled. On August 18, the Federación Estudiantil Universitaria demanded the reinstatement of the expelled students on the ground they were not guilty. On the twentieth, Subsecretary of Education Bernardo Gastélum announced that Vasconcelos had a plan to create a secundaria course of study within the prep school, a plan approved by the University Council. Since the Prepa and the university were hostile to the idea of a general secondary education outside the traditional curriculum, an attitude that disturbed the government, the timing of this announcement seems to have been an attempt to validate the Revolutionary credentials of Vasconcelos during this conflict with Lombardo Toledano as well as to threaten the students. Vasconcelos decided to prosecute students who engaged in violence, for not only had the police officer died but Professor Heliodoro Valle had been beaten by students outside the Secretariat of Public Education building. Student attempts on August 24 to get a local penal judge to quash the warrants on the accused students failed. Another group of students appeared in support of Vasconcelos. The judge blamed professional politicians who were trying to form the students into a political gang. By this point, CROM members were threatening a demonstration against Vasconcelos; observers feared it would lead to a bloody confrontation between the union and the students supporting the secretary.[21]

[20] *Excelsior*, August 18, 1923.
[21] *Excelsior*, August 19, 21, and 25, 1923. One of the students accused of assaulting Valles was Rogelio de la Selva, later to be a major politician and private secretary to President Miguel Alemán (1946–1952). The judge asserted that professional politicians were using the students for their own purposes.

The controversy in the school continued through the last week of August. Over one hundred students, Lombardo Toledano supporters, demanded the resignation of the acting director of the school. Vasconcelos then expelled Daniel Schultz and José María Ojeda, the student leaders. The school was closed but the students declared a strike. A delegation of strikers went to the CROM for help. Vasconcelos expelled two more strike leaders and, more important, three professors: Alfonso Caso, brother of the rector and brother-in-law of Lombardo Toledano; Enrique Schultz, brother of the student; and Agustín Loera Chávez. The striking faction organized a Liga de Resistencia composed of students from all the faculties to try to start a general strike. Antonio Caso broke with Vasconcelos and resigned the rectorship. The next day, the twenty-eighth, Ezequiel A. Chávez was elected interim rector and Roberto Medellín, the *oficial mayor*, took over the ENP. When the prep school reopened on the twenty-ninth, however, the Lombardo Toledano group, including some CROM members, burst into the school, fired shots, and threw projectiles at the firemen stationed there. Vasconcelos beat a retreat into the administrative offices, from which some of the students tried to extricate him. The strikers then left to try to get support from students in other university schools. The FEU, however, voted to support Vasconcelos, thus stifling the movement. By the thirty-first, the crisis was over. Three-quarters of the two thousand students had returned to class; the rest would soon follow. The Secretariat of Education suggested reductions in the professorial staff, but Chávez made an investigation that exonerated the three dismissed professors, and they were reinstated.[22]

The controversy prompted the second student attempt to obtain autonomy, one that almost succeeded. The FEU presented a bill to Congress on August 27 that would not only give autonomy to the university but would also give the FEU a representative on the University Council in addition to the students elected by each school. The FEU commission, headed by law student Luis Rubio Siliceo, lobbied with

[22] *Excelsior*, August 28–31, September 1, 1923. This use of firearms and porras was unusual. That it occurred in the 1920s refutes recent studies that assert that this practice was begun by rightists in the 1930s. For the Chávez investigation, see Ezequiel A. Chávez, "Carta al Secretario de Educación Pública," September 3, 1923, Archivo Chávez, Caja III. Chávez thanked the student federation for encouraging students to stay in class: "Chávez al Sr. Presidente y Sr. Secretario de la Federación de Estudiantes de Mexico," August 31, 1923, Archivo Chávez, Caja II bis.

individual congressmen and, by September 6, obtained the endorsement of ninety-seven senators and deputies, including José Manuel Puig Casauranc (who would be education secretary in 1924) and Pedro de Alba. Both would continue to play major roles in university politics. The proposed bill was sent to committee the next day. Vasconcelos asked for a copy in order to recommend possible changes; the bill disappeared. By the end of 1923, Vasconcelos was on his way out and Adolfo de la Huerta (interim president in 1920, secretary of the treasury for 1920–1923 and passed-over presidential candidate) had risen in revolt against the government. President Obregón and Congress had to concentrate on this serious rebellion. Bernardo Gastélum, subsecretary of education under Vasconcelos and secretary of education in 1924, recommended an autonomy plan to his friend Obregón on July 22, 1924, but the president tabled the matter, pleading lack of funds. Money was not the issue as much as his refusal to take major steps during the last few months of his term.[23]

The prep school was just one source of difficulty between the university and the state, for the latter was unhappy with the university's lack of attention to teacher preparation and lower education. The Escuela de Altos Estudios, originally conceived and operated as an unstructured, advanced, and experimental humanities division wherein unsalaried professors could offer whatever courses or lectures they pleased, had gradually assumed the task of teacher preparation. The university, however, had not committed itself to the task. In 1924, Secretary of Education Puig separated the school into the Escuela Superior Normal and the Facultad de Filosofía y Letras, thus guaranteeing that both functions would be well served. The next year, however, it lost its funding, and only regained it slowly. Puig asserted that he had forgotten to include it in the budget, but his assertion that he had forgotten to include it in the budget, but his assertion that elementary schools needed the money revealed the true purpose. The govern-

[23] The student proposal is reprinted as "Proyecto de Autonomía de la Federación de Estudiantes de México, Departamento Técnico," in Pinto Mazal, *Autonomía universitaria*, p. 109–112, and is signed by numerous students and politicians. Bernardo J. Gastélum, "La universidad autónoma y sus problemas," *Excélsior*, October 13, 1955; a copy of the 1924 proposal can be found in Caja IV, Archivo Chávez. Rodríguez, "National University," pp. 132–134, citing a Vasconcelos letter to him, asserts that Vasconcelos talked the students into returning. The best work on the de la Huerta rebellion is David Brush, "The De la Huerta Rebellion in Mexico, 1923–1924."

ment in the mid-twenties was going to emphasize lower education and the university would have to accept this reality.[24]

The controversy over the prep school continued through 1926 but centered on its curriculum. Many Revolutionaries believed that the prep school was not meeting national needs, that it should reform its curriculum to provide a general secondary education for students who did not plan to enter professional careers. During the 1920s, Moisés Sáenz, trained at Columbia University, and other education officials familiar with U.S. secondary education began efforts to create secundarias, non-college preparatory schools. It was an effort to democratize public education, but the university community, particularly in the Prepa, saw it as another attack on the university. President Calles ignored the opposition, issuing a decree on December 31, 1925, to create the new schools. Classes opened within a few months. The ENP lost the first three years of its curriculum and a building. Prep students criticized the change as the influence of Yankee imperialism and moaned that the secundarias would not be able to maintain the high and proper standards of the ENP. Some asserted that Calles, as a normal school graduate, was personally bitter toward the university. This creation of the secundarias further strained relations between the university and the state.[25]

The ENP was the foundation of the university's power. The few students who studied beyond the sixth grade did so in the ENP or a school modeled after it, hoping to enter one of the National University's schools. Receiving the *bachillerato* from the ENP meant a good job in government, business, or industry; a professional degree from the National University virtually guaranteed it. Since the ENP's creation in 1868, the system meant that the university got almost all of the best students in Mexico and/or those whose families had the resources to support them in the national capital. It also meant that the univer-

[24] Burke, "University of Mexico," pp. 262–263.

[25] Josefina Vázquez de Knauth," *Nacionalismo y educación en México*, p. 142; Juan González A. Alpuche, *La universidad de México: Su trayectoria sociocultural*, p. 72; Jiménez Rueda, *Historia jurídica*, p. 55. Luis Garrido, *El tiempo de mi vida: Memorias*, pp. 74–75, reports that this tension began under Carranza. Later, in the early 1920s, soldiers intervened in a strike and arrested students, including Garrido. That soldiers were used in the 1920s was significant, for many observers of the 1968 movement have erroneously asserted that their use that year was unprecedented.

sity got them young. The normal time in the preparatory-professional curriculum was ten years, ample time to mold minds and build loyalty. Only the very best or the wealthy graduates of other schools could hope to compete or to break into this exclusive club.

Creating the secundarias was a serious threat to both the university's power and prestige and its continued existence. Giving students the alternative of a non-preparatory education under direct government control meant that most would not go to the ENP but into the labor force without any vested interest in the university. That the government could so easily change a system that had existed for almost sixty years meant that it might just as easily lop off more of the university at some future date. More significant was the end to the university's monopolistic and privileged jurisdiction. The state's legal right to take such an action was unquestioned, but the threat to the university's habit of running its own affairs was not. As government employees directly responsible to the secretary of public education and ultimately to the president of the republic, university administrators and faculty could do little publicly about this threat. Students, through their organizations, were not similarly constricted. No doubt encouraged by some professors, they accepted the challenge of defending the university.

Student interest in this matter as well as in university governance and curriculum dated back to the founding of the university in 1910, but the lack of student organizations prohibited any sustained student effort for years. The organizers of the 1910 student congress had hoped they were building a permanent organizational base; the revolt against Porfirio Díaz in 1910–1911 dashed those hopes, as did the subsequent wars of the Revolution. Student indifference or hostility to the Revolution meant that they failed to build bridges to the victors and that these victors—military men—saw little reason to support the university. The insignificant number of students who participated in the 1910–1916 phase of the Revolution rarely fought and thus did not share the risk-taking, a common bond of the victors. To overcome this disadvantage, students needed to demonstrate that they were a sizable group that could not be ignored; they had to develop a force of their own.

The necessary organization began in 1915 when Jorge Prieto Laurens and other student supporters of the Carranza movement took steps to call the Primer Congreso Local Estudiantil del Distrito Federal, a group that would form the basis of the Federación Estudiantil Universitaria del Distrito Federal (FEU). According to Prieto Laurens, the majority of students were hostile to or had no confidence in the Revolution, so he and his friends tried to unite students in support of the Constitutionalist cause and against the counterrevolutionaries. Whether Prieto Laurens and his group or Gregorio Cristiani of the Internado Nacional (a student house supported by Carranza) called the first meeting is not clear, but Prieto Laurens was elected president when the congress actually met in 1916. The organizers represented a cross-section of higher education institutions in the Federal District. Some of the organizers, including Prieto Laurens, were also leaders of the Catholic Association of Mexican Youth (ACJM), but Catholics did not control the congress. When the congress met in 1916, delegates, elected by student assemblies in each school, came not only from the national university and the normal school but also from the schools of agriculture and commerce and the military school.[26]

The congress was successful. It got the Carranza government to declare a Day of the Student, an idea that various organizers had gotten from contact with South American students. The most important immediate achievement of the congress, however, was establishing good relations with the Carranza government. Because the organizers had been open supporters of the First Chief, he and part of his cabinet attended the congress. One result of this tie was Carranza's acceptance

[26] Prieto Laurens, *Cincuenta años*, pp. 15, 34–35, and "El verdadero proceso histórico estudiantil," *El Universal*, March 28, 1934; Miguel Torner, "Organizaciones estudiantiles," *Boletín de la Universidad* 1 (1917): 244–245; Pacheco Calvo, *La organización estudiantil*, p. 6, and "La organización estudiantil," *El Universal*, March 20, 1934, credits Cristiani as being the leader. Rodríguez, "National University," p. 87, and Lucio Mendieta y Núñez, *La universidad creadora*, p. 180 (and his other studies of the university), give virtually identical accounts; both base their work on Pacheco Calvo. The problem arises from the tendency of various authors to use *federación* and *confederación* interchangeably. This study will refer to the Federación Estudiantil Universitaria, Federación de Estudiantes Universitarios [de México], and any other similar name as FEU except when it is necessary to make a distinction. The name changed as a result of conflict in the organization. Prieto Laurens was a participant in the events, whereas Pacheco Calvo was not. A leftist, Pacheco Calvo opposed Prieto Laurens, who was a rightist in the 1930s.

Other organizers included Fernando Saldoña, Miguel Torner, René Capistrán Garza, Gabriel García Rojas, Julio Jiménez Rueda, Juan Espejel, Adelaida Argüelles, Amalia González Caballero, and Manuel Mazari.

of the idea that Mexico should assign university students to its embassies in Latin America in order to build stronger ties with those countries.[27]

The Congreso Local Estudiantil became the directive organ of the Federación Estudiantil Universitaria del Distrito Federal as well as the organizing committee of what later became the Confederación Nacional de Estudiantes. Both count the 1916 congress as their first. In the case of the CNE, this creates confusion, since it was not effectively organized until much later, even though it held national meetings in the early 1920s. The loss of various student archives in the upheavals of the 1930s makes tracing these federations difficult. Ciriaco Pacheco Calvo, the most commonly cited source, is not clear on his evidence. Since the FEU was the dominant university student organization and controlled the CNE, it is easy to confuse the two, as some writers do. In order to obtain some clarity, the history of the FEU will be approached first.[28]

The newly created FEU, controlled by the Prieto Laurens group, tried to create a pro-Revolutionary organized student class as a power in Mexican politics as well as a lobbying group for purely student interests. Its actual influence fluctuated with the personality of its presidents, many of whom started their careers in politics with this organization. In 1916, the Congreso Local adopted the proposal of Gabino A. Palma and other normal-school students to create a true national federation of students (the CNE). The FEU and the Congreso Local sent students on recruitment trips throughout the republic. The second national congress, however, would not be held until 1921 in Puebla, indicating that the organizers met with little initial success. The immediate recruitment drive was directed toward Federal District university students, who were easier to organize and could have more impact

[27] Prieto Laurens, *Cincuenta años*, p. 35, and "El verdadero"; Pacheco Calvo, "La organización estudianti]," *El Universal*, March 20, 1934.

The first student diplomats sent were Enrique Soto Peimbert, Adolfo Desentis, Pablo Campos Ortiz, L. Padilla Nervo, Rafael de la Colina, J. Manzanera del Campo, Luis Norma, and Carlos Pellicer Cámara.

[28] Torner, "Organizaciones estudiantiles," pp. 244–245; Prieto Laurens, *Cincuenta años*, pp. 15, 34, and "El verdadero." Pacheco Calvo, "La organizacion estudiantil," *El Universal*, March 22, 1934, asserts that the FEU was created in 1918–1920. Confederación Nacional de Estudiantes, *Mensaje a la juventud mexicana*, p. 41, counts this as the first congress, but 1923 and 1927 are also cited as dates the confederación was created.

on the national government. Those recruited came from a variety of other student organizations. ACJM students such as René Capistrán Garza and Julio Jiménez Rueda joined. The "Siete Sabios" —Manuel Gómez Morín, Vicente Lombardo Toledano, Alfonso Caso, Antonio Castro Leal, Jesús Moreno Baca, Teófilo Olea y Leyva, and Alberto Vázquez Mercado—were recruited, as was their friend Daniel Cosío Villegas. Leftists, under the leadership of Luis Enrique Erro, joined. The membership represented most of the brightest and most aggressive students of the era; many would dominate Mexican political and cultural life for generations.[29]

The combination of these strong but diverse personalities, confusion as to whether the FEU should intervene in non-university politics as well as seeking power within the university, and the relative unimportance of university students in a nation ruled by military men vitiated any hopes student leaders may have had about becoming a source of influence. During 1917, the FEU debated whether Mexico should join the Allies in the First World War or support President Carranza's neutrality stance, an important issue because the federación risked losing the President's blessing. The nationalistic or neutrality side, supported by Erro and Gómez Morín, won. In December of that year, Prieto Laurens, Miguel Torner, and Fernando Saldaña Galván ran on the Partido Cooperatista Nacional ticket for seats on the Mexico City council. Other students objected to this direct intervention in politics, an issue that would recur in student circles. These men and others would eventually leave the FEU for the more exciting world of urban and national politics.[30]

Between 1918 and 1921, the FEU focused on internal university issues. Organizational efforts in the Federal District were continued by

[29]Torner, "Organizaciones estudiantiles," pp. 244–247, for a report of the activities of the first year; Prieto Laurens, "El verdadero," and *Cincuenta años*, pp. 34–37; and Pacheco Calvo, "La organización estudiantil." The list of FEU presidents (1916–1932) is in Federación Estudiantil Universitaria de México, *Anuario, 1932–1933*. Brito Foucher, Caso, Castro Leal, and Gómez Morín would later become rectors of the university. Cosío Villegas, more famous in later years as an intellectual and political critic, Jiménez Rueda, and Lombardo Toledano would hold high university posts. Gómez Morín founded the Partido Acción Nacional in 1939 and Lombardo Toledano the Partido Popular [Socialista] in 1948.

[30]Pacheco Calvo, "La organización estudiantil"; Prieto Laurens, *Cincuenta años*, pp. 53–61.

Miguel Palacios Macedo, with some success, and an appeal was made to U.S. student organizations to establish more contact and interchange with the Mexican group. Inside the university, professional-school students continued to pass exams at a high percentage rate, from a low of 53 percent in dentistry to a high of 100 percent in pharmacy; academic standards were low, for it was common for 90 percent of the students of a school to pass. In these easy-going days, students had ample time to engage in politics. In 1920, the FEU was campaigning for a seat on the University Council on the grounds that there was a serious split between the students and the faculty. According to the FEU, the faculty complained that the students were undisciplined and uncultured and thus the educational institutions were inefficient, while the students complained that the professors were incompetent, unenthusiastic, and cynical. The FEU solution was to give the students the right to vote as well as speak in the council. FEU intervention to resolve a law school strike that year proved propitious, for the rector granted the organization the right to send a representative to the council.[31]

The FEU continued the efforts of the first local congress to establish close ties with students in other nations by calling the Primer Congreso Internacional de Estudiantes to meet in Mexico City in September 1921. Vasconcelos, the university rector, supported the meeting and gave the inaugural address. The official Mexican delegation included Cosío Villegas (who presided), Rodulfo Brito Foucher (FEU president), Miguel Palacios Macedo, Raul Pous Ortiz, and Francisco Río Cañedo. In spite of its "student" title, recent graduates such as Octavio Medellín Ostos, Manuel Gómez Morín, Eduardo Villaseñor, Ramón Beteta, Leopoldo Aguilar, Vicente Lombardo Toledano, and Arturo Martínez Adame were adjunct delegates. Representatives came from the United States, Norway, Japan, Germany, Switzerland, and

[31] Pacheco Calvo, "La organización estudiantil"; Miguel Palacios Macedo, letter to *New York Times*, February 16, 1919, on the pass rate, see "Labores del Departamento Universitario, 1918–1919," *Boletín de la Universidad* 2 (1919): 9–19. Alfonso Pulido Islas, in a letter to Roderic Camp, March 21, 1974, wrote that student leaders in the 1920s and 1930s (his era) had high grades; it appears that most students had high grades. On the FEU complaint, see "La representaciones estudiantiles," *Acción Estudiantil* 1 (1920): 7. This periodical was the FEU publicity document. On the council seat, see Mendieta y Núñez, *La universidad creadora*, p. 182.

most of the Spanish-speaking countries, giving the meeting its claim to international status.[32]

The international congress advocated many ideas that later became commonplace in the hemisphere, giving the meeting an importance beyond its almost totally unimportant effect in Mexico. The delegates proclaimed that university students would fight for the coming of a new humanism based on the modern principles of economic and political justice. More specifically, they advocated the abolition of the state as a sovereign moral entity apart from the people who constituted it, an entity used by minorities to dominate the majority; the destruction of the exploitation of man by man; the end of the actual organization of property, which treated human labor as merchandise and prevented the establishment of socioeconomic equality; and the integration of humankind into a universal community. Reflecting the influence of the University Reform Movement, perhaps, the congress advocated student participation in the governance of university, abolition of required class attendance, academic freedom for students and faculty, university extension systems, and people's universities.[33]

Almost immediately after this international meeting, the Second National Student Congress convened in Puebla and adopted resolutions applying some of these principles to Mexico. Organized by Arturo Vendrell, the congress was presided over by Rafael Corrales Ayala. The state governor, General José María Sánchez, disliked the opening speeches, rudely interrupted the proceedings several times by commanding the band to play, and finally left in anger. The meeting almost adjourned, but the leaders persuaded the delegates to return.

[32] *Excelsior*, September 21, 1921, reported that Vasconcelos spoke as the representative of President Obregón, that Cosío Villegas gave the greetings of the FEU, and that not as many students and professors were attending as hoped. Gilberto Freyre, the future famous Brazilian sociologist, attended. *Excelsior* thereafter ignored the meeting. The fullest details can be found in "El primer congreso internacional de estudiantes," *Boletín de la Universidad* 3 (1921): 59–98; Rodríguez, "National University," p. 126, lists the Mexican delegates.

[33] Mendieta y Núñez, *La universidad creadora*, p. 184; Sebastián Mayo, *La educación socialista en México: El asalto a la Universidad Nacional*, pp. 136–137; "Resoluciones del Congreso Internacional de Estudiantes reunido en México," in Gabriel del Mayo, ed., *La reforma universitaria*, vol. 6, pp. 75–84, presents the resolutions. This meeting was not the origin of the University Reform Movement in Mexico, as often asserted, since Mexican students had been arguing for the elements of the movement before 1918 and had contact with other Latin America students before 1921.

Cosío Villegas, incoming FEU president, delivered an impromptu speech on a poet that calmed the atmosphere. At the close of the congress the students resolved that the "student class" ought to accept the moral obligation to work for the welfare of the people and ought to intervene directly in politics and social questions so that social conflict would create economic equality. Further, students should engage in politics to elect men who would protect the rights of the people. The assembly also decided to ask Congress and state governors to enforce the anticlerical Article 3, on education, of the Constitution and to institute the teaching of socialist doctrine in schools. Interested in a student-worker alliance, the congress called for night schools for workers (Brito Foucher had been an early advocate of workers' universities), socialist unions, cooperatives, and recreation centers for the people. On educational matters, the delegates called for a national university-student federation to be governed by a five-person directory, elected by majority vote, more scholarships and stipends, exchange programs of students and faculty among schools, student discounts, similarity of curricula, the creation of a periodical press, and preference to students in administrative and adjunct professor posts. In short, the congress was trying to create a national student movement that would have real power in the universities and the nation. The chief arm of this effort was to be the Confederación Nacional de Estudiantes, whose statutes were passed at this meeting.[34]

By 1924, however, Federal District students spent most of the year watching their leaders argue over the federation presidential election, then create rival federations, and, finally, appeal to the university rector to resolve the dispute. At the elections there were three parties:

[34] *Excelsior*, October 2, 1921; Prieto Laurens, "El verdadero"; Pacheco Calvo, "La organización estudiantil," *El Universal*, March 27, 1934; Rodríguez, "National University," pp. 93–95, citing Pacheco Calvo, *La organización estudiantil*, and Mendieta y Núñez, "Ensayo sociológico sobre la universidad," in *Primer Censo Nacional Universitario, 1949*, pp. lxxii. (he also cites Pacheco Calvo), assert that the meeting was called and timed by enemies of Cosío Villegas to interfere with the international congress, that it resulted in the dissolution of the FEU, and that the third CNE congress was later called by law students. From the *Excelsior* story, it is apparent that there was no fight with Cosío Villegas. My research revealed no evidence to support this or the other two assertions. On Brito Foucher's advocating worker's universities, see Pacheco Calvo, "La organización estudiantil," *El Universal*, March 27, 1934. Although Pacheco Calvo is not entirely trustworthy as a source for these years, this statement has merit because he and Brito Foucher were ideological opponents in 1934.

Orientador Estudiantil, Renovador, and Rojo. When the outgoing administration of Lalo de Larrera declared Enrique Torres of the Escuela Libre de Derecho the victor, Cayetano Ruiz García, the loser, revolted and led his fellow national law students out of the FEU, after ransacking the offices and taking part of the files. In early April, the Rojo party and most of the schools in the Renovador party also left. Engineering and medicine followed two months later. By June 17, most of the National University schools and at least eleven others joined to create the new Federación Estudiantil Mexicana.

Two issues wedged the split between the groups even deeper: ownership of the files and a medical clinic begun in April. Before leaving the Federación Estudiantil de México, the medical and engineering students had cooperated with it to organize the clinic, hire a nurse, acquire some equipment, and promise physicians and students that the clinic would open in June. Now that they were in the new federation they wanted to take the clinic with them. The university rector, Ezequiel A. Chávez, settled the dispute by giving the clinic to the student societies of the university and of the military medical schools. The old federation received all the files generated between April 5 and September 22, except for the clinic's files. So that the new federation could make copies, Chávez ordered the files stored in an administrative office for a month. There are grounds to believe that the two groups eventually merged into a single new federation, but, since some of the files have disappeared, it is impossible to say that with certainty.[35]

This seemingly trivial incident was important because it revealed that National University students, despite the rhetoric of student unity or a student class, were interested only in a unified organization they controlled. Besides being the most numerous group inside the federation, they also commanded the support of many non-university students, including those in some normal schools, in the business school

[35] Ezequiel A. Chávez, "Fallo dictado por el Rector de la Universidad Nacional de México en la divergencia surgida entre la Federación de Estudiantes de México y la Federación Estudiantil Mexicana, a propósito del Consultivo Gratuito del Estudiante y del archivo de la Federación de Estudiantes de México," September 22, 1924, typed document, Archivo Chávez, Caja II bis; Ezequiel A. Chávez, "Informe presentado por el rector, Ezequiel A. Chávez, reunida en el paraninfo de la Universidad Mexicana, para solemnizar el XIV aniversario de la misma," Boletín de la Secretaría de Educación Pública 3 (1924–25): 46; and Pacheco Calvo, "La organización estudiantil," March 27, 1934.

(not yet part of the university), secretarial schools, and the military medical school. The key to this control in 1924, as it would be in 1929, was the alliance of law, medical, and engineering students. University law students usually controlled the federation presidency, but no mass movement was possible without the aid of the more conservative students from the technical disciplines.

That same year, two incidents brought the wrath of a labor union on student heads. Local No. 1 of the Unión de Carpinteros y Similares protested formally to President Obregón and Secretary of Public Education Gastélum about student attacks on the José Clemente Orozco and David Alfaro Siqueiros murals in the ENP and on female workers by medical students. In the first case, some students who objected to both the techniques and social content of the murals defaced them. In the second case, the medical students shaved the heads of some women workers to protest their short hair style, a style considered "un-Mexican" and "unfeminine" by traditional Mexicans. In other words, both incidents reflected class hostility. The union pointed out that short hair was necessary for the safety of persons who worked with machines and suggested that the students, non-working members of society, would have to learn this reality. Rector Chávez, into whose lap the demand for punishment was dumped, expelled the guilty medical students but could only promise greater vigilance over the paintings, since the vandals were unidentified. This satisfied the workers.[36]

That university students displayed no understanding of the working classes was not surprising, for most still came from the middle and upper strata of Mexican society. No concrete, comprehensive data exist on the socio-economic composition of National University students in the 1920s, only testimony given by former students years later. Few children of workers ever made it to the university; the few who managed to complete elementary school usually had to enter the labor force as soon as possible. Students in the university tended to congregate by social class in their voluntary associations, in residences, and in the different schools of the university. Those with lower-middle-class origins tended to choose disciplines that promised the quickest payoff,

[36] Letter of Simeón Mesiári [sic], Secretario del Exterior, Unión de Carpinteros y Similares, al Sr. Presidente de la Republic General Álvaro Obregón y al Sr. Ministro de Educación Pública Dr. Bernardo J. Gastelum, July 28, 1924, Archivo Chávez, Caja II bis; letter of Chávez to Secretario de Educación Pública, November 8, 1924, Caja II bis.

such as dentistry and engineering. Although Daniel Cosío Villegas has asserted that he and his fellow students made no such class distinctions, the available evidence suggests that he was being romantic about his own student days. Students went to the university to certify their elite status or to enter the national elite, and tended to seek out students similar to themselves. Poor students were socialized and absorbed into this new elite. Expressing some concern for workers or about social conditions was almost obligatory in the 1920s, but few student congresses gave more than lip service to these problems. The students were more interested in political power within their own federations, within the university, and within the nation at large.[37]

Their regionalistic rivalries and patronizing views of the working classes notwithstanding, the students supported the early Calles administration, which was liberal. The third national student congress, meeting during the last week of January 1926 in Ciudad Victoria, Tamaulipas, occurred shortly after Mexico enacted the organic law to implement constitutional Article 27 (which gave the nation all subsoil mineral rights) and the Petroleum Law of 1925. By asserting its right to own and control petroleum and other natural resources, Mexico was challenging the interests of the foreigners who had obtained title to these resources in earlier years and had invested considerable sums to pump oil or dig ore. The United States and other countries pressured Calles to reverse the laws. The recently formed Sociedad de Estudios Internacionales of the national law school, in a proposal signed by Rogerio de la Selva, Carlos Zapata Vela, and César Ruiz, asked the student congress to protest U.S. intervention in Mexican internal affairs. The proposal created some excitement in the nation and the congress, which debated whether to seat delegates from the society (de la Selva was seated as the fraternal delegate of a state delegation). Manuel Gudiño, the presiding officer of the congress, sent a telegram to Aarón Sáenz, the secretary of foreign relations, asking for a clarification of the issue, but Sáenz told the students to rely on the government's public statements. In its final resolutions, the student congress called for the

[37] Daniel Cosío Villegas, letter to Roderic Camp, April 18, 1973; Dr. Pedro Daniel Martínez, in his February 14, 1974, letter to Roderic Camp asserts that social interaction was determined in large measure by the socioeconomic level of the students; Clamento Bolio, letter to Roderic Camp, July 18, 1974, asserts that the great majority of the students were from the lower middle class.

nationalization of public natural resources and the passage of laws to give petroleum and mining unions preferential treatment.[38]

Other resolutions and proposals of the congress reflected a pro-Calles majority. The congress called for the redistribution of private wealth; supported unions free of government control (Calles had the support of Luis Morones's CROM, but the government controlled the union); demanded laws to support the rights of agrarian and other workers; called for the state to become socially, not just politically, active; and advocated class cooperation instead of conflict. The congress also heard proposals to institute practical and theoretical agricultural education in the upper levels of primary schools, to create polytechnical institutes, to nationalize the curricula of secondary schools and universities, and to create night elementary schools for workers. On social matters, the congress resolved in favor of extreme anticlericalism and the absolute equality of men and women (which Calles promulgated in the Civil Code of the Federal District and Territories on August 20, 1928).[39]

The delegates were not in unanimous agreement, however. The call for free unions was a slap at Calles's labor policy. The demand for the nationalization of the curriculum, even though it called for the appointment of a committee by the national Congress and the state legislatures with equal student representation, was not included in the final resolutions. Too many National University students would object to such a proposal, since it would reduce their institution's power. Conservative delegates lost on their proposed resolutions to adopt the university system in the secundarias, as well as on their demand that the congress demand that Governor Tomás Garrido Canabal of Tabasco reopen the state's schools (most of which were Catholic). The frivolous proposal of Gustavo Rubirosa that the congress adopt a treatise on sexual hygiene that pointed out the dangers of matrimony also went down to defeat.

The most serious disagreement came from the charge that the president, Gudiño, had abused his power. The congress had decided

[38] *Excelsior,* January 22, 24, 26, and February 1, 1926.
[39] *Excelsior,* January 26, 28, and February 1, 1926, printed some of the resolutions; see also Pacheco Calvo, "La organización estudiantil," *El Universal,* March 27, 1934, for some of the resolutions. Mendieta y Núñez, *La universidad creadora,* p. 185, summarizes the resolutions. Calles's position on equality can be found in Moisés Ochoa Campos, *Calles: El estadista,* p. 34.

to intervene in the dispute between the students of the Local Escuela Normal y de Preparatoria and its director, whom they accused of being a tyrant. When the Tamaulipas delegation discovered that Gudiño had altered the wording of the congress's letter to Governor Emilio Portes Gil, they and some other provincial delegates called for a vote of no confidence in Gudiño. Gudiño won, but the delegations from Tamaulipas, Guanajuato, Coahuila, and San Luis Potosí, as well as five Federal District delegates, walked out. Regionalism had reared its head again. One of the Federal District delegates who left was Ángel Carvajal, who would be president of the FEU in 1927 and a power in the CNE. The flare-up did not prevent the planned conclusion of the congress on January 31, the selection of the organizing committee for the next meeting on Oaxaca, or the election of an executive committee headed by Manuel Yáñez.[40]

Within a few months of the Ciudad Victoria meeting, another student congress, the Congreso Nacional de Jóvenes, met in the mining school building in Mexico City. Carvajal presided over the debates. Little is known of this congress or the two that preceded it. The delegates supported a number of commonplace propositions: the replacement of foreign-owned industry with Mexican industry, the right of non-governmental schools (escuelas libres) to exist, and the self-determination of the National University. One delegate argued in favor of women's rights *after* they had 'learned' to be free," a not surprising Mexican view and interesting primarily because it contradicted the women's rights resolution of the third National CNE Congress. More important than the debates was the participation of Carvajal, José M. de los Reyes, Julio Antonio Mella (a Cuban Communist student leader), Guillermo Tardiff, Sealtiel Alatriste, Arcadio Guevara, Baltasar Dro-

[40] See *Excelsior*, January 26, 1926, for the resolutions that lost. The debate over the local school and Gudiño can be followed in *Excelsior*, January 27, 31, 1926. The conclusion of the congress is reported in *Excelsior*, February 1, 1926. Pacheco Calvo, "La organización estudiantil," *El Universal*, March 27, 1934, asserts that Gudiño won the presidency as the Federal District candidate against Eduardo Balvanera, the provincial candidate, by means of illegal delegates, false credentials, and deals based on friendships, a view that Rodríguez, "National University," pp. 96–97, accepts. *Excelsior*, January 24, 1926, reported a split over procedures but did not identify the causes. That the opposition to Gudiño on January 30 came primarily from provincial students supports the Pacheco Calvo view. Rodríguez, "National University," p. 97, asserts that Gustavo Díaz Canova was elected the next CNE president, but Díaz Canova became FEU president that year.

mundo, and Luis Meixueiro B., all of whom would be leaders of the first university general strike in 1929 and some of whom would play important roles in public life for years.[41]

More important future national politicians were active in still another student organization, the Liga Nacional de Estudiantes. Unfortunately, the history of this organization is virtually unknown. It apparently existed before January 1926, when two of its members, councilmen in the municipality of Villa de Guadalupe Hidalgo in the Federal District, announced plans to start an agricultural and industrial school. Since participants and contemporary reporters often used different names for the same organization, it is possible that the liga was one of the organizations already mentioned in this work. In 1962, former member Tardiff listed a number of famous members: presidents of Mexico Adolfo López Mateos and Miguel Alemán, Braulio Maldonado, Raúl Noriega, Eduardo Hornedo, Efraín Brito Rosado, Jorge Meixueiro B., and Leopoldo Ancona. Liga members were nationalistic, pro-Revolutionary, and pro-labor. By 1928, the liga, which had committees in each National University school, advocated university autonomy.[42]

The FEU was the important student organization, however, for it was aided by the Mexican government. Carvajal won the presidency of the FEU in 1927 after a heated campaign against Francisco Doria Paz; Carvajal had the support of the rector and of Secretary of Public Education Puig. Both his secretary-general, José M. de los Reyes, and his vice-president, Alfonso Millán, Jr., would follow him in the FEU presidency in 1928. Carvajal regained the right of the FEU to name a delegate to the University Council and, at the end of his presidency, got the secretary of public education to recognize the FEU as the official Federal District student organization, the university student societies as the official representatives of their schools, and the CNE as the official organization of university students in the nation.[43] With these measures, the FEU finally got the clout its members had been seeking for years.

[41] Excelsior, March 30, 1926; Baltasar Dromundo, "Balance de la Generación de 29," in Antonio Damiano, et al. En torno de una generación, p. 66.

[42] Excelsior, January 21, 1926; Guillermo Tardiff, "Policromías: Liga Nacional de Estudiantes," El Universal, May 11, 1962. Rodríguez, "National University," p. 136; José M. de los Reyes, "El movimiento de mayo de 1929," El Universal, May 10, 1949.

[43] Pacheco Calvo, "La organización estudiantil," El Universal, March 28, 1934.

The CNE, more heterogeneous by nature, was less amenable to government control and less likely to back the government automatically. Its fourth national congress, held in Oaxaca city in late January 1927, took a firm stand against the reelection of Álvaro Obregón as president of Mexico. Although no-reelection was one of the shibboleths of the Revolution and was incorporated into the 1917 constitution, Obregón and his partisans decided in 1926 that the Revolutionary general was indispensable and had the Constitution amended to preclude immediate reelection. The move upset not only potential rivals but the nation at large because it threatened the re-creation of the continuism that characterized the Porfiriato. By the time the student congress met, politicians were announcing their desire to be elected national president in 1928. Thus, any statement by the students would be interpreted as a political maneuver by some political faction, a charge leveled by the student Alfonso Pulido Islas at the opening of the congress. Pulido Islas and four other students sent a telegram to Obregón disavowing the congress's resolution, and, in Mexico City, a group calling itself the Central Executive Committee of the Gran Partido Estudiantil Universitario announced its opposition to the congress's resolution and its support of Obregón.[44] Pulido Islas became a student leader in Obregón's presidential campaign.

The fourth national CNE congress solidified the structure of the CNE and adopted resolutions characteristic of students in those years. José Cantú Estrada, who presided over the congress, was reelected president of the permanent commission of the CNE. The delegates again supported anticlericalism, opposed U.S. imperialism in Nicaragua, saw Mexico's role as being a bulwark against U.S. penetration of Latin America, and called for workers' night schools staffed by students. In addition, the congress paid homage to José Vasconcelos, naming him "Benemérito" of the student class, a move interpreted as anti-Obregón because the two had fallen into disagreement. It may have been nothing more than an act of homage, for he was one of the most influential intellectuals in the nation, a man who served the university well and was *the* cultural caudillo of the 1920s. Some delegates

[44] *Excelsior*, January 19, 23, 1927. Pulido Islas actively supported Obregón in the campaign. Carlos Zapata Vela, a leader of this fugitive party, later became a leftist politician and served as a federal deputy and as ambassador to the U.S.S.R.

did assert that the students should run Vasconcelos as their presidential candidate. His actual presidential candidacy in 1929, supported by students, suggests that this 1927 act was political.[45]

The CNE congresses of Culiacán (1928) and Mérida (1929) continued the old refrain of the necessity of student participation in the governance of the National University, university autonomy, opposition to the government, opposition to U.S. imperialism in Nicaragua, and night schools for workers. The 1928 congress met at the same time as the Pan American Conference in Havana, and the students called on the Pan American delegates to condemn U.S. imperialism in Nicaragua and Haiti. Student splits continued. The Culiacán congress decided to elect a chairman for each debate rather than a president of the congress, a clear indication that the students were afraid of centralized power. The anti-government tone of the Mérida meeting, which elected the Vasconcelista Alejandro Gómez Arias as president, brought about the creation of the Confederación Nacional de Estudiantes Revolucionarios, which announced that it supported Gilberto Valenzuela, Vasconcelos, Antonio Villareal, and the Partido Nacional Revolucionario. The goal of the new group, according to its organizing committee (which included Zapata Vela, Dromundo, and G. Cárdenas Huerta), was to create a student political party and offer a presidential candidate that year to unify the "revolutionary" students and to make them a force in national politics. Clearly, it was designed as a rival to the CNE, which had tended to become a pro-Vasconcelos group under the leadership of Gómez Arias.[46]

The FEU also faced internal difficulties in 1928, having four presidents in one year. In the election, José M. de los Reyes was declared the winner over Alfonso Millán, Jr., but the Millán faction, not satis-

---

[45] *Excelsior*, January 18–21, 23, 31, 1927; Pacheco Calvo, "La organización estudiantil," *El Universal*, March 28, 1934. *Excelsior*, January 21 1927, and Pacheco Calvo say that Cantú Estrada was elected president, but Rodríguez, "National University," p. 99, says that Angel Carvajal was. Carvajal was elected FEU president in 1927.

[46] *Excelsior*, January 26–28, 30, 1928, reports the Culiacán congress. Carvajal and Salvador Azuela supported the resolution to rotate the presiding officer for the debates, whereas Gómez Arias opposed the move. Rodríguez, "National University," p. 104, errs in asserting that the congress met under the leadership of Carvajal. Baltasar Dromundo, "El ideal común, respuestas a la época," in Damiano, *En torno*, p. 30, asserts that various delegates fought in favor of university autonomy; *Excelsior* did not report this. The records of the Mérida congress were lost and there is some confusion as to what hap-

fied with a lesser office for their man, contested the propriety of the electoral process. As a compromise, both men resigned and Luis Meixueiro B. was elected. Before he finished his term, however, he resigned to attend a student congress in Europe. Gómez Arias took his place, thus getting a springboard for the 1929 CNE presidency. When Gómez Arias did become CNE president, Ricardo García Villalobos took over the FEU.[47]

Thus, on the eve of the first general strike in the history of the National University, a strike led by students against the government, the old dream of a unified student movement, of a student organizational base that would give them power or influence, was far from reality. That student meetings could agree on anti-Yankee resolutions or university autonomy or student participation in university governance or mild pro-labor measures could easily mislead the casual observer. Student politicians were like other politicians; they wanted office for whatever power and prestige it might bring and were as likely to use the same methods as national politicians to obtain office, notwithstanding their self-perception that they were purer. As long as real power lay in the rector's office, in the University Council, in the Secretariat of Public Education, or in the Mexican presidency, the myth of student unity or a student class could be sustained. Occasional splits in student organizations belied the myth, and student and national politicians could use student organizations to demonstrate support on national issues.

Even without true student unity, student political activity after 1910 planted the seeds and tilled the fields that produced the 1929 harvest of a university autonomy law. Students had accustomed national politicians to the idea of student political activity; some of the activists became national politicians themselves. Only a tiny proportion of the

pened. *Excelsior*, January 29, 1929, only reports that the state governor formally received the delegates. News from the congress was undoubtedly difficult to obtain because it occurred in distant Yucatán and had low priority during a time when presidential candidacies were being announced. Rodríguez, "National University," pp. 105–106, discusses this meeting, but he errs when he asserts that the CNE was officially organized at this meeting, that Gómez Arias was the first CNE president, that the CNE replaced the FEU, and that the two were practically the same. See *Excelsior*, January 23, 1929, for the CNER. I found no further evidence on it, which suggests that it was ephemeral.

[47] Pacheco Calvo, "La organización estudiantil," *El Universal*, March 28, 1934.

students were activists, but their intensity was sufficient to create the popular image of general student activism. Student advocacy of university autonomy was traditional by 1929. Limited participation on the University Council demonstrated student responsibility. The growth of the FEU and the CNE gave student activists the organizational base necessary for unified action. Through these organizations students expressed some support for Revolutionary goals as well as anti-government sentiment. What was lacking was a catalytic agent.

3. Emilio Portes Gil and the Creation of UNAM

ONLY a few events may be seen as major historical turning points; the 1929 university general strike was one of these. It merits recounting in detail. Out of that strike emerged the Universidad Nacional Autónoma de Mexico (UNAM), a gift of interim president Emilio Portes Gil. The inherent conflict between the university and the state was recognized and institutionalized. Students, long desirous of power in the university and through it the nation, moved into the seats of the mighty on the University Council and within the individual schools. The university became a democratic polity even though the state was not. Student leaders then and later recognized this anachronism and argued that the state should imitate the university; the tension between the two institutions increased. Other students and other politicians in different universities and different decades would look to the 1929 strike for guidance. Its leaders would occupy public posts disproportionate to their numbers.

That the 1929 student strike took place when the government was facing more serious problems, including the possibility of revolt, is important to an understanding of the development and outcome of the strike. The year before, President-Elect Álvaro Obregón had been assassinated by a Catholic fanatic. The assassin and his co-conspirators were tried and punished, but the death of Obregón split the ruling coalition. Some Obregonistas suspected the murder was a plot by followers of incumbent president Plutarco Calles to perpetuate their man in office.[1]

In spite of an adroit move by Calles to avoid an open and perhaps

---

[1]These events can be followed in Dulles, *Yesterday in Mexico*; Jean Meyer, *La Cristiada*, 3 vols.; and Lorenzo Meyer, with Rafael Segovia and Alejandra Lajous, *Los*

bloody battle to settle the succession issue, times were tense. Unable to extend his term beyond the November 30 deadline, Calles created an umbrella party, the Partido Nacional Revolucionario, to include all the potent politicians. This party, or confederation, was to allot the spoils peacefully on the basis of the relative strengths of the membership. The financial costs to the participants would be kept low, for each government employee was forced to contribute seven days' salary to the PNR coffers. The success of this move depended on selecting an interim president satisfactory to all factions but especially to the Obregonistas, and then on a presidential candidate who met the same qualifications, with the additional one of not having a personal following. Emilio Portes Gil, governor of Tamaulipas and a cagey politician in his own right, took the interim post. The presidential candidate was Pascual Ortiz Rubio, a virtual political unknown. The candidacy of Aarón Sáenz, a powerful Obregonista, had been rejected because he could not be controlled by Calles.

At the time, there were no assurances that this device would work and plenty of indications that the government was in serious trouble. General José Gonzalo Escobar revolted against the government in March; although the revolt ended in April, it reminded Portes Gil's government that not everyone accepted the PNR candidate. The Cristero rebellion and church-state conflict, two separate but interrelated movements, continued until June 22, when Portes Gil and Archbishop Ruiz y Flores announced a modus vivendi. The Cristeros did not lay down their arms immediately, however. The presidential election scheduled for November 17 loomed down a road potentially mined with a number of unpleasant surprises for decision-makers. The opposition coalesced around José Vasconcelos, former rector, former secretary of public education, leading intellectual, and a man with a strong following among the urban middle class and university students. Meeting resistance to their campaign efforts, Vasconcelistas began talking of possible revolt. The Mexican Communist party supported the Ortiz Rubio candidacy but quietly instigated peasant revolts, which were easily put down. In short, the government that faced the student rebellion dur-

inicios de la institucionalización. La política del Maximato, vol. 12 of Historia de la Revolución Mexicana. See Baltasar Dromundo, "Perfil de la Generación de 1929," Diario del Sureste, June 6, 1949, for a view that the government's attention was absorbed.

ing May and June had to do so with one hand tied. That some of the students were Vasconcelistas complicated matters.[2]

Nothing so important as high national policy tripped the wire leading to the student bomb in the National University. Instead, students exploded over more common and mundane issues: examination policy and the length of the preparatory curriculum. Conflict began between university administrators on the one hand and law and prep students on the other. That the administrators were government officials meant that the state would inevitably be drawn into the conflict, but administrative misjudgments created the problems. The rector, Antonio Castro Leal, had taken office on December 10, 1928; the director of the law school, Narciso Bassols, had taken office on January 3, 1929, and the director of the prep school, Antonio Caso, at about the same time. Thus, inexperienced administrators were trying to make fundamental changes during a time of national tension. Compounding the problem would be the belief of these administrators that students did not learn enough, were more interested in acquiring degrees than knowledge, and were lazy. Further, they believed that students should automatically obey the dictates of the administration and faculty.

When the new academic year began in February, Caso, ENP director, announced that the curriculum was being extended a year to total three years so that students would learn more archeology, paleontology, and other subjects. Students grumbled during the first two months of classes but took no decisive action. Alfonso Guerrero Briones, Ignacio Galvadón, and José Vallejo Novelo unsuccessfully protested to Secretary of Education Ezequiel Padilla. The University Council refused to hear a student delegation. Caso broke the strike that followed by sending mounted police into the school's patios. Galvadón and Vallejo Novelo were expelled. The students, led by Eduardo Hornedo, formed a defense committee, but the issue appeared lost and administrative authority confirmed.[3]

[2] Roderic Camp, "La campaña presidencial de 1929 y el liderazgo político en México," *Historia Mexicana* 27 (1977): 231–259.

[3] Pacheco Calvo, *La organización estudiantil*, p. 39: "La lucha de los estudiantes por la libertad," *La Nación*, October 3, 1942; Rodríguez, "National University," pp. 72–73, citing a letter from Vasconcelos; Pedro de Alba, "Las peripecias de nuestro bachillerato," *El Nacional*, August 2, 1933, on the debate in this period on the ENP curriculum.

Law students had their own complaints, and their actions would demand the attention and resources of the administration and, later, the government. Law students protested the institution of reconocimientos in place of the final oral exam before a three-man tribunal. Rector Castro Leal had announced on February 27, before classes began, that reconocimientos would be used in the law school that year. Law director Bassols pushed the issue. The students, however, assumed that they would be able to avoid them as they had done in the past.[4]

Law students had good reason to assume that they should not take Castro Leal's announcement seriously. The University Council, in April 1925, had approved a system of written and successive examinations, as had the rector and the secretary of public education. The students beat the proposal by declaring that since the new system was announced at the end of the third month of classes, instituting them would be unfair, an argument accepted by the administration. The students agreed that they would accept the system in 1926. Nevertheless, in 1926 they also resisted and avoided the switch-over. In 1927, a group of professors in the law school asked for and got a meeting on the issue; they agreed that the written exams should be instituted and made such a recommendation to the rector. The rector, Alfonso Pruneda, did not follow through, in spite of his promise to do so. In 1928, the administration allowed law professors to decide which system they would use. Some used the new system but fed the questions to the students beforehand. Others simply began passing students. The other schools and faculties in the university had gone to the reconocimiento system in 1925, thus isolating the law students. Before the 1929 academic year began, the university administration decided that law would follow the same rules as the others and passed the appropriate regulations.[5]

The reconocimiento system threatened the less serious law student. Under the examen, or prueba system, the student faced a tribunal composed of the professor of the course and two other professors. The student drew two questions from a bowl and then delivered a discourse on the one of his choice. At the end, the assistants

[4] Pacheco Calvo, *La organización estudiantil*, p. 39; Emilio Portes Gil, interview in James W. Wilkie and Edna Monzón de Wilkie, eds., *México visto en el Siglo XX*, p. 557; and Jesús Silva Herzog, interview in *México visto*, p. 674.

[5] Antonio Castro Leal as quoted in Silva Herzog, *Una historia*, pp. 37–40.

asked questions to determine the extent of the student's knowledge. Those who were eloquent orators and quick on their feet had ample opportunity to rephrase the question to suit what they knew or to dazzle the panel with oratorical brilliance. The judges found it difficult to flunk such a student, and few did. This procedure had other obvious defects as well. Class attendance was irrelevant, thus leaving students with plenty of time to engage in such non-academic pursuits as politics. No sampling of knowledge was possible. The student with poor self-discipline and study habits could do better than a brighter peer who happened to draw the wrong questions. Under the reconocimientos, the student would face written exams three times a year. The same theme for this essay would be given to only five students. Students would have to answer between two and five questions. The last examination would be comprehensive and would last two hours. Students would not have foreknowledge of the exam contents. To take the first exam, the student would have to have attended at least 60 percent of the classes; to take the others, at least 75 percent. A passing grade was six on a scale of one to ten. The final grade in the course would be determined by the arithmetical average of the three exams. Students could appeal a grade if they believed it unjust. [6]

Students protested but Castro Leal stood fast. The University Council rejected the appeal of Alejandro Gómez Arias, Arcadio Guevara (president of the law student society), and Heliodoro Gurrión that the system be abandoned. Castro Leal, in a press statement on April 27, detailed the history of the issue and reaffirmed the intention to begin in May. [7] The battle lines were drawn.

On May 4, the law students began preparing for a strike, declaring that they would strike on the twelfth if the reconocimiento system were put into effect. They named a strike committee to use direct action against any student who tried to take the exams. Alejandro Gómez Arias headed the committee, with Ricardo Villalobos as secretary; a number of committee members played important roles in this and future strikes. In a vote, 328 voted for the old system, with only 27

[6] UNAM, Facultad de Derecho y Ciencias Sociales, *Plan de estudios, programas y reglamentos de reconocimiento en la Facultad de Derecho y Ciencias Sociales,* pp. 450–451.
[7] "La lucha de los estudiantes": Castro Leal in Silva Herzog, *Una historia,* pp. 39–40.

voting in favor of the new one. The delegation sent to talk to the rector met instead with the secretary-general of the university, Daniel Cosío Villegas, who ordered them to obey the rule. Students then invaded the Secretariat of Public Education building; Arcadio Guevara asked Padilla to intervene to stop the reconocimientos; he agreed only to send the issue to the University Council. Castro Leal and the council, however, backed their earlier decision to give the exams as scheduled. On May 6, Bassols posted a notice that any student impeding classes would be expelled. His antagonistic attitude provoked the students further.[8]

By the seventh of May, the law students resorted to violence and were met by intransigence from the government. Students seized the law school building and posted guards, but firemen ran them out that night. Ezequiel Padilla announced to the newspapers that the government was more interested in educating the masses than university students and that, if the conflict was not resolved, the school would become a polytechnical school. The students also resorted to the press; Arcadio Guevara and Antonio Damiano declared that the new system was "a Yankee invention unsuited to the Latin race," thus trying to appeal to Mexican nationalism for support. They also argued that the new system destroyed private initiative. Two students who refused to obey the strike edict were stripped, doused in a pool, and ridden through the university section on a rail. Faced with riotous behavior, Portes Gil closed the school that day and warned that if the academic year were lost through a prolonged closure, the unexpended funds would be given to polytechnical schools. Efforts to enlist the support of the medical, engineering, and national prep schools failed, for students there had been using the reconocimiento system for years. When the strikers tried to retake the law building on the eighth, they found that firemen had occupied the building hours before. Upper-

[8] Pacheco Calvo, *La organización estudiantil*, p. 39; *Excélsior*, May 5, 1929; José M. Lugán, "La huelga de 29," *El Universal*, July 13, 1945. The other strike committee members were Arcadio D. Guevara, Flavio Navar y U., Luis F. Martínez, Teodosio Montalván, Norberto Valdés, Julio Serrano, Salvador Azuela, Juan Perdomo, Rafael Landa, Carlos Zapata Vela, José M. de los Reyes, and Santiago Zúñiga; see Silva Herzog, *Una historia*, p. 41. Rodríguez, "National University," p. 148, also includes Antonio Damiano. Numerous authors, including Rodríguez and Mendieta y Núñez, emphasize this committee to the exclusion of the general strike committee, which carried the burden of the general strike.

level law students appeared at the school during the day to demonstrate their willingness to take the exams and to show their opposition to the strike. Padilla argued that students who did not like the national law school system could create their own, private, law school (as he, Portes Gil, and others had done in 1912), and that the government could spend the money saved on rural education. A commission of Guevara, Gómez Arias, and Flavio Navar y U. was named to seek Portes Gil's help, but the president refused to make any deal. The strike was stymied unless the law students could find something to spark the issue.[9]

In part, Alejandro Gómez Arias and Salvador Azuela were that spark. Azuela was in some respects a professional agitator, for he had been expelled from ENP in 1923 for his participation in the student upheaval of that year. Since that time he had studied in Michoacán and worked in state and student politics. Since his return to the National University in 1929, as a law student, he had been active in the Vasconcelos campaign. Older than many of the other students, faced with a real threat to his career, and committed to an anti-government candidate, the strike gave him an excellent opportunity to demonstrate his political skills. His father, Mariano Azuela, was one of the most famous novelists of the Revolution, best known for *Los de abajo*. Gómez Arias, president of the CNE, oratorical champion, and honor student, would lead the movement. His CNE ties enabled him to recruit student support in other parts of the country. The confederation promised on May 9 that its 130,000 members would support the strike and demonstrate on the fourteenth.[10]

The strike directors knew, however, that no single individual could defeat the forces arrayed against the law students. Somehow they had to get public support, a difficult task because their demands were so self-serving. That students in other schools of the university

[9] *New York Times*, May 8, 1929; Mateo Solano y Gutiérrez, "El conflicto estudiantil," *Excelsior*, May 8, 1929; and Luján, "La huelga." The events of this movement can usually be followed in *Excelsior* the day after they occurred.

[10] Antonio Damiano, "Prolegomenas de la huelga universitaria," *En torno*, p. 15; Desiderio Horta, "Quince años de autonomía universitaria," *Así* (November 11, 1944): 13; Mendieta y Núñez, *Historia*, p. 180. On Salvador Azuela, see Mario Colín, *Salvador Azuela*, 11–12; Salvador Azuela letter to Roderic Camp, July 14, 1974; Azuela, interview with Camp, Mexico City, June 26, 1975; and Baltasar Dromundo, *Los oradores de 29*, pp. 3–39.

were unwilling to support them severely weakened the effort. The promise of the CNE to help and to send telegrams asking for support from all the other student federations in the country was at best a propaganda ploy. Telegrams of support from students in other countries and a telephone conversation with Cuban students were no more than psychological support. They could also point out that Aquiles Elorduy, Revolutionary and former law school director, had stated to the newspapers that they were right, but the salient fact was that the university administration, the secretary of public education, and the president were unyielding. Thus, on Thursday the ninth, the strikers met and listened to rallying speeches from Gómez Arias, Salvador Azuela, and others; the attacks were launched against law director Narciso Bassols and the rector, Castro Leal. Some students talked of creating an Escuela Libre de Derecho y Ciencias Sociales, in imitation of the move by Padilla and Portes Gil seventeen years before, but the circumstances were different—no political faction was willing to finance such a school. Finally, they adopted a manifesto and appointed a ten-person propaganda committee to publicize their version of the issues. They declared themselves revolutionaries at heart and against all tyrannies, especially those of Bassols and the other educational authorities. Bassols, they said, could never empathize with students. The attack on Bassols represented an effort to focus their barbs on a single individual in the hope that forcing his resignation or removal would save them from disciplinary action.[11]

The government and the administration, for their part, put pressure on the students to return to school. They thought the possibility of a general strike slight, but took precautions to prevent one, threatening severe penalties if the students misbehaved. *Excelsior* noted that the nucleus of the strike was small, that the majority of the students were signing up to return to class, and that university administrators were counting on parental support to get classes opened. Cosío Villegas, himself a former student leader, argued that the students ought to take the exams. Government officials suggested repeatedly that the country would be better off if the monies were spent on

[11] Damiano, "Prolegomenas," pp. 13–17; González Cárdenas, *Cien años*, p. 181; Horta, "Quince años," pp. 12–13; René Esclaire, "A Castro Leal y Bassols los sacamos de las orejas, dice Andrés Henestrosa," *El Nacional*, May 2, 1949.

rural or technical education. Within the FEU, the Grupo Orientador Estudiantil was formed to act as a truth squad against the assertions of the strikers and to begin a separation from the FEU. Padilla, on May 13, reminded the students that the University Council, on which they had representation, had approved the reconocimientos and that the student demand for his intervention was contradictory to the other student demand for university autonomy. By the sixteenth, the government, believing that the strike had virtually come to a standstill, announced plans to reopen the school with the reenrollment period scheduled for May 20–25. If not enough students enrolled, the school would be closed permanently.

The University Council considered the reconocimiento issue during its May 16 meeting, but made only minor concessions to the strikers. Castro Leal reminded the council that it had approved the reconocimientos in 1925, that he had notified the law students on February 27—before the opening of classes—that they would be using this exam system, and that the students began to cause trouble eight days before the first use of the reconocimientos. Law director Bassols argued that oral exams promoted mediocrity. Further, he proposed to reduce the class attendance requirement for the first exam to 50 percent and for the second exam to 66 percent and to reduce the number of reconocimientos to two. In the debate, Luis Sánchez Pontón, Vicente Lombardo Toledano, Antonio and Alfonso Caso, Fernando Ocaranza (medical school director), and Pedro de Alba (known as a friend to students) argued that the reconocimientos should be used. That these men represented both leftist and rightist currents within the university demonstrated that this issue was academic, not political. The council agreed to keep the reconocimiento system but in the proposed modified form. To give the students more time to prepare, exams were scheduled for the first ten days of July, and the second series set for November 18 to December 14. The exams would last two hours each and would not be comprehensive. Students would be notified of the exams eight days before they took place. Six was established as the passing grade on the second exam. The class attendance requirement was reduced to 50 percent for the first exam and 65 for the second. These concessions were the best the students could hope to get. The university administration sat back and waited to see how many law students reenrolled during the May 20–25 period. On the twenty-first, the rector announced that 113 had reenrolled in the law school during the first day. The strike appeared broken.

Meanwhile, the strikers had been busy trying to win support to their side. Gómez Arias announced to *Excelsior* that the students were opposed to the reconocimientos because they were done arbitrarily and that laws should be made with the consent of the governed; that is, the strikers had decided to argue not against the new and tougher exams but in favor of democracy. Student leaders and hundreds of others issued a manifesto agreeing that the nation needed more lower-level schools, as the government said, but stressing that the society also needed trained leaders such as lawyers and legislators. Fliers were issued that called SEP functionaries and the rector traitors to the Revolution. *Excelsior* commented that the students were getting financial aid. Student leader Santiago Zúñiga tried to convince the public that the issue was not the reconocimientos but the necessity of recognizing the rights of the "student class." On the eleventh, seventeen university, technical, and free schools, all part of the FEM, met to discuss the law strike. No decision to join the strike was made but a directive committee headed by Carlos Béjar, from medicine, and José Barros Sierra, from the Escuela Libre, was appointed to watch events. On the thirteenth, Baltasar Dromundo, one of the chief strike leaders, announced that the students would agree to assigned papers in addition to the oral exams but that the strikers were opposed to compulsory class attendance, preferring the voluntary system of San Marcos University in Peru. Gómez Arias and Azuela announced plans for a student stoppage in all university schools on May 17, during which a mass open-air meeting would be held. By the fourteenth, the students were declaring that this would be a general strike and that Jalapa students had announced a one-day stop as a show of support. President Portes Gil told the press that the strike was a Vasconcelos tactic. The previous day, the law strike committee met to decide what to do. Teodosio Montalván resigned from the committee for fear his Cuban nationality would compromise the movement. A delegation was sent to the rector to ask for a meeting of the strike committee with the University Council. The strikers formally demanded Bassols's resignation as well. By the evening of the sixteenth, however, the strikers had only achieved a modification of the new system. There appeared little hope that they would win. Only the new school of economics, formerly part of the law school, had joined the strike.[12]

Students of the ENP joined the strike on May 21 and quickly turned events around. Prep students had their own grievance, concerning the addition of another year to their studies, but it was the combined efforts of prep and law students that created the 60–10 vote in favor of the strike. This represented a minority of the some 1,500 prep students and did not represent the night prep students, who refused to join; it demonstrated that a minority could control events when the majority was willing to acquiesce. In essence, it was the efforts of a few that created the vote. Prep students Ignacio Gavaldón and José Vallejo Novelo, who were already being disciplined for agitation, and Ciriaco Pacheco Calvo, Efraín Brito Rosado, and Flavio Navar led the fight for the strike. Law students Azuela, José Zapata Vela, and Montalván spoke as well. When the ENP group went to tell the university authorities that the day ENP was on strike, they found the doors closed and guarded by soldiers. They went to the medical school that night to try to get those students to join the strike, but firemen opened their hoses on the students; students threw stones from the roof of the building; the rector ordered the firemen to leave; and mounted police burst onto the scene, breaking up the demonstration. The medical students voted against joining. Later that night, some medical and dental students joined in the protest demonstration against the police. Flavio Navar justified the demonstration as a protest against the use of mounted police, the firing of two shots toward the roof by policemen, the false declaration of the rector that 113 had reenrolled in the law school when only 13 had, the director of secundaria #3 for ordering his building protected, and prep director Caso for sending threatening letters to parents.[13]

May 22 was relatively quiet. Secundaria #4 joined the strike, but neither the medical nor the dental school had decided. Ex-president of the FEU Horacio Núñez was arrested, and newspapers reported that secret police were infiltrating the student ranks. Nevertheless, law students continued to reenroll.

The strike leaders realized that they had to get the medical stu-

[12]Silva Herzog, Una historia, pp. 43–44.

[13]Damiano, "Prolegomenas," p. 16; González Cárdenas, Cien años, p. 182.

dents to join if they were going to close the university, for the medical students would bring all the more conservative schools into the strike with them. Somehow the strike leaders had to polarize student opinion and create martyrs in order to rally support. For weeks Gómez Arias and Dromundo had been going to the medical school in an effort to persuade students there to join up, but they had failed because the medical students could not identify with either the law or prep school complaints. Director Ocaranza was popular in the medical school and his cool head and light hand had preserved order.[14]

At or around 1:30 in the afternoon of May 23, approximately a thousand students began a demonstration in front of the law school, but the guards posted there would not let them enter the building and called for reinforcements. Soon, the chief of the security service, Pablo Meneses, and the assistant commandant of the police, Benjamin Alamillo, arrived with help. Someone yelled that the technical police had hurt three students and were holding them hostage inside the school. Assault brigades were immediately organized to break into the school and rescue the "hostages." The firemen hooked up their hoses and drew out their hatchets. Students on the roof threw stones at the police and firemen. Some students asserted that there were six corpses inside the school and that that was why the authorities were trying to keep the students out. The officers in charge got the fighting stopped so that Guevara and newspapermen could go into the school and see that the rumors were false. Although they reported that there were no dead or detainees inside the school, they were unable to stop the agitation. The police and firemen tried to disperse the crowd peacefully. According to their version of events, a student hit a fireman with a .45 caliber pistol (which disappeared into the crowd) and, in the ensuing melee, three students, including Dromundo, were hurt. Dromundo later withdrew his accusation that he had been hit by a fireman's hatchet. Through the use of water hoses, mounted police, and police muscle, the students were driven away, but they had had the confrontation they needed. Rumors flew through the university section, asserting that six students were dead, that the police had wantonly attacked the students, and that the government was getting rough.[15]

[14] Fernando Ocaranza, *La tragedia de un rector*, p. 279.

[15] *Excelsior*, May 24, 1929, has both student and police versions of the events. See also José M. Luján, "El 23 de mayo," *El Universal*, August 10, 1945; *New York Times*,

Later that day, about 7:30 P.M., another confrontation occurred. Law and prep students had gone to the medical school to try to get their support. As director Ocaranza reported it later, the government so mishandled the situation that the medical students reversed themselves and joined. In their meeting, 75 percent of the medical students had voted against going on strike. Ocaranza got a telephone call from rector Castro Leal telling him that the students were coming to his school, that he, the rector, had sent police, and that the director was to use them against the students. Ocaranza, furious that all his efforts to keep the peace in his school were being jeopardized by such stupidity, told the assembled medical students. Nonmedical students assembled outside the building and in the nearby Plaza Santo Domingo waited for the results of the medical school meeting. Some began to hassle fellow student Enrique Acosta Raalu, accusing him of being a traitor, and took him inside the building. Fearing that he would be hurt, the police ordered that he be released and that the students leave. Policemen entered the building to rescue Acosta. Stones were then thrown at them, and the police and firemen retaliated with water bursts and a police charge. Some policemen fired their pistols into the air. Inside the building and in the plaza, a short scuffle took place until Federal District regent, José Puig Casauranc, called to the scene by Ocaranza, arrived and ordered a halt. Speaking in the name of Portes Gil, he told the students that the police and firemen would be withdrawn within ten minutes, that the law demonstrations were justified, but that now four or five schools were involved the students should quit demonstrating, for it was no longer a university but a police matter, and that they should present their grievances to President Portes Gil. He stated his concern that a student might be killed in a street confrontation between students and police.[16]

May 24, 1929; *The Times* (London), May 25, 1929; Damiano, "Prolegomenas," p. 16; Emilio Portes Gil, *Quince años de política mexicana*, p. 320; Horta, "Quince años," p. 14; and Luján, "La lucha." The government had good reason to be concerned, since the students had eight to ten pistols plus two Thompson submachine guns brought by Miguel Lanz Duret, Jr., a night or two before; see Horta, "Quince años," p. 14.

[16] Ocaranza, *La tragedia*, pp. 279–280; *New York Times*, May 24, 1929; *The Times* (London), May 25, 1929; and Luján, "23 de mayo." Portes Gil, *Quince años*, p. 320, says that the students had begun to attack faculty members, that Castro Leal had asked the Secretariat of Public Education for help, and that Padilla's office told the Mexico City government to send police.

The police-firemen confrontation with students at the medical school changed the strike from a localized to a general one. The medical students, angered at the attacks on students and the invasion of their school, voted to strike, a decision backed by the school's director. With the entry of the medical school, the schools of dentistry, veterinary medicine, and chemical sciences also voted to strike. Within a few days, every university school, almost every technical school, and almost every secundaria in the Federal District had declared themselves on strike. In the states, other schools and universities declared strikes or stops in support of the National University students.[17]

Skull-cracking swung support in favor of the university students. On the night of the twenty-third, within hours after the beginning of the medical school confrontation, two or three hundred students fought with police and firemen near the Hotel Regis in downtown Mexico City. Pistols were fired, probably by both sides, skulls were cracked, and some twenty-six persons, including Guevara, were arrested. Newspaper reports on the following day erroneously said that between two and six students were killed during the day of the twenty-third. The president of the student society of the Escuela Libre, Barros Sierra, protested that one of that school's students, Enrique M. Loaeza, had been shot. To prevent further violence, President Portes Gil withdrew all police, firemen, and soldiers from the university precincts, expressed regret at what had taken place, and asked the students to present their petitions to him in writing or in person.[18]

Student ire against both university and governmental authorities could not be deflected so easily. On May 24, orators mounted the tribune in the patio of the law school to lambaste the university administration and the public authorities. Besides the usual leaders (Gómez Arias, Brito Rosado, Dromundo, and Zapata Vela), others, such as Adolfo López Mateos (future president of Mexico), joined the militants. Strike committees were formed in each school, inside and outside the university, and delegates selected to form part of the Comité Central de Huelga, to meet that night at nine to draft a response to Portes Gil. The Escuela Libre leaders, claiming the impartiality of their school, now stated that they had to intervene because students

[17] Damiano, "Prolegomenas," p. 16; González Cárdenas, Cien años, p. 183.

[18] Portes Gil, Quince años, p. 320; New York Times, May 25, 1929. Dulles, Yesterday in Mexico, p. 464, incorrectly says that Portes Gil took these steps on May 24.

were being hurt. Orators charged university authorities with incompetence. Bassols was a principal target because of his unwillingness to debate the reconocimiento issue. Padilla had converted a local into a national issue—perhaps, in the view of Escuela Libre students, as part of a systematic attack on professional training by the government. They ended by asking Portes Gil for a radical solution to the conflict rather than a patchwork one. Bassols resigned the directorship of law, saying that he had only been trying to improve the quality of the school but was now an obstacle to any solution. The students announced a mass march for the following Monday, the twenty-seventh, to present a petition to Portes Gil. Rector Castro Leal held a 2 P.M. meeting of the directors of the university faculties and schools, during which he called for a police investigation of the overuse of force and punishment of the offenders. But more students and schools joined the strike.[19]

Delegates from all these schools met on the twenty-fifth in the law school to organize the strike and draw up a list of demands. The central strike committee named was made up of: Arcadio D. Guevara (law), José Vallejo Novelo (ENP), Alfonso De Gotari (medicine), Francisco J. Ramírez (engineering), Ramón Corona (commerce), Guillermo Alvarez (dentistry), Francisco Cañedo (Escuela Nacional de Maestros), Antonio González (electrical and mechanical engineering), Francisco Sánchez Ruiz (secundaria #3), Alejandro Gómez Arias (CNE president), and Ricardo García Villalobos (FEM president). Gómez Arias, who presided, offered to resign because his friendship with Vasconcelos, the presidential candidate, might compromise negotiations with Portes Gil. The assembly scheduled a protest march for the following Tuesday, the twenty-eighth. They tentatively agreed to demand the resignations of the rector, Padilla, Meneses, the police chief Valentín Quintana, the directors of secundarias #1, #3, and #4, and Alfonso Caso, director of the ENP. Further, they wanted the composition of the university council changed to give students equal representation with professors. At the end of the meeting, they appointed a committee to draw up their demands. This key task was given to Efraín Brito Rosado (ENP night), Modesto Sánchez (Escuela Nacional de Maestros), Miguel Monterola (commerce), Flavio Navar (law), and Eduardo Angoita (engineering). What had begun as a law school issue and had been joined by the ENP

[19] Horta, "Quince años," p. 12.

and then by the university was now becoming a crisis in Mexican education at the secondary level and above. Even private schools, such as the Colegio Francés of the Brothers of Mary, had joined the movement. In short, the government was facing a serious rebellion, serious because the students could not be treated lightly. They were the sons and daughters of prominent people, including politicians, and they were demonstrating against the government not only within blocks of the central government buildings but all over the Federal District. Student sympathy demonstrations and strikes elsewhere in the republic further tied the hands of the government.[20]

When Brito Rosado and his fellow committee members finally met Portes Gil on the afternoon of the twenty-seventh, the list of demands they gave him demonstrated a desire for revenge and a total reorganization of post-elementary education in the Federal District. First, they demanded the dismissal of Padilla, his undersecretary, Moisés Sáenz, Castro Leal, Quintana, and Meneses. Next, they wanted the resignations of all university directors and all university and Secretariat of Public Education employees responsible for reprisals against the students. Further, they demanded a full investigation to identify and punish those responsible for the events of May 23 and thereafter. Their demands on educational matters were equally extensive, and reflected their non-university support. The government was to create a council of technical schools and a council of normal schools. The secundarias were to be reincorporated into the ENP. Co-government (parity of student-professor representation) was to be instituted in the university council and the new technical and normal school councils. The University Council was to nominate three persons among whom the Mexican president could choose the university rector. The rector would lose authority, being able to vote only to break ties.[21]

The next day, the students backed their demands with a massive demonstration. Over twelve thousand students, from different schools in the Federal District, paraded for three hours through city streets to the National Palace. Portes Gil watched from a balcony but did not

[20] New York Times, June 26–27, 1929.

[21] Excelsior, May 28, 1929. The student petition is also printed in Mendieta y Núñez, Historia, pp. 183–185. See Rodríguez, "National University," pp. 150–151, for his agreement with the view that the demands included one for autonomy, drawn by medical students and sent to Puig. Baltasar Dromundo, "Balance," p. 64, also makes this assertion.

speak, pleading illness, but he promised an answer for the next day. Presumably he had to ponder the significance of demonstrations of support for Padilla that came from the Parents Society, one hundred members of the Professor Corps of Secundarias, and the National Teachers' League. Although it is not possible to know, it appears that he had taken precautions to insure that the march would be peaceful. Police chief Quintana had threatened to break the march and label the participants reactionaries, Catholics, and Vasconcelistas. Lombardo Toledano had threatened to use the CROM in a counterdemonstration. Neither threat was carried out. [22]

Portes Gil's reply to the petition was a political masterstroke, for he preempted public attention, yielded little, and split the strikers. After stating that he sympathized with the students and the university, he rejected the demands for firings on the grounds that he could not allow the students to dictate who his collaborators were; governmental authority would be severely compromised. Although he did not mention the broader political issues, the fact that there were thousands of armed Cristeros in the countryside, ongoing delicate negotiations with the Catholic hierarchy and involving Dwight Morrow, the U.S. ambassador, and the constant turmoil of the presidential election campaign meant he could show no sign of weakness. Even in better circumstances, the government could not abdicate its responsibility for postelementary education, much of which was already in Catholic hands. Instead, he offered the students university autonomy on the grounds that it would produce long-range solutions to the problems that had created the strike and would take academic disputes out of the political arena. He offered nothing to the non-university strikers, however, knowing that their interest in the strike would quickly wane. [23]

His reply, which reached the students on the twenty-ninth, only outlined the proposal he was to release to the newspapers the next day,

[22] Excelsior, May 29, 1929, says that over 15,000 marched; New York Times, May 29, 1929, says nearly 12,000. Rodríguez, "National University," pp. 151–152, cites Jorge Siegrist Clamont, En defensa de la autonomía universitaria, p. 249, for the Quintana assertion, which is also in Damiano, "Prolegomenas," p. 16. For the Lombardo Toledano threat, see José M. Luján, "Adhesiones y manifestación," El Universal, August 17, 1945.

[23] Excelsior, May 30, 1929, prints the text of his reply. His autonomy proposal is printed in Excelsior, May 31, 1929. See also Portes Gil, Quince años, pp. 342–345. Years later, he maintained this view; see Portes Gil, interview, Wilkie and Monzón de Wilkie, México visto, pp. 558–559.

but it clearly indicated that Portes Gil was giving up little. The students were to be given parity on the university council and in the academies of professors and students for each school or faculty. Henceforth, he declared, the university community was to govern itself. Nevertheless, he would name the ternas (three candidates) for the rectorship and the directorships; the council would have to choose one of the president's nominees. In short, these university administrative positions remained political appointees. He promised that the university would have full control over academic matters and be given a general appropriation each year. The document sent to Congress would substantially circumscribe this freedom, however.

Participants still debate the origin of the idea of university autonomy at this time. Portes Gil contends that the idea was original with him, that it was something that had been floating around university circles for twenty years (which was true), but that the students had considered the idea too utopian to suggest it. Students, writing later, claimed they had drawn up an autonomy proposal and sent it to Portes Gil; he said he never received it. There is no doubt that some students had been discussing the idea for months; prep school students had wanted to propose it but had been unable to write a plan in time for submission. The specific proposal that was sent to Congress seems to have come from Portes Gil, however. In the university archives, there is a typed copy of the 1924 autonomy proposal that has been redated June 3, 1929, indicating that it was the model for the Portes Gil bill. The issue is important because the strikers later claimed authorship of university autonomy and used this authorship to justify their actions during the long strike.[24]

The autonomy proposal immediately split the student ranks. The strikers, meeting on May 30, tried to close ranks by seeking to add students from the secundarias, technical schools, and normal schools

[24] For student assertions that they proposed autonomy, see Pacheco Calvo, *La organización estudiantil,* p. 42; Horta, "Quince años," p. 13; Dromundo, "Balance" and "Perfil." For Portes Gil's assertions that the idea was his, see Portes Gil, *Quince años,* p. 328; interview in Wilkie and Monzón de Wilkie, *Mexico visto,* 558–559, and "La verdad sobre la autonomía universitaria," *Así,* (November 18, 1944): 8. For the redated 1924 document, see "Proyecto de decreto de autonomía de la Universidad Nacional de México," Archivo Chávez, Caja IV. *Excelsior,* May 27, 1929, reported that the ENP advocated autonomy; Lujan, "Adhesiones," agrees with Portes Gil.

to the committees working on academic problems. Brito Rosado defended the delegation to the president, arguing that they had done all they could and thus there was no need for further debate. Dromundo also was willing to settle for autonomy because it was more than they had expected and would allow the students to stop professors from being appointed through political patronage and allow the students to fire professors who would not accept "modern" ideas. De Gotari, the leader of the medical students, also argued that university autonomy was enough of a gain and that the students should back off. Carlos Zapata Vela justified accepting the autonomy proposal on the grounds that the university had been fighting for it since 1910. Others realized what the president's letter really meant. Navar pointed out that autonomy did not solve the problems of all the students; Julio Serrano of the CNE labeled it a farce; Ciraco Pacheco Calvo argued that the students should continue to fight until their demands were met; Rosendo Béjar of medicine went straight to the point: autonomy was a myth. Teodosio Montalván, the experienced Cuban, summed up the position well: Portes Gil had shown his ability to divide the students. The debate degenerated into an argument over who had sold out and why. At the end, the strike leaders decided to accept autonomy in principle but to continue the strike.

Throughout the course of events, the students had concentrated on academic issues or the treatment of students by public forces; little or nothing was said about the rest of the Mexican population. Nevertheless, a delegation of railroad strikers came to the student meeting of May 31 and asked for support in defending themselves before the Supreme Court. A law student delegation—Antonio Damiano, Carlos Zapata Vela, Julio Serrano, Guillermo Amparán, and Ricardo García Villalobos, all student activists—was named to speak for the railroaders in the court. This was the only occasion during the long strike on which the university students showed any social consciousness.

Following two days of lengthy discussions, a student delegation met with Portes Gil on June 2 to present their list of objections to his autonomy proposal. They prefaced their remarks by asserting that they represented all university students and that they were Revolutionaries who supported workers and peasants, thus claiming their loyalty to the government and the Revolution. The theme of their objections was that more power over a larger university should be put into student hands. They wanted the National Agricultural College and School of Veterinary Medicine, secundarias, and cultural institutions such as art galleries and museums added to the university. They wanted to deny the vote to the secretary-general of the university, the treasurer, and those directors who did not head faculties or schools. They wanted the Secretariat of Public Education representative on the council removed permanently. No more than two alumni would be allowed to serve on the council and neither would have a vote. On the other hand, both the FEM and the CNE would be given a voting representative. The law should guarantee student representation on the key committees. They wanted the terna for the rector to come from the council. The council should elect the directors and name and remove professors on the basis of proposals by the respective academies. Rectors would have to have lived in the country for one year immediately before taking office (a slap at Castro Leal, who had not), but directors would not have had to live in the country for one year in their lives. Further, they wanted the student societies to continue as the official governing bodies for the students inside the university. Finally, they wanted to remove the president's power to veto student admissions. Portes Gil asked them to put their requests in writing (they had appeared the day before in *El Universal*) so he could study them.[25]

These student efforts to get Portes Gil to alter his proposal failed, as did efforts to lobby with the special session of Congress that had been called. The government had conceded as much as it planned to do. During the congressional session in the first week of June, various functionaries including Padilla testified on behalf of the bill, but its passage was a foregone conclusion. On June 5, Congress authorized Portes Gil to issue the autonomy law. Now the university had to await the promulgation of the new law by the president.

Having failed to get a concession from Portes Gil before Congress acted, the students now concentrated on continuing the strike and maintaining student solidarity while they lobbied to get the desired changes as well as something for the non-university students. They

25 "Objeciones hechas al Presidente de la República por el Directorio de Huelga Estudiantil, respecto de la Ley de Autonomía," *El Universal*, June 1, 1929, reprinted in Pinto Mazal, *Autonomía universitaria*, pp. 151–161.

abandoned their original intention of ending the strike on June 8. On the sixth day they ejected the president of a student group in the National Teachers School, accusing him of trying to break the strike. That same day, they again stated their demands that the secundarias be returned to the university, that the secondary, technical, and normal students get their demands, that the University Council name the directors from lists submitted by student societies, that the alumni have no vote in the council, that both the FEU and the CNE have representatives (without votes) in the council, that the President be able to act only on foreign degrees, that the subsidy to the UNAM be at least equal to the 1925 subsidy, and that the government accede to the student demands for councils for technical and normal schools.[26]

The non-university students began to pull out of the strike, however. On June 8, the central strike committee agreed to allow the technical and secundaria students to return to school on the nineteenth, as they requested. The plea of Gómez Arias, during a meeting of parents and students from the secundarias, to stay with the strike for another week received little response.[27]

In desperation, a group of strikers decided to force Castro Leal out of the rectorship before the new autonomy law was initiated. On June 11, two thousand students marched on the university. Some went into the rectory to demand Castro Leal's resignation, but he stepped out a side door. Angered, the students seized secretary-general Daniel Cosío Villegas and ENP director Alfonso Caso in an attempt to get Castro Leal to return, but then discovered that they were locked in. After two and one-half hours, they let the two men go but decided to occupy the building until the rector resigned. After two days, during which they were left alone, Portes Gil agreed to send a representative to receive custody of the building. In their meeting with Portes Gil, the leaders—Gómez Arias, Brito Rosado, Navar, Zapata Vela, De Gotari, Francisco Ramírez—told Portes Gil that they had confidence in him but not in Castro Leal. In all likelihood, what they meant was that they

[26] FEM vice-president Antonio Prior Martínez had been expelled for making proreconocimiento declarations to the press; see Luján, "La huelga." The Federación Estudiantil Mexicana and the Federación Estudiantil Universitaria were interchangeable terms.

[27] Pacheco Calvo, *La organización estudiantil*, p. 48.

were afraid that Castro Leal would retaliate against them if he stayed. The rector sent his letter of resignation on the fourteenth, saying that after helping draw up the autonomy law, he had done all he could. It is also likely that Portes Gil advised him to resign.[28]

Splits in the strikers' ranks continued. Women students, organized as the Sociedad de Universitarias Mexicanas and led by Carmen Rodríguez Anaya, met on the fourteenth in an effort to unite all women students and present a united front to insure that they would have *de jure* and *de facto* representation on the University Council and the FEU. Some members wanted half of the representation from each school/faculty to be female. Significantly, perhaps, Vasconcelos was advocating female suffrage. That same day, in another meeting, Gómez Arias was lambasted by Teodosio Montalván and others for having relinquished control of the university buildings without securing the rector's resignation. The next day, medical students began circulating a call for a return to class, arguing that the goals of the strike had been achieved; this forced a general meeting on the seventeenth. The upper-level medical students and those of secundaria #2 of the National Teachers School wanted to return to class. The Sociedad de Universitarias Mexicanas complained that they were not receiving a sympathetic ear. The meeting agreed to call the strike off at the end of the week in the expectation that Portes Gil would have issued the new law by that date. On the eighteenth, however, the strike committee had to meet again. This time Gómez Arias received a vote of confidence after having been accused of betraying the strikers. Brito Rosado was criticized by Serrano and Montalván for collaboration with the president. The women's group asked that they be permitted to collaborate in the strike, but the strikers agreed only to allow them to do so in the form that was necessary—in short, the men did not want to share power.[29]

---

[28] José M. Luján, "El fin de la huelga," *El Universal*, August 24, 1945; *New York Times*, June 12, 1929; *The Times* (London), June 13, 1929; *Excelsior*, June 12–13, 15, 1929.

[29] *Excelsior*, June 15, 17–19, 1929, reported this activity of the Sociedad de Universitarias but without providing background. That women were organizing was not surprising. Mexico's first International Congress of Women was held in Mérida in 1916, the first feminist congress met in Mexico City in 1921, and by 1923 there were a considerable number of women's organizations; see Ward Morton, *Woman Suffrage in Mexico*, pp. 3, 9. Women were also active in the Vasconcelos presidential campaign, which advocated female suffrage; see Camp, "Political leadership."

The Portes Gil law, announced on June 21, officially converted the National University of Mexico into the National Autonomous University of Mexico, but the details of the law were quite different.[30] The University Council was named the supreme internal authority and was to be composed of ex-officio members (the rector, the chief administrators, and a non-voting delegate from the Secretariat of Public Education) as well as elected members (two professors and two students from each school or facultad, plus their alternates; a male and a female member from the FEU; and a delegate from each alumni association recognized by the council). Faculty members elected had to have had two years of service as well as a regular appointment; they were elected by their peers for a two-year term. The students, who had to be full-time with a grade average of 80 percent or better, were elected annually by their student societies. One had to be in the highest year of the curriculum of his particular school. If 25 percent of the students of a school were female, one of that school's representatives had to be female. The FEU delegates were selected for unlimited terms by that organization. The law specified the powers of the council and the administrators, the qualifications for administrative positions, and other matters of governance. Although important for the university, these details were not as important for the immediate future as the sections that gave the president ultimate control.

The president retained both direct and indirect control. He sent a terna to the council from which it could choose the rector. The president could name extraordinary professors or conferenciantes charged against his own budget. He could veto any council resolution concerning the closing of a facultad or school, the admission of students, the revalidation of studies made in Mexico or in foreign countries, the eligibility requirements for scholarships funded by the national government, purchases of 100,000 pesos or more in a single purchase or of 10,000 or more pesos budgeted annually. He could veto any council resolution within thirty days of passage. In short, the purse strings, the choice of the rector, and the admission of students remained in the president's power, a far cry from autonomy.

The announcement of the law did not end the strike or the inter-

[30]The text is printed in *Excelsior*, June 22, 1929. See also Pinto Mazal, *El consejo universitario*, pp. 4–6.

nal bickering in the strike committee. The directors of the general strike committee immediately called for the resignations of all directors of schools and facultades (that is, council members) on the grounds that such an action would aid the reorganization of the university. The strike leaders began to attack the new law and each other. On June 22, some male students broke up a meeting of women in secundaria #6 who were discussing whether to continue the strike. During the last week of June, the students again tried to convince Portes Gil to accept their objections to the autonomy proposal. From their perspective, the most serious fault was that the president, rather than the council, would nominate the rector candidates. Portes Gil made it clear, however, that he would not yield on this point; as he put it, he did not want each school to nominate its own candidate, as had happened in Córdoba, Argentina; that is, he did not want the rectorship election to become politicized. Further, he thought the rector-president relationship should be the only tie between the state and the autonomous university. He also refused to yield to their other demands: the Museo Nacional de Arqueología e Historia and the national stadium would stay outside UNAM, the SEP (Secretariat of Public Education) would continue to have a delegate on the council, UNAM would report to the SEP, the academies in the schools and facultades would not be given the power to promote professors, and the president would keep his veto power. Public and university officials feared too much power in the hands of students; ex-rector Chávez wrote Moisés Sáenz of his fear that the students, in league with sympathetic professors, might constitute a majority and of his desire that the autonomy law specify that a measure had to have the approval of the majority of professors on the council before it became effective. Carlos Zapata Vela led a group into the music school at the request of the anti-director (Carlos Chavira) faction to close it on June 27, showing that this was not an idle fear.[31]

Women students and professors also tried to convince Portes Gil to modify his proposal in their favor. A delegation from the Sociedad de Universitarias Mexicanas met with the president on the afternoon of June 27 to plead for formal female representation, with votes, on the council. A group of professors, the Asociación de Profesores Univer-

[31] Ezequiel Chávez, letter to Moisés Sáenz, subsecretary of public education, June 28, 1929, Archivo Chávez, Caja IV.

sitarios, led by Enrique E. Schulz, Lombardo Toledano, Sánchez Pontón, and Ocaranza, persuaded Portes Gil on the twenty-eighth to postpone the autonomy decree so they could comment on it. The strike committee, fearing that this was an anti-student maneuver, broke up the APU meeting on the twenty-ninth. Brito Rosado wrested the podium from Sánchez Pontón and asserted that the presence of Palma Guillén and Sotero Prieto demonstrated that the meeting was anti-student. Zapata Vela leveled similar charges against Lombardo Toledano. Within a few years, the two would be leftist allies. This group of students represented the hard core of the strikers, the ones who would brook no interference with student demands and would use whatever means available to obtain their ends. De Gotari, Ramírez, Navar, Brito Rosado, and Zapata Vela were determined that they would not lose power to women or to professors and thought they had to use such tactics to maintain control of the strike and to guarantee their future power in UNAM.[32]

The tactic failed, however, for it split the strikers' ranks even further and caused Portes Gil to embrace the professors. Portes Gil publicly deplored the student action and allowed the APU to meet in a presidential room. The APU called for the promulgation of the autonomy law as soon as possible (thus cutting off future student efforts to amend it in their favor) and for the president to issue transitory rules. The strike directors vowed their continued opposition to anti-student professors, but it would be weeks before they would be able to drive some of them from their posts. A student group calling itself the Bloque de Estudiantes Universitarios, claiming more than 200 members, disavowed the strike committee and announced support of the APU. On July 2, the Federación de Escuelas Secundarias voted 13 to 10 to continue the strike but reversed itself in the face of strong opposition from some of the secundarias. The student society of public administration withdrew its recognition of the strike committee on the same day. Professors in each school/faculty began organizing their own societies. The strike committee found it necessary to deny on July 3 that the strike was broken, but it was, ending officially on July 11. At

[32] Pacheco Calvo, *La organización estudiantil*, p. 50. The reasons for the objections to Palma Guillén are unknown; she was a feminist. President Cárdenas would appoint her ambassador to Colombia, a major breakthrough for women. See Morton, *Woman Suffrage*, p. 17.

the end, the secundarias questioned their fate, but the strike committee could only offer the empty promise that they would get their own autonomy law.

Portes Gil emerged the victor, with his prestige and authority intact, for he had seemingly granted the university what its members had long demanded, autonomy from the state. By making the promise in late May, he had calmed a volatile situation; by delaying the fulfillment of the promise, he had given the strikers ample opportunity to argue among themselves and had secured for his government the little they could do. Henceforth, the contest would be between the state and UNAM, represented by the University Council, not between the state and students in the streets.

Having received the right to govern itself, the university community had to reorganize as an autonomous university, a task made difficult by the abrupt, unexpected change in internal governance rules and the tensions created by the strike. The first step was to install an interim administration until the council could be elected and make more permanent appointments. Ignacio García Téllez, who had strong ties to presidential candidate Ortiz Rubio, became interim rector. Luis Chico Goerne, a future rector, became law director, a post he would hold until 1933. Pedro de Alba, a leader of the newly formed Unión de Estudiantes y Professores, became director of both the ENP and the faculty of philosophy and letters. Ocaranza continued in medicine. José A. Cuevas became director of engineering. Roberto Medellín, a future rector, got chemical sciences. The autonomy decree also apparently meant that all professors lost their posts and that appointments to the faculties would have to be decided by the new council. Thus, the students would have ample opportunity to dictate the administrative and professorial composition of the new university.

Even before the new council was elected, prep students mounted their campaign to block the new curriculum. Under the leadership of Guerrero Briones, they met on July 13 to discuss the issue. When ENP secretary José Romano Muñoz stated that it was too difficult to change the plan at that late date and that all they might expect was a compromise, the meeting exploded into a heated debate. The students created a committee headed by Guerrero Briones to devise a student alternative to present to the new council and rector. Carlos Ramírez Zetina, who would play a major role in future student politics, served on this committee. The ENP opened a few days later with the old plan, but Alba promised that they would work on a compromise. [33]

Council and academy elections filled the last two weeks of July and provided a test of the ability of the strike leaders to retain power. There were limitations that precluded all strike leaders from obtaining posts. Since only four students (two delegates and two alternates) from a single school could be selected for council membership, few of the fifteen-person law school strike committee could be chosen. Further, the grade qualifications and class year requirement disqualified some. Gómez Arias and Julio Serrano, members of the law strike committee, were elected to the council; Gómez Arias had also headed the general strike committee. The engineers ignored the strike leaders, but they did reject José A. Cuevas as director in favor of Mariano Moctezuma by a 132 to 9 vote, an action that would have greater significance in days to come. Guerrero Briones and Vallejo Novelo, a member of the general strike committee, were elected to the council by the day ENP students. Brito Rosado was selected by the night ENP students. Guillermo Alvarez, from the general strike committee, was elected to the council from dentistry. Antonio Damiano, from the law strike committee, was elected to a law academy post, representing fourth-year students, and Baltasar Dromundo got an academy post, to represent first-year law students. Most general and law strike committee members, however, failed to get council seats. [34]

Portes Gil shocked the new council on August 1 by sending a rectorship terna composed of politicians close to himself. His primary choice, García Téllez, the interim rector, had been a federal deputy and oficial mayor (the third highest post) in Gobernación before assum-

[33] *Excelsior*, July 14, 16, 1929. Pedro de Alba, "Escándalos y algarados estudiantiles," *Novedades*, October 6, 1953, says that when he took over he got rid of the prefect system and relied on the self-discipline of the students. Further, he asserts that part of the 1929 victory was the right not to study. His careful handling of the students allowed him to avoid solving the curriculum issue as the students wanted.

[34] Pacheco Calvo, *La organización estudiantil*, p. 52, lists the student representatives on the council.

ing the rectorship. During the week prior to his nomination, he had advocated making UNAM a socialist university, a statement he had had to clarify on the university's opening day by defining socialist to mean being useful to society. Salvador Urbina, a Supreme Court justice, had been treasury undersecretary during de la Huerta's presidency; José A. Cuevas, an engineer, had just been defeated for the directorship of the engineering college; his nomination was obviously a direct slap at the university.[35]

The student members of the council immediately called a meeting to decide who to support, but on August 2 the council rejected all three nominees as being unqualified. Gómez Arias argued that some were ineligible because they were under forty or held public posts. Brito Rosado threatened another student strike because they were anti-student. Antonio Caso, author of the council communique to Portes Gil, criticized the nominees for not being published scholars.

The council and the president locked horns, for Portes Gil refused to back down. In his view the members of the terna had the necessary prestige and Revolutionary qualifications for the post; he refused to send another list. The council recognized that UNAM had not escaped political partisanship, so, on August 7, the members elected Urbina by a 53 to 9 margin over García Téllez. One additional vote was annulled and Cuevas was ignored. Urbina was seen as the least politically partisan of the three and the most adventuresome. Because he had been elected to spite Portes Gil, Urbina publicly refused the post and told the council to show more respect for the president's terna, thus protecting his own political career.[36]

Before the rectorship issue could be settled, however, the council's attention was diverted by outbursts within the university. The council had named Juana Palacios as director of the Escuela Superior Normal, but the students, through their academy, protested and announced their support of Manuel Barranco (who had been criticized in the council by Gómez Arias for being too pro-U.S.). The real objection to Palacios, however, was that she was female; she stayed. On August 14, a group of public administration students broke into a council meet-

[35] Luján, "La lucha," p. 12.
[36] Ibid.

ing to prevent the election of Luis F. León as director of their school. Ironically, the election was not scheduled for that day. Two days later Manuel Centurión, interim director, resigned because he had been attacked in the council. No doubt these incidents strengthened Portes Gil's resolve to put a strongman at the helm of UNAM.

The government began politely to threaten the council to elect one of Portes Gil's candidates. *Excelsior* reported a rumor on August 23 that the president was going to nominate Dr. Atl (Gerardo Murillo), Manlió Fabio Altamirano, and Antonio Díaz Soto y Gama as a new terna, thus suggesting that an alternative terna would be worse. In the same story, the newspaper also reported that the Chamber of Deputies was thinking about cutting the UNAM budget. Portes Gil soon denied the terna story, but its origin appears to have been calculated. The council quickly elected José López Lira as interim rector so that the university could continue to function. Nevertheless, the same deputies in the Chamber began suggesting on August 24 that they would not approve UNAM's budget, putting the money instead into rural schools. On the twenty-ninth, Portes Gil told the council to choose from the two remaining candidates. The next day, the Secretariat of Public Education announced that 460,000 pesos would be cut from the budget because the National Agricultural School was not in UNAM. The council unanimously approved a motion requesting a new terna. On the thirty-first, *Excelsior* reported that the budget cut would be 680,000 pesos. In case the council was not getting the message, some deputies suggested that the president appoint the rector, who, in turn, would appoint the directors from ternas supplied by the academies. The rector would be able to reject a terna, however, giving the president's man enormous power. Further, they suggested that the professors be appointed in the same way as were the directors, that the rector could replace professors who did not "work for the benefit of the university" (that is, do what the rector wanted), and that the rector could veto council acts and could also remove administrative personnel according to the civil service law. The president would become the final arbiter of rector-council disputes.

The pressure worked, for, in the tempestuous three-hour session on September 3, the council elected García Téllez. Cuevas got only two votes; Portes Gil's two votes (an interesting commentary on the reality of the situation) were treated the same as the three blank votes. The vote was easy to understand; as Gómez Arias put it, it was to prevent the suicide of the university.[37]

UNAM entered a period of relative peace in the fall of 1929. García Téllez would complete his three-year term, a feat rarely repeated by UNAM rectors. The assassination of Germán del Campo, student leader and Vasconcelista, on September 20, deeply disturbed many university students, not only because Germán was popular but because it was threatening; they did not start another strike in the university, however.[38] Vasconcelos went down to defeat in November, crying fraud and hinting at a possible revolt, but nothing happened other than his voluntary exile. Many of the 1929 strike leaders had been Vasconcelistas as well; perhaps his defeat had a chastening effect. So much time had been lost because of the strike; most students tried to catch up to prepare for the exams. The law students found that they had to take the reconocimientos after all. The ENP curriculum change was killed by the strike, but the plan of studies was changed in 1930 and changed again in 1931.[39] Castro Leal and Bassols were driven out of their posts, a victory for the strikers, but Bassols would return to haunt UNAM in the 1930s as secretary of public education. Gómez Arias, the single most important strike leader, almost immediately became part of the UNAM establishment as a professor and thus uninterested in causing more trouble.

In later years, the strike leaders, calling themselves the Generation of 1929, would claim that they had achieved university autonomy and that they were one of the great generations of twentieth-century Mexico, comparing themselves to the Ateneo de la Juventud and the Generation of 1915. In 1949, they published newspaper articles and pamphlets, and held a banquet, to celebrate their glorious conquest.[40]

[37] Horta, "Quince años," p. 14, says that strong student-professor agitation carried García Téllez to the rectory, but his meaning is unclear. My view is that Portes Gil wanted a strong man.

[38] Germán del Campo was the son of Ángel del Campo, noted nineteenth-century author; see Mario J. Santromán, "Bodas de plata de la autonomía universitaria," El Universal, May 17, 1954.

[39] Alba, "Las peripecias."

[40] See the anthology edited by Antonio Damiano, En torno, which includes articles by many of the principal leaders. Some of the articles were published at least once in newspapers. Other sources referring to the Generación de 1929 include Raúl Noriega, letter to El Nacional, June 19, 1949. Ángel Torres, "Sí hubo generación universitaria en

Various student strike leaders later took pride in their role in creating and sustaining the strike and in the acquisition of autonomy for the university. Some have asserted that autonomy was their idea, one they forced on Portes Gil, and that the Generation of 1929 had been one of the major groups in twentieth-century Mexican public life. It is true that some of the strike leaders—García Villalobos, Guevara, Dromundo, and Gonzáles Ramírez—had known each other well since ENP days, having congregated at the Casa de Troya or been active in FEM or CNE politics, but the responsibility for the strike lies not with a select few but with the leaders of the Escuela Nacional Preparatoria, for it was the prep group that radicalized the strike and created the confrontation conditions of May 23. Mendieta y Núñez has claimed that the law school students were responsible for university autonomy. Other participants have said that the idea came from the medical school. Portes Gil has repeatedly asserted that he knew nothing of student desires for autonomy in 1929 and that he simply picked up on an idea discussed by university people for years. The truth appears to be that some university students in 1929 advocated university autonomy but that there was no Generation of 1929, working in concert, to obtain it. Rather, Portes Gil used the idea to escape from a difficult situation. The claims about the Generation of 1929, instead, seem to be a romanticization of former times by men not wanting to admit that their motives in striking and shutting down the university were selfish.[41]

Easy as it might be to focus on the activities of student leaders or on street tactics, the most important lesson from the strike must be learned by examining the role of the government. It was the decision of government officials to use force on May 23 that drove medical

el año 1929, dice Martínez Mezquida," *El Nacional*, May 11, 1949; Alberto Morales Jiménez, "La generación de 29 ni está corrompida ni es retrograda," *El Nacional*, May 2, 1949, and "No han permitido actuar a la generación universitaria del año 1929, dice Reynoso," *El Nacional*, May 3, 1949; and Rubén Salazar Mallén, "La generación de 1929," *El Universal*, June 15, 1944. For a list of members, see *El Universal*, May 9, 1949. An example of the view that there was no such generation is Leopoldo Salazar Viniegra, "¿Quién empujo a la 29?" *Excelsior*, April 12, 1949.

[41] For the claim that the ENP had a major role, see Dromundo, "La Escuela Nacional preparatoria," in Damiano, *En Torno*, p. 26, but Agustín Rodríguez Cambas, medical school leader, asserts that Dromundo is wrong; see his article "La revolución universitaria en Mexico," *El Dictamen*, April 16, 1949. See Mendieta y Núñez, *Historia*, for the claim that the law school was responsible. Damiano, "Prolegomenas," p. 16, says that the idea came from medicine. The Portes Gil view has already been cited.

school students and with them thousands of others into what had been a localized event, one that promised to peter out soon. The use of violence by the government was counterproductive, for it was polarizing. It was the government, in the person of Portes Gil, that stopped the violence, defused the situation, split the strikers, and isolated UNAM from other educational institutions in the Federal District. Had the national situation not been tense because of events unconnected with the university, the national government might have acted differently. Regardless of this, however, Portes Gil emerges from the events as an extremely skillful politician who stepped in to save a situation created by his less competent subordinates. He deserves more credit as a molder of contemporary Mexico than he usually receives. Whether one credits Portes Gil or other officials, it is clear that the government was responsible for both the course and the outcome of the strike.

4. The Semi-Autonomous University, 1929–1933

MANY Mexicans feared that the Revolution died with Obregón in 1928 and sought to resuscitate it by seeking the selection of a leftist as the presidential candidate of the Partido Nacional Revolucionario in 1933. In the last years of his presidency, Calles had become more conservative (leftists suspected the influence of U.S. Ambassador Dwight Morrow) and was able to select conservatives such as Pascual Ortiz Rubio and Abelardo Rodríguez as presidents for 1929–1934. Calles was the power behind the throne, the Maximum Chief. Political wits joked that Ortiz Rubio and Rodríguez could make no decision without first consulting Calles, but all three shared a conservative outlook. The left resisted this political trend when it could and, recognizing the reality of political life, maneuvered to get one of its own into the presidency.

National politics in 1933 was consumed by these efforts to shift the nation leftward. The debate over socialist education was, among other things, an effort to redefine the political agenda. The crisis of capitalism in 1929 and the early 1930s strengthened the arguments of leftists. Even Franklin D. Roosevelt's New Deal aided the Mexican left, for an activist state with a concern for social justice was emerging in the very heart of the world capitalist order, thus undercutting the arguments of many conservatives.

The left was fortunate in 1933 in having Lázaro Cárdenas as the PNR candidate. Cárdenas was acceptable to a broad range of politicians. As a Revolutionary general, he had the respect of the army. As a reform governor of Michoacán, he had proven both his dedication to social reform and his ability to govern. His youth encouraged Calles to believe that he could be controlled. Shrewd as a politician, Cárdenas would marshal the support necessary for the nomination and then the support necessary for him to emerge as master of the nation.

Until 1933, however, the national political scene was relatively quiet. Calles, Ortíz Rubio, and Rodríguez were not dramatic activists in these years, and much of their time and effort went to coping with the economic depression. The direction the government would take was not immediately clear either. One had to watch and wait to see which direction Ortíz Rubio would take and then do it again when he resigned and Abelardo Rodríguez took his place.

The peace that followed the 1929 strike might have become permanent; the new law did not create the ideological struggle of 1932–1933 nor the crisis of October 1933 that prompted the government to jettison the university. Portes Gil's intention had been to neutralize the university as an active participant in national politics by creating a mechanism that would allow university members to settle their disputes without appealing to the national government and embroiling it in petty squabbles. In a sense, he sought to contain intra-UNAM factionalism in much the same way as the PNR contained political struggles.

Student representation on the council in the first two years after the promulgation of the new organic law worked well. Student parity with professors did not create discord. The electoral qualifications for the students almost insured that those elected would be persons who accepted the system as it was, who were similar to the professors. Gómez Arias, Azuela, Brito Rosado, Pacheco Calvo, and other student leaders banded together (opponents called their group the "mafia") to control the FEU, CNE, and the election of fellow student councilors by the academies and, as they saw it, to defend UNAM from the state, protect academic freedom, and make the institution a social critic. They had little confidence in García Téllez, believing him to be nothing more than a political hack. Their skill allowed them to ally with powerful faculty councilors—Alba, the Caso brothers, and Luis Chico Goerne— to pass proposals and play an important role in making university policy. Significantly, García Téllez complained of faculty absenteeism and of students not completing their courses, rather than of student politics, when he reported to the council in June 1931.[1]

From this power base inside the University Council, the mafia reached out into the national and international arenas. At the CNE

[1] Ignacio García Téllez, *Informe que el . . . rector de la Universidad Autónoma rinde al H. Consejo Universitario.*

meeting in Monterrey in February 1930, they led the delegates in the demand for autonomy for state universities, a Universidad del Norte in Saltillo, and the creation of a research and social action institute to work on national problems. In December of that year, through the CNE, they were hosts to the Primer Congreso Iberoamericano de Estudiantes. The idea for the congress and the confederation formed from it was not theirs, having originated at the 1928 Paris meeting of the International Student Federation when Antonio M. Imbert of Spain and Rodolfo Barón Castro of El Salvador pushed for it, but they reaped the credit. Although the Mexicans had agreed to sponsor the conference earlier, they had to wait until 1930, when the domestic political situation was calmer. By that year, the government was willing to help, for having delegates from Spain, Argentina, Bolivia, Colombia, Costa Rica, Cuba, Honduras, Nicaragua, the Dominican Republic, and Uruguay come to Mexico increased national prestige.[2]

Through the congress, Mexico seemed to be taking the lead in the Latin American University Reform Movement away from Argentina. The congress resolved in favor of university autonomy, co-government, voluntary class attendance, academic freedom, competitive examinations for teaching posts, research institutes, seminars, publication of monographs, and the end of final examinations in favor of papers. The delegates demanded that universities become agents of social change, studying national problems and disseminating their findings to the general public. The delegates also condemned the dictatorships of Gerardo Machado in Cuba and José Uriburu in Argentina, taking special note of the anti-student policies of both regimes.

The mafia fared well in these activities because its members shared similar views on procedures, policies, and goals with other members of the council. Nothing in the governance system guaranteed the continuance of this consensus. Instead, the system offered the opportunity for other politicians, within and outside of UNAM, to use the elections and posts obtained for their own or non-university ends or both. Since the national political system precluded non-PNR politicians or dissi-

[2] *Excelsior*, January 30, 1930; Rodríguez, "National University," pp. 209–212; and Mendieta y Núñez, *La reforma universitaria integral*, p. 23. For the Iberoamerican congress, see Pacheco Calvo, *La organización estudiantil*, pp. 64–66; Rodríguez, "National University," pp. 214–219; Mendieta y Núñez, "Ensayo sociológico sobre la universidad," in UNAM, *Primer censo universitario*, lxxxiii.

dents from gaining national power and made it difficult for PNR politicians to climb the political ladder, the UNAM system became one means of obtaining influence. By controlling student and faculty elections, ambitious politicians could gain control of the university. As a prestigious national institution with a large budget, UNAM was worth having. Patronage, status, and the chance to mold national ideology were the payoffs.

Vicente Lombardo Toledano, erstwhile professor, university administrator, labor leader, Marxist ideologue, and politician, exploited the opportunity to control UNAM. Concerned that Mexico had lost its revolutionary zeal under the presidents since Obregón, having developed into a Marxist from a Christian Democrat, and having extensive experience in and knowledge of UNAM, Lombardo Toledano took steps to build his own coalition, the antimafia, within the governance system in order to take over the university.

The antimafia consisted of a number of different elements. Many students had become concerned that the mafia would never leave office or the university and that the opportunities for others were being blocked. Further, the apparent contrast between the failure of capitalism demonstrated by the depression of the early 1930s and the Soviet Union's success during the same crisis, added to Mexico's own revolutionary tradition, created an ambience in which radical politicians could work. Lombardo Toledano recruited Luis Martínez Mezquida (a 1929 leader), Efraín Escamilla Martínez, and Perfecto Gutiérrez Zamora to lead the antimafia fight by infiltrating and capturing control of the FEU and CNE. That Narciso Bassols, also a Marxist, was the secretary of public education from 1931 to 1934 helped. Bassols had ample reason to want the ouster of the students responsible for his own departure from the law directorship.[3]

The blows began falling in June 1931, even before Bassols took over the education post from Puig. The government had been careful during the 1929 strike to avoid the union of UNAM students with those in technical schools, both to isolate the university students and to give more emphasis to technical and vocational education. One step in 1931 was to create a Federación Estudiantil de las Escuelas Técnicas, Indus-

[3] John Britton, *Educación y radicalismo en México*, I, 12, 27; Raúl Puga, "La autonomía de la Universidad Nacional," *Revista de Revistas* (October 22, 1933): 12–14; Mendieta y Núñez, *Historia*, p. 187; and González Cárdenas, *Cien años*, pp. 192–193.

triales y Comerciales independent of the FEU. Brito Rosado, FEU president, charged that the SEP authored this move, but Puig and his assistants denied all culpability. The second blow fell a few days later in Mexico City at the eighth national CNE meeting, which began June 10.[4]

The fight began ostensibly as a credentials issue, with the provincial students and technical school students demanding control of the organization. The CNE, despite its national name, had been run by UNAM students in the Federal District. The antimafia, seeking to consolidate the control it had been gaining, exploited this regionalistic sentiment. Within minutes after president Horacio Núñez opened the meeting, the assembly divided into two groups amidst the cry "¡Arriba la provincia!" Núñez nominated a credentials committee from each faction after the original committee was rejected. The mafia committee won, 60–44. Rather than resolving the problem, the election widened the split over the next two days. When the mafia committee's report was accepted by a 59–48 vote, the antimafia group, backed by the state delegations of Campeche, Veracruz, Tabasco, Puebla, Yucatán, Coahuila, and Sonora, as well as the new technical student federation and some FEU members, accused the mafia of accepting false credentials while rejecting legitimate ones and threatened to create a rival group, the Congreso Nacional de Estudiantes. The issue turned on the accrediting of the technical students, since their addition would throw the majority to the antimafia. Brito Rosado argued against their inclusion in the CNE because they had not been in the CNE for four months as required.

When, on June 12, Escamilla Martínez passed out lists of all the credentials presented, Brito Rosado again objected to the inclusion of the students from the new federation and added a new element by denying that Pacheco Calvo was his candidate for the CNE presidency. Instead, he asserted that he had no candidate, although the provincial students were actively campaigning for theirs. Núñez finally appointed one person from each side—Pacheco Calvo and Martínez Mezquida—to help Escamilla Martínez decide on the disputed delegations. As a leftist, Núñez probably intentionally gave the majority of the committee to the antimafia. The final result was the election of Martínez Mez-

4 *El Nacional,* June 7, 1931.

quida of the antimafia as CNE president. The mafia was left with control of a weakened FEU.[5]

Politicians had not yet finished with the old student leadership. By September, a Frente Revolucionario Estudiantil de Jalapa was attacking the CNE as unrepresentative of the students and of only being interested in influencing public opinion. The Liga de Estudiantes Revolucionarios (also called the Juventud Revolucionaria) led by Ernesto Rubio Rojo publicly attacked the FEU, CNE, and the Iberoamerican federation for the same reasons. The Liga was a pro-Calles group that had been active in the Ortiz Rubio presidential campaign.[6]

The political environment of the university changed in 1932; only some of the changes directly involved students. As part of the continued conflict between the state and the Catholic church in Mexico, President Ortiz Rubio had issued a decree withdrawing recognition of credits from Protestant and Catholic secondary schools. Graduates of these institutions would henceforth have to take an exam from the education ministry to be admitted to the university. Since these schools fed students into UNAM, and since the decree would determine the admission patterns of the institution, many students were directly affected. Inexplicably, none of the regular student organizations protested.

Most students who thought about political matters followed the nationalist and progressive views of the CNE. In an open letter to the Pan-American Student Congress meeting in Miami, the CNE asserted that U.S. and Mexican students were poles apart in views. The CNE position included demands for absolute equality among peoples, the condemnation of imperialism, non-intervention in the internal affairs of other countries, and the importance of respect for other cultures and traditions. Specifically, the CNE questioned whether U.S. students knew what their country was doing in Nicaragua, Cuba, the Dominican Republic, Puerto Rico, Haiti, Columbia, Spain, and Mexico.[7]

In spite of this CNE support of Mexican foreign policy, the university suffered other attacks in 1932 from the national government.

[5] *Excelsior,* June 11–13, 1931.
[6] They might have been ephemeral organizations organized to split student ranks. No further notices of their activities have been discovered during the research for this work. *Excelsior,* June 11–13, 1931; *El Universal,* September 18, 1931; and *El Nacional,* November 11, 18, 1931.
[7] *New York Times,* January 2, 23, 1932.

When UNAM fired a number of employees in an economy move without giving them the required three months' severance pay, process servers attached the furniture in the university secretary's office. One thousand students organized a twenty-four-hour guard to block any more process servers. The government finally transferred ninety thousand pesos to resolve the dispute, but the issue raised questions about the juridical status of the university. It was being treated as a private corporation rather than as a government agency with sovereign immunity. Rector García Téllez was of little help, for he had taken leave to campaign for a federal deputyship. In July, Bassols circumscribed UNAM further by forbidding it to recognize foreign degrees except for internal purposes, since, he argued, such a step affected professional licensing and foreign policy, both prerogatives of the state.[8]

The split in the student ranks continued during the summer of 1932 as the antimafia fought to keep control. At the CNE meeting in Toluca in late June and early July, the FEU attacked CNE president Martínez Mezquida, charging that he was biased, but the CNE refused to recognize the FEU. It also refused to recognize the technical student federation with which it had just recently allied. These changes were not student-inspired. Lombardo Toledano attended the CNE meeting. Another of his henchmen, Gutiérrez Zamora, assumed the presidency when the delegates decided to forbid the reelection of officers. The delegates adopted positions more leftist than those of the mafia, asserting that the Revolution had stalled and that it lacked ideological consistency. Almost a month later, on July 25, CNE officers led an anti-Machado demonstration in the ENP amphitheater; the police arrested a few demonstrators but avoided a confrontation. By the fall of 1932, then, there were at least three student groups of some importance: the CNE under the control of Lombardo Toledano, the FEU as the last bastion of the mafia, and the technical student federation controlled by the national government.

The FEU was reorganized in 1932. The former Federación Estudiantil Universitaria del Distrito Federal (also called the FEU and the FEM) disbanded and a Federación Estudiantil Universitaria, limited

[8] New York Times, March 18, 1932, Excelsior, March 18, 1932; and Narciso Bassols, "Declaración sobre las razones que dice tener la Universidad para considerarse competente para la revalidación de títulos procedentes del extranjero," issued July 8, 1932, reprinted in Antonio Luna Arroya, ed., La obra educativa de Narciso Bassols, p. 39.

to UNAM students, was created in its place. Meeting on August 6, the provisional president, Roberto Patiño Córdoba (who also would serve as law student president), turned the FEU over to Alfonso Guerrero Briones, the former prep school militant of 1929. Then the entire FEU met on August 23 in an amicable session. Outwardly, it appeared the UNAM students were again united and might use their organization to defend their interests.[9]

These hopes were dashed, however, when the FEU met on November 26. Vice-president Luis Gijón and another officer accused Guerrero Briones of dictatorial, arbitrary, and secretive action, asserting that he was meeting with a conservative coalition of Gómez Arias, Antonio Díaz Soto y Gama, and José M. de los Reyes to plot the reelection of Alba as ENP director even though there were serious irregularities in the ENP administration. Two officers, José Rivera Albarrán (who would play an important role in future events) and Rubén Aguirre, moved that Guerrero Briones step aside from the presidency and become president of the debates. In a vote by schools, the motion lost nine to one. Two other delegates then moved that the FEU unanimously reject the "absurd charges," remove the two challengers from office, and give emergency powers to Guerrero Briones. The motion passed. The FEU went further, calling for the CNE to stay out of the director elections taking place in November and December because it was not an UNAM organization.

The fight within the FEU was part of a long-term strategy by leftists to gain control of UNAM and force it into a more progressive course. UNAM was essentially a traditionalist institution that prepared students to assume elite positions. Its curriculum differed little from what it had been in 1910 except for the incorporation of such previous non-university schools as business and the creation of an economics faculty inside the law school. In the midst of an economic depression in a poor, underdeveloped country, UNAM was making little or no effort to meet the special needs of society by training students in science, technology, and the management sciences. Instead, it drained large resources from the national budget to educate a relatively small number of persons for the overcrowded liberal professions. The 1929 autonomy law and its practical operation promised little in the way of change in spite of student protestations of interest in making the university a servant of society. University critics believed that, unless persons committed to the masses and national needs gained control, UNAM would continue to be unresponsive.[10]

The first step was to elect a sympathetic rector at the regularly scheduled elections in September 1932. Roberto Medellín became the progressive candidate against José González Ureña and Basilio Romo. Lombardo Toledano, recently elected director of the small but leftist plastic arts school, eloquently backed Medellín. Few councilors realized at the time, however, that Medellín was a front man for Lombardo Toledano. Some members began complaining of Medellín's administrative style by November, accusing him of unfairness in the distribution of scholarships (he was giving them to his supporters) and of being inaccessible. Medellín denied the charges publicly and bided his time.[11]

The hidden agenda behind Medellín's election was revealed in the directorship elections in November, when Lombardo Toledano sought election as ENP director, a position he had held in 1923. Part of the split in the FEU that month had been over what one student leader called the imposition of Lombardo Toledano as ENP director with the aid of the rector, part of the council, and Bassols. The FEU in December adopted one resolution specifying that its members did not want him as ENP director and another adopting the censure resolution of the ENP student society, which condemned the councilors who supported Lombardo Toledano and the rector. Instead, the ENP student society had voted unanimously in November for the continuance of Alba in the directorship.[12]

The issue split the ENP students into two militant factions. One group, perhaps the majority, resisted all efforts to put Lombardo Toledano into office. They were supported by Díaz Soto y Gama, the old Revolutionary, and Lauro G. Caloca, a former Senator and still an active politician. To them, the "imposition" of Lombardo Toledano by Bassols meant the loss of university autonomy and a reduction of their own influence. Lombardo Toledano, on the other hand, enjoyed the

[10] See Lombardo Toledano's statement to the council that UNAM ought to serve the state and train technicians, *Excelsior*, December 3, 1932.

[11] *Excelsior*, September 8, 13, and November 9, 1932; Silva Herzog, *Una historia*, p. 59.

[12] FEU, *Anuario*, pp. 57–58.

support of the first-year prep students led by Carlos Madrazo, a radical from Tabasco who was initiating a long career as a politician. On November 26, when the academy met to elect the director, some students tried to disqualify some of the most prominent Lombardo Toledano supporters, accusing them of having made a deal with the candidate, Díaz Soto y Gama, himself a candidate and perhaps sensing defeat, argued that their votes could not be counted, hoping to reduce the number of voters below the quorum of thirty-one. Alba overruled him, however, and Lombardo Toledano won easily with twenty-two votes over the fourteen of Díaz Soto y Gama and the one of a third candidate. The thirty-seven-vote total meant the quorum maneuver was doomed to failure. Much to the surprise of those present, many, including student secretary José M. de los Reyes, had switched to Lombardo Toledano when it appeared that he was winning. After the election, both groups went to *Excelsior* to complain about the other. The Díaz Soto y Gama group threatened direct action and a strike if Lombardo Toledano actually tried to take office, but the fact that he had been elected legally would forestall such an action.[13]

Lombardo Toledano and his supporters did not fare as well in the other schools. Ignacio Chávez, a respected cardiologist with leftist sentiments, easily won the directorship of medicine, but he was his own person, unlikely to toady to anyone. Héctor Villagrón García won in architecture with the support of Gómez Arias, in spite of Lombardo Toledano's accusation that he was a Catholic (meaning that he was a tool of the church), but the vote was close, 32–26. In commerce, Lombardo Toledano supported the student favorite, Roberto Casas Alatriste, who won.

None of these were as important as the law directorship, however, for law students, activists by tradition, would supply the bulk of future politicians. To block leftist control of the school, Rodulfo Brito Foucher ran in alliance with remnants of the old mafia, some antimafia members, and a group led by Patiño Córdoba, the latter two fearing the influence of Lombardo Toledano. Roberto A. Esteva Ruiz, a political moderate, had the strongest support in the academy, but neither he nor the leftist Enrique González Aparicio, the third candidate, lined up enough support. During the pre-election debate, which supported

13 *Excelsior*, November 19, 26, 27, 1932; Mendieta y Núñez, *Historia*, p. 188; Baltasar Dromundo, *Mi calle en San Ildefonso*, pp. 172–173.

González Aparicio, students smashed windows and doors to enter the meeting room, forcing the academy to recess. The CNE immediately denied responsibility to *Excelsior* and demanded that persons of "known religious affiliation" (Catholic activists) not be elected directors. Many believed that the CNE was responsible, however, and when the law director was finally elected by the council on November 30, Brito Foucher won with thirty-eight votes to twenty-two for González Aparicio and five for Esteva Ruiz.[14]

These elections heralded a fundamental change in the internal politics of UNAM. Students had disagreed before and outsiders had used students as tools. What was different was the threat of and use of force. Not only had students disrupted the law school education but porras (gangs) had entered the fray in other schools. Although these initial porras appear to have been leftists under the control of Lombardo Toledano, the use of such groups would not be limited to the left. Brito Foucher, as law director, began to build his own cadre of shock troops to impose his will on the school and, he hoped, to prepare for his election as rector. Further, Catholic students, alarmed by the animosity toward their religion and themselves, had begun to organize to combat the leftists.

Much of the student conflict of the 1930s in UNAM would be ideological conflict between traditionalists, led by the Unión Nacional de Estudiantes Católicos, on the one hand, and reformers, led by Marxists and radicals, on the other. Intermingled with these events, as both cause and effect, would be the efforts of the state to establish complete control over the educational system and to alter its mission and scope so as to provide the skills needed for a modernizing society. This state activity would produce a hysterical reaction by traditionalists, particularly Catholics, who thought civilization itself was threatened.

Because the participants in the church-state conflict have shown each other little quarter in their zeal to credit themselves with the noblest and their opponents with the basest motives, scholars need to be extremely careful and precise in examining any facet of the conflict. Unfortunately, the historiographical tendency has been for historians to side with one group or the other. Modern scholars trained in the positivist and logical positivist traditions find it almost impossible to

---

[14] *Excelsior*, November 19, 30, and December 1, 1932; Mendieta y Núñez, *Historia*, p. 188.

take a mystery religion and its institutions seriously. From their perspective, anyone who professes to believe such nonsense is benighted, fanatical, or deceptive and is, consciously or unconsciously, an exploiter of human credulity. Defenders of the faith often use the same or worse descriptions of their opponents, for they believe that only Christianity knows what reality is. This attempt to dichotomize the population makes it difficult to deal in shades of gray, but the conflict of the 1930s cannot be limned in black or white. Hence, it is necessary to detail the history of the most important Catholic university student organization in order to understand the events.

The Unión Nacional de Estudiantes Católicos (UNEC) was an unusual Catholic organization in that it had little direct contact with the church hierarchy or other Catholic organizations. It was organized and sponsored by the Society of Jesus, thus being able to bypass the principal Catholic young men's group, the Asociación Católica de la Juventud Mexicana, and Acción Católica, the umbrella lay organization formed in 1929 after the modus vivendi with the state. UNEC was nominally a part of Catholic Action, but the relationship was so weak that it took a major effort on the part of the church leadership to force UNEC into Catholic Action in the early 1940s, and the coercion caused the practical dissolution of UNEC.[15]

UNEC was created with limited goals. Its immediate predecessor had been the Confederación Nacional de Estudiantes Católicos (CNECM), created in 1926 to combat attacks against Catholic schools by the anticlerical Calles government. Its members were drawn primarily from these schools. By 1931, this threat had declined and the members were entering the university, where they met hostility because of their religiosity and where the prevailing secular views threatened their religious beliefs. The organizational meeting of UNEC was to take place days before the celebration of the Convención Iberoamericana de Estudiantes Católicos (CIDEC) in December 1931. Led by Ramón Silva Martínez, a Jesuit who had been a collaborator of Acción Populaire Francaise, UNEC was to be a leader in the Jesuit effort to organize university students in Spanish-speaking countries into a

[15] Sources for UNEC are Luis Calderón Vega, *Cuba 88: Memorias de la UNEC*, an account by a former president and its principal historian; Joseph Ledit, *Rise of the Downtrodden*, pp. 68–73; E. R. Gottshalk, "Catholicism and Catholic Action in Mexico," p. 49. No further citations will be made.

unit that would fight to reestablish Catholic predominance in universities. A second important goal of UNEC was to give Catholic university students the moral support and guidance they needed to face the pressures of the secular and hostile university and to provide acceptable Catholic answers to the pressing social and economic issues of the day.

Much of the internal life of UNEC revolved around its headquarters at Calle Cuba #88 in the old university quarter. Here, the students congregated to debate issues, worship, use the library, and socialize. It would become the staging base for forays into other student organizations, the university, and the nation at large. Students were organized into subgroups by academic discipline—Lex (law), Bio (medicine), and Labor (engineering, architecture, and chemical sciences). They shared a common periodical, *Proa*, which contained literary efforts and religious, political, and social news.

Most of 1931 was spent preparing for the Iberoamerican convention in addition to the organization efforts for UNEC. The convention was very much a Mexican affair. The organizing committee consisted of budding Catholic lay leaders and politicians; many would be founding members of the Partido Acción Nacional in 1939. Some would play important roles in later Iberoamerican congresses in Rome (1932), Lima (1939), Bogotá (1942), and Santiago, Chile (1944). They spent most of 1931 in issuing a program, inviting delegates, collecting funds, and soliciting support from other Catholics. Since the meeting was timed to celebrate the 400th anniversary of the "apparition" of Our Lady of Guadalupe, the patron saint of Mexico and, according to some views, of Latin America, the congress was in part a Mexican effort to dominate Catholic student movements in Hispanic America.[16]

The Jesuits planned to use the meeting to demonstrate that it was possible to support both Catholicism and Revolution as part of their goal of training a generation capable of functioning in Revolutionary Mexico. In this light, few of the conclusions of the convention were surprising. Protestantism was condemned for fostering birth control, divorce, and practices that would "cause society to dissolve into anar-

---

[16] Confederación Iberoamericana de Estudiantes Católicas, *Convocatoria* and *Conclusiones aprobadas*. The organizers were Salvador Noriega, Luis Islas García, Enrique de la Mora y Palomar, Ernesto Santiago López, J. J. Perez Sandí, J. Jesús Toral, Luis de Garay, and Manuel Ulloa Ortiz.

chy." In addition, the conventioneers contradictorily asserted that Protestantism was a nursery of Communism and that its members were agents of U.S. capitalist penetration of Iberoamerica. As a counterpoise, the delegates lauded Catholicism as a common bond and encouraged greater ties with the National Catholic Welfare Conference (the Catholic Action organization in the U.S.).

On the agrarian question, one of the burning issues of the day, the delegates attacked both Liberalism for fostering haciendas and egoism and the Revolution for creating insecurity in land titles, which debilitated production and experimentation. Rather than criticizing agrarian reform and the ejidos (collective or communal farms) emerging from it, the delegates saw reform as necessary and the ejidos as an appropriate solution to the problem. Their fire was concentrated on the application of a homogeneous solution to a heterogeneous problem, the lack of technical and moral education for agricultural innovation, and the failure to provide the recipients of the redistributed land with the means of cultivation. They attacked the creation of new haciendas owned by politicians. Not surprisingly, they also complained about the constitutional prohibition against the church's owning real property. In toto, however, the posture of the delegates and therefore the UNEC was surprisingly progressive, since many churchmen had fought agrarian reform since its beginning.

On labor questions, the delegates held somewhat similar views. They called for the enforcement of the labor provisions of the Constitution and the federal labor law, one of the most advanced in the world. CIDEC expressed particular interest in artisans, miners, workers outside the basic industries, and the unorganized, for they had the least protection against the evils of capitalism. Miners and other workers in dangerous occupations were the most likely to respond to "red socialism" (Marxist-Leninism) and needed special attention for that reason alone, for only that brand of socialism threatened the freedom of workers. Female workers were singled out as a special class. They needed higher pay, better legal protection, educational opportunities in or near factories, better hygienic conditions in which to work, better factory recreational facilities, and the enforcement of the existing maternity benefits. All workers should have an eight-hour day, annual vacations, the right to participate in the operation and management of enterprises, and shares in the profits, particularly through stock ownership. The state should procure cheap, clean housing for workers, help establish cooperatives and savings associations, end child labor, and prohibit the employment of women in dangerous factories.

The delegates also addressed a scattering of other social problems. Emigrating to the United States was to be discouraged, in part because of the dangers of Protestantism. Urban population concentrations were to be avoided, for cities were corrupt and inhumane. Poverty was to be wiped out by the application of scientifically organized charity along Swiss lines. The government was called upon to make major efforts to wipe out disease.

That these statements were liberal for the day can easily mislead the casual observer into believing that CIDEC and UNEC were more progressive than they actually were. Compared to New Deal liberals in the United States as well as to many fellow Mexicans, the delegates displayed more social conscience and willingness to restructure property relationships in favor of workers. The principal instrument of the envisaged new order, however, was the recognition by workers and employers that they were interdependent, that they should love one another and work for the common good. The delegates were careful to counterbalance claims to rights with an equal emphasis on duties, to liberty with responsibility. In short, social problems could not be addressed outside the teachings of the Catholic church. The appearance of the papal encyclical *Quadragesimo Anno* in 1931 meant that Catholics could take more liberal positions on social issues than they had in the past, but it did not mean that they could call for a worker-peasant state. Instead, they followed a line of thought that led to a corporate state, although not along fascist lines.

During the rest of the 1930s, UNEC members would spread these views to university students inside and outside Mexico City. Manuel Ulloa Ortiz, the first president (1931–1934), had minimal overt involvement in national student politics, but Armando Chávez Camacho (1934–1936), Daniel Kuri Breña (1936–1938), and Jesús Hernández Díaz (1938–1941) became leaders of the CNE and the chief opponents of leftist students. After the founding of PAN in 1939, UNEC began to decline because the new political party performed many of its functions. Later presidents—Luis Calderón Vega (1941–1942), Manuel Cantú Méndez (1942–1943), and Guillermo Castillo Hernández (1943) presided over the last troubled days of UNEC before the Jesuits disbanded it rather than yield control to Catholic Action. Thereafter the Jesuits spent their efforts organizing and operating the Universidad Iberoamericana in Mexico City, Calderón Vega and Cantú Mendez were also active PAN members and must have found it difficult to keep their two different roles separate.

Leftist students had also begun to organize within the hemisphere and, at the May 1933 Congreso Iberoamericano de Estudiantes in San José, Costa Rica, issued their program for the next few years. Prominent among the participants was Efraín Escamilla Martínez, the secretary-general of the congress. According to their proclamations, the delegates believed that capitalism was in its last hours and that the young people of Iberoamerica had to lead the masses to a better future. University students were to form an advance guard that would raise the consciousness of workers and aid them by intervening in the internal affairs of manual workers' associations, helping them solve their problems by studying economic and technical problems of the working class, reforming existing legislation, and providing free professional help. On other matters, the delegates resolved against private schools in favor of state-controlled education that emphasized social conscience and anti-imperialism. In short, the students identified with the working masses, condemned capitalism and imperialism, and promised to work for a worker-oriented society.[17]

Encouraged by the San José conference, student leftists and their non-student allies accelerated their efforts to take over UNAM. Their control of the CNE gave them a national voice, but it was the FEU that actually controlled student politics within the university. Their first step, then, came almost immediately after San José as they began organizing for the FEU presidential elections of June and July 1933. Almost simultaneously, the leftists would announce the convocation of the Primer Congreso de Universitarios Mexicanos, to be held in the national prep school amphitheater in September. This ostensibly was an effort to coordinate higher education in the republic to create interinstitutional cooperation. The hidden agenda, revealed at the congress, was to facilitate leftist control. So that non-leftist students would not be alerted to their goals, the leftists delayed announcing the dates

[17] Confederación Iberoamericana de Estudiantes, *Segundo Congreso Iberoamericano de Estudiantes*.

and site of the tenth CNE congress until after the FEU elections and with only one month's notice of the actual meeting. The plan, then, was to move from control of the CNE (accomplished the year before) to the San José congress (May) to the announcement of the universities' congress (May) to the capturing of control of the FEU (May–July) to the announcement of the CNE meeting to the CNE meeting itself, and then immediately to the Primer Congreso. The non-leftists would be caught off guard and the momentum established would be too great to overcome.

The choice of the leftist or antimafia candidate provoked unusual discord in the FEU electoral process and led to polarization and violence. The candidate was Alonso Garrido Canabal, a chemical sciences student and brother of Tabascan governor Tomás Garrido Canabal, one of the most radical and anticlerical men in politics. His efforts to drive religion out of his state would later be fictionalized by the English novelist Graham Greene in *The Power and the Glory*. To enforce his views, the governor organized a paramilitary group, Redshirts, who terrorized the governor's opponents. Alonso would bring Redshirts to Mexico City to help him control the student election, thus introducing pistoleros into the university. Garrido Canabal's candidacy frightened not only conservatives but some leftists as well, partly because his brand of radicalism was sui generis and partly because they did not want the family to gain a power base in the capital.[18]

Garrido Canabal enjoyed the backing of both university and non-university people. Rector Medellín, secretary-general Jiménez Rueda (a former Catholic activist), and ENP director Lombardo Toledano used all their powers to get him declared the victor. Martínez Mezquida and day ENP student president Carlos Madrazo (a Tabascan radical) led the UNAM student forces. Technical students, outside UNAM, also joined the fray. Although proof is difficult to obtain, there are grounds to believe that education secretary Bassols helped as well; the anti-leftists certainly thought so, and such a move was consistent with his career.

Law director Brito Foucher (a long-time Tabascan rival of Garrido

[18] The following account of the election is taken from Mendieta y Núñez, *Historia*, pp. 188–189; González Cárdenas, *Cien años*, p. 104; *Excelsior*, June 11, 13, 17, 18, and July 7, 1933; and Horta, "Quince años." No further citations to these sources will be made.

Canabal) and student leader José Vallejo Novelo led the opposition. When Brito Foucher learned that Alonso Garrido Canabal was to be the leftist candidate and that Vallejo Novelo, José Rivera Albarrán, and José Pavía Crespo, all law students, were running for the FEU presidency, he asked law president Octavio González Cárdenas to call a law student assembly to choose a single candidate. Vallejo Novelo won. Because of this association with Brito Foucher, his opponents would successfully label him a tool of the clerical reaction, but his real goal was complete university autonomy. He led the Partido Autonomista Universitaria, a law school group formed for that purpose. Covertly joining the battle were UNEC members.

Garrido Canabal was declared the victor, but his opponents disputed the results. On June 10, Vallejo Novelo won in philosophy and letters (a conservative school), 87–69, and in veterinary medicine, 29–13, but the next day law and medicine students invaded the ENP before the urns were opened to insure that he would not win there. On the eighteenth, Brito Foucher asserted that engineering had sold its votes to Garrido Canabal for 2,500 pesos. The Partido Autonomista Universitaria announced on July 7 that it recognized Vallejo Novelo as FEU presidency and complained of CNE intervention in the elections. Commerce students withdrew from the FEU. The true results are hard to determine. The intervention of university administrators, the terror tactics of the Redshirts (who brandished pistols), and the work of the CNE and the technical students must have had some effect on the outcome, but the amount is problematical. González Cárdenas, years later, asserted that Garrido Canabal won, but the law students, unaccustomed to losing control of the FEU, refused to recognize the new president or to cooperate. From the election until the successful October strike, the law students would be the principal opposition to the leftists' plans.

Although it is clear that the leftists planned to take control of the university, these efforts were only part of a more general effort by leftists to elect one of their own as president of the nation in 1934. Pascual Ortiz Rubio, president until 1932, and Abelardo Rodríguez, president from 1932 to 1934, were conservatives. Social and economic reform efforts in the nation had virtually stopped, even though the depression had increased suffering. The 1934 election (the campaign began in 1933) offered the first opportunity to turn the nation in a new direction. Much of 1933 was spent in trying to influence the selection of the presidential candidate and, once he was selected, to campaign for him in order to gain influence in the new administration. Leftists rallied around General Lázaro Cárdenas, the reform governor of Michoacán.

Twenty-five student organizations fused on July 13, 1933, to create the Partido Nacional Estudiantil Pro Cárdenas and call a convention in Morelia, Michoacán, for July 16–21. The officers of the old national student party were deposed and a leftist group led by Alejandro Gómez Maganda, president, and Natalio Vázquez Pallares, organizer, put in their place. Baltasar Dromundo of the 1929 strike and Roberto Patiño Córdoba, soon to be law student president, participated, but no other officers or committee members would come from the traditional UNAM student leadership. García Téllez, the former rector, participated, however, for he had ties to Cárdenas. Significantly, federal deputy Froylán C. Manjarrez, who would be one of the chief advocates of "socialist education" and later would be director of *El Nacional* (the PNR newspaper) under Cárdenas, played an active role, indicating that the meeting was endorsed by the future president.

The convention was replete with socialist oratory and calls for a classless society in Mexico. Both the convocatory document and the convention resolutions called for a radical transformation of capitalist society, the proletarization of the university (which was considered to be a bastion of privilege and reaction), the socialization of wealth and education, and the advent of the class struggle. The university presented a special problem for the delegates. Some wanted to force it to teach scientific technology and socialist principles; others wanted to cut it loose from the government and thereafter ignore it. The delegates knew what their central purpose was, however; they declared themselves in favor of Cárdenas's nomination by the PNR and of his election to the presidency in 1934.[19]

If centrists and rightists missed this signal that the left was on the move and that the university would be a target, the tenth CNE congress in Veracruz, August 25 to September 2, provided another one. Not all of the 120 delegates from twenty-one states were socialists— some liberals and Catholics attended—but the convention was social-

[19]Mayo, *Educación socialista*, pp. 56–67; Alberto Bremauntz, *La educación socialista en México*, pp. 164–166; and *El Nacional*, July 24, 1933.

ist from start to finish. Bassols sent a personal representative, as did Governor Gonzalo Vázquez Vela (who would follow Bassols as education secretary); two Tabascan federal deputies and Senator Alcides Caparroso, a confidante of Tomás Garrido Canabal, monitored the credentials committee, which was controlled by socialist students. Thus, a socialist voting majority was insured. Early in the convention, held in the assembly hall of the stevedores' union, some students and stevedores discussed creating a worker-student alliance, but nothing came of it. The purpose of the congress was to present the claim that virtually all university students supported socialist goals; the delegates changed CNE rules to include automatically all university students as members.[20]

Some of the resolutions passed were commonplace. The delegates stated their opposition to obligatory military service. They again condemned dictatorships in Latin America and their ally, U.S. imperialism, asserting that these blocked the development of the class struggle; they vowed to work for the overthrow of the dictatorships and the end of U.S. interventionism.[21]

Sexual education provoked a long, heated debate even among progressive delegates. The controversy over sexual education had begun in Mexico the year before and would last into 1934. The controversy is a complex subject with a detailed history of its own. The proposal itself was simple and straightforward. Beginning in mid-elementary school, students would be taught the essential principles of plant reproduction; as they grew older, they would be taught personal hygiene, human reproduction, and sexual responsibility. Advocates believed this necessary because of the pandemic proportions of venereal disease, "natural" children, sexual perversion, abortions, and the unwillingness of parents to assume responsibility for sex education. Many parents, however, would see this as a direct attack on parental prerogatives (the claim traditionalists would make). Bassols and the government came under severe attack for the program and finally retreated in the face of opposition. The CNE, however, approved the proposition at its convention.[22]

[20] Mayo, *Educación socialista*, pp. 68–71. The students were Gutiérrez Zamora, Guillermo G. Ibarra, and Santiago López.

[21] Mayo, *Educación socialista*, pp. 70–71.

[22] Mayo, *Educación socialista*, pp. 71–72; Britton, *Educación y radicalismo*, I, 97–103.

Socialist education, the other major controversial issue considered, was the only one that could generate more heat than sexual education. Its proponents called for the radical transformation of Mexico into a socialist state. The CNE focused on schools, particularly the university. Private education was to be abolished, for they believed it only served the bourgeoisie. Universities (UNAM was the real target) were to become national research centers to attack national problems. They were to train professionals with a socialist conscience who would work for the creation of a socialist society controlled by workers. The CNE vowed to work in accordance with the socialist principles of the Iberoamerican student federation stated in the recent San José meeting. Lombardo Toledano came to the last session of the CNE congress to give his stamp of approval. Two of his supporters, Guillermo G. Ibarra and Manuel Boneta, had been elected CNE president and secretary-general, respectively. They would carry this support of socialist education into the Primer Congreso de Universitarios Mexicanos, scheduled to meet in UNAM September 7–14.

The overt agenda of the first university congress gave little hint of what was to come. UNAM had previously ignored the state universities, seeing itself as a giant among pygmies, as *the* university that other universities unsuccessfully tried to emulate. But the economic crisis, the decline of public support, the growing hostility of the government, and the accession of more public-spirited administrators to top posts combined to reduce that snobbism. The stated goals of the congress were to create inter-university cooperation, to establish student and faculty interchanges, to standardize practices, and to define the role of the university sector vis-à-vis the needs of society, focusing on scientific and technical education. To emphasize the importance to the government of this first effort at institutional cooperation, the organizers arranged for President Rodríguez to serve as honorary president and to give the opening address. Further, Secretary of Education Bassols was made an honorary officer. UNAM officials such as Medellín and Jiménez Rueda dominated the presidium, but other rectors, such as Enrique Díaz de León of the Universidad de Guadalajara, also had conspicuous roles, and this bolstered the claim that it was a national meeting.[23]

23 University delegates came from virtually every state in the nation. This was the most comprehensive meeting of higher education people in the history of Mexico. See

The deck was stacked, however. Besides Bassols, Medellín, and Jiménez Rueda, the reform group also had Lombardo Toledano, Martínez Mezquida, Boneta, Díaz de León, and Gutiérrez Zamora in key positions. They controlled the organizing committee and wrote the agenda. Medellín set the tone in his opening address, warning that the government considered the university a backward institution. Two days later, on September 9, the press prematurely revealed the position the congress was to take by printing an abstract from the position paper prepared by Díaz de León. The Guadalajaran rector argued that since culture is the product of the ruling class, universities, which mold culture, should become revolutionary agents and serve the needs of a worker state by emphasizing the social functions of professional careers and by teaching technical subjects.[24]

Stirred by this premature shot, delegates and outsiders anxiously awaited the full salvo to be delivered, as everyone knew, by Lombardo Toledano when he presented his committee report. Few could doubt the position he would take, for his public career had been evolving leftward since he graduated from UNAM in 1919, nor could they doubt the importance of his remarks, for he was a rising political star. He had entered politics early, serving as chief clerk of the Federal District in 1921 and as interim governor of Puebla in 1923. He became a leader of CROM in 1923 and did not break with the leadership of its boss, Luis Morones, until 1932. In 1933, he was creating a new labor union, the Confederación de Trabajadores Mexicanos, which would become powerful once Cárdenas became national president. As a labor leader, politician, and intellectual, he had stated his views in numerous articles and books. Now, in front of the nation's educational leaders, he would use his considerable oratorical talents to persuade this friendly crowd to make his views the official ideology of Mexican universities.[25] Since he was not an orthodox Marxist, he did not call for a class

---

[24]"This created a debate within the committee. Mayo, *Educación socialista*, pp. 75–78; Mendieta y Nuñez, *Historia*, p. 190; Bremauntz, *Educación socialista*, p. 166. See Gabino Palma, "La universidad mexicana del futuro," *El Universal Gráfico*, September 9, 23, 1933, for Medellín's statements on the proper goals of university education.

[25]Biographical data can be found in Roderic A. Camp, *Mexican Political Biographies, 1935–1975*, pp. 183–184. See also his comments on his own career in Wilkie and Monzón de Wilkie, *México visto*. Robert Millon, *Mexican Marxist*, discusses his thought.

Bremauntz, *Educación socialista*, p. 166, for a list of the state universities that sent delegates.

struggle or violence to overthrow the capitalist regime. His approach was gradualist; he believed that the means of production and distribution must be socialized by a strictly scientific regime but that this necessitated the transformation of society. It was the universities' job to lead this change by teaching professors, students, and, through them, the nation that human history had been the evolution of social institutions toward a classless society based on the people's ownership of property. An ethics professor, he went on to argue that the nation must also be taught the ethics of a classless society. Universities must become active agents of social and economic change; faculty and students should be obligated to spend a year in national service. The clincher, however, was his assertion that Marxism must be the only ideological basis for university teaching.

By insisting on a Marxist monopoly, he overstepped the limits of tolerance. Many educated Mexicans of diverse political viewpoints were aware of national problems. The widespread, conspicuous poverty was a constant reminder. Many were annoyed that UNAM had provided no leadership in solving these problems, preferring instead to produce unemployable professionals, caterers to the rich, or titled social parasites. The pervasiveness of Marxism in educated and labor circles meant that the terminology of the left was not frightening. His call, however, for the implantation of a foreign ideology as the sole philosophical underpinning of university education was more than most could bear. Mexican nationalists feared that Lombardo Toledano was trying to turn the nation into a Soviet satellite.[26]

Amidst the explosions and debates that followed approval of Lombardo Toledano's proposition came Antonio Caso, sallying forth to do battle against this threat to academic freedom. When he had seen that the congress was rigged, he had resigned his honorary office, but he accepted the challenge to debate Lombardo Toledano. The debate was filled with high drama. Caso was no ordinary man; he was a giant as a philosopher, teacher, and administrator, and was the grand old man of Mexican letters. As a university student and young professor he had fought positivism with Bergsonian intuitionism. Now he saw himself fighting a newer form of positivism. More poignant, however, were the special circumstances. He had taught almost everyone in the room, in-

[26] Frederick C. Turner, *The Dynamic of Mexican Nationalism*, has an excellent analysis of the xenophobic character of Mexican nationalism.

cluding his opponent. His brother Alfonso and Lombardo Toledano were brothers-in-law. Master versus pupil, a classic confrontation, drew the attention of the nation.

Caso made what would become a traditional defense of academic freedom. Universities, he argued, were cultural communities for research and teaching that must search for the truth and seek the good of all. Agreeing that the university must aid in the solution of social problems, he argued that it could not perform its mission if it was oriented toward only one social system. Diversity was a strength that must be preserved. The competition for ideas was the best means of finding the truth.

Lombardo Toledano countered that Caso misunderstood reality, that he was a dreamer. He asserted that the university had never been neutral, that academic freedom meant that students were taught to serve the bourgeois state. Students should not leave the university without formed opinions, without a definite ethical code. Academic freedom must agree not with past truths but present and future truths. One should only be free to teach reality, meaning, in this case, Marxism. The goal of the university should be to improve the lives of the proletariat, not, as it currently was, to serve only the needs of the bourgeoisie.

Neither was going to agree, and neither was going to win the debate. When Caso argued that the university did not have to have a creed, his opponent argued that it could. When Caso suggested that a creed cannot be imposed, Lombardo Toledano countered that Gabino Barreda had imposed positivism on the ENP over protests and that it could be done again. Lombardo Toledano slapped at Caso's humanism, for which he was known, by asserting that one should not discuss eternal values when people were hungry. Caso may have won, however, because his opponent argued that he would prefer a Catholic to a bourgeois school, for the latter was chaos.[27]

The daily metropolitan press quickly joined the debate. Both *El Universal* and *Excelsior* attacked the pro-Marxist proposal and favored the anti-Marxist side but opened their pages to both groups. *El Nacio-*

[27] Juan Hernández Luna, "Polémica de Caso contra Lombardo Toledano, sobre la Universidad," *Historia Mexicana* 19 (1969): 87–104; Mayo, *Educación socialista*, pp. 81–98; Juan Hernández Luna, "Una jornada del maestro Caso en favor de la libertad de cátedra," *Filosofía y Letras* (January–March 1947).

nal, the "government" paper, was cagier, but finally came out against the Lombardo Toledano proposal. President Rodríguez personally opposed the proposal but allowed the debate to continue. In the face of this opposition, Medellín sent a circular on September 21 to all his directors claiming that the press was distorting the congress's resolution by printing fragments, that the university community should await the full report, and that students, faculty, and administrators would be consulted before a policy change was implemented. Few believed him.[28]

Students joined the action, but to drive Medellín and Lombardo Toledano out of UNAM. UNEC members had been harassing Lombardo Toledano for a year, heckling his speeches and setting off stink bombs. Before this, under the leadership of Hernández Díaz, they had wrested control of the plastic arts student society from him. Medellín, by supporting the Marxist position, had made himself the target of their wrath. Because of the general uproar over the issue, the UNEC group could covertly join with the more broadly based effort led by Brito Foucher to oust the rector and the ENP director. Brito Foucher caucused with dissident students to devise the strategy of obtaining the express support of the law students, then the full law academy, and then the students in other schools to force their opponents out by resignations or firings. Because Lombardo Toledano had timed the congress to coincide with the closing of UNAM for vacations, this group had ample time to marshall its forces.[29]

Caso and Lombardo Toledano rejoined the debate through the newspapers. Most of what they wrote repeated the stance they had taken in the congress. Caso accused his opponent of being trapped in positivism (a slur, because that philosophy was identified with the hated Porfirian dictatorship) and ignorant of the facts when he asserted that positivism was the essential core of Mexican liberalism. Caso denied that positivism had ever been dogma in the ENP. Once again, he stressed that academic freedom (libertad de cátedra) was essential to

[28] Mayo, *Educación socialista*, pp. 105–107, 109; Gaxiola, *El presidente Rodríguez*, p. 319; *Excelsior*, September 15, 1933; *El Universal*, September 17, 1933; and *El Nacional*, September 17, 1933.

[29] Calderón Vega, *Cuba 88*, pp. 78–79; Mendieta y Núñez, *Historia*, p. 192. The students were Brito Rosado, Patiño Córdoba, Mejía M., Vallejo Novelo, and Rivera Albarrán.

the university's mission. Lombardo Toledano restated his position that the university must be responsive to the needs of the people, that the people needed a classless, socialist society, and that it was the duty of the university to help create such a society. UNAM, in his view, had always been political but must now support the proletariat instead of the bourgeoisie.[30]

The most telling blows against the Marxist advocates during the newspaper war came from the left. Enrique González Aparicio, a former student activist and now a young Marxist university professor, attacked Lombardo Toledano's understanding of Marxism, pointing out that a state-supported university could not be Marxist unless the state were. Further, to be a Marxist university, full control would have to be given to the workers, thus forcing Lombardo Toledano and 90 percent of the faculty to leave. Pablo González Casanova (the elder; his son would be UNAM rector in the 1970s), an extreme leftist, categorized the Marxist proposal as nothing more than a pre-election maneuver and took a stance in favor of academic freedom.[31]

The Brito Foucher group launched its public opposition on September 25, calling together a plenary session of law students. Over the next two days, these students, the director, and the faculty would debate the Marxist issue and agree to resist it. On the twenty-sixth, the organizers of the opposition managed to hold three separate meetings. At the first meeting, agreement was reached to defend the principles of academic freedom and university autonomy. Salvador Azuela had come out in favor of this position publicly, which aided the Brito Foucher group. The law students went further than making pronouncements, however: they agreed to organize a protest delegation and send a delegation to President Rodríguez and Bassols to explain their point of view. Faculty members joined in the second meeting of the day. Brito Foucher, Eduardo Pallares, and Luis Chico Goerne spoke in favor of academic freedom. Having lined up both student and faculty support, the opposition held a formal meeting that evening of the law school academy. The academy resolved against the Lombardo Toledano proposition. Significantly, support for this resolution came from all parts of the political spectrum.

[30]Mayo, *Educación socialista*, pp. 82 ff.; *Excelsior*, September 15, 1933; *El Universal*, September 17, 1933.

[31]Mayo, *Educación socialista*, pp. 114–119, 120.

Lombardo Toledano's views were supported by professors Luis Sánchez Pontón and Miguel Othón, but they represented a small minority.[32]

Several factors accounted for the strong opposition in the law school to the Marxism proposal. Many of the law students and faculty were traditionalists, in part because legal studies emphasize regulation and order. Equally important, however, was that the Marxist proposal threatened almost everyone in the school. If Marxism became the philosophical basis for teaching, virtually all of the faculty would find themselves unprepared to teach; their past experience and training would be largely irrelevant. Even the left would suffer, for Lombardo Toledano's brand of Marxism was his own, and his control of UNAM, which is what the proposal meant, would preclude their participation.

Other schools did not join the law school protest immediately. The reasons are not clear. One participant[33] has suggested that the CNE and FEU had almost complete dominance over the other schools, thus preventing the organization of any opposition. Perhaps the scientific and technical disciplines could not imagine how the proposal could hurt them. That Medellín, a scientist, backed the proposal probably pacified many people in these schools. Regardless, the law school appeared isolated, but was adamant.

Opposition generated some movement, however. Protests filtered in from the countryside from citizens and from other universities. UNEC was quietly lining up what forces it could muster. Medellín, feeling the pressure, issued a statement, printed on September 27, saying that what he was trying to do was to open debate, not impose Marxism. He went further, professing his desire for a socialist criterion to create a just distribution of wealth as suggested in the extreme interpretation of the ideas of Pope Leo XIII. By shifting drastically away from Marxism and then trying to use reform Catholicism as a philosophical justification, Medellín tried to pacify the Catholic-conservative opposition. In doing so, however, he undercut some of his own support; Díaz de León accused him of betraying the congress.[34]

[32] González Cárdenas, *Cien años*, p. 195; Mayo *Educación socialista*, pp. 114, 120; Mendieta y Núñez, *Historia*, p. 193. The professors speaking for the resolutions were González Aparicio, Antonio Carrillo Flores, Miguel Palacios Macedo, Esteva Ruiz, and Manuel Gual Vidal; the students were Patiño Córdoba and José M. Walls Herrera.

[33] Mendieta y Núñez, *Historia*, p. 194.

[34] Mayo, *Educación socialista*, pp. 120–121; Mendieta y Núñez, *Historia*, p. 192.

The dispute might have dragged on for weeks in the newspapers and finally petered out with a Lombardo Toledano victory had not Brito Foucher and his group created an incident. The conservative law students asked Brito Foucher to demand that the CNE vacate its offices in the law school on the grounds that the CNE had illegally interfered in local student elections and had adopted an anti-student attitude. Brito Foucher complied on September 29. The CNE officers refused to leave, so the director ordered the custodial staff to move the CNE files to a meeting room; the CNE resisted with force. The CNE claimed that the rector had given them the space and only he could make them move. Both waited until October 9, when Brito Foucher posted a formal notice that the CNE was to vacate within twenty-four hours. Again the CNE argued that the director was overstepping his authority. On the tenth, a group of law students raided the CNE offices, pulled out the files and some furniture, and set them on fire. They showed no concern that this action contradicted their professed belief in academic freedom and freedom of belief. Both sides were intolerant; the struggle was to be for total control of UNAM.[35]

The attack on the CNE offices shocked the university community and prompted a strong response from the law faculty. Most of the professors signed a joint letter of resignation as a protest against the turmoil in the school. They argued that students were studying less, classes were being disrupted, and political maneuvering was making academic life impossible. They vowed not to return until order was restored, but they were vague as to who was to blame. Brito Foucher, as director and as an instigator, bore major responsibility, but the professors strongly opposed the Marxist position of Medellín and Lombardo Toledano.[36]

Two aspects of the mass resignation are striking. That they resigned simultaneously suggests planning with the goal of throwing the school and the university into a greater crisis and forcing the council to act. Equally interesting was the composition of the group, which included four future rectors (Manuel Gómez Morín, Antonio Caso, Chico

[35] Mayo, *Educación socialista*, p. 123, and Mendieta y Núñez, *Historia*, p. 194, say the ejection occurred on the tenth, but I have followed *Excelsior*. See also González Cárdenas, *Cien años*, p. 196.

[36] The resignation can be found in Mayo, *Educación socialista*, p. 124, and Mendieta y Núñez, *Historia*, p. 194. *Excelsior*, October 11, 1933, asserts that all resigned. See also *New York Times*, October 12, 1933.

Goerne, and Luis Garrido) and other prominent (then and future) directors and politicians (Mariano and Salvador Azuela, Trinidad García, Antonio Carrillo Flores, Manuel Gual Vidal, Daniel Cosío Villegas, Andrés Serra Rojas, Eduardo Villaseñor, and Juan J. Bremer). Some of the men would join Gómez Morín in founding the Partido Acción Nacional six years later; others would develop close ties with the government.

One reason for the mass resignation was the attack on Brito Foucher that came the same day. A group of university directors met on the afternoon of the tenth to give Medellín a vote of confidence and to demand the law director's resignation. He refused to resign. The council went into emergency session that night. During its long session, Medellín and Brito Foucher exchanged recriminations. The former charged the law director with having stirred up trouble since last May, when he intervened in the FEU elections. Brito Foucher countercharged that the rector was taking orders from the CNE and Lombardo Toledano and had lost the support of the law school. When it became clear that he was going to lose, Brito Foucher, joined by the student Andrés Iduarte, argued that the council could not dismiss him because charges had not been brought before the Court of Honor. The council, on the motion of Martínez Mezquida, a student, voted 47 to 4 to fire him, the procedural question notwithstanding. Outside the meeting, a student group headed by Bernardo Ponce and Rivera Albarrán clashed with another headed by Garrido Canabal and including cinematography-union members.[37]

The law students officially declared a strike in favor of their director and against Medellín and Lombardo Toledano. They also announced their support for the protesting professors. How many law students supported this strike cannot be determined, but the strike leadership was conservative: Patiño Córdoba, Mejía M., and Ponce. Except for a few economics students, no other school supported law; medicine specifically decided to support Medellín. The university directors also announced support for the rector. In short, it appeared that the strikers were isolated.[38]

[37] Mayo, *Educación socialista*, pp. 124–126; Mendieta y Núñez, *Historia*, p. 195; *Excelsior*, October 11, 1933; and González Cárdenas, *Cien años*, p. 196.

[38] *Excelsior*, October 12, 1933; González Cárdenas, *Cien años*, p. 196; Mendieta y Núñez, *Historia*, pp. 195–196; and Mayo, *Educación socialista*, pp. 195–196.

Undaunted, the law strikers made several unsuccessful efforts on October 12 and 13 to take the rectory and the ENP by force to drive their opponents out. When they made their first charge, Medellín called the police. The appearance of mounted police firing into the air drove the future lawyers and their supporters into the law school building, whence they counterattacked with sticks and stones. Fortunately, the police withdrew before anyone was seriously injured. That same day, the twelfth, approximately a thousand students paraded down Juárez Avenue, the main street, protesting the rector's action and the use of police. Lacking martyrs, the march was ineffectual. A group of philosophy and letters students, led by Juan Sánchez Navarro and Leopoldo Baeza, declared their support of the strike but could not carry their school with them. Most students stayed out of the university quarter, not wanting to get caught in the crossfire. On the thirteenth, the strike committee sent a delegation to Medellín and Lombardo Toledano to ask them to resign. Medellín tried to calm them and agreed to receive a delegation, but, when they reached the door, it was slammed shut and a torrent of rocks, bricks, and tiles came flying down from the rooftops, where a group of students and workers had stationed themselves. After fleeing to temporary safety, the strikers launched another assault. To penetrate the large wooden door in this attempt to gain control of the building, they concocted a Molotov cocktail from siphoned gasoline and set the door afire. When this failed, they again took refuge. [39]

Events threatened to take a more violent turn as the strikers issued demands and stiffened their resolve. Firemen and mounted police fought for an hour to drive the strikers back. Tensions rose. An accident could set off a chain of lethal events. Lombardo Toledano brought more workers to aid his students in another assault on the law school. Law students obtained a vial of nitroglycerine to blow up the university door. Rumors circulated that Luis Morones, Lombardo Toledano's labor union rival, was supplying the strikers with pistols and other weapons. Thus, the confrontation in the narrow street was broadening to become a battle between rival labor unions as well as an intra-university struggle. The strikers finally issued their demands: (1)

[39] The metropolitan press covered these events; *Excelsior* gave the most extensive coverage. See also González Cárdenas, *Cien años*, p. 197; Mayo, *Educación socialista*, p. 127; and Mendieta y Núñez, *Historia*, p. 196.

the resignation of Medellín, (2) the resignation of Lombardo Toledano, (3) the suspension of the practice of using federal stipends to students as political tools, (4) the end of Bassols's intervention in the university, (5) the suppression of "professional" students, and (6) full autonomy. No mention was made of labor union intervention, probably because both sides were guilty. Most of these demands were internal matters, including the stipend and the professional students issue. The council could take steps to make sure that the stipends (becas) were not distributed on a political basis and dismiss persons who were only nominally students. As important as the content of the demands was the determination of the strikers to continue until they were met.[40]

Alarmed by this and other similar situations in the country, various groups tried to change the situation. Conservative and moderate Jalisco students and citizens began to revolt in the Universidad de Guadalajara when Díaz de Leon declared it a Marxist university. Durango students revolted, demanding university autonomy for their institution. UNEC had a hand in both movements. On the thirteenth, the UNEC group pulled together the leaders of the state student groups and overthrew the Lombardo Toledano officers of the CNE. In a clever tactical move, the victors put Guerrero Briones, a leftist, in the presidency while putting Chávez Camacho and Luis de Garay in less visible positions. Hernández Díaz led the school of plastic arts on strike. The most important university directors switched positions and asked Lombardo Toledano to resign. He agreed under protest. Behind the scenes, Antonio Caso and others quietly worked for a more permanent solution.[41]

This secret effort to resolve the conflict is still shrouded. Caso and fifteen professors began drafting a plan of university reorganization. Perhaps this group also participated in the meeting held in the law office of Hilario Medina, a 1917 constitutional convention delegate. The law office meeting resolved to rewrite the university's organizational chart, demand Lombardo Toledano's resignation, and review Brito Foucher's dismissal. They blamed Lombardo Toledano for causing the trouble and vowed to resign irrevocably if he did not leave. Since Jim-

[40] *Excelsior*, October 14, 1933. The demand can also be found in the other works on which this section is based.

[41] *Excelsior*, October 14, 1933; Mayo, *Educación socialista*, pp. 205–218. See these sources for the data in the following paragraph as well.

énez Rueda attended the meeting; it appears likely that Medellín was seeking a compromise solution, one that would protect him. The law students called off the planned attack on the university building in the belief that Medellín had agreed to fire Lombardo Toledano.

Still more pressure was needed, however. Lombardo Toledano reneged, claiming that the continuation of the strike violated the agreement. In response, several prominent professors, including Ignacio Chávez, resigned to protest this reversal, thus undercutting his strength in the university. On the other hand, ENP and chemical science students restated their support for the controversial labor leader. The shift away from Lombardo Toledano increased, however; Vallejo Novelo wrested control of the FEU from Garrido Canabal. Veterinary medicine and the day ENP students joined the strike. The dental school gave a vote of sympathy. Medical students said they could not strike because they were celebrating the centennial of the school, but they were sympathetic. The strikers began planning a mass demonstration for the fifteenth. Of special significance was the formation of a mixed committee of strike leaders and prominent professors, many of whom had not publicly supported the strike. Reassured by the growing support, Rivera Albarrán led an assault on the rectory and threw out Medellín. Lombardo Toledano resigned.[42]

The government finally acted on October 14 to end the conflict. The escalating violence, particularly the ejection of Medellín, could no longer be ignored. President Rodríguez had exhausted his patience; he announced he was sending a full autonomy bill to Congress, one that would completely separate UNAM from the state. The government, he said, could not ignore the expulsion of Medellín nor the physical damage to the university. The situation threatened lives and the legitimate interests of the city's population. Since the government did not want to intervene in the internal affairs of the university, it planned to give UNAM its own resources and withdraw all control. In testimony to congress, Bassols, author of the bill, went further. Since UNAM refused to serve the national interest but blamed the state for all its problems, the government was washing its hands of the university. Henceforth, UNAM (as essentially a private university) could do what it

[42] González Cárdenas, Cien años, pp. 197–198; Mayo, Educación socialista, pp. 127–131; and Mendieta y Núñez, Historia, pp. 197–201. The mixed committee was Palacios Macedo, Caso, González Aparicio, Gual Vidal, Carrillo Flores, and Chico Goerne.

wanted; the government was going to spend public funds on basic scientific and technical education.[43]

Alarmed, the mixed committee tried to interview Rodríguez to discover his intentions. He refused to see them, but the assistant attorney-general, José Ángel Ceniceros, unofficially told them that the views of the law students would be taken into account. Surprisingly, this meaningless assurance seemed to pacify the mixed committee.[44]

Both the new CNE and the leftist Federación de Estudiantes Revolucionarios issued statements in an attempt to influence the government. The CNE applauded full autonomy but expressed concern over future government financial support. The revolutionary students issued a laundry list of demands. They wanted Medellín and Jiménez Rueda out (both resigned when the autonomy proposal was announced) as well as Chávez (even though a leftist, he did not tolerate student politics), the end of stipends and admission exams, the direct election of the administration, the ejection of the Iberoamerican confederation and the CNE, the abolition of obligatory military service, and the end of Bassols's and police intervention in the university. They capped their demands with a call for solidarity with Cuban students fighting the Machado dictatorship. The length of the list and the inclusion of a number of issues irrelevant to the situation at hand vitiated its impact.[45]

Congressional approval of the Bassols law was a foregone conclusion. Both houses passed the bill on October 17, the Senate not even bothering to debate it. The Chamber of Deputies' debates revealed the depth of anti-UNAM sentiment in government circles, where it was widely believed that UNAM refused to be more than a bastion of conservatism and reaction. Bassols had to convince some wavering deputies to vote for complete separation by reassuring them that, if UNAM could not govern itself under full autonomy, the state would take full control. To encourage this development, the law gave UNAM its buildings and a ten million peso endowment, from which it would earn less than eight hundred thousand a year, considerably less than the three million peso subsidy it received in 1933. The intention, as one delegate succinctly put it, was to starve the university to death.[46]

[43] Gaxiola, *Rodríguez*, pp. 318–321; Mendieta y Núñez, *Historia*, p. 200. The Bassols testimony is reprinted in Pinto Mazal, *Autonomía universitaria*, pp. 200–220.

[44] Mendieta y Núñez, *Historia*, p. 200.

[45] *Excelsior*, October 16, 1933.

[46] *New York Times*, October 18, 20, 1933.

The mixed committee called off the strike on the eighteenth and began to reorganize the administration. The members vowed to continue their demand for more state aid, however. On the twenty-third, a constituent assembly, over which Caso presided, named Manuel Gómez Morín as provisional rector. The new rector appointed Salvador Azuela, the 1929 hero, as official mayor, the third highest position. Vasconcelos supporters and the UNAM strikers of 1929 were now moving into key positions.[47]

The 1933 conflict was not over, however, because UNAM had to be reorganized under the new law and some means found to finance it. Further, UNAM voted to support the student strikes in Guadalajara and Durango because it was necessary to defend the principle of autonomy. What occurred in October 1933 was a truce, not a victory. Lombardo Toledano was out and the Marxist proposition defeated, but the university still had to survive in a hostile environment likely to become more so with the election of the leftist Lázaro Cárdenas as president of Mexico in 1934.

[47] *Excelsior*, October 24, 1933; Mendieta y Núñez, *Historia*, p. 200; Mayo, *Educación Socialista*, pp. 163–164.

5. The Struggle for Survival, 1933–1935

TRADITIONAL Mexico was battered and routed by the left between 1933 and 1935. Cárdenas meant not only to rule but also to change the nation. Once nominated for the presidency, he campaigned throughout the nation as no one had ever done before, listening and talking to thousands and gaining their support. His allies moved simultaneously to block actual or potential opposition. Not recognizing what this meant, Calles supported Cárdenas until 1935, when it became clear that the power had shifted to the young president. Cárdenas had gained so much power by then that he had little difficulty in sending Calles and his closest associates into exile. Change came quickly. Socialist education had been adopted by constitutional amendment. Lombardo Toledano organized a pro-Cárdenas national labor union; peasants were being given land and organized to support the government; and Calles's supporters were being removed from office or isolated. UNAM, a stronghold of traditionalism, had been amputated from the body of the state.

The divorce between UNAM and the state, decreed by the 1933 organic law, threatened the survival of the autonomous university. The combination of governmental animosity, leftist hostility, and the inability of the endowment to fund the operating budget seemed to guarantee bankruptcy and a return to complete governmental control within a few short years. Even the university's juridical status was unclear, for it might be either an autonomous state agency or an independent institution chartered by the national government. If it were the former, it could reasonably make a claim on the public purse; if not, not. The resolution of this legal question would depend on the occupant of the presidency and the political climate in which he operated. All the signs available in the fall of 1933 portended ill, since leftists were in the ascendancy and expected to elect one of their own, Lázaro Cárdenas, to the presidency in 1934. If the relatively conservative Rodríguez government had been willing to abjure its relationship with UNAM, university members could expect worse from his successor. Moreover, the money might run out before relations could be improved. Survival, then, was the central issue for UNAM after 1933.

The national fight over socialist education complicated the issue. The movement to mandate a socialist ideology for education resulted in the amendment of constitutional Article 3 to that effect in October 1934. Massive resistance began almost simultaneously with the inclusion of a socialist education plank in the Partido Nacional Revolucionario platform in December 1933, and would continue until 1937, finally ending when the constitution was amended again in 1946 to remove the language offensive to conservatives. UNAM, both as a conservative institution and as a defender of academic freedom, would resist socialist education. Its leadership would fight hard to prevent the university's being included in the proposed change. University students would divide into three groups: proponents of socialist education, led by the Lombardo Toledano cadre; opponents, led by the UNEC cadre; and the apathetic. The first two groups would fight inside student organizations and the university and outside in the streets while the bulk of the students, opposed to socialist education, watched and ducked. In short, UNAM became a battleground, with fights spilling over into state universities. Each student fight, regardless of the victor, alienated some sector of the public and seemed to prove that the university was incapable of self-government.[1]

More general political events created complications. For the first thirteen months or so of university autonomy, university officials faced the uncertainties created by the change in national presidents. Although Cárdenas was likely to be less sympathetic to UNAM than Rodríguez, there was the possibility that he would disassociate himself from his predecessor at least to the extent of taking a fresh look at the relationship. Even if he turned out to be as hostile as some university officials must have feared, the particular form that hostility might take would remain problematical until he had been in office for a few months.

[1] The socialist education controversy has been the subject of numerous articles and books. The best single study is John A. Britton, *Educación y radicalismo en México*, vol.

In the summer of 1934, ex-President Calles, still a major political force and more conservative than Cárdenas, threw his weight behind socialist education in his Grito de Guadalajara speech, asserting that children belonged to the state. The subsequent power struggle between the two, ending in Calles's exile in 1935, meant that UNAM became a pawn in the struggle.[2]

Backing Cárdenas in this struggle was Lombardo Toledano, who thus enhanced his political clout at a time when he was angry with the university and capable of creating enormous difficulties for the institution. His rising influence must have sent shivers down the spines of university administrators. Their hope was that he would be too busy with the organization and operation of his new labor union, the Confederación de Trabajadores Mexicanos, the Universidad Obrera in 1936, and his political career, all of which would generate opposition, to attack UNAM. The Universidad Obrera, an idea promoted by students for years, was founded by the labor leader with government subsidies. It was not a university, for it taught elementary-school–level courses and politics.

That Cárdenas shifted Mexico leftward, fostered the creation of the Confederación Nacional Campesina (peasants' or farmers' confederation), redistributed land with both hands, encouraged the creation of ejidos, castigated the rich, created the Instituto Politécnico Nacional, and sided with the Republicans in the Spanish Civil War did not auger well for the university. The rise of fascism and other forms of right-wing authoritarianism, particularly on the Iberian peninsula, with which many Mexicans had a love/hate relationship, made defenders of academic freedom and traditional values easy targets. Even leftists who opposed socialist education or the assault on the university were reluctant to speak out in such a climate. The university would have few overt political friends.[3]

I: *Los años de Bassols (1931–1934)* and vol. II: *Los años de Cárdenas (1934–1940)*. See pages 138–139 for the text of the amendment.

[2] Calles had not previously been a proponent of socialist education; his support in the summer of 1934 no doubt emanated from his anticlericalism and his desire to stay in the mainstream of politics after his presidential term ended. Nevertheless, Cárdenas asserted his own authority and excluded Calles from decisions. Both had supporters within UNAM, and elements of the struggle between the two would appear in university squabbles.

[3] The history of the Cárdenas period is still being written, but there is a substantial

Not all of these problems were known in mid-October 1933, when the students and professors began meeting to reorganize UNAM, but the participants realized that the institution faced difficult days. Two groups, the strike committee and the mixed pro-university reform committee, initially worked on the reorganization, but they shared overlapping memberships. Significantly for the future, Luis Chico Goerne, law school director, presided over the October 17 strike committee meeting and would serve on the program committee of the other group; in 1935 he would be elected rector. Antonio Carrillo Flores, a young law professor, would also be involved in both groups; he would become one of the most powerful men in Mexican public life after 1945, and his brother, Nabor, would be rector in the 1950s. Antonio Caso continued to play an important role, presiding over the general assembly of students and professors on the eighteenth (the group declared the official end of the strike) as well as the October 23 meeting at which Manuel Gómez Morín was elected interim rector and Azuela became oficial mayor. The latter meeting also appointed a committee to produce an organizational plan for a new University Council by the next day. By the twenty-eighth, the new council had been elected, and on November 1 it officially elected Gómez Morín as rector.[4]

Information does not exist that fully explains why Gómez Morín was chosen, but the reasons seem self-evident, if not somewhat ironic. Gómez Morín had a distinguished university career. He had been a student leader with the support of Lombardo Toledano. Before graduating, he became a professor and served as secretary of the law school during 1918 and 1919. He was law director from 1922 to 1924. As a student he had been one of the Siete Sabios, the Seven Wise Men of Greece, one of the most brilliant intellectual groups in twentieth-century Mexican history (Lombardo Toledano was also a member). He had an equally distinguished political career, holding important posts in the finance ministry in the 1920s, including the post of undersecretary of finance, 1919–1921. He was the principal author of the organic law

———
[4] In addition to the coverage provided by such newspapers as *Excelsior*, see Mayo, *Educación socialista*, pp. 162–165. The committee charged with the organizational plan was Ignacio Chávez, Miguel Palacios Macedo, Azuela, Hugo Rangel, and Ignacio Mejía.

literature on the subject. The best interpretive study is Arnaldo Córdova, *La política de masas de Cardenismo.*

for the Banco de México, the central bank, as well as its first director. As a private lawyer, he had developed a corporate practice that put him in constant touch with the rich. Having benefited from the mobility created by the Revolution, he did not oppose it, but as a Catholic, traditionalist, and technocrat he abhorred some of what he saw. As a moderate with tremendous national influence and with intense loyalty to his alma mater, he seemed the only one capable of leading the institution through its inevitable turmoil. He had been treasurer of the 1929 Vasconcelos campaign and enjoyed close ties with Ignacio Chávez and the Azuelas, who also participated in that campaign. That one of his principal opponents would be his old friend and rival was perhaps not an unconscious touch of irony.[5]

Both the new rector and the new council knew that the legal status of UNAM was in doubt. Bassols had testified to Congress on October 17 that when the new law was passed, UNAM would be *a* university of the republic instead of *the* university, but the council approved a report of the Juridical Commission on November 27 that claimed that the institution *was* an autonomous state agency. Since the document had been written by Manuel Gual Vidal, Trinidad García, and José Ángel Ceniceros, the assistant attorney general of the country, it carried an authoritative tone, but it was not final. The Supreme Court would eventually have to rule on UNAM's status, but that would come later.[6]

The council did not move so quickly to reorganize the internal structure of the university, waiting to give the new rector a major role in the process; the new statute was not promulgated until March 1, 1934. A purge committee (depuración) was appointed in October 1933 to decide which professors and students should be expelled, but not many were and the committee was short-lived. Instead, the new statute tried to make internal political machinations more difficult. Indirect elections of councilors were instituted. The school/facultad academies met in two groups, one for professors, the other for students. Each of these groups elected representatives to the general academy of

[5] Donald J. Mabry, "Manuel Gómez Morín," in Harold E. Davis, et al., *Revolutionaries, Traditionalists and Dictators in Latin America*, pp. 112–118. The best study of Gómez Morín is Enrique Krauze, *Caudillos culturales en la Revolución Mexicana*, which compares him with Lombardo Toledano.

[6] The Bassols testimony can be found in Pinto Mazal, *Autonomía universitaria*, pp. 200–220. The council's conclusions are in ibid., pp. 227–233.

the school/facultad, which then selected those who would sit on the council, guaranteeing, as well, that there would be student-professor parity. The professors had to be part of the academy from which they were elected and hold a regular appointment. The students had to have been enrolled for two semesters without having failed any course. The rectors, directors, CNE representative, and two alumni representatives held ex-officio membership, but the CNE member, as well as the official mayor and the department heads, had only an informative role.[7]

In order to depoliticize the institution and increase internal discipline, election rules were altered substantially. The rector was to be named by a direct, secret, absolute majority vote of the council; he could be removed at the petition of fifteen councilors, or of department heads if two-thirds of the council agreed. The rector nominated the directors from the six most senior professors of the respective school/ facultad; the council then ratified or rejected the nomination. Students, except as councilors, were given no role. Directors could be removed by petition of ten councilors or their respective academies, if a majority of the council agreed. The rector was given veto power on university matters, but could be overridden by a two-thirds council vote. The administration assumed the right to apply collective sanctions on students or professors if their actions resulted in the closing of a school/facultad.

The refusal to give the student organizations a vote on the council and to remove the FEU provoked a debate in the latter organization. The FEU met on March 16, 1934, to discuss what student societies should do in light of this development. The philosophy and letters delegates, perhaps the most conservative, argued that the FEU no longer should be the representative organization of the student societies since the societies had been formed to resist the state, a purpose no longer necessary under the new autonomy. Besides, they argued, the student organizations had never represented the genuine students but had been led by agitators with personal interests at stake. Instead, each department of a school/facultad should create research institutes or seminars and its own student society. These new societies would send a delegate to the council of the school/facultad. The council would have its

[7] For this and the following paragraph, see Pinto Mazal, *El Consejo Universitario*, pp. 9–14, and *Autonomía universitaria*, p. 15; Mayo, *Educación socialista*, pp. 166–167.

own triumvirates. Whatever hope these delegates had of depoliticizing student organizations while giving their own facultad (which had the most departments) greater power were dashed when the FEU refused to accept the idea. The FEU only agreed to cease forcing students to join student organizations.[8]

Gómez Morín took his own steps to make internal political activity more difficult. The indirect election system of the new statute, which he had had a hand in formulating, was just one step. The other was to control the council meetings, required weekly. For years, the meetings had been long and tumultuous, sometimes being reduced to shouting matches as different factions sought to impose their will. Gómez Morín moved the council session into a smaller room that could not contain many non-members, met the council infrequently, and then adjourned it after twenty minutes of announcements. As authoritarian as this behavior was, he was able to do it because council members knew they needed him to save the university.[9]

His greatest problem and success were in finding the money to keep the university open; the ten-million-peso endowment could not long fund the normally three-million-peso operating budget. His first step was to reduce expenditures, eventually slashing them by almost half. He cut his own salary from 2,000 to 400 pesos monthly as a signal to the rest of the university. Many administrators and professors agreed to work without pay, possible because they had other sources of income, from either their principal jobs or personal wealth. Others were fired. Any expense that could be postponed, was. The university began selling supplies to students. When these reductions were insufficient, he campaigned among alumni (some of whom he had taught during his career), friends of the institution, and business contacts, many of whom were interested in preventing a leftist takeover of the university. U.S. Ambassador to Mexico Dwight Morrow donated fifty thousand dollars for law books, and Puig Casauranc donated a printing press. These private donations represented 253,000 of the 572,000 pesos donated. Since Mexico does not have a tradition of private support for universities, public or private, the task was difficult. That Gómez Morín had

[8] *El Universal*, March 17, 1934.
[9] Josefina Vásquez de Knauth, *Nacionalismo y educación en México*, p. 151; Desiderio Horta, "Quince años de autonomía universitaria," *Así* (December 2, 1944): 20–22.

the talent and contacts necessary to do it must have been a primary reason for his selection as rector. Government money was still necessary, however, since even these reductions and donations were incapable of balancing the budget.[10]

To obtain this governmental aid, the new rector had to convince President Rodríguez and members of his government that, no matter what UNAM students might do, the university itself would do nothing to attack the state. To put it another way, Gómez Morín had to disassociate the official university from the actions of some of its members, particularly students who led crusades for university autonomy in the states and against socialist education in the nation. Tighter discipline within UNAM and the reduction of student power in the administration of the university were thus logical steps toward improving university-state relations as much as they reflected Gómez Morín's administrative style. When a group of students sacked the offices of the Secretariat of Public Education on January 12, 1934, Rodríguez did not accuse the university of having fomented the attack. When student tumults on April 7 necessitated police intervention, Rodríguez complimented Gómez Morín on his efforts to calm the students.[11]

No administrator, state or university, could control the CNE and its leadership, however, and prevent it from compromising UNAM. The organization actively intervened in struggles in other universities. Its leaders did not even wait until UNAM was reorganized, jumping into the fight in Guadalajara in October 1933, flush with their victory over Lombardo Toledano. Since few doubted that Gómez Morín and his administration personally opposed socialist education, the CNE actions were seen for a time as part of a general UNAM (and conservative) assault on socialist education. To proponents of this fundamental change, university autonomy and academic freedom became code words for the preservation of conservatism and traditionalism in higher education. Thus, a full debate on whatever intrinsic merit these ideas might have had was prevented.

The Universidad de Guadalajara struggle began when the rector, Díaz de León, backed by Jalisco Governor Sebastián Allende (a Calles

[10] Manuel Gómez Morín, interview of December 11, 1964, in Wilkie and Monzón de Wilkie, *México visto*, pp. 173–174; Rodríguez, "National University," pp. 243–246; Armando Ramírez, "La revolución universitaria de 1933," *La Nación*, October 10, 1942.

[11] Gaxiola, *Presidente Rodríguez*, pp. 323–325.

man), decided to impose Marxism on this second most important university in the nation. Both the state of Jalisco and its capital, Guadalajara, were bastions of Catholic conservatism, so the massive student-citizen resistance was not unexpected. On October 24, the students asked UNAM for help in their strike for academic freedom, co-government, and a tuition reduction; the constituent assembly of UNAM expressed sympathy but took no action. The next day, federal troops forced the Guadalajara students out of the building they had taken, but the students tried to take it again on the twenty-sixth. When more than 150 were arrested and jailed, the remainder began a hunger strike that compelled the governor to free the prisoners on the twenty-eighth. President Rodríguez sent Aarón Sáenz on an unsuccessful mediation mission. When Allende closed the university, Guadalajarans sent a delegation to Rodríguez to seek his positive intervention.[12]

While these events were taking place, Durango students were making similar demands for the Instituto Juárez. Again the CNE responded to the call for help, and some parents organized to support their student children. Unlike Allende, Governor Carlos Real watched and waited.

In response to these events, which they had had a major role in creating, CNE leaders organized a committee to study and publicize the issues. No one in authority would be gulled by these statements, since they knew the details, but the commission could pressure the government through public opinion. Rodríguez responded that he would disregard the comments, for the events were a state, not a federal, matter. On November 3, the CNE issued a manifesto declaring that these struggles were just autonomy fights, like that of UNAM, but the manifesto's attack on the Veracruz CNE congress and on the Congreso de Universitarios undercut this claim.

Guerrero Briones, CNE president, and his cohorts continued to press the attack during the first weeks of November. In Guadalajara, they helped organize the Comité Reinvindicador de los Derechos Estudiantiles, which petitioned the governor. On November 6, they staged a rally at which Guerrero Briones, Raúl Clavo of the leftist Federación de Estudiantes Revolucionarios, and Ignacio Mejía of the

[12] Accounts of the struggle in Guadalajara and Durango can be found in *Excelsior*, October 13, 1933; Armando Ramírez, "La revolución universitaria"; and Mayo, *Educación socialista*, pp. 205–220.

FEU spoke, a combination designed to prove that this was not a right-ist movement. When the Durango governor demanded, on November 8, that the CNE justify its actions in his state, Mejía and others quickly went there.

Governor Real compromised in the face of this pressure. Durango students had demanded an autonomy law similar to that of UNAM, except that the governor would nominate the rector and the preparatory curriculum would be returned to the state government. Talks between the protagonists broke down temporarily, after acts of violence in mid-November, and the CNE asked Rodríguez to intervene in both states, but the two sides finally reached agreement a few days later. The Instituto rector would be named by the governor from a list prepared by the Instituto council; education would be laicized (but not made socialist); the institution would be governed by both statute and council regulations, and would submit its budget to the state government annually.

Why the governor did not try to destroy the student movement or close the Instituto is not clear. Distant from the seat of power and governing a sparsely populated state, he may have decided that compromise was more important than total victory. He may not have been a partisan of socialist education, or he may have been waiting for events to develop nationally before he took more decisive actions.

The Guadalajara situation was entirely different. Both the governor and the rector were leftists in a conservative state and must have felt besieged. Cristeros had been active in Jalisco in the late 1920s and many were still anxious to break the power of the government. Also, the state and the university were too important for the national government to allow its will to be thwarted. Violence was quick to surface, as it did when students were arrested on the eve of a November 17 meeting. On the twenty-first, the Guadalajara affair was debated in the national Chamber of Deputies, and that body unanimously agreed that the clergy and the reactionaries were backing the students.

The CNE denied the charge and made counterclaims the next day. The leaders argued that the state should not intervene in university affairs nor try to impose sectarian ideologies and high fees (an interesting set of arguments). Further, the CNE branded Allende unreasonable and, contradicting its earlier position against state intervention, asked for presidential aid.

The Guadalajara students, supported by the CNE, elaborated on their demands. They wanted academic freedom, the restructuring of the university so that its administrative arrangements resembled UNAM's, better libraries and laboratories, reduced student fees, and the expulsion of the administration.

On November 27, the two sides compromised. Students got representation, promises of better facilities, and a reduction of fees for poor students. The governor agreed to name the rector and directors from a list approved by the university council.

This partial student victory was temporary, however. On the first of February 1934, after the PNR had endorsed socialist education, the governor demanded that the students respect authority and warned that he would not allow enemies of the Revolution to attack Revolutionary institutions. Leftist-rightist fights continued in the university until October 1934, nevertheless, so the governor closed the university. Conservatives organized the Universidad Autónoma de Guadalajara in 1934, which UNAM recognized in 1935 and to which it gave financial aid in 1936. The state reopened the state Universidad de Guadalajara in 1934–1935. For the next forty years or so, students of the respective universities fought sporadically in outbursts of unresolved tension.[13]

This division of university students into rival camps of leftists and rightists became common after its beginning in 1934, and represented a major departure in the development of student political activity. There had been leftist and rightist groups within the CNE and the FEU, but student opposition to the state had been sufficient to maintain at least the semblance of unity. Even the battle between the mafia and antimafia had been conducted within student organizations. But socialist education, both as an ideological issue and as a stalking horse for the struggle to control Mexico, split the student ranks into two warring factions and eventually contributed to the effective demise of the Confederación Nacional de Estudiantes. By capturing control of the CNE and turning it into an instrument of conservatism, UNEC leaders

[13]Mayo, Educación socialista, pp. 218–219; René Capistrán Garza, "Calles vive aún. El caso de la Universidad Autónoma de Guadalajara," Mañana (May 31, 1947): 44–45; and Nemesio García Naranjo, "La Universidad Autónoma de Guadalajara. No debe suspendarse la obra de cultura," Novedades, June 11, 1958. This university attracted large numbers of medical students from the United States in the 1960s and 1970s.

discredited the organization as the representative of university students, making it, instead, into a single-issue lobby. The organization lost its force once the issue did.

Conservative control of the CNE was consolidated during the May 1934 national convention in San Luis Potosí. Leftists attended, but they were unable to control either the credentials process or the convention itself. The validity of the delegations from Tabasco, Chiapas, and Oaxaca were immediately impugned during the first session on May 6. Two Tabasco delegations, one headed by Alonso Garrido Canabal, claimed to represent students in that state. After a long debate over several days, the convention admitted the more conservative delegation, whose members lived in the Federal District because they were enemies of the governor; the governor of San Luis Potosí intervened in the struggle by impeding the arrival of the Garrido Canabal delegation's railroad car. Both Oaxaca delegations were seated, but only the conservative group was given the right to vote. The presidential elections proved to be the true test of who now controlled the CNE. Armando Chávez Camacho, of UNEC, became president, but the leaders were shrewd enough to select Coquet, a liberal, as vice-president. During this hectic year (1934–1935), the CNE presidency would change hands several times: Chávez Camacho resigned within a few months, then Coquet resigned as president on November 5, 1934, the presidency passing to Daniel Kuri Breña, also of UNEC, and finally to Manuel Pacheco Moreno, of UNEC, in July 1935. These UNEC members were the ones who, with their cohorts, controlled the CNE. At the end of the meeting, the leftist Tabasco students and the delegations from Campeche, Guerrero, and Sinaloa left disgruntled.[14]

CNE opposition to socialist education was hidden within the resolutions of the congress, which in part represented a version of Catholic social philosophy similar to that of *Quadragesimo Anno*. Much, of course, was a rehash of their arguments in favor of academic freedom and university autonomy, of government fiscal support but not control of higher education, of student concern for social problems (usually ex-

[14] *Excélsior*, May 7–9, 1934; Mayo, *Educación socialista*, pp. 271–283; *El Universal*, April 5, 1934; Calderón Vega, *Cuba 88*, pp. 89–90; R. Vega Córdova, a delegate from Guerrero, in *El Universal*, June 7, 1934; and Rodríguez, "National University," pp. 249–252. The leftists were José Vallejo Novelo, Ignacio Mejía, Benito Coquet, and Enrique Ramírez y Ramírez.

pressed in terms of the need for seminars and institutes), and of governance of the university itself. They came out against final exams and class attendance and in favor of lower fees for poorer students as well as parity with professors on governing councils. They demanded an end to scholarships (becas) because these limited the liberty of the students, and they also wanted admission to the university separated from grade averages. To offset the loss of student fee income, the CNE called for the state to create an endowment for universities and to require professionals to pay an annual fee to the university. In addition, the CNE formally called for the adoption of these measures (including university reform) in each university in the nation.[15]

The CNE's stands on social and political issues deserve special mention because these were the issues on which it would split with the leftists. The key to its efforts would be the organization of an Instituto de Estudios Sociales that would conduct studies and arrange for week-long seminars in various cities to teach professional ethics, labor legislation, and the history of proletarian revindication in Mexico and the world; comparative analysis of fascism, communism, liberalism, socialism, and social catholicism; imperialism (which they opposed internally and externally); and social hygiene, among a long list of issues. Further, they wanted to establish a national system of night schools to operate in small and isolated population centers to reach out to villagers. They called the agrarian problem the nation's largest and lamented that some had made it into an armed fight. The CNE wanted a minimum wage for the working class, federalization and unification of primary education, and cheaper school textbooks. In sum, they again expressed sympathy for the poor and the workers but sought to redress these grievances through education and social legislation rather than through a change in the ownership of the means of production and distribution.[16]

Within weeks of the congress, CNE leaders intervened in the dispute between state authorities and students of the Instituto Científico y Literario in the state of Mexico. The students demanded that the in-

[15] *La Opinión* (Los Angeles, California), June 3, 1934; Mayo, *Educación socialista*, pp. 281–282.

[16] Mayo, *Educación socialista*, pp. 281–282, saw these statements as a conventional statement of *Quadragesimo Anno*; *El Universal*, June 15, 19, 1934, and *Excelsior*, July 10, 1934, carried reports on CNE views.

stitution be given autonomy and the endowment it had lost in 1890 in addition to seats on the governing council. When the director refused, the students declared a strike and seized the university building. The CNE, FEU, and the state primary teachers' league announced support of the strike; Governor Leopoldo Suárez Ocana retaliated by closing the school. Fearful that this would be a permanent closure, alumni, led by Fernando Ocaranza, jumped into the fray. Through their negotiations, Ocaranza became director, academic freedom was guaranteed, and by June 11 the autonomy demand was dropped. In September, however, the Federación de las Juventudes Socialistas tried to reopen the issues by attacks in the press, but failed.[17]

More important for the long-term development of UNAM were the organizational and propaganda efforts of leftist students. One group revitalized the Partido Nacional Estudiantil Pro Cárdenas in May as part of the presidential election campaign. The party called for the abolition of private schools, socialist education, and a state inspired by Marxist socialism. Although students participated, the party was actually a creature of professional politicians such as Antonio I. Villalobos, Froylán C. Manjarrez, and García Téllez, who were trying to entice students away from the CNE and into the Revolutionary cause. The outcry against socialist education had risen to such proportions by May that Narciso Bassols had to be shifted from the education ministry to the gobernación (government) ministry. Although the Partido Nacional Estudiantil Pro Cárdenas was an ephemeral electoral organization, it formed one segment of the Confederación de Estudiantes Socialistas de México (CESM), created in the summer of 1934.[18]

The conservative conquest of the CNE, solidified in May, forced socialist students and their backers to create their own organization if they were to compete for student sympathy and combat the conservative assault on socialist education. The initial organization efforts ran into some difficulty, probably because of the July presidential election, for El Nacional, which supported the CESM, announced on June 9 that the constituent assembly would be held in Jalapa, Veracruz, under the organizational effort of Universidad de Veracruz student president Francisco García R. and Governor Gonzalo Vázquez Vela. The meeting actually began on July 29 in Álvaro Obregón, Tabasco, under the lead-

17 Mayo, *Educación socialista*, p. 307; *Excelsior*, June 10, 1934.
18 *Excelsior*, May 7, 1934; *El Nacional*, July 31, 1934.

ership of the governor, Garrido Canabal, and ENP student Carlos A. Madrazo. The stated purpose of the meeting was to show that the Mexican Revolution had ideologically prepared young people, that is, that the CNE did not represent Mexican students but was a conservative, clergy-backed group. Both Cárdenas and the PNR endorsed the CESM, signaling as well their support for socialist education. UNAM students, through the CNE (now headed by Coquet) and the FEU (headed by Ignacio Mejía), announced their opposition to the inclusion of UNAM in the socialist education requirement. From the left, the Federación de Estudiantes Revolucionarios, led by Guadalupe Peraza E., called the socialist student congress demagogic, reformist, and fascistic in its views of education. These opposition statements revealed little except that the CESM was just one leftist group among several; not revealed were its ties to one group of Cárdenas politicians.[19]

Some of the events of the CESM meeting reveal clearly that the primary purpose in creating the confederation was to offset the CNE attacks on socialist education. The newspapers *Excelsior, El Universal,* and *La Prensa* were lambasted as reactionary (all opposed socialist education), and *El Nacional* was lauded. In their conclusions, the delegates announced that capitalism was bankrupt, that the academic freedom issue was an attempt of the privileged to preserve their privileges, that education should have a scientific, socialist orientation at all levels, that teachers who refused to follow this line should be fired, and that students should join the class struggle. In a closed session, they named commissions to inform Cárdenas and Calles of the resolutions approved, to ask Cárdenas to establish a state university in Tabasco, and to ask Calles to intervene to bring about the immediate implementation of socialist teaching. Of course, they censured Gómez Morín and the CNE.[20]

Even though the delegates unanimously supported these resolutions and agreements, they were far from unanimous in their views. Both Cárdenas, the president-elect, and Calles, the gray eminence of Mexican government in these years, supported socialist education, but the power struggle between the two, which would culminate in the exile of Calles in 1935, had already begun. The delegates were split into

[19] *El Nacional,* June 6, 7, 9, and July 10, 28, 30, 1934; *Excelsior,* July 31, 1934.

[20] Mayo, *Educación socialista,* pp. 284–293; José Horta, "¡Reclama a su presa un río!" *Así* (December 30, 1944): 34; and Dulles, *Yesterday in Mexico,* pp. 618–619.

the two rival camps. During the meeting, someone proposed that Calles be named Maestro de la Juventud, but the suggestion was met with silence until Alonso Garrido Canabal (a Calles ally) finally signed up to speak in favor of the proposal. Again, silence reigned. Then a small Yucatecan man stood up and shouted, "¡Yo acuso!" and attacked Calles as not being a socialist, calling him an obstacle to the development of the Mexican Revolution. Before he finished, Redshirts came into the galleries. When another delegate stood up and declared that Calles's personality could not be judged and that he was therefore declared Maestro de la Juventud, the Redshirts came onto the floor. The Yucatecan student went into a circle formed by Cardenistas led by Lombardo Toledano, who hurried him out the door of the theater so he would not be killed. During the fight that occurred outside in the dark streets, the sound of a strong blow to the head by a club filtered back into the theater. This incident served warning to the Cardenistas that the Callistas would resist with force.

The socialist education campaign generated even more heat in university circles between August and November as the Chamber of Deputies committee headed by Alberto Bremauntz drafted and redrafted a constitutional amendment and the opponents and proponents escalated their activities. Bremauntz and his cohorts were determined to revolutionize Mexican education from top to bottom as one step in creating a true socialist state. In part, perhaps, their efforts were an attempt to rally the left and the proletariat behind the first leftist president Mexico had had in years and to finish with clerical influence permanently. That Bremauntz specifically planned to include the universities in the socialist education requirement insured opposition not only from UNAM but also from most university students in the nation.

Both the CNE and FEU actively campaigned against socialist education and its application to universities. The FEU met in August and the assembly, led by Brito Rosado, Sánchez Navarro, and Coquet, unanimously proclaimed against the Bremauntz proposal. Even Gómez Arias, who defended socialism, attacked this proposal. In the newspaper article, Coquet expressed surprise that the issue had resurfaced and argued that the economy had to be socialized before education could be. The University Council also entered the fray by declaring in favor of academic freedom. When police began patrolling the university precincts, arresting and then releasing students as harassment, Coquet issued a warning that continuance of such a practice would lead to violence. Elsewhere in the republic in August, the CNE backed students in Puebla, Zacatecas, Michoacán, and Coahuila who resisted efforts to make their universities socialist. UNEC leaders, many of whom were CNE officers, led these fights, but their previous anonymity was being lost and their participation became a major issue in itself.[21]

This growing concern about the nature of the CNE leadership erupted on August 11 when Vallejo Novelo and José Rivera Albarrán attempted a coup. The national directive council of the CNE met on Saturday in the prep school to discuss plans for the fight against socialist education, but the meeting was disrupted when the dissident group labeled the CNE leaders as reactionaries acting against UNAM's interests and demanded their resignations. Coquet suspended the session and moved his delegates to the law school. The dissidents, who included not only Rivera Albarrán and Vallejo Novelo but also Rogerio de la Fuente, law student president, and Ignacio Mejía, remained behind to elect their own CNE officers. The Coquet group then purged the dissident officers and replaced them with more UNEC members. During the next few days, the two groups argued as to which represented the majority of the nation's university students, each side producing telegrams and organizational documents to support its claims. The philosophy and letters and the commerce student societies withdrew from the FEU to protest its pro-dissident stand. The CESM announced that neither CNE group could legitimately represent student interests. The FER not only took the same position but also dismissed the CESM as a government-sponsored organization organized to support the "false" socialist education. Because both CNE groups agreed on two points—that 95 percent of university students espoused some form of socialism and that the government was the enemy—reconciliation, when the dissidents began proposing it on August 17, was possible. The CNE closed ranks on the twentieth, in order to resist the government, but the split was not healed; two separate organizations would be created in 1935.[22]

[21] Mayo, *Educación socialista*, pp. 304–305, 314; *Excelsior*, August 8, 1934.
[22] *Excelsior*, August 12–20, 1934; *La Prensa*, August 14, 1934; *El Universal*, August 12, 1934; and Mayo, *Educación socialista*, pp. 301–303.

Student opposition to socialist education mounted as the date for the Chamber debate drew near and as events in the states polarized opinion. In Hidalgo, the governor declared his support for socialist education in August. On August 27, the Zacatecas governor issued a similar declaration. The ensuing strike in Zacatecas turned bloody in mid-September. Coquet, accompanied by Kuri Breña and Manuel Pacheco Moreno, went to Zacatecas city to speak to a crowd against socialist education, but the local police would not let the crowd into the plaza. While the three went to send a protest telegram to President Rodríguez, the police fired their Thompson submachine guns at the crowd, killing one person. In Michoacán, a Bloque de Jóvenes Revolucionarios announced its support of socialist education. On September 15, Melchor Ortega, governor of Guanajuato, sent his legislature a bill on cooperativist education that declared that individualism would be replaced with socialist education. In early October, the legislature closed the Ateneo Fuente because its students had demonstrated against socialist education. Bremauntz, writing several years later, gave a long list of those who opposed socialist education: the Frente Único de Izquierda of Rivera Albarrán, the Partido Renovador Estudiantil, most UNAM students, the Mexican Communist Party (until 1938), the Escuela Libre de Derecho, the Academia Mexicana de Jurisprudencia, the Barra Mexicana de Abogados, the FEU of UNAM, and the CNE, as well as Catholic and conservative organizations.[23]

The effects of this struggle on a single institution can be illustrated by briefly tracing events in the Universidad de Nuevo León in Monterrey. As was true of Guadalajara, Monterrey was a conservative center; Monterrey was also the second most important capitalist center (after Mexico City) in the nation. The Regiomontano rich were and are tightly knit and determined to protect their own interests. The university first opened for classes on September 25, 1933, under the sponsorship of Governor Francisco A. Cárdenas, but he resigned in late December of that year. In mid-August, the interim governor appointed Dr. Ángel Martínez Villareal, a Mason and Communist party leader in Nuevo León, as rector. His opponents would argue that he was ineligi-

[23] Mayo, *Educación socialista*, pp. 307–309, 315; *El Universal*, August 28, 1934; *La Prensa*, August 31, 1934; *La Prensa* (San Antonio, Texas), August 18, 1934; and Alberto Bremauntz, *La educación socialista en México (antecedentes y fundamentos de la reforma de 1934)*, pp. 302–315.

ble because he was under the required age and held a government post (in the ayuntamiento of Monterrey).

When the rector and Governor Quiroga tried to make it a socialist university, the students rebelled and took control of the central building on September 26; CNE/UNEC leaders hurried to the scene. On the twenty-eighth, Quiroga met with ex-president Calles and president-elect Cárdenas to discuss strategy; after also meeting with legislators, he nullified the university's organic law. Federal troops occupied university buildings on the twenty-ninth. On October 1, the Federación de Estudiantes Socialistas was created with the help of the CESM. The next day, students shot at each other. On the third, the governor announced a five-person committee to organize a Universidad Socialista de Nuevo León to replace the former institution. When these plans were finally announced in November, they stipulated that a university student had to join the FES and the Instituto de Orientación Social (a Marxist-oriented, government-sponsored agency) in order to enroll in the university. Classes reopened on November 20, but an organic law was not passed until September 1935, in time for the socialist university to be dissolved. During the year from September 1934 to September 1935, the university became another political football in a game that involved a son of ex-president Calles as a gubernatorial candidate for Nuevo León in 1935. The election, violent and disorderly, was annulled in August 1935. Various members of the organizing committee of the university quit in late August, and the institution was allowed to die. By the end of the year, Calles and his friends were preparing for exile and the peak of the socialist education controversy as it affected universities had passed.[24]

Mexico City, however, was the focal point of the struggle over socialist education, and its streets and meeting rooms were fully occupied by partisans during October. On September 17, the proposed Bremauntz version of the amendment to Article 3 was published, with the accompanying applause of Carlos Madrazo in the name of the CESM. The version excluded universities, a victory for the opposition, but the inclusion of all post-elementary education (thus affecting university preparatory schools) and the possibility that Congress might add a university section kept university students agitated. Some, of

[24] Tomás Mendirichaga Cueva, "La Universidad Socialista de Nuevo León," *Humanitás* 9 (1968): 361–388.

course, opposed socialist education at any level and would agitate against it. On October 3, students took to the streets to demonstrate against the amendment, an act to which the National Revolutionary Block in the Chamber of Deputies objected on the fifth, calling the CNE and the FEU a bunch of clerical-inspired reactionaries. *El Nacional* editorialized the same day that UNAM was anti-Revolutionary, the students were anti-government, and the movement was being led by the clergy, reactionaries, and Gómez Morín; on the other hand, the paper asserted that technical students were pro-revolutionary. Gómez Morín published a letter in *El Universal* the same day asserting that the government was trying to defraud the autonomy granted in 1933 but calling upon students and professors to return to their studies and attendance, to call the amendment fascistic and to demand the total seizure of power to create a dictatorship of the proletariat.[25]

The opposition movement became more violent. On October 10 and 11, students stoned the offices of *El Nacional.* On the twelfth, members of the National Parents' Union paraded through the streets in a protest demonstration. As they neared the National Palace, university students joined the march and stoned policemen. Some fifty-five persons were arrested and an unknown number injured. The next day, the FEU met to consider whether it should continue to be a leader in the anti-socialist education fight and to join a united front. By a 9-4 vote, the school representatives decided to continue, but signs of a split were present. Philosophy and letters, one of the conservative schools, voted against continuing. Representatives of both the day and night prep schools voted with the majority in spite of their personal support of socialist education. The delegates debated the advisability of calling a strike so near vacations and when the university was divided. On the seventeenth, however, students rioted in the university sector, attacking buses and cars, and the FEU meeting that day was

of calling a strike so near vacations and when the university was divided. On the seventeenth, however, students rioted in the university sector, attacking buses and cars, and the FEU meeting that day was

Carlos Sánchez Cárdenas, David Vilchis, and Germán Lizt Arzbide in sympathy for fellow students in Zacatecas, Monterrey, and Puebla. The FER met in the prep school, with leftists David Alfaro Siqueiros, stoppages (mini-strikes) in UNAM that day as a demonstration of their to quit using violence and agitation. Nevertheless, students launched students were anti-government, and the movement was being led by

[25] Mayo, *Educación socialista,* pp. 316–320; "La impunidad estudiantil y la agitación clerical," *El Nacional,* October 5, 1934; Manuel Gómez Morín, letter, *El Universal,* October 5, 1934; *Excelsior,* October 7, 1934.

constantly disrupted as the organization named strike committees to prepare for a strike.[26]

The crisis created by the student anti-socialist education campaign had reached major proportions. President Rodríguez announced on October 18 that new disorders by the students would be energetically repressed and schools closed. *El Nacional* editorialized that the riot the previous day was carried out by "professional students," agitators, clericals, and spiteful politicians, and asserted that the government was justified in repressing them. Rivera Albarrán called a meeting of the CNE to discuss what role the organization would play if a strike were declared; Coquet objected that only he, as CNE president, could call such a meeting. UNAM's medical school declared itself on strike, and police and students from the medical, law, and prep schools fought. The UNAM council met, appointed a committee to ascertain the government's attitude toward the university, and then voted to close the university until such an official policy statement was issued. The Universidad de Guadalajara was closed that same day by the governor. Students in other universities, both closed and open, declared their opposition to the government's plan; higher education was virtually brought to a standstill, and few secondary-level or elementary schools in the capital were functioning peacefully, since UNAM students were disrupting classes and being chased out by saber-waving policemen.[27]

The general strike in UNAM that all sides had been anticipating came on October 20 after President Rodríguez announced his continued hostility toward the agitation, the university, and the council decision to suspend classes. Gómez Morín and the council had announced their disapproval of the strike movement when they met on October 19 and disavowed any complicity in the events, blaming instead irresponsible elements. Rodríguez, on the twentieth, disagreed and threatened to pursue the matter vigorously; he also criticized the council for suspending classes. In a letter to the council's commission on October 23, 1934, he justified his posture by saying that students

[26] *Excelsior*, October 14, 18, 1934; *New York Times*, October 12–13, 1934; Mayo, *Educación socialista*, pp. 319–320.

[27] *Excelsior*, October 18, 1934; *El Nacional*, October 18, 1934; *New York Times*, October 19, 1934; and Mayo, *Educación socialista*, p. 321. Mendieta y Núñez, *Historia*, p. 202, has his description of events on pages 212–213 suggests otherwise.

were using the university as a cover while they traveled throughout the country agitating against the amendment to Article 3; since the university had not disowned them, he considered UNAM as hostile. In response to the president's hostility, law students met on the twentieth and declared a strike, demanding that the government give UNAM enough money to guarantee its autonomy. They declared their solidarity with the working class and the anti–socialist education students in the nation and said they were not striking against the university administration. Both the FEU and the FER announced support of the, strike. The entire university followed shortly.[28]

Faced with government hostility and the inability to influence events, Gómez Morín resigned on October 22. He had asked law student president Rogelio de la Fuente to end the strike and had pleaded with other students to call the strike off, but to no avail. When he tried to resign on the twenty-second, the council voted 23–21 to reject his resignation, but for all practical purposes he was through, even though his resignation was not official until November 1. The close vote in the council demonstrated that he had lost support, even though a majority of the schools, meeting on the twenty-third in response to a council request, had voted to end the strike. Law, by a 227–200 vote, and medicine, by a 461–206 margin, voted to continue and did. When the council met again on October 26, it gave the rector a month's leave and named Dr. Enrique O. Aragón to act in the interim.[29]

UNAM soon returned to normal. The amendment to Article 3 had been passed on October 20, taking the wind out of the students' sails. The council reopened the university on October 29, accepted Gómez Morín's resignation on November 1, and began the process that eventually led to the selection of Fernando Ocaranza as rector on November 26. The government arranged a pro–socialist education rally on October 28 to try to demonstrate that the students were not the majority. The amendment to Article 3 did not include the university level nor did it apply to all other schools, so both sides won a partial victory. The Marxist left had again been kept out of control of UNAM. Ocaranza was

[28] *Excelsior*, October 18–24, 1934; *El Nacional*, October 18–19, 1934; letter of Abelardo L. Rodríguez to Ezequiel A. Chávez, Antonio Caso, Trinidad García, and others, Archivo Chávez, Caja IV; *New York Times*, October 21, 1934; Mayo, *Educación socialista*, pp. 320–323; Mendieta y Núñez, *Historia*, pp. 213–215. The council's commission included Ignacio Chávez, Antonio Caso, and Trinidad García.

[29] *Excelsior*, October 22–24, 1934; Mayo, *Educación socialista*, pp. 322–323.

given the task of picking up the pieces and keeping the university alive for a while longer.[30]

The choice of Ocaranza to head UNAM in these difficult days provides an interesting insight into the internal political process as well as into the distribution of power. The new rector, who had received his medical degree in April 1900 from the military medical college, had served on the University Council for twelve years, eight of them as director of the medical school. He was known and trusted by students, including his former students Ignacio Chávez and Gustavo Baz, and faculty alike. A classical liberal and a hero of the right for his role in the Instituto Científico y Literario struggle, he could be trusted not to deliver the university to the socialist education faction. In his memoirs of this period, he explained how he was selected and unconsciously revealed the extent to which he was a creature of student politics. According to his account, he was approached in September (he must have meant November) by three members of the student federation, who asked him to attend a meeting of professors and students in the National Museum on a matter of importance to the university. The professors were Ezequiel Chávez, Antonio Caso, Alfonso Caso, and Pablo González Casanova (the elder); the students were the leaders of the student federation. Ocaranza was persuaded that he was the only possible alternative to Chico Goerne, whom the group saw as demagogic and tied to the rising leftist regime. Ocaranza saw Chico Goerne as the candidate of Rodríguez and Cárdenas and had promised to vote for him. With Ocaranza's acceptance of his candidacy, the campaign was launched. Chico Goerne withdrew and Ocaranza got all but two votes, one of which went to Mario de la Cueva, who would later be rector.[31]

Accepting the rectorship under these circumstances meant that Ocaranza was dealing from a position of weakness. He would normally have had difficulties because he was not an UNAM graduate, a fact his opponents would use when convenient, but to accept as the instrument of students who themselves were considered enemies of the state seems especially foolhardy. As he himself saw the situation, years later, his firmest support came from the CNE—specifically from Kuri Breña,

[30] Silva Herzog, *Una historia,* p. 77.

[31] Fernando Ocaranza, *La tragedia de un rector,* pp. 217, 229, 258–259, 365–366, 369–370; Silva Herzog, *Una historia,* p. 77; Arturo Arnáiz y Freg, "Fernando Ocaranza, treinta y tres años de enseñanza médica," *Novedades,* December 18, 1944.

Pacheco Moreno, Chávez Camacho, Carlos Ramírez Zetiña, Bernardo Ponce, and Leopoldo Baeza y Aceves (almost all of whom were UNEC activists), yet he credited the members of "Bios," "Lex," and "Labor" (the constituent groups of UNEC) as the initiators and directors of the university opposition to socialist education and the 1934 strike. Writing only of the medical school, he identified the militant Catholics and the Communists as extremists who made the proper functioning of the school impossible. Thus, by accepting the rectorship from and relying on the CNE, he was delivering himself and his administration into the hands of extremists and revealing his political naiveté.

Not surprisingly, student politics almost guaranteed that his term would be foreshortened. Elected November 26, 1934, he resigned on September 17, 1935, frustrated by his inability to find even temporary solutions to the fiscal and political problems UNAM faced. Almost constant agitation marked his ten months in office. Groups agitating inside the university and, at times, in the nation at large were numerous. Ocaranza identified some in his memoirs. The extreme left was backed by Ramón Denegri (former cabinet secretary under Calles) and Alberto Tejada (governor of Veracruz). A moderate left group was backed by General Francisco Múgica. The CNE, by the summer of 1935, was flirting with Saturnino Cedillo, governor of San Luis Potosí and presidential aspirant. Pro-Calles forces continued to try to influence events. Garrido Canabal's Redshirts and the Goldshirts (a quasi-fascist group) intervened. Within the university, he identified other groups: the Communists, usually poor and to whom he sometimes gave money individually; the demagogues, with José Rivera Albarrán being the most noteworthy; the exploiters, who were always trying to extort money out of students, especially new ones; the "saviors" of the university, as the 1929 pro-university reform group identified themselves; and the CNE leaders. Students in specific schools created problems as well. Chemical science students struck. Law students viewed the rector with coldness, in large part because he was not from their school. The extreme left agitated constantly in plastic arts. In short, there were enough politically motivated student groups with outside support to convert UNAM into a bubbling cauldron.[32]

The year 1935 was marked by constant maneuvering and infight-

[32] Ocaranza, La tragedia, pp. 418–420.

ing among the various student organizations. In November 1934, the pro-Calles Liga de Estudiantes Revolucionarios, led by Ernesto Rubio Rojo but backed by PNR president Manuel Pérez Treviño and by Luis L. León, changed its name to Juventud Revolucionaria in an attempt to co-opt the leftist youth and add another element to the ex-president's power base. The FEU, for its part, lambasted Calles in a November 20, 1934, manifesto, calling him the strongest bourgeois capitalist in Mexico and his life the grossest negation of socialism. To the leaders of the FEU—president Efrén R. Beltrán, Brito Rosado, Vallejo Novelo, and Rogelio de la Fuente—the PNR, odious to the people, headed the counterrevolution, and the corrupt government had failed to follow through on the Revolution. The solution was for Cárdenas to break with Calles. In January, the FEU, the FER, and the CNE joined forces to protest the attacks on students by Redshirts in Coayacán in December and after more than 1,500 students threw stones at the headquarters of the Redshirts. Cárdenas found it necessary to counter that only the PNR represented the Revolution and to demand that strikes in schools cease.

In March, controversy continued. Beltrán, Kuri Breña, Héctor Mata González, and Enrique González Rubio led a mass protest meeting in the ENP amphitheater against police attacks on students in Guadalajara. One student suggested that it was time to organize a terrorist group like the ABC in Cuba. Also in March, the Partido Revolucionario Estudiantil, led by Ranferi Gómez Díaz, launched a tirade against the conservative elements in UNAM and announced its desire to unify all the "genuine" university people. Leftists protested against U.S. intervention in Cuba and against fascists, Redshirts, and Goldshirts on March 17, 1935; Kuri Breña of the CNE announced that his organization was not part of this movement. Carlos Sánchez Cárdenas led the Frente Único de Estudiantes, Maestros y Campesinos. On April 10, Rivera Albarrán announced his "resignation as secretary-general of the CNE, saying that his Marxist position was incompatible with holding the office and calling for an end to agitation inside UNAM. On May 21, UNAM was closed to prevent further rioting by students who were protesting a Supreme Court decision against university control of secondary schools. Three days later, the newspapers carried notices of a split in the FEU. In late June, a Lombardo Toledano group burst into a law student meeting called to debate the presidency of

José M. Walls Herrera and his (and the CNE's) involvement with Governor Cedillo (who was feted by the CNE that month). They were ejected. The meeting itself was interesting, for the FER was trying to take control of the law student society from Walls Herrera, but he was saved by this unknown group, identified only as "gobiernista." It is possible that Walls Herrera even arranged the assault. [33]

The Catholic leadership of the CNE suffered its own problems with internal power struggles and its efforts to disassociate itself from traditional Catholic philosophy. On July 9, 1935, the officers announced plans to reorganize the federation, re-examine the delegations accredited to it, and forbid the election of officers who were involved in confessional or national political activity. Two days later, the FEU rejoined the CNE. On July 15, delegates began gathering in Monterrey to celebrate the annual convention, having successfully resisted the efforts of the CESM to get the state governor to block the meeting. Efforts to stop the meeting did not end there; on the fifteenth, as they were leaving a session, two students were shot to death in the street. The assassin, apparently a Callista, was not punished. Thousands attended the funeral and protested. On the sixteenth, the delegates received news that the brother of Rodulfo Brito Foucher had been assassinated in Tabasco, where he was active in the gubernatorial campaign. Students in Mexico City, led by the FEU, arranged a mass march on the National Palace, attacking Garrido Canabal and Calles and calling for Cárdenas's intervention to stop the repression. In light of these events, leftists were unable to capture control of the CNE; Kuri Breña turned the reins over to Pacheco Moreno.

The resolutions passed resembled prior congresses, calling for a law to protect workers and peasants and for regulations requiring students and universities to work or create solutions to social problems. The single most important item to come out of this congress was the call for graduates of professional schools to repay society for their education by giving a year to social service, an idea that was eventually adopted in the medical school. Of course, the delegates also opposed

[33] *El Nacional*, November 17, 1934; Federación Estudiantil Universitaria, "Manifesto de los universitarios de Mexico," *Omega*, December 8, 1935; *Excelsior*, January 8–9, March 18, May 24, June 27, 1935; *La Prensa*, March 12, 1935; *El Nacional*, March 12, April 11, June 27, 1935; *New York Times*, May 22, 1935; *El Día*, June 27, 1935; *El Universal*, June 27, 29, 1935.

socialist education and called for an amendment to Article 3. They adopted the Catholic position that parents had the right to educate their children as they pleased.[34]

Although these student political activities complicated UNAM-government relations, they were less important than the decision of the University Council to attempt to thwart the government's socialist education plans. Some background is necessary here. In January 1935, Archbishop Pascual Díaz announced that religious persecution was worse than it had been between 1926 and 1929. In March, the government jailed the archbishop and others; when he was released shortly thereafter, he sent a letter to Cárdenas complaining of the persecutory tactics of education minister García Téllez (who had vowed that all efforts would be employed to destroy the Catholic church) and that government employees had been fired because of their religious beliefs. García Téllez had decreed that secondary education would no longer serve as preparation for the liberal professions (thus trying to cut off the flow of students into UNAM). President Cárdenas ruled that private schools either had to adopt socialist education or close; some eighty did close in Guadalajara, sparking protest demonstrations.[35]

Ocaranza, prompted by the UNEC members of the council, confronted the government by proposing that the university return to its five-year preparatory curriculum and allow students to enter it without finishing their secundaria studies. García Téllez responded by decreeing that secundaria studies had to be completed before preparatory certificates would receive official recognition. Ocaranza appealed to the Supreme Court for a writ of amparo to block the government, claiming that, because the university was autonomous, the government had no right to intervene. The court supported the executive branch, and students rioted. In the council, Bernardo Ponce advocated

[34] *El Universal*, July 9, 1935; *Excelsior*, July 11, 16–20, 1935; Mendirichaga Cueva, "La Universidad Socialista," pp. 370–374; Rodríguez, "National University," pp. 256–273; Confederación Nacional de Estudiantes, *El XII Congreso Nacional de Estudiantes, Monterrey, Nuevo León. Estado y educación. Servico Social*. This last document contains information on the events and the resolutions of the meeting. *El Nacional*, July 17, 1935, reported that a Congreso de Estudiantes Campesinos announced for socialist and practical education and castigated UNAM as a bastion of the privileged and the conservative; the timing suggests that this was done to offset the CNE. Mayo, *Educación socialista*, pp. 379–380, also provides an account of the CNE congress.

[35] Dulles, *Yesterday in Mexico*, pp. 626–628.

a general strike, but Antonio Caso's caution prevailed. The council agreed with the suggestion that an Escuela de Iniciación/Extensión Universitaria be created as a means of expanding the preparatory curriculum. Such a tactic would be justified by asserting that the university was simply trying to complement rather than compete with government efforts to educate.[36]

UNAM had gone too far and its leaders had provided the government and leftists with the opportunity to regain control. Although Ocaranza had managed to get a two-million-peso subsidy from Cárdenas, when he asked for an additional one in August 1935 to offset the 306,000-peso deficit, Cárdenas refused. On September 6, Ocaranza reported the facts to the University Council (without mentioning the five-year preparatory curriculum); the council decided to ask Cárdenas to bail out the university! That UNAM would consider expanding its curriculum in the face of penury perhaps documents the unreal world in which the council had been living. When the Council went into closed session, a leftist porra, led by Rivera Albarrán, tried to break in, demanding Ocaranza's resignation. Repulsed, they turned to attack José González Jáuregui of the FEU and a plastic arts student and to demand that either Luis Enrique Erro or González Aparicio (who had just returned from the Soviet Union) be named rector. Surprisingly, law student president Walls Herrera prevented their expulsion. The day after the incident, Ocaranza announced that he was not a politician and that he did not aspire to high political office. He would not comment on the previous day's events. The CNE announced its support of him (perhaps a kiss of death), but was itself denounced on September 8 by the FEU headed by Beltrán, which also denounced the FEU of González Jáuregui (of UNEC). In a secret session the council again considered the university's situation vis-à-vis the state, deciding that it wanted to keep its liberty, autonomy, and government subsidy. González Aparicio charged that leftists were being replaced by rightists on the council; Antonio Caso denied it and threatened to resign because he could not agree to socialism as the doctrine of the university. González Casanova threatened to resign as well. González Aparicio apologized.[37]

[36] Dulles, *Yesterday in Mexico*, pp. 626–628; González Cárdenas, *Cién años*, pp. 208–209; Armando Ramírez, "La revolución universitaria", *New York Times*, May 22, 1935; Mendieta y Núñez, *Historia*, pp. 215–216.
[37] *Excelsior*, September 7–10, 1935.

On the tenth, two important steps were taken. The council voted 25–11 to suspend university operations until the state defined its attitude toward the university (and sent more money). Ocaranza reported on his conversation with Cárdenas and a possible modus vivendi. The state would create secundarias of a university type that would be controlled by a technical and managerial group of two professors named by the education ministry and two named by UNAM. The secretary of education and the rector would take turns presiding. The extension courses would constitute the first two years of these. The council approved the compromise plan and appointed a committee to deliver it to Cárdenas. A detente appeared possible.[38]

Rivera Albarrán, however, complicated the issue by leading a group in a temporarily successful takeover of university buildings on September 11. The group was called the Ala Izquierda or the Frente Único Pro-Reforma Universitaria and included members of the FER, Juventudes Socialistas de la Republica, Federación de Estudiantes Socialistas de la Federal District, and Communist Youth, among others, numbering some 150 in all. They claimed to be liberating the university from those who had bankrupted it and asked that Cárdenas give them control, with autonomy and a subsidy, but Walls Herrera and a law school group (which included Alfonso Corona del Rosal) recovered possession on September 14. The gesture was futile, since UNAM was closed and since Cárdenas was unlikely to give the university to a self-proclaimed group.[39]

The power struggle became more complicated on September 12. The Chamber of Deputies expelled seventeen pro-Calles congressmen because of a gunfight in the Chamber the day before. Inside the university, a group of law students and professors formed a mixed committee to repudiate the administration and to call for the creation of a directory to take over the university. The ground was being cut from under Ocaranza.

Cárdenas's response on September 14 to the council's appeal brought the resignations of Ocaranza and his associates on the seven-

[38] *Excelsior,* September 11, 1935; Mendieta y Núñez, *Historia,* p. 216; González Cárdenas, *Cien años,* p. 209; Mayo, *Educación socialista,* p. 412.

[39] *Excelsior,* September 12–13, 1935; *New York Times,* September 13, 1935; *The Times* (London), September 13, 1935; González Cárdenas, *Cien años,* p. 209; Mendieta y Núñez, *Historia,* p. 217; Mayo, *Educación socialista,* pp. 413–415.

teenth. The president blamed UNAM's troubles on its refusal to adapt to the new social realities and to its attempts to thwart the social reforms of the government. If the government were to fund UNAM, the institution's autonomy would have to be limited to purely technical matters; further, the government was drafting a law to accomplish that purpose. Senate spokesman Juan de Díos Bátiz announced that the government would not aid the university as constituted, since it was led by reactionaries, and that Cárdenas was going to give two million pesos to create an Instituto Politécnico Nacional. Ocaranza called a council meeting for Tuesday, September 17. Before it convened, a group of 150 (the majority of whom were councilors) met in the school of philosophy and letters to decide what to do. When the council itself met, the rector, all but one director, and some of the elected councilors resigned. The remnant named Balbino Dávalos, an elderly ex-diplomat, as provisional rector. In a public statement, the council argued that the government had made it clear that academic freedom and autonomy were going to disappear. Ocaranza complained of the vices of student politics and claimed not to have favored any group.[40]

While the Frente Único continued to hold the buildings, Walls Herrera called together students and professors to form a directory to reorganize the university and present a united front against the government. Surprisingly, Octavio Lozano, an employee, was included, the first time that the academics had ever recognized the importance of employees. That a worker, three liberal heroes of the 1929 strike, and Ramírez y Ramírez from the FER were participants made it difficult for Cárdenas or others to assert that reactionaries still controlled UNAM.[41]

The reorganizational plans approved at this meeting were also designed to pacify the government and preserve university autonomy. A

[40] *Excelsior*, September 14, 18, 1935; *New York Times*, September 14–15, 1935; González Cárdenas, *Cien años*, p. 210; Mendieta y Núñez, *Historia*, pp. 217–218; Mayo, *Educación socialista*, pp. 415–420. The law school mixed committee included professors Roberto Esteva Ruiz, Agustín García López, and Manuel Moreno Sánchez and students Corona del Rosal, Augustín Peña, Francisco G. Toabada, and Raúl Rangel.

[41] Mendieta y Núñez, *Historia*, pp. 218–219, citing *El Universal Gráfico*, September 19, 1935; Mayo, *Educación socialista*, pp. 420–421. Professors Gómez Arias, Brito Rosado, Salvador Azuela, and Enrique González Rubio and students Leopoldo Baeza, Manuel García Rodríquez, Enrique Ramírez y Ramírez, and Walls Herrera (FEU president).

new council would be elected by majority vote of the students and professors to carry out the reorganization under existing university statutes. Professorial slots would be filled on a competitive basis, but a "free university" (or parallel lectures) in each school/facultad would guarantee ideological diversity. Student fees would be reduced and scholarships would be given to needy students. Graduates and students would perform social service in order to strengthen ties between the university and the working class. The directory appealed to Cárdenas for a state subsidy and the continuance of autonomy; that is, for the president to withdraw his proposed new organic law.

Not everyone in the university agreed with the directory. In a September 20 meeting, philosophy and letters professors resigned en masse, demanding academic freedom, a government subsidy for UNAM, private financial aid, and the creation of a fight and defense committee to resist the government; in an act of futility and bad judgment, they recognized Dávalos as the legitimate rector (he was out the next day). The success of the directory would mean that these professors would lose the influence they had gained under Ocaranza. From the left, Ramírez y Ramírez declared that the clerical elements had to be expelled, that they could no longer be allowed to hide behind university autonomy and academic freedom. The CESM took an almost identical stance. The Ala Izquierda also agreed but went further, suggesting that the council be elected from candidates of the left, center, and right to solve the crisis (and thus guarantee seats to its members).[42]

Other groups maneuvered in favor of their own interests during the election days of September 20–23. Chávez Camacho and Kuri Breña joined with Ángel and Alfonso Caso, David Thierry, and René Barragán to argue that, since the mass resignations, the government no longer needed to destroy UNAM's autonomy and create a socialist university. The point of the mass resignations, they asserted, was to demonstrate that the bulk of the students were fighting for academic freedom. On the twenty-first, a new radical group of students and professors, the Unión de la Izquierda, announced their goal of ejecting the reactionaries who were posing as liberals (the 1929 group). The next

[42]Mayo, *Educación socialista*, pp. 422–423.

day, the FER withdrew from the directory; and the Ala Izquierda announced that it would not participate in the elections. The Vanguardia Estudiantil Universitaria, a leftist group of unknown origin and duration, also attacked the election. Despite these efforts of the left to stop the elections, they proceeded as scheduled; the new council was elected on the twenty-third and, in turn, elected the new rector.[43]

Secret bargaining, based on an accurate appraisal of the reality of the situation, determined the election of Luis Chico Goerne as rector by all but three votes. Although a practicing Catholic, Chico was not fanatical but instead identified himself with the Revolution. As a former law school director, he could count on the support of the most politicized school. The actual negotiations leading to his election were conducted by Juan José Bremer, a German-Mexican, who made a deal with UNEC, Gómez Arias, and Azuela. The clericals believed Chico would protect them. Azuela was to be given a high administrative post. The deciding factor in his selection, however, was his personal friendship with Luis I. Rodríguez, private secretary to Cárdenas.[44]

Through this connection, Chico persuaded the president to substitute a national council on higher education (Consejo Nacional de Educación Superior y de Investigación Científica) for the planned takeover of UNAM and to trust the new rector to maintain order in what would be a pro-Revolutionary university. The law creating the new council was passed before the end of September; its teeth would be in the government's power to regulate the exercise of the professions. Cárdenas still had the fiscal whip; he was unwilling to supply funds until he was sure of what he was getting. Chico sold the land the university had been holding for a new campus (Ciudad Universitaria), thus obtaining 700,000 pesos to cover the deficit and supply operating capital.[45]

Having spent two years in open conflict with the national govern-

[43] Mayo, *Educación socialista*, pp. 423–425; Mendieta y Núñez, *Historia*, p. 219; *New York Times*, September 25, 1935.

[44] Mendieta y Núñez, *Historia*, p. 219. Mayo, *Educación socialista*, pp. 425–426; Horta, "Quince años," *Así* (December 9, 1944): 28–30; Silva Herzog, *Una historia*, p. 77.

[45] Mendieta y Núñez, *Historia*, pp. 219–220; Mayo, *Educación socialista*, pp. 426–428; Horta, "Quince años," *Así* (December 9, 1944); *Excelsior*, September 29, 1935; *New York Times*, September 29, 1935.

ment, UNAM now appeared headed toward a rapprochement, but with its autonomy intact. Student groups had gained power by forcing out two rectors and by choosing the third. As observers surveyed the scene in October 1935, they must have wondered how long this new rector would last, whether he could control student politicians long enough to build a working relationship with the national government and get a return of a regular subsidy, and whether he could avoid a government takeover of UNAM.

6. Rapprochement, 1935–1944

THE rapidity of social and political change fostered by Cárdenas produced successful demands by 1940 for a period of consolidation and stability. To be politically aware in the 1930s was to live through more change than the nation had ever seen before or since. Workers emerged as a political force with some weight, winning job disputes with the aid of the government and being given control of the nationalized railway system. Land was redistributed on a massive scale, usually into ejidos (communal farms). Foreign-owned companies had their property expropriated in 1938. Businesses and industries of any size were forced to join formal interest groups. The government party was reorganized and strengthened as an instrument of control. Spanish Republican refugees from the rightist Franco forces were welcomed. These and other events occurred so quickly and with such fundamental consequences that even Cárdenas began to pull back in the last years of his administration. The selection of the moderate Manuel Ávila Camacho as the government party's candidate for the 1940–1946 presidency promised to bring the social peace that many demanded.

The election of Chico Goerne proved to be a turning point in the history of both UNAM and student activism, for the new rector effected a rapprochement with the national government and initiated the policy of using porras to control students. His successors, Gustavo Baz (1938–1940), Mario de la Cueva (1940–1942), and Rodulfo Brito Foucher (1942–1944), would continue the latter practice, but Brito Foucher would begin moving UNAM toward confrontation again, in part to further his personal dream of a political career, only to be driven out by students and their political allies. The rapprochement, however, would last beyond any of these individuals. Chico Goerne, considered a radical lawyer, shifted the university toward support of Cárdenas and the

Revolution. His ouster in 1938 would be the result of his misuse of his power and UNAM monies, not dissatisfaction with his support of the government.

For the political right to continue controlling UNAM after September 1935 would have been suicidal for the university. Cárdenas, already in a power struggle with ex-president Calles, could ill afford to allow political enemies to continue to use the university as a privileged bastion from which to send sorties against the government. But the weight of the autonomy tradition and the considerable loyalty UNAM was able to command argued against a frontal assault, particularly of the kind Lombardo Toledano had tried in 1933. Thus, the selection of Chico Goerne, whom Cárdenas found fascinating, was politically shrewd. How this decision was reached is still hidden.

Chico wasted little time in disassociating himself from the old guard who had controlled UNAM, even though he had used UNEC votes to win the rectorship. His first move was to pay off the heroes of 1929 by appointing Salvador Azuela as head of the new Department of Social Action.

Cárdenas was serving notice that education would no longer be a privilege of a few, that the economic and social organization of the country as well as the government itself could no longer be at the mercy of a privileged minority in higher education. Thus, he was creating a National Council of Higher Education and Scientific Investigation, composed of fifteen presidential appointees and one representative from each government department, to reorient higher education to serve the collective ends. Further, the government planned to use its power to regulate the exercise of the professions. That Cárdenas was moving away from UNAM's monopoly of higher education was no idle threat; federal deputy Luis Enrique Erro had announced on September 6 that the government was creating an Instituto Politécnico Nacional. It was officially founded the next year. No one doubted that this was a direct slap at the national university. In short, university-state relations in the early fall of 1935 were seriously strained: the Cárdenas government, with Gonzalo Vázquez Vela as secretary of public education, was on the attack against an impoverished UNAM.[1]

[1] Excelsior, September 29, 1935; New York Times, September 29, 1935; Britton, Educación y radicalismo, II, 73.

Chico, more sympathetic to Cárdenas than his predecessors had been, began disassociating himself and his administration from conservative opposition to the state. He created a Department of Social Action to carry out the long-suggested social service projects (ironically, advocated as often by conservative as by liberal students). Cárdenas thought he finally had a socially conscious university. During the October 22 council meeting Chico charged that the university had become clerical and that, even though he was himself a Christian, the university had gone too far to the right. He demanded and got, by a 45–21 vote, the power to appoint the director of the Escuela de Extensión Universitaria, thus guaranteeing that it would not become a center of resistance to the government. In mid-March 1936, some student groups, controlled by Chico and his close associate Juan José Bremer, began a public campaign to discredit Gómez Morín and Ocaranza, accusing them of making UNAM a refuge for the clerical right. Both former rectors denied the allegations, and after allowing several days of newspaper publicity to drive home the point, Chico, Pacheco Moreno (one CNE president), and Roberto Fernández Morán (an FEU president) called off the attack, seeking to avoid a division of the students. The purpose of this charade, however, had been accomplished: Chico had demonstrated where his sympathies lay.[2]

But Chico played a double game. Bremer, his henchman, had persuaded UNEC members to vote for the "radical" Chico because, as a practicing Catholic, he was more acceptable than a Marxist. Once in power, the new rector secretly began to undermine UNEC and the conservatives by using university money (part of which came from the land sale) to guarantee the election of friendly, leftist officers of the FEU, ignoring UNEC and the CNE for months and putting leftists on the payroll of university extension. Additional monies were used to pay porras (often professional boxers) to "discipline" recalcitrant students. Even though these moves did not go entirely unnoticed by the right, since Chico was making a public play to Cárdenas, the fact that he aided the conservative Universidad Autónoma de Guadalajara by incorporating it into UNAM in 1936 and allowing it to keep the fees it collected confused the issue. This incorporation meant that students received UNAM degrees, necessary because degrees were licenses to

² Excelsior, October 23, 1935; Mayo, Educación socialista, pp. 427–428; Horta, "Quince años," Así (December 9, 1944); Excelsior, March 13–18, 1936.

practice a profession and education authorities refused to recognize UAG degrees.

Both the Chico administration and UNAM in general benefited from this strategy. Cárdenas, impressed by the new university posture as well as by Chico's mastery of student politics, resumed the university's subsidy. Covertly at first, money dribbled into university coffers, but in 1938 the president secured the passage of the Ley de Embudo (Funnel Law), which overtly raised the subsidy to one million pesos. Chico used this money and funds obtained from the sale of university land to pay extra salaries to himself, his friends, and his allies. UNAM was able to pay its personnel and expand its programs. Chico and Bremer did not use the new money to reduce fees, however; instead, they gave discounts to cooperative students.[3]

Much of the success and survival of the Chico administration depended on student politics. Students had driven rector after rector from office and had the power to veto the selection of a new one. By their loud and sometimes violent demonstrations against the state, they had threatened the survival of the institution. UNEC's capture of the CNE in 1933–1934 and subsequent anti-government, anti–socialist education campaign had not only alienated the new Cárdenas regime but had spawned a number of leftist student organizations, each determined to destroy the CNE and capture control of UNAM. Chico had to control both ideological groups, supplant the right with the left, and control the leftist UNAM student groups in order to maintain his own power base. To understand how this delicate strategy worked in practice requires both background information on leftist student organizations (the CNE has been described) and detailed accounts of some events.

The Confederación Estudiantil Socialista de México (CESM) continued to push for socialism in Mexico. Meeting in its second national congress, in Uruapan, Michoacán, on October 8, 1935, the delegates again demanded that education be based on dialectical materialism and teach revolutionary consciousness. Specifically, they called for free schools for workers' children as well as free primary schools for all (the assumption being that non-workers could afford to send their children to post-elementary schools). They repudiated UNAM, asserting that it

[3] Horta, "Quince años," Así (December 9, 1944); Rodríguez, "National University," p. 287.

had fallen into disrepute because it was controlled by the church and a neo-Porfirian caste. They noted the "violent" right-wing reaction to the CNESIC and the IPN and demanded that UNAM be put at the service of the country. University students, they argued, should be children of workers and peasants. The resolutions they passed addressed a wide range of issues, few of which directly concern us here.[4]

The persons included in and excluded from the CESM congress are worth noting, for the roster suggests that this was an important organization. Carlos Madrazo continued as a leader, but Ángel Veraza presided. Other important participants included Alejandro Carrillo, Enrique Ramírez y Ramírez, Juan Gil Preciado, and Roberto Hinojosa (from Bolivia). But the CESM did not include all those who belonged to the organization, for a group of Jalapa students withdrew from the CESM in November and created the Frente Único Estudiantil Revolucionario because the CESM's state committee had ignored them and taken non-representative students to the Uraupan congress.[5]

The goal of the CESM was to unite leftist and progressive students under a single banner in order to gain control of the nation's universities and of education in general. The eight archbishops of Mexico, in January 1936, had raised the ante by forbidding Catholics to send their children to socialist schools. In the countryside, socialist education advocates and rightists battled: right-wing fanatics cut the ears off some three hundred teachers between 1935 and 1939. To support socialist education, the Primer Congreso de Estudiantes Normalistas was held in December 1936, during which the delegates advocated the teaching of sex education to mothers, women's rights, equal pay for equal work, government housing for teachers, and a minimum salary for teachers, in addition to declaring themselves against war, fascism, and imperialism. The Aguascalientes delegation, which included UNEC members, withdrew, asserting that the other delegates were not students. In March 1936, Lombardo Toledano, Madrazo, and the CESM organized the first congress of socialist students of Puebla as part of this national campaign to create a leftist student bloc.[6]

By mid-May 1936, leftist students had united sufficiently to begin

[4] Roberto Hinojosa, *La justicia social en México*, pp. 19, 21–22, 39–48; Mayo, *Educación socialista*, pp. 405–408.

[5] Hinojosa, *Justicia social*; *El Universal*, November 3, 1935.

[6] *The Times* (London), January 20, 1936; Knauth, *Nacionalismo y educación*, p. 158; *El Nacional*, December 31, 1935, and March 17, 1936.

planning a national congress to create a new Confederación Nacional de Estudiantes to replace the one controlled by the rightists. The rightist CNE, on March 12, 1936, announced plans for a celebration to pay homage to Carranza on May 20; Carranza, to the leftists, did not belong in the Revolutionary pantheon. The leftist organizing committee included delegates from the major university-level leftist organizations.[7]

Missing from the list was the Federación Estudiantil Universitaria of UNAM, which was also opposed to the conservative direction taken by the CNE. As the single most important student organization, its lack of participation was significant. In part, president Fernández Morán and his officers did not want to share power; in part, Chico, who financed them, wanted to maintain his and the university's independence in national politics.

In reaction to this leftward shift, particularly in leftist control of student organizations, the CNE unsuccessfully attempted in the May-June FEU elections to regain control and push Chico out. Although Chico had been able to bring most of the student organizations under his control and to guarantee the election of officers sympathetic to and supportive of his position, the May-June 1936 elections exploded in his face and the right made a serious effort to push him out of the rectorship.

The CESM went beyond national boundaries in its effort to assume national leadership of university students. Just as the CNE had hosted an international congress in 1921, so too did the CESM in 1936. Using funds provided by Jalisco governor Everado Topete, the CESM invited eminent socialists to the Primer Congreso de Estudiantes de América. Foreigners who accepted the invitation for the Guadalajara meeting included Ramón Grau San Martín and Carlos Prío Socarrás (Cuba), Waldo Frank (United States), Roberto Hinojosa (Bolivia), Raúl Haya de la Torre and Luis Alberto Sánchez (Peru), Alfredo Palacios (Argentine), Maxim Gorki and Jorge Dimitroff (USSR), and José Ortega y Gasset (Spain).[8]

[7] *Excelsior*, March 11, 1936; *El Nacional*, May 13, 1936. They were Luis Mondragón and Ramírez y Ramírez (FER); Trinidad López and José Rivera Alberrán (Ala Izquierda Estudiantil); Julio Aguilar and Luis Torres (Federación Nacional de Estudiantes Normalistas); Julio Marín, Carlos Sánchez Cárdenas, and Ambrosio González (Federación Juvenil Comunista); and Carlos Rubio and José M. Borrego (CESM).

[8] *El Nacional*, May 22, 1936; *Gráfico*, July 7, 1936.

UNAM student leaders split into two factions. The FEU was headed by Roberto Fernández Morán, but a rightist group calling itself the Directorio claimed that it actually won the FEU elections. These latter students from UNEC and/or the CNE asserted that the elections had been fraudulent and that Chico had not been impartial. A law professor, Gabriel García Rojas, stepped in as a mediator and nullified the elections in architecture, chemical sciences, commerce, engineering, and law on or about May 11. It is not clear whether García Rojas had authority to intervene (Chico later said he did not) or whether both student groups agreed (the Directorio did but its members were out of power). *Excelsior* reported that the major reason for the conflict was the desire of those out of power to take office so they could get jobs in the university, since almost all FEU directors were university employees or professors, including Fernández Morán and Aguirre E. *Excelsior* also asserted that student elections were conducted like those of the PNR—in violation of the election rules. There was some ideological basis for the student division: the opposition feared Marxist professors and did not want non-Marxists replaced with Marxists. To a point, they were friends of the rector. They did not like Gómez Morín, because they saw him as weak and vacillating, nor did they like Ocaranza, because he deserted at a time of danger. It would be a mistake to see one group as clerical or the other as Marxist. García Rojas announced that both groups were out.[9]

The Directorio refused to leave, however, until the Fernández Morán group quit. They argued that Chico was showing partiality and that the Commission of Honor did not have the right to judge them. They asserted that Fernández Morán and Aguirre E. had been named to posts in University Extension.

Chico now disassociated himself from García Rojas and began backing Fernández Morán's group more openly. Chico asserted that García Rojas had volunteered and not been appointed and that the Commission of Honor was not a commission but just three professors who had been asked to mediate. The FEU contended that García Rojas was a rightist who had not been invited to intervene and that Aguirre

[9] *Excelsior*, May 15, 1936. Unless otherwise noted, this account is based on *Excelsior*.

had resigned several days previously. In the intervening days since the argument had begun, the FEU had discovered that it would have the support of leftist students. On May 17, the Ala Izquierda announced that it was going to sit out this argument, but gave its vote of support to Chico for having put UNAM at the service of the nation. The Ala offered to give free classes in the prep school and University Extension.

The result was that the Fernández Morán group maintained control of the FEU, discovered that Chico would not support its opponents, and joined with other leftists to drive the conservatives out of student organizations. The CNE responded with attacks on the FEU. On May 20, the student presidents of law, economics, medicine, chemistry, engineering, dentistry, commerce, plastic arts, the prep school, music, philosophy and letters, and veterinary medicine declared that the CNE was a right-wing clerical group, denounced the CNE campaign against student leaders, and stated that they had no disagreement with the FEU and that the FEU was *the* recognized student organization. If the CNE attacks continued, they said, they would not be able to hold back the FEU.

In response, a CNE-UNEC group (including some professors) assaulted the FEU offices, bringing forth demands for expulsions. The FEU specifically demanded that Jesús Guiza y Acevedo and seventeen students be expelled for a year because they were betraying the university and student causes. There was also a demand that the rector be impartial. On the twenty-third, the CNE issued a call for all students to maintain the fight for autonomy, academic freedom, and sincere social service (an allusion to their contention that the social service program of the university was demagogic and, in some cases, nonexistent).

The leftists decided to reorganize the Confederación Nacional de Estudiantes because, they asserted, the clerical conservatives in control did not truly represent university students. Pacheco Moreno, CNE president, countered that his group could not be thrown out and that they had telegrams of support from student organizations in the states of Chihuahua, Querétaro, Tamaulipas, México, Hidalgo, Coahuila, and Guanajuato. This CNE announced plans for a national congress later in the summer at which the issues of the balance of the Mexican Revolution and humanistic orientation in universities would be addressed. The leftists created a committee led by Fernández Morán and Rómulo Sánchez M.[10]

As the days passed into June, the argument heated up, drawing the rector further into the fray. The Directorio accused the rector of malfeasance, asserting that Chico paid professors who did not meet their classes, put relatives into high posts, and favored Communists on the UNAM police force. Further, it said that the university had two million pesos. These facts, they explained, accounted for the student fights. Chico made a categorical denial. Students from the states entered the argument by saying that they had come to the capital to study at great sacrifice and were tired of student fights and discord and hoped that the forthcoming XII CNE congress would define student organizational relationships. The Directorio accused Chico of partiality and claimed that UNAM had three months of life and that the two million from the sale of land had been used to buy student leaders. Further, they asserted that Chico, Azuela, and others were paid to teach but did not.

Chico called a public meeting to defend himself and had to stop a strike attempt the same day. He claimed that *Excelsior* was misleading students and the public. He told the meeting, which *Excelsior* claimed was attended mostly by administrators, that he would only stay as long as he had support. He defended his actions by saying that the council had not met often because the problems UNAM had had with the state gave him little time to call it and that the council and the CNE had approved this procedure. He defended the selection of his nephew Carlos Chico Alatorre as secretary to the law school on the grounds that the law director had recommended him. Further, he claimed that he needed people close to himself in whom he had confidence. He said he got permission not to teach and did not take any money, that, in fact, he had given up a decent law practice in order to serve the university. He asserted that all of the accounts were in order. He then appointed a committee of Aragón, Ochoterena, Fernando Lanz Duret, Silva y Aceves, and Fernández Morán to draft a statement of defense. The Directorio sent a telegram, which Chico read, in which it said that it had been invited to attend this meeting but would not because only

[10] *El Nacional*, May 27, 1936; *Excelsior*, May 26, 1936; *El Universal*, May 26, 1936, and June 1, 1936.

the council could conduct university business. The assembly gave Chico a vote of confidence. Chico promised to convoke a general student assembly and a council meeting to decide what to do about this conflict.

As the assembly ended Jesús S. Sodi and other students seized the university extension building where the meeting was being adjourned, ejected some participants, and tried to start a strike. Chico persuaded them to desist, however, and promised to talk with them about their complaints. The Sodi group then went to *Excelsior*, where they announced their demand that Rivera Albarrán, Francisco Valencia, Carlos Sánchez Cárdenas, and Roberto Fernández Morán be fired as professors and Rubén Aguirre E. be fired as secretary of university extension because they had no university antecedents and because Rivera Albarrán, Valencia, and Sánchez Cárdenas were Communist party members and thus enemies of academic freedom. They claimed that a boxer had hit a student after talking to the rector. They said a strike was declared but they were not sure it would occur.

On June 2, events got more exciting. In an interview with *Excelsior*, secretary-general Bremer answered some of the charges. He asserted that the strike had failed, that Rivera Albarrán and Sánchez Cárdenas were not professors, that Aguirre E. was not an officer of the FEU, and that Fernández Morán had a brilliant university career and would give up the FEU presidency when elections were again held. The Ala Izquierda again announced its support of Chico and of Rivera Albarrán. *Excelsior*, for its part, accused Chico of violating university law and of ruling like a dictator. That same day, some 30 or 40 students and boxers of the Rivera Albarrán group assaulted the CNE offices, breaking up the furniture and carting off the CNE files. The Directorio reported that the FEU group was using boxers, pistoleros, and other outsiders to beat up students to break the strike that had been declared. That night, some students stoned the *Excelsior* building.

June 4 was little better. *Excelsior*, which was partisan, noted that Chico had not disavowed the assaults. The extension strikes continued. A group of professors asserted that almost everyone who had taught in extension the previous year had been replaced, but the Bloque Unificador Estudiantil de Extensión Universitaria countered that only incompetent professors had been fired. The CNE displayed a copy of its letter to Bremer, in which it had argued that professorial posts should be filled by competition (oposición) and that, if this could not be done, the university should insure ideological diversity. In the school of plastic arts, a group of boxers and pistoleros (*Excelsior* said they worked for Chico) broke up a meeting being held to discuss the events. Leading the pack were Brito Rosado and Salvador Moreno. They used tear-gas bombs. The plastics arts students demanded that Chico resign.

On June 5, it appeared that calm might return. Chico issued an official announcement deploring the violence. *Excelsior*, finding no evidence of a strike and concerned that its articles were stirring up trouble, announced that it was no longer going to print the various accusations.

Leftist students were not willing to terminate their drive to destroy the conservative CNE of Pacheco Moreno. They disowned the CNE directors, claiming that the majority of students backed the leftists and that all the schools and university authorities supported Chico. They formed purge committees to rid the schools of conservative officers. They justified their June 2 attack on the CNE as a reprisal for the CNE-sponsored or sanctioned assault on the University Extension building and the CNE use of rockets and other threats to try to start a strike. They also claimed that rightists had used tear gas and guns in the plastic arts school to stop those students from supporting Chico. [11]

Chico and his supporters, thus encouraged, decided to rid the university of the rightist troublemakers. On June 6, Chico held a meeting with students and professors in the prep school amphitheater during which Azuela, Brito Rosado, Gómez Arias, César Ortiz, Raúl Rangel, and José Elizalde attacked the CNE. The assembly passed a series of resolutions to be presented to the council when it met on the eighth. Along with giving Chico a vote of confidence, the assembly agreed to keep Guiza y Acevedo out of UNAM for publicly attacking the administration; agreed not to allow Islas García, Chávez Camacho, or Antonio Aguirre Salas to enroll, claiming they were non-students who served outside interests; and voted to suspend for one year six others for having publicly vilified the rector and the university. Of interest was the support that Agustín Yáñez, later a major novelist, gave to these resolutions. On the eighth, the council in a rowdy meeting voted 40–22 to accept the resolution after a heated debate between Chico

[11] *El Universal*, June 5, 1936.

and Chávez Camacho, during which the latter accused the rector of being a Catholic (saying he had seen him praying in church) and of having betrayed the Chávez Camacho group, which had supported him. But these rightist leaders were out. For the sake of appearance, Chico did appoint an investigating committee a few days later; it cleared him of all charges. The CNE tried to get the attorney general to investigate the attack on its offices, but nothing came of that. A group of philosophy and letters students issued a memorial against the expulsion of Guiza y Acevedo and claimed that because of the tumultuous nature of the council meeting, with the attendance of numerous non-members, it was not a valid meeting.[12]

New statutes, officially approved on June 16, 1936, increased student power on the council. In addition to two students to be elected from each facultad/school, the president of the student society of each facultad/school would be a council member, thus balancing each directory with the student president. The FEU was allowed to send a voting delegate, but the CNE was given only a voice. The rector, four non-school/facultad directors, two alumni, the oficial mayor, the head of Social Action, and the head of the department of accounts and administration were also council members; the total membership was well over one hundred. The council was given the power to fire personnel when one-third of those present agreed and could remove professors with more than three years' service. Elections were to be supervised by a triad of student, a professor, and a director. The council assumed the obligation of determining the validity of the elections of student society representatives, thus making these societies implicit official organs of the university, a move that would cause trouble because it embroiled the administration in some ugly fights it could have avoided.[13]

In a relatively quiet FEU election in July 1936, Francisco López Serrano, running on the blue ticket, won the presidency over Isidro

[12] *Excelsior*, June 7, 9–10, 1936; Armando Ramírez, "La revolución universitaria de 1933," *La Nación*, October 10, 1942.

[13] UNAM, *Estatuto de la Universidad Nacional Autónoma de México;* Pinto Mazal, *El Consejo Universitario*, pp. 14–17; César Sepúlveda, "Student Participation in University Affairs: The Mexican Experience," *The American Journal of Comparative Law* 17 (1969): 386. Alfredo Chavero, commerce director, had resigned his post on June 13 because student leaders and non-students had been causing trouble since 1934; he wanted nothing to do with the new rules; see *Excelsior*, June 14, 18, 1936.

Castorena, the red ticket candidate; both were law students. The only significant issue raised during the campaign came from the FEU and law students, who asked the attorney general to arrest Luis Magaña Velasco for the murder of a student in 1927, calling him a henchman of Senator Gonzalo N. Santos of San Luis Potosí and that state's strongman. On the twenty-sixth, the law student society issued a call for an end to national pistolerismo and again accused Santos of having authored murders.[14] Santos, a conservative rival to Cárdenas, was sympathetic to rightist UNAM students. These denunciations resulted in no actions, however.

Student agitation did not end but became more complicated and even ludicrous. The conservatives announced their plans for a CNE meeting to be held in September, eventually deciding on Nuevo Laredo as the site. Chico failed to persuade the governor of Tamaulipas to block the meeting. The leftists charged that a meeting so far from Mexico City and so close to the United States was proof that the conservative CNE did not represent Mexican students. Women technical students decided in July to organize the Federación Feminina de Escuelas Técnicas to defend feminist interests because they claimed that the FET directors, who lived on the government budget, were only interested in currying official favor; they also said they were tired of political agitators preventing them from studying. The normal school federation announced a 48-hour strike on July 9 to protest the expulsion of some Puebla normal school students. On July 28, the FEU held a mass assembly and decided not to participate in either the leftist CNE congress scheduled for Mérida or the conservative one in Nuevo Laredo because both groups were extremists. The FEU called for a grand congress of students to create a representative national student organization. The conservatives announced they had majority support and would have delegates from the states and that they did not recognize the Federal District leaders. By August 7, there was the possibility of three student congresses, each claiming to be national. A group calling itself the Delegaciones de los Estados disavowed both CNEs; it was refused affiliation with the FEU because it did not represent a majority, so it decided to meet in Mérida at the invitation of the governor. The FEU president announced that his organization did not support

14 *Excelsior*, June 17, 20, 21, 1936, and July 22, 1936; *El Nacional*, July 8, 1936.

the Mérida congress, contrary to the claims that group had been making.[15]

Of the two CNE congresses, the one in Mérida proved more interesting. The conservative Nuevo Laredo congress reaffirmed its desire for independence and its support of academic freedom and autonomy, denounced Chico, and elected Federico Rodríguez Hicks as its president. The organization continued to exist but increasingly played a minor role in student politics, becoming a small right-wing pressure group. The FEU sent a delegation to the organizing-committee meeting of the leftist congress in Mérida, but decided not to participate when the committee reported on September 3 that the delegates were not students and that it was going to be a pseudo–student congress financed by the government in order to get proclamations of student support of the government. The government verified its role by using the Mexican Navy's ship *Querétaro* to transport the students to Mérida.[16]

A close examination of the personnel and program of the Mérida congress reveals its true purpose. Under the leadership of Jorge Octavio Acevedo, the delegates assembled for the opening session on September 13. Most delegates were closely tied to the Cárdenas government. They issued a vote of sympathy for Republican Spain and a salute to fellow leftists elsewhere, called for the federalization of all education, asked that UNAM become a dependency of the executive branch, lambasted imperialism, and called for students to unite with workers to bring about socialism.[17]

No UNAM rector could ignore the twists and turns of student politics, whether they were internal or external to the university. The 1936 statutes, giving students almost half the voting seats on the council and requiring only a one-third vote to fire personnel, meant that a rector who could not count on student support could not survive. The

[15]*Excelsior*, June 24, July 29, August 7, 25, 29, 30, 1936; *Gráfico*, July 7, 1936; *El Nacional*, July 9, 1936; *El Universal*, July 29, 1936.

[16]"Confederación Nacional de Estudiantes, *Estado y Educación*; Rodríguez, "National University," pp. 287–290; *Excelsior*, September 2, 4–6, 14–15, 1936.

[17]*Diario del Sureste*, September 14–18, 19, 1936; Rodolfo Jiménez Barrios, "El Congreso de la C.N.E.," *Diario del Sureste*, September 19, 1936, p. 3. The delegates included Alejandro Magaña (Juventudes Socialistas de México), Isidro Castorena, Antonio Acevedo Gutiérrez, Carlos Sánchez Cárdenas, Enrique J. Encinas, Luis Torres Mesías, and José E. Elizalde (who was elected president).

FEU had only one vote, but many, if not most, of the other student delegates followed the lead of the FEU. Hence, to control the FEU elections was to guarantee a solid majority on the council, for the rector usually controlled most of the directors.

When it appeared in the summer of 1937 that he would lose control of the FEU, Chico threw his resources into the student presidential elections to guarantee the victory of his candidate. The clerical faction supported José Campillo Sáinz, but the leading candidate in the early stages of the process was Humberto Olguín Hermida. Realizing that if either won, he would lose control of the FEU, Chico backed Héctor Mata González, a chemistry student and thus an unlikely winner since he was neither from law nor medicine and was backed primarily by the "fossils" or perpetual students. Two hours before the first balloting in a school, Bremer persuaded the UNEC faction to join forces with Mata González, putting their man Campillo Sáinz in the second spot, in order to keep the "Communists" out of power. Word of the deal spread, however, and many students voted for Olguín in protest, including Catholics. With anti-Mata González and anti-Chico sentiment mounting, the rector decided to force the election results.[18]

Few precise accounts of the internal workings of school elections exist, but the several that are extant indicate what happened. On August 2, Olguín, on the green ticket, soundly beat Mata González (red ticket) in the Juárez Hospital by 104–99, in the General Hospital by 122–33, and in the medical faculty by 166–125, or 392–257 in the medical school overall. The balloting was turbulent. Nevertheless, Arturo Ruiz de Chávez, head of the FEU technical department, announced that the Olguín group, seeing that they were losing, had assaulted the ballot boxes and students in an attempt to force new elections. Much the same happened in the engineering school. Chico promised to stay out of the dispute but broke his word.[19]

Administrative support and a tactical error on Olguín's part insured Mata González's election. The university treasurer shelled out money to buy votes and, when that appeared to be failing, issued pistols to selected students and toughs. Olguín accepted the overt support of the Juventudes Socialistas, thus lending credence to the charges that he was a Communist and scaring the conservatives. When

[18] Horta, "Quince años," *Así* (November 16, 1944): 24–25.
[19] *Excélsior*, August 3, 1937; Horta, "Quince años," *Así* (November 16, 1944).

the results were in on August 14, Mata González was declared the victor by eleven schools to five.[20]

Chico's machinations in the election cost him more than it was worth, for the university again blew up in his face, this time with long-term consequences. Late on the night of August 10, a group of law students led by José Bello seized university buildings and declared a strike against Bremer and other high administrators (but not Chico) in an attempt to stop the Mata González victory, claiming that administrative manipulation made the elections fraudulent. In addition to assurances that Olguín would be FEU president, they wanted Bremer, Azuela and his assistants, and treasury officials fired. Chico hurried to the law school to meet with strikers (some of whom were not students) and threatened to resign if the strike were not ended. When he promised to fire Bremer, Olguín gave the order to vacate the buildings by morning. Not knowing of this deal, which Chico abrogated the next day, some pro-Olguín students accused their man of treason. Olguín left when word got out that the "strikers" had come from the Consejo Nacional de la Educación Superior and the Juventudes Socialistas.[21]

On the morning of the eleventh, FEU president Arturo Milhé (López Serrano had resigned earlier in the year) convoked a mass meeting to support the administration. Chico, Azuela, Bremer, and other aides of the rector came. Chico simply thanked the assembly, leaving the dirty work to his subordinates. Azuela first pleaded, "Why me?" but then charged that the attack on UNAM was the work of Narciso Bassols, working through the Consejo Nacional. Bremer denied his role in manipulating the elections, claiming he was opposed to outsiders using students for their own political ends. Softened up, the assembly gave a vote of confidence to Chico, declared the Consejo Nacional and its president, Enrique Díaz de León, as well as Luis Enrique Erro, responsible for the assault. The Consejo Nacional would deny the charges.[22]

The Consejo Nacional had become an issue because it was moving

[20] Horta, "Quince años," *Así* (November 16, 1944, and December 23, 1944); *Excelsior*, August 15, 1937.

[21] *Excelsior*, August 11, 1937; Horta, "Quince años," *Así* (December 23, 1944); Carmen Cira Guitán Berniser, "Las porras: Estudio de caso de un grupo de presión universitaria," p. 7.

[22] *Excelsior*, August 12, 1937; Horta, "Quince años," *Así* (December 23, 1944); and Guitán Berniser, "Las porras," p. 9.

into direct competition with UNAM, in spite of what the university community had thought in October 1935 when it supported its creation. Instead of being a research and planning unit, it had created six secundarias, a school for preparatory teaching, and an industrial museum. The consejo had begun to argue that state universities suffered severe problems and would either have to be reformed or abolished. Many directors or supporters of the Consejo Nacional had strong ties to the socialist wing of the Cárdenas administration. This was no idle threat. On August 12, 1937, the consejo announced plans to open university centers in Michoacán and Jalisco. The stakes for UNAM were being raised. [23]

Two other versions of the August upheaval warrant mention. CNE (conservative) president Federico Rodríguez H. declared the assault a Communist plot. Pro-Olguín students told *Excelsior* that the August 11 meeting was phony because most of those attending had been bused from University Extension by Bremer. They declared that they, students, had seized the buildings and had released them because of Chico's promise. They promised a meeting on the twelfth. [24]

The anti-Chico meeting on August 12, 1937, turned into another bloody confrontation. Two versions of the event exist. What appears to be the UNAM version claimed that members of the Juventudes Socialistas, having been given the rector's permission to use the prep school amphitheater to hold an anti-Chico administration meeting, took the law school meeting room by surprise and met resistance. Francisco Robledo, president of the day prep students and one of the intruders, wounded a medical student in the hand with a .45-caliber pistol shot. The socialists were ejected, but some trapped non-student intruders, wearing overalls, confessed that they had been sent by the Consejo Nacional. The Juventudes Socialistas denied their involvement and counterclaimed that Bremer had sent toughs to attack their headquarters with stones and gunfire.

Another version put forth by a group of students (they showed their credentials to *Excelsior*) claimed that they were holding a protest meeting against Bremer, the treasurer, and a group of students who were also professors. Chico was applauded when he arrived. The rec-

---

23 *Excelsior*, August 2, 5, 12, 1937.
24 *Excelsior*, August 12, 1937. The pro-Cárdenas directors and supporters included Xavier Icaza, Alejandro Carrillo, Juan O'Gorman, and Enrique Díaz de León.

tor told them that he could not fire Bremer because they were friends. Shortly thereafter, Bremer-paid students led by Valero Recio broke into the meeting and began beating people with sticks and firing pistols at the protesters. CNE (liberal) president José E. Elizalde and Francisco Robledo were injured. The offended students reported to *Excelsior* that Chico had betrayed them and that they were now going to try to oust him. Chico's friend spread the rumor that Chico might resign to end the conflicts, and the law director claimed that the police came in answer to his call and arrested three of the eight intruders detained (the other five escaped). All were armed and five were "dressed in the *camisetas blancas* worn by Communists," and three in overalls.[25]

The Chico forces cleaned house. Four hundred student guards kept intruders out of the university. Seven students were expelled, and Daniel Bravo and Castorena were fired from their university posts for being Redshirts. The council decided to investigate the roles played by professors Leopoldo Ancona and Vallejo Novelo in the events. On August 14, the university directors gave Chico a vote of confidence and began planning for a council meeting.[26]

After more violence, the effort to oust Chico and his group fizzled out when Cárdenas announced his support of the rector. Student guards and socialist students conducted a shootout early in the morning of the sixteenth, but no one was hurt; the police broke it up. The football team (U.S.-style) sided with the conservatives. Robledo asserted that UNAM authorities were responsible because they were trying to impose the Mata González ticket and using porristas to do it. Milhé, reflecting the Chico line, claimed that the attack on the university was a plot to paint the university as reactionary so that Cárdenas would cut off funds. Olguín, however, speaking in the name of the Partido Revolucionario Estudiantil, said that the Juventudes Socialistas were not causing the trouble but that it was a progressive movement that wanted to reform teaching, democratize higher education, and convert student groups into instruments of the popular culture. The extension professoriate rallied behind the rector, claiming outsiders were responsible for the discord. The council meeting on the sixteenth con-

[25] *Excelsior*, August 13, 1937; *New York Times*, August 14, 1937.
[26] *Excelsior*, August 14–15, 1937; *New York Times*, August 14, 1937. Those expelled were Elizalde, Octavio Rivas Cid, Castorena, Francisco Castro Garrido, Bello, Robleda, and Juan Estrella.

firmed the expulsions and firings. Chico offered to hold new FEU elections if anyone doubted that the Mata González group won. The clincher, however, was the telegram from Cárdenas announcing that money for UNAM was coming.[27]

Chico survived this second attempt because his subordinates took the heat and his opponents challenged his authority with extreme measures. By using Bremer as his point man, the rector was able to divert the sniper fire away from himself. When he stepped forward to defend his aides, he was able to claim, implicitly, that he was being a loyal boss. By the time Chico himself came under attack, his detractors had attacked an institution (the Consejo Nacional) favored by Cárdenas and fired pistols. Cárdenas had little choice but to defend the principle of executive authority by supporting Chico, who was loudly asserting that UNAM supported the Revolution. The claim that Redshirts were involved (whether true or not) damaged the opposition, for Cárdenas would not support the pro-Calles Garrido Canabal. Socialist students began to reorganize under the patronage of Luis I. Rodríguez, Governor of Guanajuato and friend of Cárdenas, and wait for another day.

In the long run, Chico had undercut his authority with many professors and students, particularly in the medical school, whose members quietly began looking for some grounds to justify ousting the rector. Moreover, he had now openly betrayed both leftist and rightist students. The CNE-UNEC would not attack Chico as long as their members thought he would keep their socialist rivals out of power, but they would not support any rector who favored Marxism. In February 1938, this CNE sent Pacheco Moreno, Gonzalo Chapela y B., and Luis Calderón Vega to Saltillo to rally conservatives when the Coahuila governor tried to impose Marxism on the Ateneo Fuentes, the state university of Coahuila. Socialist students reorganized in October in a meeting sponsored by the Durango governor and Luis I. Rodríguez. Chico and UNAM would hear from the left again. Mata González announced in mid-October that the FEU had nothing to do with the Durango group nor with the CNE meeting in Querétaro of September-October. Chico had to increase his payoffs to students and professors to keep the peace; he could not afford another outburst of violence.[28]

[27] *Excelsior*, August 15–17, 1937; Horta, "Quince años," *Así* (December 23, 1944); *New York Times*, August 17–18, 1937.

[28] Horta, "Quince años," *Así* (December 23, 1944); Rodríguez, "National University," pp. 290–291; *Excelsior*, October 16, 1937.

The socialist student congress in Durango, coming so soon after the August upheaval, hinted at the Cárdenas government's attitude toward UNAM. The purpose of the meeting was to replace the CESM with the Confederación de Estudiantes Socialistas Unificados de México because the leadership of the former had sold out for money and to unite leftist students in the fight againt capitalism, conservatism, and fascism. The CESUM traced its lineage back through the CESM to the Lombardo Toledano group of 1933; Carlos Madrazo and Ángel Veraza provided continuity. The organization had links back to 1929 as well, for Baltasar Dromundo was an active participant. The most important group backing the new organization was that clustered around Luis I. Rodríguez; the delegates' expenses were paid, and they had the use of a special car of the National Railways to transport them from Mexico City to Durango. Although the delegates promised to point out the contradictions of the Cárdenas regime before world leftists, many of their resolutions supported the Cárdenas line. They vowed support for the Confederación de Trabajadores Mexicanos, the federal labor law, the Confederación Nacional Campesina, federalization of education, and Cárdenas's opposition to the conservative UNAM. In foreign affairs, they excoriated German, Italian, and Japanese imperialism, capitalism as inherently imperialistic, and right-wing regimes in Latin America. They applauded Raúl Haya de la Torre and APRA in Peru, Manuel Azaña of the Spanish Republic, and Cuban leftist students. UNAM and the CNE drew volleys of fire, the latter as the "Confederación Nacional Eclesiástica" that espoused an "advanced" social philosophy. Significantly, the delegates criticized those who attacked the Consejo Nacional.[29]

The CESUM would not strike against Chico until the rector was fighting for survival against allegations of fiscal mismanagement and corruption. Late in April 1938, reports began circulating that UNAM salaries were in arrears, with hints that the reason lay in Chico's use of the funds for illegitimate purposes, among which was the bribing of student leaders. Chico called a meeting of directors and student leaders to assert that the amount that salary payments were in arrears was

[29]Manuel González Calzada, *Juventud Izquierdista de México. Congreso Constituyente de la C.E.S.U.M.*, with a foreword by F. León de Vivero, printed at government expense by D.A.P.P., the government propaganda agency; Confederación de Estudiantes Socialistas Unificados de México, *Estatutos y Conclusiones del Congreso Constituyente de la Confederación de Estudiantes Socialistas Unificados de México.*

small and thus inconsequential. The professors' federation supported Chico; on May 9 the group issued a denial that it planned a work stoppage because some salaries were not being paid. Since most of the directors and student leaders were creatures of the rector, their support was a publicity ploy. The professorial support is more puzzling, but perhaps understandable in light of the fact that their salaries were not their principal income. Chico's maneuver did not guarantee him security, for student elections were being held and a medical school committee was investigating the university accounts.[30]

Chico successfully prevented a prep school fight when the losing ticket tried to start a strike by accusing the FEU delegates of fraud, but his position was becoming more perilous. The dispute encouraged the anti-Chico forces to press their attack. If they could create sufficient student opposition, Chico would tumble.[31]

On May 11, law students ejected from their building a group of students and non-students who were trying to hold a meeting to disavow the rector and push him out of office. Law student president Diodoro Rivera Uribe then organized a pro-Chico meeting at the rectory, which was followed shortly by a similar show of support from prep students. Another law student group, the Comité Pro Reorganizador, joined the anti-Chico movement. The Frente Progresista, part of the FEU, dismissed this latter move as a plot by a traitorous university functionary. No one identified this person or the non-students who were thrown out of the law school.

In spite of these demonstrations of student support, Chico was unable to resist the pressure exerted by medical faculty members, joined by law faculty members, to open the books for a careful examination. The medical group, led by Gustavo Baz, had been unhappy with Chico since the fraudulent student elections in their school the year before. They were the ones responsible for the rumor of mismanagement and would not accept Chico's argument that anyone could have examined the books on April 27. The law professors who supported the medical faculty demands came from among the most prestigious faculty members and from the political left and right. A group of law students, calling themselves the pro-reorganization committee, joined

[30] *Excelsior,* May 1, 9–10, 1938.
[31] *Excelsior,* May 1, 1938.

the anti-Chico movement. Hoping to contain the inquiry, Chico volunteered to aid the investigation.[32]

Whatever hope the rector might have had of surviving the investigation disappeared as leftists, both student and non-student, and FEU supporters began battling. On May 14, a noisy meeting in the law school, attended, according to *Excelsior*, by a majority of Communists or street people, demanded Chico's resignation. On the sixteenth, members of the CESM and followers of Olguín took control of the law and commerce schools between two and three in the morning, to be ousted by the police later that day after a bloody battle between leftist and rightist students. One student died in the melee. The FEU quickly disclaimed any responsibility for the death. Such an incident polarized opinion and encouraged anti-Chico factions to act.[33]

During the first days of June 1938, various groups jockeyed in an effort to control the financial audit. The Chico administration tried to keep the investigating committee to a small number of friendly persons. The medical group refused to join the administration committee and left the June 1 meeting in disgust. Law professors Roberto Cosío y Cossío, Agustín García López, and Lucio Mendieta y Núñez informed *Excelsior* by letter that the law group had not been invited to the meeting but was determined to participate in the investigation. On the third, the university faculty agreed to a mixed committee of seven to conduct the investigation, but the medical faculty, almost ready with its report, and some law professors left to follow an independent course of action. Chico began producing letters of support from the directors, but a premature release of the medical report on June 6 made all these efforts pointless.

The rumors of the contents of the medical school report leaked out of the meeting on June 6 and sent shock waves through the university. Chico must have known what would happen, for, after having the council minutes read and approved, the university auditor announced

[32] *Excelsior*, May 12–13, 1938. The law professors were Octavio Medellín Ostos (brother of the former rector), Luis Garrido (a future rector), Mario de la Cueva (a future rector), Antonio Carrillo Flores (director of Nacional Financiera, the government development bank, 1945–1952 and treasury secretary, 1952–1958), Agustín García López, Alfonso Teja Zebre, José Castro Estrada, and Vicente López.

[33] *Excelsior*, May 15, 17, and 19, 1938; Frank C. Kluckhohn, *New York Times*, May 17, 1938; Horta, "Quince años," *Así* (December 23, 1944).

that the rector wanted to wait until the medical school report (being presented at another meeting) was available before reading his report; the council recessed until 7 P.M. Baz, an ex-officio member as a director, announced that he was not trying to get the rector to resign, but the findings of his school's committee could have little other result. They found that the books did not balance; that money was missing; that funds were being shifted from account to account; that the rector and the finance committee were constantly creating teaching and administrative posts; that professors were being paid before they were hired; that lump appropriations, especially for building repairs, were being made without requiring any details of expenditures; that high officials, including the rector, official mayor, and treasurer were collecting additional salaries for other university posts; that the finance committee members were being paid unusually high salaries; that FEU president Hector Mata González, CNE president Roberto Carriedo, and most of the persons who participated in student politics were receiving university salaries; that the rector had covered the 1937 deficit by selling university property; and that some non-students were being paid out of funds reserved for students. The treasurer in a June 15 letter to Chico confessed to having stolen 35,000 pesos; the previous day, university officials of the new regime had issued a report proving that the above charges were just the tip of the iceberg.[34]

Chico did not resign until continued pressure from professors and students made his position untenable. The council, meeting on June 7, gave the rector a vote of confidence, at which point the medical school delegation left. One of the medical committee members said that the published newspaper reports of their findings were not the committee report and that they were not accusing Chico and his administration of theft. Chico pleaded that no one pointed out how he had saved the university economically. Gómez Arias unleashed his oratorical skills in support of the rector, but a more telling act was the resignation of Mariano Azuela (brother of the student leader) from the council on the grounds that the council was controlled by Chico. The medical professors created a Directorio Depurador (purge committee) and withdrew recognition of the rector and the council, soon joined by professors and student leaders.

[34] *Excelsior*, June 7, 15–16, 1938. Treasury figures revealed that each strike cost twelve thousand pesos and that the rector had paid five hundred pesos for a meal for student leaders.

fessors and students from the law and prep schools. In a mass student meeting, Chico defended his actions and promised not to resign, but did so the next day, June 9. Bremer, Gómez Arias, and the treasurer followed suit. The students had joined the opposition; Cárdenas had cut the subsidy.[35]

In spite of his claims of disinterest, medical director Gustavo Baz became the new rector, after several days of confusion. The medical school group initially designated Leopoldo Salazar Viniegra, a leftist, as interim rector, but he resigned on June 11. Julio Jiménez Rueda, a former Catholic and student activist who shifted to the left, presided over many of the Directorio Purgador meetings. Most of the directors were fired. The purge committee did not please most students and professors, even though it contained leftists as well as two people from the academic freedom (rightist) group. The leftists wanted to insure that professors would outnumber students two to one on the new council. On June 11, Baz was named interim director by a 27–5 vote over García López; he promised that his stay would be brief and that he would quickly call rector elections. Aurelio Manrique had nominated a student for the rectorship and resigned the prep school directorship because of student opposition. Mario de la Cueva resigned as oficial mayor and was replaced by Salazar Viniegra. The purge committee issued rules for the election of a Constituent Council on which each school would have two delegates, plus alternates. In an interesting commentary on the Chico regime, the election rules specified that no student delegate could have served or be serving in any teaching or administrative post. A minority whose votes equaled 75 percent of those obtained by the majority in a school was entitled to one of the seats. By the time the rector elections were finally held on June 21, Baz was the only candidate, but received only 53 of the 81 votes cast. Medellín Ostos, the leftist candidate, who had withdrawn, received 28 protest votes.[36]

Gustavo Baz and Mario de la Cueva, his oficial mayor and replace-

[35] *Excelsior,* June 9–10, 1938; Horta, "Quince años," *Así (December 23, 1944), says the key act was Cárdenas's decision to cut the university subsidy, which Chico took as a sign of no confidence. This is the only reference I saw to this, but it is a logical surmise.

[36] *Excelsior,* June 10–22, 1938; *New York Times,* June 13, 1938; Armando Ramírez, "Revolución universitaria," October 10, 1942. The leftists were Salazar Viniegra, Aurelio Manrique, and Medellín Ostos; the academic freedom (rightist) group included Agustín Yáñez and Mario de la Cueva.

ment, tamed the students and moved UNAM closer to the government. After sixty-six sessions, the council approved new statutes on December 19, 1938, that made political activism more difficult. In some ways they resembled the rules for the Constituent Council election, for students had to have a grade average of eight out of ten and not be university employees. Students and professors got equal representation, but the students lost the votes of society presidents and the FEU. In a switch, no councilors could be reelected. More important than structural changes, however, were Baz's relation with Cárdenas (as one of his personal physicians) and his organization of a group of student pistoleros or porra, the Pentathlon Deportivo Militar Universitario, recruited primarily from U.S.-style football players, who kept the peace. Baz left the university in 1940 to take over the Secretariat of Health, leaving Mario de la Cueva in his place. When Cueva issued a report for the 1938–1942 period, he could report that there had been no strikes or disruptions and that the university was conducting classes normally. He was in error in two ways: it was a peace by terror, and university students had fought in 1938 with vocational students in one instance and with taxi drivers in another. Neither incident, however, directly involved the university. This peace enabled Baz in 1940 to secure the exemption of college preparatory schools from the regulations enforcing Constitutional Article Three.[37]

To single out Baz as the rector who effected a reconciliation between Cárdenas and the UNAM is to ignore the achievements of Chico Goerne. When Chico became rector in 1935, the Cárdenas government, exasperated as much by student upheavals as by the conservative, anti-government stance of university leaders, was ready to remold the university into a state agency. By giving Cárdenas part of what he wanted—support of the Revolution, social service, extension efforts toward workers, and more peaceful student politics—Chico rescued both autonomy and academic freedom. Student criticism of the action against Chico or his administration failed as long as Cárdenas

[37] Horta, "Quince años," *Así* (December 23, 1944 and January 6, 1945); Miguel Castro Ruiz, "La compleja crisis universitaria de 1944," *La Nación*, July 16, 1951; *Excelsior*, August 17, 27, 1938; *New York Times*, August 17, 27, 1938, and February 5, 1940; Pinto Mazal, *Consejo Universitario*, p. 17; Ramírez, "Revolución universitaria"; Mario de la Cueva, *Informe de la rectoría, 1938–1942*; Gustavo Baz, *Informe que rinde el Rector de la U.N.A.M. al H. Consejo Universitario, sobre las actividades desarrolladas por la Universidad hasta el 1 de febrero de 1939*.

supported the rector. That Chico used toughs and bribes to control the students or that he and his friends profited from university funds, not common behavior for public officials, caused few problems until medical professors decided to bring Chico to heel. One can speculate that Baz's political ambition was a major factor in the anti-Chico movement. By June 1938, Chico had alienated both left and right (although it is doubtful that either could have been pacified). He could still count on the vocal support of his paid student leaders, but nothing would allow him to ride out the storm, as he had done in the past, after a student was killed. Whether the murderer was from the CESUM or the FEU was irrelevant: blood-stained hands could not hold the university reins. Baz, the hero of the anti-Chico forces, reaped the harvest sown by his foe. Baz's relationship with Cárdenas accounts for much of his success as rector, as did that of Cueva, who listened carefully to his predecessor, but Baz could not have become rector had Chico not cleared a path.

The political environment changed during the last years of the Cárdenas government. In 1938, the PNR was reorganized into the Partido de la Revolución Mexicana (PRM), with four constituent functional sectors. Cárdenas began toning down radicalism. The Jesuits ordered UNEC to stay out of university politics and to join Catholic Action. By 1939, most politicians began maneuvering for the next year's presidential elections. Manuel Gómez Morín organized a new opposition party, Acción Nacional (PAN), pulling into it many students, professors, and administrators who had been active in the university struggles of the 1930s.[38]

PRM politicians organized a youth wing, the Confederación de Jóvenes Mexicanos, in 1939, giving the party student support and a constant presence inside the national university. The CESUM was dissolved. Carlos Madrazo became the first CJM president, followed the next year by Ángel Veraza. The organizers were a stellar group of main-line politicians: Lombardo Toledano, Alejandro Carrillo, General Heriberto Jara, and Alfonso Corona del Rosal (head of the military youth). For years afterward, officers would move upward to important political posts. A brief list is suggestive: Juan Gil Preciado, Enrique

[38]On the shift of Cardenismo, see Albert Michaels, "The Crisis of Cardenismo," *Journal of Latin American Studies* (May 1970): 51–79; on UNEC, see Calderón Vega, *Cuba 88*, pp. 171–184; on Acción Nacional, see Mabry, *Mexico's Acción Nacional*.

Ramírez y Ramírez, Guillermo Martínez Domínguez, and Leopoldo Sánchez Celis. Neither the PRM nor its successor, the Partido Revolucionario Institucional, would ignore the political importance of university students.[39]

The election of General Manuel Ávila Camacho in 1940 signaled the beginning of a more conservative cast to politics. The "Gentleman President" brought leftists and rightists into his cabinet, publicly announced his belief in Catholicism, appointed a conservative to head the education ministry, and had Constitutional Article 3 amended to remove all reference to socialism. The Cárdenas reforms were allowed to stand, but monies were diverted to projects to increase agricultural and industrial productivity. Close cooperation with the United States increased after Mexico entered World War II in 1942, and Mexico reaped economic benefits. Miguel Alemán, his successor, would go even further in favoring business, industry, and commercial agriculture. Alemán was almost hostile to the labor movement. He was also something of a Cold Warrior, for he greatly admired the United States and tended to follow its lead. The success of the Revolution began to be measured by increases in the gross national product and by other economic data. In politics, participants were expected to endorse this definition of the Revolution or be called reactionaries or foreign (un-Mexican) radicals.

[39] See *Excelsior*, April 16, 1939, for a report on the organizational meeting. Confederación de Jóvenes Mexicanos, *Veinticinco años, cuadernos para la juventud, No. 4*, provides historical information. Virtually no research has been done on the government party's recruitment efforts in UNAM because of the difficulties of research; this author touches on the issue in later chapters. See Roderic Camp, *Mexico's Leaders: Their Education and Recruitment*, for a valuable analysis of the relationship between university life and political recruitment. Carlos Madrazo was the president of the Central Executive Committee of the Partido Revolucionario Institucional, the ruling party, in 1964–1965. Lombardo Toledano created the Partido Popular (later Socialista) as opposition to the government in 1948. Alejandro Carrillo became a federal deputy in 1940 and subsequently served in such posts as secretary-general of the CEN of PRI for 1939–40 and continued from Sonora. Heriberto Jara was president of the Federal District and senator in government posts. Alfonso Corona del Rosal was regent of the Federal District from 1966 to 1970 and, ironically, bore substantial responsibility for the student crisis of 1968. Juan Gil Preciado eventually rose to be secretary of agriculture (1964–70). Ramírez y Ramírez, active in the Mexican Communist party, was a founder of the Partido Popular and was a federal deputy (1964–67) under that party's label. Guillermo Martínez Domínguez served in numerous government posts and rose to be director of Nacional Financiera (1970–74); his brother Alfonso also became a powerful politician. Sánchez Celis became governor of Sinaloa (1963–67) and, ironically, one of those responsible for the ouster of Madrazo from PRI leadership in 1965.

Much to the dismay of the Ávila Camacho government, a student strike and a series of demonstrations erupted in the polytechnical system beginning on March 4, 1942. With UNAM finally under control, the government had little reason to expect trouble from university-level students, for the other major institution of higher education, the Instituto Politécnico Nacional (IPN), was a tightly controlled state agency with no claim to autonomy. IPN students, however, wanted the status and benefits enjoyed by their UNAM rivals. The strikers, some 25,000 strong, from the ranks of prevocational, vocational, and professional schools, demanded professional titles (instead of certificates), an organic law giving the system almost as much authority as that of UNAM, better teachers, laboratories, and equipment, and regulation of the rural medicine major. When the government used the army on March 6 in an effort to break the strike, two persons died and ten others were wounded. The students contemplated using a silent protest demonstration. On March 12, Ávila Camacho promised that the students would get the professional titles they desired, even though it required a constitutional amendment. The strike ended the next day.[40]

Although the Ávila Camacho government had more serious matters to consider, some government officials intervened in UNAM in 1942, trying to control the election of the rector. From his cabinet position, Baz tried to continue to control UNAM. To replace Cueva, who was stepping down, Baz chose Salvador Azuela. The clerical faction, however, had regained much of the strength it had lost when Baz was rector and, allied with Octavio Véjar Vázquez (a Baz enemy, and secretary of public education), it supported Rodulfo Brito Foucher. Brito had lost political wars in UNAM and Yucatán (where he lost a brother to an assassin) and was determined to win this time. He let the Baz group know that if they used violence, the Brito group would retaliate with guns. On the morning of the election, Azuela withdrew. Eight council members, including Jesús Silva Herzog, who tells the story, cast votes for Azuela as a protest against Brito and what they considered to be his fascistic tendencies.[41]

Brito needed little time to confirm the suspicions of the critics

[40] *Excelsior*, March 5–14, 1942; *Diario de Yucatán*, March 5, 1942; *New York Times*, March 7, 1942.

[41] Horta, ""Quince años,"" *Así* (January 6, 1945); Silva Herzog, *Una historia*, pp. 79–80; *Diario de Yucatán*, June 14, 1942; Rodríguez, "National University," p. 293. Rodríguez misunderstood the manner of Brito's election and the nature of his rectorship.

who thought he would be a right-wing dictator. In his inaugural address, he claimed that "the most important post in Mexico after the Presidency of the Republic is the rectory of the University." Some suspected that he planned to be a presidential candidate in 1946. At the end of his first year, he claimed that he had abolished the assaults and exploitations common during enrollment periods and hazing, gotten the majority of students to keep the rough minority in line, stopped students from starting vacations early, and ended marches and demonstrations. Despite his claim that this was done voluntarily, he raised the use of porras to a fine art. No one dared oppose him for fear of being physically assaulted. Even though he made UNAM more conservative, conservatives have seen his administration as a disaster. Leftists were determined to drive him out at the first opportunity.[42]

Using the occasion of the directorship elections in July 1944, the left made its move. When the old Revolutionary Antonio Díaz Soto y Gama, now very conservative, won the prep school directorship by an 89 to 50 vote over Agustín Yáñez, a moderate leftist, the latter protested, claiming that Brito Foucher had manipulated the election. Yáñez may have had the covert support of members of the government; no documentary evidence has been found to validate this hypothesis, but the rapidity with which Yáñez appealed to President Ávila Camacho suggests it as a strong possibility. First, however, incidents had to be created before the government would intervene. When Brito Foucher called a meeting on July 17 in the ENP amphitheater, the Díaz Soto y Gama group refused to let Yáñez speak. Brito, however, offered to hold new elections, but Yáñez refused. The two factions scuffled in Bucareli street when Yáñez returned with professors and students from the law school. Yáñez announced that he would seek presidential intervention to solve the "student" conflict. The ENP dispute was just the opening salvo.[43]

The pivotal events would start on July 19 in the veterinary medicine school, a surprise because its students usually played a passive role in student politics. Law students and professors had lamented the

[42] Silva Herzog, *Una Historia*, p. 80; Horta, "Quince años," *Así* (January 6, 1945); Rodulfo Brito Foucher, *Balance de la labor realizada por la actual administración universitaria durante un año, 1943*; Castro Ruiz, "La compleja," pp. 12–13; Guitán Berniser, "Las porras," pp. 12–14.

[43] *Excelsior*, July 7, 1944; *Diario de Yucatán*, July 18, 1944; Horta, "Quince años," *Así* (January 6, 1945); Castro Ruiz, "La compleja."

appearance of factions as a result of the directorate election, but pro-Yáñez students in veterinary medicine set off incendiary bombs and called a strike against the new, pro-Brito director. The police quickly released the students when they were arrested. Brito sent FEU president Rafael Huacuja H. and his porra into the fray, but this use of force backfired when victims complained to the press. [44]

The rector defended himself in the press and tried to insure that Ávila Camacho would not ignore the contents of his telegram. In Brito's version of the events, eleven of the fourteen director elections took place without incident and student objections in commerce had been met. Only in veterinary medicine and the ENP were there problems, even though the rector had offered to hold plebiscites. He accused Yáñez of getting aid from outside the university, charging specifically that an assault group had been recruited in the Sindicato Único de Empleados y Trabajadores of the central department of the Federal District to take over university buildings on July 24 as a simulated "student" strike. Police protected the university that day so that classes could continue, but unidentified armed men watched from the street. Yáñez, for his part, claimed that Brito lied about the plebiscite offer and was using gangs to suppress dissent. Yáñez asserted that he had been threatened himself on two occasions. [45]

Violence forced Brito to resign on July 27. Yáñez students, firing rockets, seized the law school building to hold it until new director elections were held in veterinary medicine, commerce, university extension, and the ENP. Hours later, at 2 A.M. on the twenty-fifth, Brito sent Huacuja's pistoleros to try to throw them out. These well-muscled men (many of them recruited from the football team, and many of them professional students) used heavy sticks, as they had been doing since the days of Chico Goerne and as they did in street battles at the prep school later that day. Believing their opponents were armed, they took pistols when they went to the veterinary school to break that strike. When the strikers began throwing stones and tiles, fifty Brito toughs and five policemen forced their way into the school. Shots were fired. A law student died and hundreds were injured. Students carried the body through the streets. Leftist law professors immediately resigned and demanded Brito's resignation. When his claim that a politi-

[44] *Excelsior*, July 20–21, 1944; *Diario de Yucatán*, July 20, 1944.
[45] *Excelsior*, July 24–25, 1944.

cal group had instigated the trouble, his appeal for presidential aid, and his promise to hold a plebiscite went unheeded, he resigned, acknowledging that he and his administration had to bear responsibility for the death. Díaz Soto y Gama and many of the pro-Brito administrators followed suit.[46]

Neither the left, which forced Brito out, nor the right, which tried to maintain control, could fill the vacuum created by the fall of the administration. The Revolutionary Directory (as the victors called themselves), led by Manuel Gual Vidal, "fired" the council and the directors and named the secretary-general, Samuel Ramírez Moreno, as interim rector. Jiménez Rueda, speaking for the council, claimed that the Directory had no such authority. When the Directory elected eightyfour-year-old Pedro Argüelles as rector, he announced that he recognized Ramírez Moreno, now the council's man, as the legitimate rector. Octavio Medellín Ostos of the Directory charged that the council was trying to cover up what it had done under Brito. The council countercharged that Lombardo Toledano was intervening in an attempt to obtain the rectorship. CNE president Ignacio Muriel de la Maza called for conciliation and justified the creation of the Directory on the grounds that the secretary-general had resigned. Outside observers must have been baffled and amused.[47]

The struggle continued through the first week of August, reaching new levels of confusion. Just after midnight on August 1, a rump council (126 regular and alternate members) elected José Aguilar Alvarez as the new rector; many preferred Ángel Carvajal, the student leader of the 1920s, but his name was withdrawn when the members realized that a Supreme Court justice was ineligible. Friends of the Directory claimed that the election was illegal because there was no legitimate quorum. Medellín Ostos admitted that the Directory itself was illegal, but he argued that it was necessary because the "legalists" had no moral authority. The dispute provided some comic relief when José M. de los Reyes, the old student leader, stormed the ENP in an effort to win the rectorship.

Rancor continued. Aguilar Alvarez, who began to pick up support

[46] *Excelsior*, July 26–28, 1944, incorrectly asserts that more than one died. See also *Diario de Yucatán*, July 26–28, 1944; Horta, "Quince años," *Así* (January 6, 1945); Castro Ruiz, "La compleja."

[47] *Excelsior*, July 29–31, 1944; *Diario de Yucatán*, July 30–31, 1944.

even within the Directory, unsuccessfully tried to persuade the Directory to yield. The CNE, unhappy with both factions, "named" Carvajal as rector. In a last effort to get support, the Directory issued a manifesto to explain its position and elected Gual Vidal as rector. The manifesto was of more than passing interest, for it called for autonomy of the facultades and schools, genuine academic freedom, a nonpolitical and strictly academic system for rector elections, fiscal management by bonded experts (patronato and fideicomiso), and a reorganized council, with student-faculty parity, focused on academic matters. When these efforts failed, the Directory announced on August 3 that it would hold Constituent Council elections, followed by an open rector election, which was won by Gual Vidal.

Tired of the dispute, Ávila Camacho acted. He called Gual Vidal and Aguilar Alvarez to his office on August 5; they promptly resigned. Two days later the president named the six living ex-rectors (Gómez Morín, Ocaranza, Chico Goerne, Baz, Cueva, and García Téllez) as a committee to create a constituent University Council that would select a new rector. No one complained of this violation of university autonomy and the law, partly because the situation seemed to demand drastic action and partly because the ex-rectors chose Alfonso Caso, brother of Antonio, a relative of Lombardo Toledano, and a moderate.[48]

The selection of Alfonso Caso closed a major period of UNAM history and ushered in a new one. Since Chico Goerne became rector ten years before, UNAM had ceased to be a conservative sanctuary from which attacks against the government could be launched. Brito's conservatism and obvious political ambitions prevented him from using UNAM as he wanted: no one would let him. Caso would reorganize university governance to exclude student participation.

Brito Foucher's ouster dramatized the metamorphosis of student politics and university-state relations. Until Chico Goerne assumed the rectorship, student politicians usually demonstrated against increased academic rigor or against government policy. Beginning

[48] *Excelsior*, August 1–8, 1944; *Diario de Yucatán*, August 2–8, 1944; Antonio Carrillo Flores, "El problema universitario de México," *Así* (February 3, 1945); Carlos Pérez Abreu, "La Universidad de México," *El Nacional*, October 5, 1946; Salvador Pineda, "Cuatrocientos años de vida de la Universidad," *Hoy* (September 26, 1951): 18–19; Silva Herzog, *Una historia*, p. 81; Horta, "Quince años," *Así* (January 6, 1945); Castro Ruiz, "La compleja"; Rodríguez, "National University," pp. 296–297.

in 1935, the nature of student activism and the selection of student leaders changed substantially. Each rector between 1935 and 1944 "bought" leaders of official student organizations, manipulated student and therefore director elections, and used porras against opponents. The targets of student protests and attacks became internal rather than external. The state reaped the harvest and then sowed this fertile ground by reassuming the subsidy and organizing a youth wing of the official political party. Baz and Cueva followed the precedent set by Chico but with more skill, aided no doubt by Baz's political connections. Rather than a bastion of conservatism and reaction out of which came guerrilla-like attacks on cherished government programs, UNAM, through its supportive statements and social service projects, became a partner in the Revolution. It was Brito Foucher's conservatism and apparent political ambitions that necessitated his removal; his use of porras was a convenient excuse. The state would not allow him to use the university as his personal, conservative power base.

7. The Long Peace, 1945–1961

ECONOMIC growth captured the public imagination more than politics in the second half of the 1940s and in the 1950s. The institutionalization of political life, symbolized by the creation of the PRI, produced moderate to conservative presidents who tended to administer the state rather than generate much excitement. Few elections were more than rituals. Even the 1952 election with four candidates was a shoo-in for PRI candidate, Adolfo Ruiz Cortines. Adolfo López Mateos had even less difficulty in defeating his opponent. Governments of the period discouraged political in favor of economic activity, giving subsidies to business and industry, building infrastructure, and holding labor in check. The economic boom, begun during the Second World War, accelerated under such government stimulus, first given in abundance by President Miguel Alemán. Getting a bigger slice of the bigger economic pie attracted more effort than gaining political office or trying to change a system that was producing what some came to call the "Mexican Miracle."

The reorganization of UNAM in 1944–1945 returned the university to its pre-1929 relationship to the state as an agency of the national government. Few persons have realized, even now, the significance of this change, in part because confusion inside the university seemed to demand decisive action. That Ávila Camacho acted illegally in having the ex-rectors name an interim rector or that the new organic law (the Caso law) specified that UNAM was a decentralized state agency disturbed few, for most interested parties were glad that someone was bringing order out of chaos and that the student politicians would be stripped of their ability to control the institution's destiny. Some students understood what was happening and fought it, forcing out rectors until 1948, when Luis Garrido, through shrewdness and government support, backed down striking students, took office, and kept the peace for years. UNAM-government relations became so close that the latter funded a new campus and the former did not intervene in fights between the government and the IPN. Not until the rectorship of Ignacio Chávez (1961–1966) did UNAM and the state return to systematic opposition.

The organic law of December 1944 and the general statutes of 1945 must be understood in order to comprehend this change in university politics, for they provided the legal and structural framework in which the participants operated. The key change was the creation of the Junta de Gobierno (governing board), selected by the junta when vacancies occurred through resignations and by the council when they occurred through death, incapacity, or mandatory retirement. Students and professors lost the power to choose the rector and the directors; the junta did that. The council could only nominate candidates. The staffing of the council was changed substantially as well. The student societies and federations as well as alumni associations lost their council seats, and the chief of Social Action and the professorial and student federations lost the right to speak. The goal of the indirect election system was to prevent demagoguery. Professors of the same specialty or area of study who had at least three years of service could elect an elector and an alternate. These electors, who had to have four or more years of service, chose the sixteen councilors, who had six or more years of service, were Mexican by birth, were not administrators, and had not committed any grave offenses against university discipline. They served four-year terms. The students could elect one elector and alternate for each specialty or class; these electors chose sixteen councilors for two-year terms who had to be Mexican by birth, be in the last three years of the curriculum with two years in UNAM, have a grade average of eight, and have no serious disciplinary record. The remainder of the sixty-odd-member council included the rector, directors, institute directors, and an employee representative. Jurisdiction over university property was given to the patronato. The rector's veto could be appealed by the council to the junta.[1]

By complicating the governance system, the farmers clearly intended to depoliticize UNAM so that it could fulfill its teaching and

---

[1] Ley Orgánica de la Universidad Autónoma de Mexico," February 6, 1945, in Hurtado Márquez, *Universidad Autónoma*, pp. 198–207.

research mission. The junta was to be a group of distinguished persons far above the parochial maneuverings of student and faculty organizations or of individuals and thus able to exercise their trusteeship with dispassionate concern for the good of the institution. At the same time, they were selected from the ranks of UNAM alumni and even from those currently holding university posts so that they would understand the university and be credible within it. The first junta, named by the constituent council, was indicative of the kinds of persons who would serve: Antonio Caso, Ignacio Chávez, Manuel Gómez Morín, Fernando Ocaranza, Abraham Ayala González, Ricardo Caturelli, Gabino Fraga, Mariano Hernández Barrenechea, Federico Mariscal, Antonio Martínez Baeza, Alejandro Quijano, Manuel Sandoval Vallarta, José Torres Torija, Alfonso Reyes, and Jesús Silva Herzog.[2]

Neither the eminence of the junta nor the new governance system nor the overt support of the president could assure internal peace. Alfonso Caso wanted to leave his interim rectorship as quickly as possible after getting the new law instituted but had to wait until March 23 before his successor, Genaro Fernández Mac Gregor, was chosen. Students and professors had continued to agitate during this three-month search for a rector, scaring off numerous candidates. The junta persuaded Fernández Mac Gregor to take the rectorship only after his law partner, Alejandro Quijano, pressured him into it. That the new rector had not been part of UNAM since 1922 was significant; the junta was desperate. The new rector asserted that UNAM ought to stay out of the political arena and be a teaching and research institution, an unlikely occurrence. In April, students and professors organized the Nacional Directorio Universitario to intervene in the 1946 presidential election. All the candidates for student society posts attended.[3]

Fernández Mac Gregor learned the hard way that student politics

[2]The junta election took place on January 22, 1945; see *Excelsior*, January 23, 1945, and Miguel Castro Ruiz, "El frentepopulismo malogra en 1945 una favorable conjuntura de la Universidad," *La Nación*, July 23, 1951, p. 12; Rodríguez, "National University," p. 303, incorrectly asserts that, by statute, the Mexican president chose the junta. Mendieta y Núñez, *La reforma universitaria*, p. 25, asserts that the rector can manipulate junta membership so that its members are in his absolute confidence. If the rector enjoys presidential support, it is likely that he and his supporters can control the junta; if he does not, he cannot remain in his post.

[3] *Excelsior*, March 23–24 and April 8, 10, 1945; Silva Herzog, *Una historia*, p. 94; Castro Ruiz, "Frentepopulismo," p. 12.

had not been banished; medical students exploded in November 1945 over that old student complaint, exams. Ignacio González Guzmán, director of the medical school, had enforced the policy of not allowing students who had failed exams in previous terms to take the exams of higher courses. The rector, who supported his medical director, was willing to set another period of preordinary exams for these "irregular" students and to extend the regular exam period so that those who passed the first could take the second. The irregulars, however, threatened to strike if their demands were not met; they had seized control of the medical building and announced the "imminent" resignation of the director. The rector was meeting his first true test of strength vis-à-vis student politicians.[4]

To win, the medical students had to enlist the support of other schools by identifying an issue around which all could rally or by provoking an incident, preferably with student blood flowing, that would turn students against the administration. The rector had to maintain the overt support of the Mexican president and avoid falling into any of the traps dug by the dissidents. Both sides understood the ritual that would have to be followed during the ensuing weeks.

The initial stages consisted of testing the will of the other side and jockeying for position. On November 12, the students criticized the rector for hiring unpopular administrators, for suppressing Greek and Latin classes, and for allowing Communist students to agitate. When a small delegation came to interview him, he took them back to the ENP amphitheater and told the assembled crowd that their demands were illegal and that he would not tolerate disruption of the university. The dissidents went back to the medical school and tried to start a riot. The medical faculty, however, gave its support to the rector and director. The University Council, at the suggestion of José Vasconcelos, who was still active in university politics, unanimously censured the medical students' actions. Round one went to Fernández Mac Gregor.

The second round began the next day when the strikers seized the main university and ENP building for a few hours. The rector was visiting the secretary of public education, Jaime Torres Bodet, and escaped capture. The FEU and the leaders of the student societies an-

[4] Accounts of this strike are taken from *Excelsior*, November 12–30, 1945; no further citations will be made.

nounced their support of the strikers and stopped the posting of preordinary exam dates (extra time at the end of the academic year appealed to them, too). Francisco Santamaría Rodríguez, president of Iniciación Universitaria Nocturna, tried to undercut the rector's governmental support by accusing him of violating the presidential order that those who had had a hand in the ouster of Brito were supposed to stay out of university activities. He asserted that Yáñez and García Máynez (the secretary-general) should be excluded. On the fourteenth, FEU president Luis Horcasitas announced that fourteen schools had joined the strike. A group of medical school agitators asked for an interview with the president hoping he would intervene on their side. Fernández Mac Gregor, however, lost his patience; when the strikers took control of his offices, he moved to the Biblioteca Nacional and ordered the strikers to vacate the rectory in forty-eight hours. The strikers responded by giving him twenty-four hours to resign. Round two went to the strikers.

Fernández Mac Gregor won the third round because Ávila Camacho supported him. The rector moved the medical and dental exams to sites unoccupied by the strikers, in the process telling the press that the strikers did not control fourteen schools. He expelled Horcasitas, Santamaría Rodríguez, and four others on November 15. When that did not stop the strike, he expelled a hundred more the next day. The FEU, meanwhile, had been granted an interview with Ávila Camacho on the sixteenth to present their case, and vowed to stand firm. The rector knew what the president would say, however; he announced that the strike would soon end.

The students quickly realized that they were in trouble. Ávila Camacho refused to see them. Horcasitas then sent a committee to the rector to ask for conditional exams for that year only. Six student leaders went public with the charge that the strike was the work of students who had failed more than three exams.

The momentum continued to shift in favor of the rector. The Mexican Senate announced its support of the rector. The strikers began calling for a hunger strike, an act of desperation. The rector announced that he was thinking of referring the matter to the attorney general. Horcasitas, seeing little hope, tried to reverse the tide by asserting that a Communist headed a group trying to make the ENP a Marxist school. On the eighteenth, the student presidents asked Ávila Camacho to intervene, not because the rector was wrong but because he was too strict. The next day, Fernández Mac Gregor turned the disciplinary cases over to the attorney general.

Classes resumed on November 30, but only after a few more exciting days of agitation during which students and parents tried to force the rector to back down. On the twenty-first, the strikers disavowed Fernández Mac Gregor and clamored for Ignacio Chávez in his place (ironic because Chávez was strict on academic standards and would be ousted as rector in part because of these views). The offer of prep school professors to mediate was ignored, as would be all others. The CNE claimed that the expulsions were too harsh, but few paid attention to that moribund organization. The rector stood firm. On the twenty-fourth, some parents and faculty members took some buildings to support the strikers while other parents interviewed the president's wife. Torres Bodet announced that his office would stay out of what was not an SEP matter, thus implicitly supporting the rector. The dissidents finally give up and classes resumed. Fernández Mac Gregor proudly announced that no deals had been made.

The strike ended Fernández Mac Gregor's career as rector, however. He offered his resignation on February 20, 1946, claiming ill health (the common euphemism for being fired), but was given a year's medical leave instead. It seems likely that he was forced out. The government supported him during the strike because it was necessary to establish the authority of the new law, but his inability to control events meant that he could not stay. Further, his treasurer had stolen 100,000 pesos and disappeared when the conflict began. After a decent interval, the rector left, resigning definitively in February 1947.

Salvador Zubirán, although interim rector for the first year, proceeded as if he were the regular rector, which he became in February 1947. By September 1946 he had launched a capital fund campaign to raise ten million pesos to build a new campus, long a dream of the university. President Ávila Camacho promised half a million pesos from the national lottery. Zubirán also began to hire full-time professors to raise teaching and research standards.[5]

Neither these significant steps, supported by the government, nor the restructured university governance system could maintain Zubirán (or any other rector) in power in the face of determined stu-

[5] El Nacional, September 25, 1946; Silva Herzog, Una historia, p. 94.

dent opposition. The most important job of the rector was to maintain order inside the university; national political leaders did not want to contend with university affairs while they were coping with more serious problems. No one believed that the rector or his aides could prevent *all* student demonstrations and strikes, for small groups could disrupt the institution, but the rector was supposed to contain these demonstrations. If he could not, as Zubirán could not in the spring of 1948, he would be forced out.

The political climate in which the 1948 strike took place differed substantially from that of three years before. Miguel Alemán had closer ties to his alma mater than did his predecessors. He would bring many UNAM graduates into high positions in his government. He would also fund the construction of the new university campus to be built some ten miles from the old university section. As a political conservative with business ties to the United States, he was responsive to the anti-communism of this Cold War period. As he shifted Mexico even further to the right, some leftist politicians withdrew from the government political party (Partido Revolucionario Institucional) to form the Peoples Party under the leadership of Lombardo Toledano.[6]

The reform impulse of the Mexican Revolution resisted the new pro-business, anti-Communist proclivities of the Alemán regime. Losing in the general political arena, progressives turned their attention to university students in the hope of securing a power base. But the organic law of the university seemed to preclude the kinds of political activity that had been so fruitful in former years. Unless the law were amended or abolished, little hope existed for political activists. The left was fortunate in 1948, however, for the clerical right, represented by the Confederación Nacional de Estudiantes, became a momentary ally as it, too, tried to abolish the organic law for the same reasons. The events of April to June 1948 suggest that the UNAM struggle in that period was a proxy fight of larger, non-university political forces.

Nothing in the April 6 demands of the Comité de Estudios de Jurisprudencia suggested the turmoil that was to follow. This committee of ten, claiming to speak for all law students, called for technical changes in the curriculum and in procedures: the creation of an agrarian law seminar, different hours for seminars, seminars that focused

[6]Roderic Camp, "Education and Political Recruitment in Mexico: The Alemán Generation," *Journal of Inter-American Studies and World Affairs* 18 (1976): 295–321.

only on the technical aspects of thesis writing, language requirement changes, use of five specialists for the professional examination jury, more books, allowing persons who passed the fourth year to enter seminars, and easing of the class attendance requirements for ordinary exams. All but the last were academically defensible, and the council approved the changes on April 15.

The threat to the system was a procedural question. The organic law had created technical councils for each school, composed of students and professors, that had the power to change the curriculum and procedures, subject to council approval. By making direct demands of the rector and the council, the comité was ignoring the law and thus seeking to destroy it. By issuing the petition as an ultimatum, giving the administration ten days in which to respond, the comité was signaling its true intentions as clearly as by its agitation while awaiting the council's response. Although some charged that they were Communist agitators, Zubirán saw them as enemies of the university who wanted to use the institution for their own ends. This view was supported by the actions of the leaders, who, when the council denied the class attendance demand, led a contingent of some two hundred to the medical school in an effort to start a strike.

For the rector and the council, the important issue became whether to allow the students, a tiny minority, to use the tactics that disrupted the university before the new organic law was passed or to set an example by strictly enforcing university regulations. They decided on April 16 to enforce the rules and apply sanctions. The administration received strong support from the schools of medicine, engineering, architecture, chemical sciences, commerce, music, and plastic arts, which condemned the agitators. The school of dentistry was divided. The comité appeared beaten.

The next step was violence. On Saturday morning, April 17, Zubirán went to the law school to explain to the assembled students that most of their petition had been granted, but the leaders called him a liar. About 9:30 A.M., they persuaded the law students to declare a strike. Prep school students, whose petition to the council against increased fees had been rejected out of hand because the language was insulting, joined the strike as well. The strikers, led by Francisco López Portillo and Helio Carlos Mendoza, took control of the rectory and ordered Zubirán out; he refused to leave. After negotiations, the leaders tried to escort Zubirán out of the building to safety, but on the way another group of students blocked his path, refusing to let him leave until he resigned. After several hours of watching his office being ransacked and suffering the indignity of physical harassment, he signed the letter of resignation. The chief of police finally arrived and freed him from his captors. The students then closed the medical, dental, engineering, and extension schools; disavowed the authority of the rector, council, and junta; and announced their plan to create a directory to reorganize UNAM. They were betting that they could provoke a general strike.

Their efforts gained momentum in spite of this insult to the rector. *Excelsior* accused the strike leaders of being Communists trying to replicate the recent left-wing riot in Bogotá. Policemen who had been given custody of the university buildings by the strikers were assaulted on the morning of the nineteenth by the strikers, who had decided to retake the buildings. The police threw tear gas against prep school demonstrators who were fighting with building materials taken from a nearby truck. Four hundred students marched to protest against the rector. More ominously, the leaders of the technical school federation (representing over sixteen thousand students in the IPN system) and of the normal school promised to join the strike. Since the government had created the IPN as a rival to UNAM and tightly controlled the former, possible student unification was a serious threat. Even medical students, who had previously opposed the law group, joined the fray by complaining that the university authorities did not listen to student complaints and arguing that the students, professors, and employees of each school should choose new authorities. They accused the administration of using secret police to spy on students and professors. Some medical students, however, denounced the strike, blaming it on agitators and fossil students of law, ENP, and extension. The CNE condemned police intervention and called for a pacific solution. Street fights continued, however, and the police arrested López Portillo and four others, calling them Communist agitators.

Zubirán's efforts to clarify events and obtain more popular support met mixed results. He asked parents to control their children; the (Catholic) Unión Nacional de Padres de Familia announced its support of the rector. Zubirán denied that the strikers had closed the university, insisting, instead, that most schools were functioning normally until *he* closed them. The Communist party issued a statement of support for both the strikers and the rector, hoping to avoid blame and consequent repression while maintaining a pro-student stance. The party asserted that a group it had expelled, citing Carlos Sánchez Sánchez as an example, was collaborating with the Jesuit-backed Conejos (a secret student activist group formed before World War II) to create problems for the rector, who represented progressive forces in UNAM. The Communists specifically denied that the strike leaders listed by name were PCM members.

The Communist label destroyed the effectiveness of those to whom it was attached, but the strike gained momentum as students reacted against the hard line adopted by Zubirán. The conservative school of commerce joined the strike on April 20, 1948; the IPN students announced their moral support. Economics students issued a statement supporting the justice of the law student demands but refused to join the strike because outsiders (agitators and police) were manipulating events (Silva Herzog, the power in the school and a junta member, opposed the strike). UNAM-IPN efforts to conduct a giant protest march on the nineteenth failed when only 600 demonstrators assembled. Rumors of corruption and mysterious disappearances of participants added fuel to the student fires in spite of the denial by the patronato that there were irregularities in the new campus fund or the lack of substantiation of the charges that some students had disappeared. The assertion that students were being kidnapped or murdered would recur in student movements. Prep students accused Zubirán of using boxers (thugs) as bodyguards to threaten students.

Equity and academic issues reappeared in the squabble. Prep and extension students complained of increased fees and argued that Zubirán was operating UNAM as if it were a private school. Further, they complained of Zubirán's policy of expelling students who had failed a course three times and of using entrance exams for both public and private school graduates.

President Alemán played a curious role in these events. The secretary of the presidency, Rogelio de la Selva, a former student activist, met privately with strike leaders, an action that convinced them that they had government support. On April 21, Alemán publicly told students to calm down, return to class, use the legal procedures of the organic law, and not allow themselves to be used by outside agitators.

Nevertheless, student leaders from a number of schools began organizing a grand commission to find a solution. Some students demanded punishment of the university authorities for using the police. Perhaps this continued militance in the face of the presidential statement affected Alemán. His next step remains a puzzle, even to Silva Herzog, a participant, who relates the story. On the morning of April 22, Alemán called the junta to his office. Since it was short notice, only Alfonso Reyes, Ignacio Chávez, Manuel Sandoval Vallarta, Silva Herzog, and, possibly, Gabino Fraga went. After hearing the history of the events, Alemán assured the junta members that Zubirán had his full support. When the junta reassembled that night, however, Zubirán told them that Alemán had pressured him into resigning.

Elated at this easy victory, the strike leaders picked up support and increased their demands. Now they wanted the resignations of all the directors, subdirectors, and secretaries of the schools and institutes, that is, the entire administrative staff. The CNE petitioned the junta to give the students parity on the technical councils and the University Council. Secundarias 1, 4, and 14 joined the strike, as did university students in Puebla and San Luis Potosí. The technical student federation began debating whether to join.

The strikers, led by Helio Carlos Mendoza, became more intransigent. They refused to recognize the authority of Alfonso Ochoa Ravivé, the interim rector appointed by the junta, charging he was part of Zubirán's clique. When the junta ordered them to return the university buildings by April 27, they announced a big demonstration for that day. The university directors threatened to close UNAM for the rest of the year if the students did not obey the junta. The students failed to find their own rector, however, first asking Gustavo Argil, oficial mayor of the Health ministry, then asking Andrés Serra Rojas, who told them to quit. On the twenty-seventh, the junta closed the university, warning that the schools in rebellion would not reopen until the buildings were returned and a majority of the students were willing to return to class. Nabor Carrillo Flores (brother of Antonio, and soon to be rector), Yáñez, and Alberto Borajes led a group of professors who wanted to close the school for the year. On the twenty-eighth, engineering professors threatened to quit if the students did not return to class within a week; architecture professors adopted a similar position.

In the midst of apparent success, the student ranks split. Some students designated Antonio Díaz Soto y Gama as rector on the night of April 29, 1948. Once he accepted, they planned to give him control of the buildings and return to class. The old Revolutionary, now a conservative, agreed on May 1 but insisted that his election be ratified by the students and faculty. Mendoza's strike committee balked at this choice, claiming that the old man had been chosen by the Conejos (actually, students from the CNE and the strike committees of medicine, ENP, dentistry, extension, economics, and commerce were involved). Mendoza's strike committee recognized the junta but wanted guarantees that one of the members of its terna (Salvador Azuela, Raúl Carrancá Trujillo, and Andrés Serra Rojas) would be chosen rector by the junta, that the junta would receive the committee's petition, and that the new rector would have to consult with the strike committee in the selection of new directors.

The students continued to argue among themselves during the next few days while the junta tried to find someone to take the rectorship. When the majority of students of nine schools asked the junta on May 2 to reopen the university, the strike committee refused. Medical students rejected the strike committee terna because it did not include a medical doctor. The FEU called a student meeting for the night of May 4, but the strike committee blocked it. A group calling itself the Juventud Demócrata Anticomunista asserted that Communists were leading the strike and called for its members and UNEC to counteract them. The strike committee tried to reopen the university on May 6, but the junta refused. The Communist members of the committee withdrew, claiming the others were opportunists, while three CNE expresidents accused the student leaders of being members of professional bureaucratic cliques and socialites and the current CNE leaders of being traitors to that organization. By May 8, the central strike committee was facing a coalition (Comité Pro Autonomía Universitaria), composed of the Directorio Central Mixto Universitario, FEU, the Grupo Liberal Depurador Universitario, and UNEC, that vowed to continue the strike until the university problems were solved. They rejected the agreements reached by the junta and the central strike committee. The junta, after offering the rectorship to many persons, including former attorney general Francisco de la Vega, finally got Andrés Serra Rojas to accept the job on May 9.

By this time the divisions within the university could not be healed so easily. Serra Rojas refused the rectorship when the students would not let him enter the rectory by the front door. The directorio switched its support to the junta, and most schools reopened by the thirteenth, but the FEU continued in opposition. The junta began considering Ángel Carvajal, Veracruz governor, as a possible rector, but he was ineligible because of his government post and in any case did not want the job. The directorio joined the boomlet for Esteban Manzanera del Campo (a member of the Partido Acción Nacional), a surprise because he was a conservative, but when vacations started on May 16, to last until the twentieth, the junta had not found a new rector.

On June 1, 1948, the junta finally found a man, Luis Garrido, who could restore order and face down Díaz Soto y Gama, who was still claiming the rectorship. Garrido had had a distinguished career as a penalist, lawyer, and sociologist. He had just reopened his law office after leaving a post with Seguros de México, S.A., when Alejandro Quijano called him late at night to beg him to take the rectorship. Other junta members took turns pleading with him to accept in order to save the university. Reluctantly, he agreed. The next day, he surprised everyone by going to the rectory, walking alone through the front door, and taking the oath of office.

Conservative students met the same day, however, and, supported by José Vasconcelos, named Díaz Soto y Gama as rector. The conservative "rector" attacked the junta as Communist and promised to guarantee university autonomy and academic freedom. The CNE announced its support of the old Revolutionary, who lambasted Garrido, the junta, Lombardo Toledano, and Cárdenas in a June 5 meeting while pledging his work to "God and Christ." Unprovoked, Garrido patiently waited for Díaz Soto y Gama to discredit himself further. The irrationality of the old man swung support in favor of Garrido. On June 3, a group of Sotistas went to Garrido to tell him that they had unleashed forces they could not control. On the fifth, Manuel Gual Vidal, secretary of public education, announced his support of Garrido.[7]

[7] *Excelsior*, April 16–June 16, 1948, describes these and the following events. See also Miguel Castro Ruiz, "De como la universidad tuvo dos rectores simultáneos," *La Nación*, July 30, 1951, pp. 12–13, a conservative view; Silva Herzog, *Una historia*, pp.

Fortunately, Garrido explained his view of the strike and his strategy in his memoirs, giving scholars a rare glimpse into the relationship between UNAM and the national government. As Garrido later interpreted the strike, it had begun because of student demands for a rendering of accounts of the campus fund campaign and dissatisfaction with the law school director. The students wanted the director fired and the junta abolished. This latter demand was part of the student desire to return to an autonomy law that gave students power. The strike had been made more difficult because the university employees supported it, the government refused to tip its hand, and few persons, including the directors, were willing to commit themselves to a rector who might lose. At first, Garrido inspired little confidence; his private secretary died during a hernia operation, having been hit earlier by strikers, and Garrido and his family were threatened and maligned. Nor did Vasconcelos's apology for having supported Díaz Soto y Gama help, for it was delivered in private. Garrido knew that he had to have the public support of Alemán to stay in office. He asked Gual Vidal for money to pay the employees; when the secretary got the president's approval and delivered the check, Garrido had photographs of it printed in the newspapers. The employees, directors, and professors returned to work.[8]

Díaz Soto y Gama and some students remained a problem until mid-June. By June 8, classes had resumed in all schools except the ENP. That day, however, the Garridistas beat the Sotistas in a pitched battle in the law school. The Garridistas recovered the rectory on the ninth and Garrido moved into his office. The press identified non-students in the fray. Both sides used porras that day and the next, when the two sides fought again, this time with tear gas and Molotov cocktails. Garrido knew he had won when a group of professors, many of them PAN and former UNEC members, called for the resignation of both rectors and a plebiscite to elect a provisional rector, and the professors knew they had lost. Garrido won most of the strikers to his side when he confronted them alone and promised to listen to their just demands.

95–96; Juan González A. Alpuche, *La universidad de México*, pp. 85–89; Luis Garrido, *El tiempo de mi vida*, pp. 261–268; Manuel González Ramírez, "Glosas al Pastor," *Novedades*, June 14, 1948; Rodríguez, "National University," pp. 311–315.
[8] Garrido, *Tiempo*, pp. 261–266.

mands. When Garrido rejected the Díaz Soto y Gama plan that they both resign, the old Revolutionary quit.[9]

Garrido won—and stayed in the rectorship until he voluntarily left in 1953—because he understood power and its use. He fired the law director in order to pacify the students but refused to expel the strike leaders as the junta, through Ignacio Chávez, suggested. He was not going to create martyrs. He remained calm in July and August 1949 when university and polytechnical students exploded over the killing of two students in Morelia by the army. The deaths created an ominous chain reaction, but the rector managed to control it. His role in the Morelia conflict reveals his political sophistication.

Some UNAM students wanted to use the Morelia conflict as an excuse to create problems in their own institution, but Garrido outsmarted them. The army had been sent into action in Morelia to break up student demonstrations over the expenditure of a million pesos by the Michoacán governor, José M. Mendoza Pardo, for an open-air theater so his daughter could dance the ballet. The students demanded that the monies be spent for schools, hospitals, and safe water supplies. UNAM students, led again by López Portillo and Mendoza, demanded that the governor and the army commander be punished for the deaths. Garrido publicly announced that their indignation was justified. Thousands marched in protest in Mexico City on August 3, 1949, threatening a national university strike if the government continued to do nothing about Morelia. When a mass meeting on August 4 degenerated into a struggle between the FEU and the directorio that had been formed, including a struggle for the microphone between López Portillo and Genaro Vázquez, the rector kept his peace, waiting until August 7 to call for calm. Nor did he intervene when twenty thousand students went on strike on August 12, closing UNAM and occupying the rectory. He did not try to exploit the split that developed between UNAM and IPN students.[10]

[9] *Excelsior*, June 9–16, 1948; Garrido, *Tiempo*, pp. 266–268. *Excelsior*, June 11, 1948, identified the professors as Mariano Azuela, Jr., Manuel Ulloa, Héctor González Uribe, Luis de Garay, Santiago Oñate, Jesús Toral Moreno, Rafael Preciado Hernández, and Carlos Ramírez Zetina. All but Azuela, González Uribe, and Oñate were Panistas and former UNEC members.

[10] *Excelsior*, July 30–August 19, 1949; Garrido, *Tiempo*, 313; *Hispanic American Report 2*, nos. 8 and 9 (1949). Rodríguez, "National University," pp. 319–320, incorrectly

By being sympathetic to the student cause but aloof from specific events, he kept UNAM relatively calm and proved to the government that he knew how to govern. Recognizing his ability, the secretary of government, Adolfo Ruiz Cortines, called Garrido for advice. Garrido argued that his former student, Mendoza Pardo, had to go. Ruiz Cortines balked because of the precedent. Garrido offered to write a private letter to the governor suggesting that he resign. The secretary called back to ask Garrido to get the students to go back to class with the promise that Mendoza Pardo would resign. He did, they did, and the strike ended August 18.[11]

Even with political skills and government support, Garrido had a tough job because he was presiding over a rapidly expanding university filled with students hoping to use UNAM as the vehicle for entry into well-paying jobs and higher social status. By 1949, when the first university census was published, UNAM had 23,527 students (82 percent male) instead of the 8,154 it had in 1929 or the 17,090 in 1940 (it had 30,278 in 1953 when Garrido left office). Although the mean average student age was 22, the modal average was 19.5. Over 84 percent lived in the family home. Thirty percent of the parents were businessmen (comerciantes), 21 percent were employees, 21 percent professionals, only 9.5 percent workers, and 6.4 percent farmers; that is, they came primarily from the middling social strata. Only 18 percent had mothers who were wage earners. Most of the students worked part-time to finance their education; their average monthly income ranged from 126 pesos for night prep students in extension to 700 pesos for graduate students. Although only 27.6 percent were born in the Federal District, most had lived there for years. In contrast to UNAM students of the 1920s and 1930s, the 1949 students came less frequently from the upper strata. Instead, they represented the ambitious, upwardly mobile lower-middle strata that was riding the wave of postwar prosperity.[12]

These students created few problems for Garrido even during the few times they got involved with the poorer and more militant stu-

---

asserts that this was a general strike in the spring. Genaro Vázquez later became a guerrilla leader between 1968 and 1972.

[11] Garrido, *Tiempo*, pp. 313–314.

[12] UNAM, Instituto de Investigaciones Sociales, *Primer Censo Universitario*, pp. 23–49 ff.

dents of the IPN. When IPN students went on strike in May 1950, in a curricular and IPN leadership dispute, the FEU declared its neutrality, thus blocking the efforts of some UNAM students and professors to draw UNAM into the strike. When a water fight in June 1951 between vocational and ENP students escalated into a more general UNAM-IPN fight, resulting in the destruction of UNAM dental school labs, Garrido and Gual Vidal cooled tempers and effected a reconciliation between the FEU and the Federación Nacional de Estudiantes Técnicos (FNET). Garrido quietly acquiesced in the temporary closing of UNAM in June 1952 in the face of the IPN protest demonstrations and the July presidential elections. The rector not only used an even hand in dealing with the various political factions within the UNAM but also took positive steps. In September 1949 he defended free expression before the Frente Anticomunista, which wanted him to censor the university press. In 1951 he opened the Escuela Nacional de Ciencias Políticas y Sociales, which quickly became one of the most serious and lively political forums. Most of the faculty and students were leftists.[13]

The most interesting UNAM student political activity between 1948 and 1953 came from the efforts of Catholic students to resurrect the CNE as a political force. Jorge Siegrist Clamont, FEU vice-president, organized the XIX CNE Congress in Monterrey for September 27–30, 1951, at which he was elected president for a two-year term. The Monterrey congress called for a revival of the 1929 and 1933 student activist traditions, a return to the 1929 autonomy law, and a campaign against the "corrupt and subversive forces" in higher education. To the CNE, fraudulent student elections had put the university in the hands of outside agents. Further, the university was training technicians instead of emphasizing philosophy and humanism. The revitalized CNE condemned social capitalism because it led to exploitation and extremes of wealth but did not want it replaced with "Stalinist totalitarianism." What the CNE wanted was what PAN was propagandiz-

[13] *Excelsior*, May 25–28, 1950; *Hispanic American Report* 3, nos. 6 and 7 (1950) and 5, no. (1952); *New York Times*, May 26, 1950, and June 21, 1952; *Excelsior*, June 24–28, 1951, June 21, 1952, and June 27, 1976; Luis Garrido, "La libertad de pensamiento y expresión en la Universidad," *Discursos y mensajes* (Mexico, 1952): 57; and "La Escuela Nacional de Ciencias Políticas y Sociales," *Ciencias Políticas y Sociales* 13 (January–March 1967): 17–33.

ing nationally, and at least four of the CNE leaders—Hugo Gutiérrez Vega, Manuel Rodríguez Lapuente, Fernando de la Hoz, and Javier Blanco Sánchez—were PAN activists.[14]

Siegrist Clamont's CNE never became the student political force he hoped for. Few UNAM schools sent delegates to the congress. Law and engineering from UNAM, the Escuela Libre de Derecho, and the Instituto Tecnológico de México were the only Federal District schools represented. More serious than this, the CNE split into two groups at the Durango congress of 1953 when Siegrist Clamont was reelected after a pitched battle between his supporters and those of Armando Ávila Sotomayor. Ávila Sotomayor's newly erected CNE, tied to PAN, published the newspaper *La Reforma Universitaria*, which took a stridently anti-Communist line. Siegrist Clamont used porras to beat up his rival and destroy his bookstore. Given these divisions, it is not surprising that neither CNE lasted.[15]

The close relationship between the university and the state in the 1950s vitiated the effectiveness of student organizations, particularly the CNE. Alemán supported Garrido, a fact so obvious that few politicians, student or otherwise, thought it profitable to stir up discord within UNAM. The president's support of the new university campus was the most obvious sign, but those close to the seats of power had additional evidence. When Garrido's term was about to end (May 31, 1952), Alemán's secretary to the presidency, de la Selva, asked each junta member to reelect Garrido for another term so he could finish Alemán's sexenio. They agreed. When Garrido finally resigned in February 1953, the junta chose Nabor Carrillo Flores as the new rector. Nabor's brother, Antonio, had been named secretary of the treasury the year before. Siegrist Clamont asserts that the two brothers named the junta members. Whether they did or not is unproven, but such a close relationship meant that the government would not attack UNAM as long as the two were in office.[16]

[14] Confederación Nacional de Estudiantes, *Mensaje a la juventud mexicana*: Confederación Nacional de México, *que será presentado al Congreso de la Unión*; Mabry, *Mexico's Acción Nacional*, chapter 4, details PAN views.

[15] Jorge Siegrist Clamont, *Trayectoría histórico-jurídico de la Universidad de México*, as cited in Guitán Berniser, "Las porras," pp. 29–38.

[16] Silva Herzog, *Una historia*, pp. 117–131; Siegrist Clamont, in Guitán Berniser, "Las porras," p. 33.

The opening of the university city in 1954 isolated the students from such government buildings as the National Palace, making effective demonstrations more difficult and thus providing an additional reason for the decline of university-state conflicts in the 1950s. To reach these buildings from the campus, students had to travel over ten miles by city bus in a system that was not as well developed as it would become by the end of the decade. In fact, the senior class of the law school tried to boycott the new campus on February 4, 1954, when ordered to move. They claimed that the campus was too far from the city, lacked communications, and was not ready for use. This issue of isolation, often disguised as protests over the bus system, was the most volatile issue for UNAM in the 1950s.[17]

UNAM students in the decade did become sporadically active on anti-imperialist and anti-Communist issues. The FEU blocked the Mexican-American Trade Fair, scheduled for the UNAM campus in May 1954, because they did not want the campus commercialized, especially by an imperialist country. In June of that year, thousands demonstrated against U.S. policy in Guatemala because the U.S. was helping to overthrow a legitimate government. The local press accused the demonstrators of being Communist. By May 1955 the press and some governmental members launched an anti-Communist campaign, claiming that Communist cells in UNAM were becoming a threat.[18]

Law students started a traditional strike in September 1955, but it petered out when other students refused to join and vacations began. The students demanded the right to take extraordinary exams when they had attended only fifteen classes (25 percent of the total) and ordinary exams when they had attended only thirty. The strike produced violence among the students. Abelardo Gutiérrez Montonya, president of the law student society, was shot several times in the chest, and this dampened the enthusiasm of the strikers. The FEU unsuccessfully called for a massive demonstration to support the law student demand. Carrillo patiently waited for vacation to begin on September 12, counting on the end of classes to end the strike, which it did.[19]

[17] *New York Times*, February 5, 1954.

[18] *New York Times*, April 7, 1954, and May 15, 1955; *Hispanic American Report* 5, no. 6 (1954), and 7, nos. 5 and 8 (1955).

[19] *Excelsior*, September 1–11, 1955; Letter of Eliseo Rangel Gaspar and Agusto Velasco S. to University Council and Technical Council of Law, September 9, 1955, in

Students in other Mexican universities were not so quiet in the 1950s, however, and the decade was peppered with strikes and demonstrations. University students in Mérida wrecked the offices of the *Diario de Yucatán* in May 1953 because the paper had opposed their strike in favor of higher pay for professors. Federal troops were used in Mérida in late 1955 to quell fights between students and workers and to bottle up students inside the university. In 1956, students of the Escuela Nacional de Maestros struck for fifty-six days, those of the Escuela Normal Superior for two and one-half months, those in Morelia struck as well, those at twelve normal schools struck, and those at the IPN embroiled the city in controversy for several months. In May 1957, students at the private Universidad Autónoma de Guadalajara brawled with their counterparts at the Universidad de Guadalajara until federal troops intervened. San Luis Potosí students seized buses and tried to force the resignations of city and state officials in November 1959, and soldiers were used to suppress students strikes and riots in Puebla in October 1959 and in Oaxaca that same month. Students of the Escuela Nacional de Maestros went on strike in March 1960; assaulted the secretariat of education building, the PRI building, and *El Universal*; and demanded the abolition of the granaderos (riot police) and Article 145 of the penal code (which imposed harsh penalties for "disturbing the public order" and trying to dissolve society).[20]

The Instituto Politécnico Nacional strike in 1956 deserves further comment because of its scale and because UNAM students stayed out of it. The 25,000 IPN students walked out on April 12 demanding that the director (rector), Rodolfo Hernández Carzo, and six other administrators be fired and that the government concede a number of points. They wanted new hospitals for the schools of rural and homeopathic medicine, a six-year construction plan for the institute, more and better dormitories, more scholarships, increased pay for interns, more buses and trucks for the school, more class hours, an organic law granting autonomy and student participation in governance, and more prevocational schools. Street fighting between students and police broke

_____

[20] *Hispanic American Report* 6, nos. 3–5, 9, nos. 4–10 (1956); 10, no. 5 (1956); and 13, nos. 3–4 (1960); also *New York Times*, May 14, 1957, November 28, 1958, October 4, 1959; *The Times* (London), May 1957, March 26, April 2, 1960.

Archivo Estudiantil, Hemeroteca Nacional, Caja I; *Hispanic American Report* 8, no. 9 (1955).

out immediately and would continue throughout the strike. On the seventeenth, students roamed the streets stoning buses and beating up the drivers and passengers. The government and the press tried to brand the strike as Communist-inspired, which it was not, but the Communist party openly supported the movement and sent brigades to help. That some of the students berated the United States as an imperialist power no doubt convinced some that the Communists were behind the movement.

UNAM students remained aloof. Both the FEU headed by Alberto Cinta Guzmán and the one headed by Carlos Ontiveros decided not to participate, in part because it was directed by leftists. Finally, on June 17, the students ended the strike when the government promised to reorganize the IPN and appoint a committee that would include student members to work out details. Police were stationed on campus, however, and would remain there until 1958. [21]

In the late summer and the fall of 1956, students of UNAM and IPN did cooperate to a limited degree when they protested the closing of dormitories and dining rooms. As a result of demonstrations in downtown Mexico City, the government forbade demonstrations by student organizations. The IPN dorm was reopened on October 1, but soldiers were posted to prevent further fights between leftist and non-leftist students. The police arrested Nicrando Mendoza, the leftist student leader, thus pulling him out of the vortex of events. The UNAM dining room issue never reached the same degree of intensity. Student political parties made its reopening an issue in their elections but directed most of their energies toward raising money from private sources and lobbying the government and UNAM to fund it permanently. Student complaints that pistoleros and police were abusing students were ignored. [22]

Why UNAM students remained calm in spite of the numerous op-

---

[21] *Excelsior*, April 13–June 18, 1956, for daily strike news; *Hispanic American Report* 9, nos. 4–6 (1956); *New York Times*, April 13, 18, 1956; *The Times* (London), April 16, 1956; "Las huelgas del Politécnico y la Normal parecen ser solo la iniciación de un periodo intensivo de proselitismo rojo entre la juventud mexicana, dentro de un plan que comprende a todo Latinoamericano," *Reforma Universitaria* (April 20, 1956): 7, 8, for a right-wing CNE view.

[22] *Hispanic American Report* 9, nos. 8–10 (1956); see the correspondence and handbills in Archivo Estudiantil, Hemeroteca Nacional, box dated 1956, 57, 58, 59, for the dining room issue.

portunities provided by the student strikes and demonstrations of 1956 remains as much a mystery as why so many outbreaks occurred. The pre–World-War-II idea of forming a student class or movement died in the 1930s, in part because the creation of IPN broke UNAM's monopoly on higher education in the Federal District. The postwar expansion of higher education further fragmented student culture, making the creation of a common cause difficult. More often than not, students of *the* university saw little in common with students of *the* institute, much less normal school students. Inside UNAM itself, the proliferation of small political groups and the manipulations of national political parties made unified action almost impossible. Finally, the political skill of Nabor Carrillo and his administration, helped by the rector's close ties with the government, must have played a role in maintaining the peace.[23]

The 1958 upheaval over the bus system, however, closed student ranks and produced a serious crisis. Students depended on the bus system to transport them to and from school and work. For UNAM students, who had to travel the greatest distances, cheap, reliable buses were a necessity. The urban and student populations were expanding faster than the bus service. Since the bus companies were privately owned, increases in the number on the streets or the state of their repair were tied directly to profits desired by the owners. When the bus companies proposed in January 1958 to raise fares, the FEU threatened to strike. The owners backed down temporarily but announced on August 13 that fares would increase eleven days later. Fare increases had to have governmental approval, a procedure that gave students leverage.

UNAM students began to mobilize in opposition. On the twenty-second, some students, primarily from the law school, took control of a bus terminal, overcoming the drivers defending it, took sixty buses to the campus, and burned the terminal. Political and social science students, aided by secundaria students, seized five buses in another part of the city. The police did nothing. That night, however, Mexico City regent Ernesto Uruchurtu, meeting with students, agreed to give the students special bus fares. The use of soldiers to surround the UNAM

[23] On national political parties working in the universities, see Servio Tubio Acuña, "Discurso," *Gaceta de la Universidad* (March 14, 1960): 4.

campus and the efforts of police to recover the buses, however, provided a common cause not only for UNAM students but also for students in other institutions.[24]

The random violence changed into a strike with ominous overtones by August 24. The police recovered some of the buses, but the students, who controlled the university campus, held scores of buses as ransom for their demands for a fare rollback and the release of arrested students. They promised to keep the university closed until after the presidential State of the Union address on September 1 and to burn the vehicles if their demands were ignored. Soldiers, surrounding the campus and picketed in nearby streets, had to break up fights between students and drivers. The former accused the drivers of using pistoleros, but the drivers threatened a bus strike if they did not receive protection against the students. Equally important, Demetrio Vallejo, the radical new secretary-general of the railroad workers' union, and student leaders from the IPN, ENP, and the Escuela Normal Superior announced their support. UNAM, IPN, and the Normal students formed a tripartite alliance, a first in the history of the nation.

Neither the students nor the bus group knew how to break the stalemate that had developed. The students drove the buses to the Zócalo on the twenty-third and demonstrated there again on the twenty-sixth, but they appealed to President Ruiz Cortines to resolve the conflict. The city government warned the students that it would not tolerate anarchy. Carrillo saw the conflict as being leaderless, with deep social origins, but not as a move against the government. He promised that neither the army nor the police would invade the UNAM campus.[25]

Presidential mediation might have ended the conflict quickly had not other groups seized the opportunity to present their own grievances. On the twenty-seventh, the government agreed to suspend the rate increase temporarily, get better service for the students, and im-

[24]Gerardo Estrada Rodríguez, "El movimiento estudiantil UNAM 1958–1968," Sociology Thesis, UNAM, 1969; *Excelsior*, August 23, 1958. Estrada Rodríguez, a participant, based his thesis on *Excelsior*. I will make no further citations to these sources on this strike.

[25]Two interesting sidelights of this dispute were the support of Ricardo García Villalobos, UNAM law director, and the negotiating role of Benito Coquet, secretary of the presidency.

prove supervision through a transportation commission in which students would have a voice. The students, through their Gran Comisión Estudiantil, agreed to a truce. They would temporarily allow buses to negotiate the streets, avoid violence while propagandizing the ideas of the movement and recruiting support, hold a student vote on the government proposals, and not hold the mass demonstration they had planned for the twenty-ninth. Carrillo asked the comisión to calm down its followers. Some IPN students, not bound by the comisión, took over the IPN administration building and ejected the director and secretary-general. Workers began to join the students that day, and by the twenty-ninth the strikers could announce that railroaders, teachers, petroleum workers, telegraph workers, and other "popular" elements would join the mass demonstration. The worker groups had serious economic and governance grievances against the government, which held their wages down and subverted union leaders; these grievances led to serious strikes in 1958–1959. By August 29, for example, the army had been used to stop fights between granaderos and petroleum workers.[26]

Very quickly, perhaps because of the persuasive speech of Andrés Serra Rojas, perhaps because of fear of army action, the students began seeking accommodation with the bus companies and the government. Meeting early in the morning of August 30, the students decided to accept the presidential offer with amendments: worker participation on the transportation commission, a study of city ownership of the bus system, unionization of the drivers, higher workers' wages, freedom for those arrested, the removal of the soldiers, and the promise of no reprisals. They continued to plan the mass demonstration downtown, but in *support* of the government.

The movement climaxed with this demonstration of some 40,000 in the Zócalo on August 30, but not without a last-ditch effort to revive it. At the demonstration the students praised Ruiz Cortines and agreed to return the buses. New elections for petroleum workers were promised by the government, thus meeting one of the student demands. As the crowd began dispersing, however, some groups began to destroy the buses and threaten the comisión. The comisión asserted that the Communist party, PAN, and FEU (an unlikely combination) were in-

[26] For the 1958–1959 railroad strikes, see Evelyn P. Stevens, *Protest and Response in Mexico*, chapter 4.

terfering. Further violence occurred during the next few days as some unidentified groups tried to prevent the return of the vehicles. The comisión, for its part, announced that the solution was in government hands and disappeared.[27]

The 1958 bus conflict reveals a number of important variables in student political activity since the restructuring of UNAM in 1945. The organic law was incapable of handling such a crisis because the students were not protesting either academic policy or university governance. Instead, they were striking out against a system that directly affected their daily lives. Because IPN and Normal students were similarly affected and had their own grievances against the government, which had direct control over them, they were willing to unite with UNAM on this issue. So, too, were some unionized workers. The quasi-alliance between students and workers was short-lived and based on opportunism; students abandoned their allies. The single most important reason why the UNAM-based strike did not become serious and was not turned against the university was the relationship between Carrillo and the government. As a result, the police and the army were not used against the students; had they been, nothing could have held the students back.

The importance of the relations between the UNAM administration and the national government had been a constant factor in the history of student strikes. Events of the 1960s would revalidate this observation. Nabor Carrillo would retire from the rectorship in 1961, after eight successful years of internal peace. His successor, Ignacio Chávez, would face constant harassment, in part because of his views on academic quality, in part because he and President Gustavo Díaz Ordaz (1964–1970) held antagonistic political views. With presidential support, a shrewd rector could survive; without it, he was doomed.

---

[27] As late as September 1, one group denied that the movement had ended; see "A la opinión pública, a nuestros compañeros estudiantes," *Hoja Universitaria* 1 (1958), in Archivo Estudiantil, Hemeroteca Nacional, Caja II.

8. The Problems of Giantism, 1961–July 1968

THE 1960s were exciting years politically, not because Mexico changed much but because people tried to force the government out of its pro-capitalist, authoritarian policies. People in other countries were also trying to restructure their societies, a fact that must have encouraged Mexicans interested in change. Pressures from the left encouraged López Mateos to declare that he was as far left as one could be within the constitution. Carlos Madrazo, as president of PRI, tried to democratize the party's nomination process until President Díaz Ordaz stopped him, but Madrazo inspired others by his actions. Ex-President Lázaro Cárdenas reappeared on the political scene in 1961 when he participated in the creation of the leftist National Liberation Movement. Pressures to democratize politics led to the creation of the party deputy system in 1963 to guarantee some Chamber of Deputies seats to opposition parties. As it became more evident that economic growth was creating new elites little interested in social justice, protests mounted. By the late 1960s, the New Left, based within the nation's universities, was actively seeking confrontation with the conservative government of Gustavo Díaz Ordaz.

The return of sustained and consequential student activism in 1961 marked the beginning of what proved to be a turbulent decade. Toward the end of that decade, in 1968, student activism reached massive proportions and, from the government's viewpoint, threatened national security and domestic order. The many commentators and scholars who have written on the student movement of 1968 have called it either a major turning point in Mexican history or an event that revealed the true nature of the political system. Few have examined the revival of student activism in the 1960s or focused on the students themselves. The events of 1968 had antecedents just as did those of 1961. This chapter explores the revival of UNAM student activism and the movement of the university into confrontation with the government.

To understand the problems faced by Ignacio Chávez (1961–1966) and Javier Barros Sierra (1966–1970) as rectors of UNAM, one must have a clearer concept of UNAM students. Regardless of who was ultimately responsible for pushing Chávez out of the rectorship in 1966 or for the beginnings of the 1968 movement, UNAM students themselves played a major role. Further, the ability to govern UNAM and the reaction of UNAM students to events depended in part on the ambience in which students lived. Much has been written on Mexican society and government—their exploitativeness, repressive character, and authoritarian policies—but little on the university itself, one public institution with which students had constant contact. Yet the sheer number of students and the university's policies regulating them surely had an effect on their perceptions of reality and their willingness to take to the streets.

The UNAM over which Chávez was elected to preside in 1961 was substantially different from the university in 1929, when it received its autonomy. In 1929, UNAM had only 8,154 students, all but 17 percent of whom were enrolled in the facultades and escuelas. By 1944, the year the Caso law was proposed, the student population had increased to 22,239 with 25.7 percent in the ENP. When Chávez became rector in 1961, however, the number of students had increased to 66,860, with 34.5 percent in the ENP. Thus, by 1961, the enrollment had increased by 820 percent over 1929. Even though Chávez slowed the rate of growth between 1961 and 1966, UNAM had 78,094 students in the latter year, 38 percent of whom were ENP students. Although the 957.7 percent increase in student enrollment since 1929 was spectacular, the ENP's growth by 2,140.3 percent was even more so, far outstripping the 715.2 percent increase in the facultades and escuelas. The very number of students by itself made UNAM a more difficult institution to govern.[1]

Such increases in the student population changed the character of student life. The 1,388 ENP students of 1929 could at least recognize, if not know, each other. Ambitious student leaders could easily work

[1]González Cosío, *Historia estadística*, p. 74.

such a constituency, especially since classes were confined to a single building in the university sector of the city. Although matters were more difficult for student leaders in the facultades and escuelas, which totaled 6,766 students in 1929, many of the same conditions obtained. By using one's own school or facultad as a power base and allying with peers in other schools, an effective coalition could be forged. Life could be based on friendships and close observance of one's peers. Not so in the 1960s, when the ENP, with branches scattered throughout the city, contained over 20,000 students, by 1966 over three times as many as UNAM itself in 1929. Nor could it occur in UNAM with its twenty-nine facultades and escuelas (including the ENP) and 87,462 students in 1967. UNAM not only had to create branch campuses for the ENP but had overflowed the university city. Equally important, its students were scattered in residences throughout the Federal District. No organization or ideology could unite them.

Instead, they were faceless individuals working within one of the largest bureaucratized institutions in Mexican life. Student-faculty ratios increased as UNAM faced the difficulty of funding classes as rapidly as students clamored for them. As late as 1958, the ratio was 5.5 students to 1 faculty member in the ENP and 7.9:1 in the facultades and escuelas, but these jumped in 1959 to 12.5:1 and 12.1:1. When Chávez took over UNAM in 1961, UNAM's student-faculty ratio was 12.4:1; when he left in 1966, it was 13.4:1, a substantial increase when one remembers that many professors taught only one course. Perhaps more serious, however, was the growth in the number of university bureaucrats. In 1960, there were 1.67 faculty members for each administrative post; in 1961, 1.43; but in 1966, 1.02. In part, this probably represented the use of administrative titles to raise salaries as well as the growth of serious research institutes, but the effect was to create a huge bureaucracy that consumed more of the budget than did teaching and research. By the late sixties, at least, the individual student lived in a mass society of more than a hundred thousand persons (students, faculty, administrators, and support staff) in a nation of over fifty million.[2]

Most of the students came from the middling social strata of the Federal District, where they lived with their families and worked. Ac-

[2] Ibid., pp. 100–102.

cording to 1964–1966 data, almost 58 percent were born in the Federal District; in the ENP this proportion surpassed 68 percent. Only 2.3 percent of all UNAM students (and virtually no ENP students) were born outside of Mexico. Eighty-nine percent lived in family-owned or -rented property. Eighty-three percent were economically dependent. The average monthly family income in 1964 was 3,440 pesos, an amount 219 percent over the national average of 1,077, and 25 percent higher than the Federal District average. ENP students, as a separate category, had fewer resources on which to draw, for their average monthly family income was 2,701 pesos, which was 151 percent over the national average but 2 percent less than the average in the Federal District, where they lived.[3]

It was the "wealthier" students who managed to continue into the facultades and escuelas, for family income levels there averaged 3,854 pesos, some 358 percent above the national average and 40 percent more than the Federal District average.

Data, though incomplete, on the occupations of those who supported the students corroborates the view that UNAM students were not representative of the national or Federal District populations. Forty percent were employees (empleados), 19.6 percent businessmen (comerciantes), 15.2 percent professionals, 12.8 percent workers, and 2.6 percent farmers. Other data for UNAM students in 1968 are consistent with this general pattern. Almost 70 percent were supported by their parents, the vast majority of whom had not attended vocational or preparatory schools. Over 76.8 percent of these heads of families worked in middle sector occupations; only 17.5 percent were workers and farmers. By 1968, 71.4 percent of these families had incomes

[3] UNAM, Dirección General de Servicios Sociales, *La población estudiantil universitaria: Datos sociales y económicos*, which excludes the Instituto de Química, Summer School, and Escuela de Capacitación para Bachilleres; Fernando Pérez Correa, "La Universidad: Contradiciones y perspectivas," *Foro Internacional* 14 (1974): 398; Gerardo Estrada Rodríguez, *Los movimientos estudiantiles en la UNAM 1958–1973*, *Deslinde*, 51 (1974): 8, 10; "Los universitarios: sus condiciones económicas su procedencia social," *Gaceta de la UNAM*, March 1, 1969, pp. 2–6; Raúl Benítez Zenteno, "El estudiante de la Escuela Nacional de Ciencias Políticas y Sociales," *Revista Ciencias Políticas y Sociales* 7, no. 23 (1961): 43–91; and Marta R. Jiménez C., "Alumnos irregulares de la ENCPS," *Revista Ciencias Políticas y Sociales* 8, no. 29 (1962): 445–457, contain the data used in this and the following paragraphs. See also Sergio Zermeño, *México: Una democracia utópica. El movimiento estudiantil del 68*, pp. 60–61, for data on appropriations and for student frustrations.

within the 1,300–6,999 peso per month range, higher than the national average; 51.9 percent had incomes between 1,500 and 5,000 pesos. In the National School of Political and Social Sciences (ENCPS) in 1960, average monthly family income was 5,337 pesos (416.3 percent above the national average). This school, which taught diplomacy, journalism, political science, and social science, was an important source of student activists in support of the left.

Although few students came from affluent families, a surprisingly small percentage of them held jobs. An UNAM source in 1969 asserted that less than 30 percent of the students did. The 1964–1966 data offer a clearer picture of student employment. In the law school, 14.9 percent worked; in commerce, 12.8; in engineering, 10.9; in medicine, 7.7; and in architecture, 6.1. Students worked an average of six and one-half hours a day. Those in the facultades and escuelas earned, on the average, 1,314 pesos (22 percent above the national average) but those in the ENP earned two-thirds that amount. In the ENCPS in 1962, 47 percent worked.

Few students actually received their professional titles, and the percentage of irregular students remained high during the sixties. Of the 15,229 students who completed their studies, only 30.7 percent received their titles. Many fell behind in their studies by not taking exams on schedule or never writing and defending their professional thesis. University-wide, irregularidad among all students averaged 39.18 percent. Between 1960 and 1966, the problem grew, except in the medical school. Why so many students did not complete their studies is not clear, for the extent of the problem cannot be explained by student employment, family poverty, or student participation in strikes or political parties. In the ENCPS, one of the most politicized schools, only 16.3 percent of the irregulars belonged to a political party—and 10.7 of the regulars did too. This difference cannot explain much. Perhaps the growth of the problem reflected the effects of mass education with its impersonality; perhaps the youth cult so popular in the world in the 1960s had an effect. Regardless, such conditions must have engendered frustration.

Students had no single focal point within UNAM. They lived throughout the Federal District (over 81 percent used buses), and they were too numerous to congregate regularly at any single point. No student organization united them. The CNE was irrelevant; the FEU was split into rival factions. Instead, the politically concerned, a minority, were fragmented into scores of political parties and groups, even within the same facultad or escuela. The old idea of a generation, students in the same class or year in school who developed a sense of community from common classroom and extracurricular activities, was virtually dead, although the term was still used. The size of any given class was such that students had to be subdivided into groups that moved through the curriculum together. Perhaps only the most politically or academically committed could attain the sense of camaraderie that allowed for common goals and action. Alienation and anomie must have been prevalent.

UNAM may have been unmanageable by the 1960s. Faculty fragmentation equalled that of the students. Although the creation of full-time faculty positions had begun in the late 1940s, UNAM had to rely on part-timers; enrollments expanded so rapidly that administrators had to hustle to recruit enough people to teach. Salaries were not high enough to allow many persons to pursue teaching and research as a full-time vocation. In spite of many comments to the contrary, however, there is little evidence that the part-timers were poorer teachers than others; often they were persons who brought their daily work experience into the classroom. But, since their non-academic jobs were their principal source of income, it is hard to believe that they were as committed to UNAM as the full-time faculty. Their occasional relationship to the university meant that administrators could exercise little control over them. As the institution grew in size, the administration also grew and more authority was delegated to directors and department heads. UNAM increasingly became a place that operated out of sheer inertia, an institution honeycombed with personal fiefdoms.[4]

Few persons should have had any doubts in January 1961 as to why Ignacio Chávez was elected rector. His reputation as a serious scholar and disciplinarian had developed over three decades. An internationally eminent cardiologist, he had been director of the medical school, the General Hospital, and the National Institute of Cardiology, as well as rector of the University of Michoacán in Morelia. As a leftist, he was acceptable to those members of UNAM who thought them-

[4] See Larissa Lomnitz, "Carreras de vida," *Plural* (March 1976), and "La antropología de la investigación científica en la UNAM," unpublished paper, for analysis of the internal workings of UNAM.

selves progressive. To the right, he was a man who would create order out of the chaos into which they were convinced the university had fallen. He would raise academic standards, reestablish discipline, and restore the academic and fiscal integrity of the university. In short, he would send shock waves throughout UNAM and constantly be embroiled in controversy, but he could not be bought off.

Those who opposed Chávez and the new order he promised first tried to prevent his election and then tried to prevent him from taking office. The junta refused to be intimidated by the threat that Chávez would never be allowed to take office: it elected him at a mid-January meeting. The opposition group, led by presidents of several FEUs, supported by Agustín García López, former secretary of communications, pressed the issue. García López cried fraud when he was not elected and called for non-violent resistance. Early in the morning of January 21, the pro–García López group took over the rectory tower and the radio station, demanding that the junta reverse the election. Chávez responded by promising to end pistolerismo and the paying off of student leaders and to create a unified student organization. Since he would not be inaugurated for three weeks, he could wait for tempers to cool. On the twenty-third, however, the rectory was fired on by occupants of an automobile. Little mass opposition to Chávez could be staged, however, until vacations ended in February. When they did, several thousand students, according to one source, joined the anti-Chávez movement, but Chávez took the oath of office on February 15 in the faculty of sciences building while students exploded small tear gas bombs. He had first thought to have the ceremony in the home of Luis Garrido, junta president, but decided it necessary to run the gauntlet of stones and insults lest he compromise himself from the very beginning.[5]

Chávez wasted little time in clamping down. Within two weeks of his inauguration, he sent word that he would deal only with students, their parents, or their tutors, not with agents, self-appointed or otherwise. General student problems and issues had to go through established channels. Further, all members of the university community were told to behave properly. When the Easter vacation period ap-

[5] Garrido, *Tiempo*, pp. 397–398; Estrada Rodríguez, "Movimiento estudiantil," pp. 34–43; *Excelsior*, January 21–29, 1961; *The Times* (London), January 23 and February 16, 1961.

proached, the rector notified the directors and faculty that classes could not be dismissed early. In August, when two student groups from economics fought and the school director punished two student leaders, some rightist students charged that the leftist administration (including the rector) was persecuting them for ideological reasons, but Chávez refused to budge. Disciplinary regulations were printed and distributed. The university security police force was strengthened, bringing complaints from student activists. Chávez's opponents would accuse him of using the police and porras to stifle dissent and create an authoritarian regime, an assertion that few bothered to question.[6]

Chávez revealed his attitude toward student political activity when he attended the law school student society inauguration ceremony in August 1961. Students from the law school would play a central role in his ouster in 1966. The outgoing president, Javier Aguirre, boasted of his efforts (unsuccessful) to lower required class attendance to 50 percent. The new president, José Luis Alonso, who would be a constant thorn in the side of Chávez, mocked his predecessor's goals, asserting that the law students were dedicated to Marxist-Leninism. They should attack U.S. imperialism, the commercial press, and clerical politics. Chávez could not resist these challenges. He first questioned the validity of having a leader who would argue that his school should only have to attend half the classes while other schools obeyed the regular rules. Then he turned to Alonso, stating emphatically that what the new president had said was acceptable for a political group but not for the university, because it violated university rules and was an improper use of the student societies. In Chávez's view, the fundamental task of a student was to prepare for a career. This hard line had initial success, for 1961 was a relatively peaceful year.[7]

Student activists were not to be curbed by exhortation, nor could they be unified into a single organization, even when it was the rector who supported it. In early November 1961, Ricardo Valdez, president of the constituent assembly of the Federación Universitaria de Sociedades de Alumnos (FUSA), presented Chávez with the statutes of

[6] *Gaceta de la Universidad*, March 6, 1961, p. 2, and May 15, 1961, p. 1; Ignacio Chávez, *Informe al honorable Consejo Universitario* (1962), p. 19.

[7] Ignacio Chávez, "Exhortación a los estudiantes," *Gaceta de la Universidad*, September 18, 1961; *Gaceta de la Universidad*, February 19, 1962, contains the university statutes, including disciplinary rules; and *Gaceta de la Universidad*, February 26, 1962.

the new organization, which purported to represent all the students in the twenty-nine schools and facultades of UNAM. Chávez praised the group for its unification efforts and encouraged the members to respect the political beliefs of others, obey their constitution, and disprove the black legend of university student politics. To the University Council, months later, he reiterated his desire for a single student federation but noted that many groups claimed the title. In fact, the creation of FUSA had little effect on the organization and activity of the numerous political groups inside UNAM. Nor was FUSA unified, for rival factions were fighting to control it. Led by Carlos A. Cruz Morales, a new executive committee (claiming to represent ten ENP units, two facultades, and four escuelas) asserted in late September 1963 that the committee headed by Juan González Jáuregui was illegal, that his term ended in April 1962. Apparently the Cruz Morales group, supported by Chávez and claiming eighteen of the twenty-nine units, was trying to wrest control from both the right-wing group led by González Jáuregui and the left-wing group led by Walter Ortiz and Jesús Ochoa. Which was legitimate is not known; each accused the others of electoral chicanery. The legitimacy of the FUSA officers continued to be debated into 1964. Student leaders could always get a round of applause by attacking FUSA as a tool of Chávez, as Rodolfo Urquiza did in front of President Adolfo López Mateos during UNAM's opening ceremony in February 1964.[8]

Much of the attention of student activists in the early 1960s was attracted to national and international politics rather than to UNAM. The success of Fidel Castro in Cuba captured the imagination of leftist students throughout Mexico. Left- and right-wing students struggled, sometimes violently, for control of a number of Mexican universities. Throughout the spring and summer of 1961, students fought in the University of Puebla, forcing the state governor to take control. In October, the national government arrested six students (five Cubans and one Guatemalan), accusing them of pro-Castro agitation and subversion among Mexican students. Mexico City dailies began printing editorials against communism in the universities and hinted that Chávez

[8] *Gaceta de la Universidad,* November 6, 1961, pp. 1, 8; Chávez, *Informe,* p. 18; *Excelsior,* September 21, 1963; Comité ejecutivo de la sociedad de alumnos [of Philosophy and Letters], "Manifesto," October 8, 1963, in Caja 636, Archivo Estudiantil, Hemeroteca Nacional: *Excelsior,* February 8, 1964.

was a conspirator. In April 1962, conservative students at the University of Nuevo León paraded through Monterrey to protest the free textbook program, which they saw as supporting communism. In 1963, in Puebla and Michoacán, students took to the streets as the left and the right contested for power. UNAM, surprisingly, remained relatively quiet, although some of its students participated in these struggles.[9]

Chávez's efforts to raise academic standards and control the growth of the university riveted the attention of UNAM students and eventually contributed to his downfall. Late in 1961, he announced that admission to the escuelas and facultades would henceforth be based on grades and written exams; the era of automatic entrance from the prep schools was over. By November of that year, fifteen thousand of these exams had been administered and an appeal committee created. This step, which would block thousands from obtaining UNAM professional degrees, or from at least trying to do so, had become necessary because the university could not yield to enrollment pressures and make even a pretense of quality. Half of the entering students, according to Chávez, had serious academic problems their first year. Since the prep schools were not sorting the students, UNAM would, a move advocated by engineering students early in the year.

In 1964, Chávez expanded the ENP curriculum (which meant that other prep schools did too) from two to three years to increase the knowledge of the graduates and to spread enrollments through another year. Graduates of private prep schools tended to do better on admission exams than ENP students, so the latter were faced with an additional year of study but with no guarantee that they, and not the private students, would be admitted to the professional curricula. Chávez also tried to strengthen the faculty by hiring more full-time professors, hiring and promoting those who had terminal degrees, and keeping less qualified persons in the adjunct status. Most of the latter were in the ENP system. One result was that UNAM's enrollment grew 11.5 percent in 1961, 5.5 percent in 1962, less than 0.1 percent in 1963 and 1964, and only 1.8 percent in 1965. In 1966, during which Chávez was rector for only a few months, enrollment grew 5.7 percent; the next

[9] *Hispanic American Report* 14, nos. 7 and 8 (1961), 15, no. 2 (1962), and 16, no. 2 (1963); *New York Times*, October 30, 1961; David Spencer, "The Impact of the Cuban Revolution on Latin American Student Politics," in David Spencer, ed., *Student Politics in Latin America*, p. 95.

year it rose 12 percent. ENP enrollments were maintained at 34–35 percent of the university total during the Chávez years but jumped to 38 percent in 1967. Prep students and their friends fought these tighter standards, contributing to Chávez's fall.[10]

Before continuing with the protest movement from the ENP, however, it is necessary to turn to the controversies in the law school, for the students from both would combine to throw Chávez out in 1966. Trouble began in May 1962 when José Luis Alonso led a group of students protesting the election of César Sepúlveda as director of the school; they asserted that he was elected illegally, but the real complaint was that Sepúlveda was a strict academician like Chávez. Alonso's group declared a strike and took control of the law building, but they failed to gain support from any other students except some in ENP #5 in Coapa, where the building was seized. After twelve days the movement faded and Alonso and four others were expelled. They accused Chávez of being a rightist; Chávez claimed that non-university people backed the movement. Having passed this initial test of power, Chávez and Sepúlveda proceeded to clamp down on the law school and the ENP system (the third year of the ENP curriculum was added in 1964).[11]

The next round began in 1964 when some student activists tried to mobilize an anti-Chávez strike, using the ENP curriculum issue. The timing also reflected the fact that 1964 was a presidential election year in which the conservative Gustavo Díaz Ordaz would take over from the more liberal López Mateos, who had supported Chávez. Rodolfo Flores Urquiza, president of the law student society, sounded the first gun during the opening convocation in February by accusing Chávez of repressing student initiative and politics with hired bully boys and university police, illegally trying to control FUSA (which he said students

[10] *Excelsior*, November 7, 1961, contains Chávez's announcement on the exams; *Gaceta de la Universidad*, April 17, 1961, reports the plea of engineering students for higher standards; *New York Times*, July 15, 1962, summarizes the Chávez reforms and their effects; enrollment figures can be found in González Cosío, *Historia estadística*, pp. 74, 76; Rafael Segovia, "Mexican Politics and the University Crisis," in Richard Fagen and Wayne A. Cornelius, Jr., eds., *Political Power in Latin America: Seven Confrontations*, pp. 313–314, provides a good description of Chávez, his reforms, and UNAM.

[11] *Excelsior*, May 15–20, 1962; Chávez, "Declaraciones del Rector de la UNAM," *Gaceta de la Universidad*, May 14, 1962, and *Informe*, p. 19.

repudiated), and precipitously creating the three-year curriculum in the ENP. Flores Urquiza was applauded—but so, too, was Chávez when he defended the new curriculum and argued that only 20 percent of the prep students had been rejected for admission. The convocation, which President López Mateos was attending, was out of control, and the administration could not regain it.[12]

Within a month, Flores Urquiza started a movement in the ENP to overthrow Chávez and abolish the changes he had made. In various prep schools, on March 9, students demanded the abolition of the entrance exams and the three-year curriculum; they also demanded salary increases for their teachers, and expressed the unjustified fear that salary cuts were forthcoming. When university police failed to master the conflict that erupted between the demonstrators and themselves, the riot police (granaderos) were sent to the scene. Most of the action took place in the original prep school building on San Ildefonso street. The trouble continued the next day as leaders stole buses in the neighborhood of the Coapa prep school and drove them to the Zócalo. Failing to arouse support from other students, a group took control of the rectory and vandalized offices. Law, ENCPS, and economics students announced support for the demands but condemned the violence. By March 12, the movement splintered over the issue of violence and attempts by left- and right-wing political groups to take control. Flores Urquiza and Julián Rojas Abraham were expelled for a year. A third leader, Miguel Castro Bustos, a non-student porrista who had been arrested in February for assaulting a policeman and defrauding students, was delivered to the regular police; he would continue to agitate in the university, however. The student organization of Coapa disowned the student president there and planned new elections. Chávez had again survived.[13]

The issue of salaries for adjunct professors continued throughout

[12] *Excelsior*, February 8, 1964; *Testimonios*, a FUSA publication, gives a detailed account in the issue dated March 20, 1964. It can be found in the student archives of the Hemeroteca Nacional.

[13] *Excelsior*, March 10–13, 1964; *Testimonios*, March 20, 1964; Ignacio Chávez, "El alto espíritu universitario repudia a los falso lideres," *Gaceta de la Universidad*, March 30, 1964; *Excelsior*, February 6, 1964. The political groups were Trotskyites, PAN, Communists, Movimiento Nacional de Liberación, Corporación de Estudiantes Mexicanos (Jesuit), and Movimiento Universitario de Renovadora Orientación (MURO, an extreme rightist group).

1964, damaging Chávez's position. In August, Coapa professors complained that the salaries of adjunct professors decreased 22 percent while those of regular professors increased 40 percent. Chávez disagreed with their statements and asserted that the real complaints stemmed from the system of ranks and demands for better performance. Most professors benefited from the Chávez salary and rank policies, but change unnerved many who were unaccustomed to strong leadership.[14]

Chávez needed professorial support in March and April 1966 when students, led by Flores Urquiza, rose in revolt against Sepúlveda and then Chávez himself. The rector was reelected on February 13, 1966, but Sepúlveda's term lasted into May, giving his opponents ample time to agitate against him. Chávez's support of Sepúlveda in the face of this agitation was one reason he came under attack. The movement began on March 2 with the release of the law student manifesto, copies of which were sent to President Díaz Ordaz, university officials, and the metropolitan press. Although Sergio Mendival was president of the group, it was Flores Urquiza, the FEU representative, who wielded the influence. The manifesto acknowledged that the law students lacked organization and a collective conscience and that the school had an alarming number of irregular students, but argued that the regularization (make-up) exams were scheduled without taking student views into account. The students also complained that some of the professors listed on the group rosters never appeared and that some groups had no professors. In addition, the manifesto called for the end of required theoretical forensic practice. Finally, the students wanted more student participation in decision making. Interestingly, the manifesto ignored the increase in class size from sixty to seventy.[15]

The manifesto leveled serious charges against Sepúlveda. It asserted that he flunked 80 percent of the students, fired fifteen professors without justification, hired incompetents to replace them, took reprisals against professors who disagreed with him, was negligent in

[14] *Gaceta de la Universidad*, August 31, 1964. Segovia, "Mexican Politics," p. 314.
[15] Ernesto Flores Zavala, *El estudiante inquieto*, pp. 3–7. The author, law director from September 1966 until September 1970, gives the most systematic and detailed account of the movement. Tarsicio Ocampo V., comp., *Mexico, huelga de la UNAM, marzo-mayo, 1966: Documentos y reacciones de prensa*, anthologizes press coverage: it provides useful background reading. The following paragraph comes from these same sources.

not establishing courses and make-up exams, ruled as a dictator, and expelled students who disagreed with him. That the expelled students listed in the manifesto had a history of disruptive behavior made little difference to the petitioners. The manifesto announced a student meeting on March 8 to plan action.

Little might have come of this movement had Sepúlveda and Chávez not misused their power. Just before the March 8 meeting, Sepúlveda suspended Esiridión Payán Gallardo for one month and Leopoldo Sánchez Celis Duarte for two months for distributing subversive propaganda and plastering walls with posters. This action seemed to confirm the charges made in the manifesto. Equally important, however, was the fact that Sánchez Celis was the son of the governor of Sinaloa, a man with powerful friends. The governor sent pistoleros to lead porras from the law school and the Coapa prep school to drive Sepúlveda and Chávez from office. Chávez, for his part, used the university police against the students, thus almost guaranteeing student unity.[16]

Sepúlveda's last chance came during the second week of March. After several meetings on the eighth and ninth, the law students wrote a petition and threatened a strike if it were not answered in twenty-four hours. The demands were numerous. They wanted changes in the group assignments speeded up: three partial exams during the year and exemption from the final exam for those who had an 80 percent average and had attended 80 percent of the classes; the end of required forensic practice; the immediate resolution of the problem of groups without professors; intensive courses to help students catch up with their class; special exams administered by the professors who taught the courses; the end of plans to create a criminology major within the law school; and the reinstatement of those expelled. The criminology issue reflected the students' fear that government agents would be introduced into the school or that the "purity" of the law school would be sullied or both. Chávez responded to the petition by saying that it was an internal matter of the law school. Sepúlveda, arguing that the movement was started by non-university interests and that he would not be

[16] Flores Zavala, *Estudiante*, p. 7; "Boletín informativo del comité del huelga de la Escuela Nacional de Ciencias Políticas y Sociales," mimeo, May, 1966, and "Análisis de Secretaría de Gobernación," in Caja 1966, Archivo Estudiantil, Hemeroteca Nacional; Guitán Berniser, "Las porras," pp. 23–24.

intimidated, further antagonized the students by refusing to receive a delegation, telling them that they would have to go through the technical council of the school, adding another month to the suspension of Payán Gallardo, and expelling Flores Urquiza, Enrique Rojas Bernal, and Francisco Dantón Guerrero. The law student society, meeting on March 11, decided to strike on the fourteenth if no agreement were reached by then and the disciplined students not reinstated. A comité de lucha (fight committee) headed by Flores Urquiza, Jesús Aguila, Yeuchiel Moreno, Miguel Limón, Ernesto Luque, and Juan José Bremer (son of the 1930s university official) took command of the movement.[17]

When the students thought Chávez had reneged on his promise to intervene, they declared a strike on March 14. According to the students, Chávez had promised the partial exams, exemptions from finals, changes of groups when there were scheduling conflicts, and an effort to start make-up courses, and had also promised to speak to Sepúlveda about the suspension of Payán Gallardo and Sánchez Celis and, if Sepúlveda would not budge, to have them tried before the university tribunal. These agreements had to be approved by the student general assembly. The fight committee argued that these accords had no standing because they had not been reached by the student assembly or an authorized group. Fearing that the movement might end, some nine hundred students took the law building on the morning of March 14, overcoming the resistance of the watchmen. The next day, economics students joined the strike and added demands, the most important of which was the abolition of Article 82 of the university statutes, which gave the university administration the right of summary expulsion.[18]

Although Chávez has been maligned as an autocratic and intransigent rector, an assertion that would rationalize his ouster, the events of the week after the taking of the law building suggest that there was

[17] Flores Zavala, *Estudiante*, pp. 7–12; "Boletín informativo"; Ramón Ramírez Gómez, "Análisis del reciente movimiento estudiantil universitario de México," *Historia y Sociedad* (supplement, Spring 1966): 12–14; anonymous Mexico City correspondent, "The University Crisis in Mexico," *Minerva* 4 (Summer 1966): 588–589. The Ramírez Gómez article contains factual errors. Bremer received a top-level post in the Echeverría administration and became director of the Instituto Nacional de Bellas Artes, a step down, under López Portillo.

[18] Flores Zavala, *Estudiante*, pp. 14–15; "Boletín informativo"; and Ramírez Gómez, "Análisis," p. 14.

little that he could have done to restore order. Numerous commentators have asserted that non-university interests (variously identified as Díaz Ordaz, Sánchez Celis, the government, PRI, and the United States) had decided to oust the rector. A conspiratorial theory such as this is difficult to prove, because conspirators cover their tracks. In this case, however, some strike leaders made the assertion. Bremer, Limón, Luque and Mendival, all leaders, were booed at a student meeting and Bremer was struck with a tile. On the seventeenth, the four resigned from the movement, asserting that outsiders had gotten involved. They specifically identified Flores Urquiza and Ladislao Hernández as agitators who served non-university interests. Shortly before this, the Comité Juvenil Renovador of the PRI announced its support of the strike, perhaps an indication that Díaz Ordaz had decided that Chávez had to go. The students added four more demands to their petition to Chávez on March 21, calling for the firing of Sepúlveda, abolition of Article 82, regulation of the university, and creation of a student cooperative cafeteria in the law school. More significant, however, was the sending of information brigades to the prep schools and professional facultades and schools, a technique that would be used again in 1968.

The fight committee had no intention of accepting Chávez's answer to the petition; the goal was greater. Chávez agreed on March 28 to add professors so that groups could be changed, to solve the problem of classes without teachers, and to institute partial exams and final exam exemptions. He said that the forensic practice issue had to go to the technical council and the abolition of Article 82 to the University Council. He agreed to send the suspension cases to the tribunal. He argued that the criminology major was only being discussed in the technical council. New rules could be devised by the proper authorities for the university police, and the cafeteria would be reopened when renovation of the building was complete, although students would not operate it because they lacked the expertise. He refused the demand for make-up courses and exams because they would perpetuate the problem of irregularidad, and he refused to fire Sepúlveda because he had no authority to do so. He pointed out that Sepúlveda had only forty-two days to serve and that the real reason for the strike was to drive him out. In short, Chávez granted most of the student demands, and student leaders had met with him on the thirty-first, so they must have known. The economics students withdrew from the strike because their demands had been met. On April 4, however, the fight committee voted to continue the strikes, claiming that Chávez was laying a bureaucratic trap, that nothing would come of the promises. Between April 7 and April 10, Flores Urquiza and Dantón Guerrero were expelled from the committee, which debated whether they were traitors.[19]

For a few days in April, Chávez appeared to have won. He announced on April 11 that he had been reasonable but was now going to apply sanctions. The next day he expelled Flores Urquiza, Dantón Guerrero, Sánchez Celis, Payán Gallardo, and José Enrique Rojas. That same day, however, students in Prepa #2 fought policemen and granaderos; the violence was spreading. On the thirteenth, the strike committee decided to try for a national strike. Chávez conducted a poll of the law students through newspaper coupons and announced that 5,308 of the some 7,000 students wanted to return to class. Chávez sent a letter to parents of prep students, a tactic that ended the strikes in those schools. On April 18, ten fight committee members met with Chávez and announced that they were pulling out because the movement had been taken over by outsiders.[20]

Events of the last of April suggest that the student movement was not designed to oust Chávez. Javier Barros Sierra, who succeeded Chávez, has argued that there was general student discontent with the conduct of higher education. Others have elaborated on this theme, stating that students wanted to democratize the university, have better teachers, improve general social conditions in the nation, and participate in the benefits of modern life. The student-written documents in the Hemeroteca Nacional student archive support this view. So, too, did the actions of UNAM and other students. On April 20, representatives of eleven of the twenty-eight law schools in that nation met, criticized the Mexican government, and called for a national university strike. The student organization to which the secundarias, prep schools, universities, and the IPN belonged also issued a call for a national

---

[19] Flores Zavala, *Estudiante*, pp. 21–33; Liebman, Walker, and Glazer, *University Students*, p. 181, assert that Flores Urquiza and Rojas Abraham were feted after the strike by the president of the Chamber of Deputies and the editor of *El Día*, a prominent PRI deputy, thus proving that the government was behind the strike. That is thin evidence on which to base such a conclusion.

[20] Flores Zavala, *Estudiante*, pp. 30–35; Silva Herzog, *Historia*, pp. 144–149; "Boletín informativo," p. 5; Sepúlveda, "Student Participation," p. 388.

strike. That all these students were cooperating for the first time indicates that the UNAM movement was symptomatic of widespread discontent and not just an anti-Chávez move.[21]

What seems to have been the deciding factor was the ability of movement leaders to exploit events. Sepúlveda, on April 22, asked Chávez not to include him in the law school terna for the May director election, thus giving Chávez the opportunity to sacrifice Sepúlveda in order to defuse the strike. That same day, prep students assaulted the strikers in the law school building because the latter had beaten one of their leaders a few days before. The movement appeared to be splintering again. Chávez announced the results of his newspaper poll and the reopening of classes in unoccupied buildings. However, Carlos Castro Osuna led economics students back into the strike and joined forces with law students to take over the unoccupied buildings, beating returning students in the process. The ENCPS group now rejoined the strike and demanded that the Federal District attorney general prosecute Chávez and other administrators on criminal charges. The movement had blocked Chávez and taken the offensive again.[22]

The incident that spelled the end of the Chávez administration was accidental. On April 26, fifteen students went to the rectory to talk to Chávez. Thousands of students milled outside the locked and guarded structure. Francisco Villalobos, a porrista, entered through the window but was struck so hard by a police official inside the building that his skull was cracked. The students then stormed the building, joined by employees. Chávez and many of his colleagues were held captive, and after six hours he resigned. Administrators and professors by the score also resigned. The junta refused to accept the forced resignation but did accept a new one made on April 28.[23]

[21] Javier Barros Sierra, 1968. *Conversaciones con Gastón García Cantú*, pp. 27–28; two examples of documents in the student archives of the Hemeroteca Nacional are Comité de Lucha de la ENCPS, "Sr. Director de la Escuela Nacional de Ciencias Políticas y Sociales," and the Comité de Huelga of the ENCPS mimeographed notice concerning monopolies, Yankee imperialism, and the grand bourgeoisie. See also the interpretations in *Historia y Sociedad* (supplement, Spring 1966) of Mauricio Swadesh T., "La huelga estudiantil a través de unas ventas," pp. 10–11, and Elí de Gotari, et al., "La reforma universitaria democrática," pp. 3–7, and "Proposiciones concretas para la reforma universitaria," pp. 7–9. Flores Zavala, *Estudiante*, pp. 35–37, details the calls for a national strike.

[22] Flores Zavala, *Estudiante*, pp. 37–39.

[23] Flores Zavala, *Estudiante*, pp. 39–43; "Boletín informativo," p. 4; "The University Crisis," pp. 589–590; *Excelsior*, April 27–29, 1966.

The junta refused to let the movement leaders take control of the university or name the new rector. Six facultades and escuelas and seven ENP units (less than half the total) formed, on April 28, the Consejo Estudiantil Universitario, composed of three members from each facultad, escuela, and institute in the strike, and the General Secretariat, composed of one-third of this group. The CEU issued a programmatic statement calling for a more democratic university governance system, the abolition of the university police, revision of the three-year prep curriculum, automatic entrance for ENP students, and freedom of speech and association inside the university. Delegates from architecture, sciences, engineering, and film studies abstained from voting and those from commerce and chemical sciences walked out. Within days it was clear that the CEU had split along science versus humanist–social science lines. Even though the professors' union (SPUNAM) supported the governance demands, the junta refused to yield the right to make decisions; it was not going back to the pre-1945 strong council system that the students wanted. On May 5, the junta named Javier Barros Sierra as rector. Six days later, the CEU gave the rectory to the new man.[24]

Why Barros Sierra was chosen as rector has fostered speculation about the origin of the movement. The new rector had been an engineering professor and then director of the UNAM engineering school, but he had more recently been minister of public works under López Mateos and then director of the Petroleum Institute. That a person would move from political circles to the UNAM rectorship, an unusual occurrence, might mean that the government was behind the student movement, that Díaz Ordaz disliked Chávez and put a friend in his place. Such a scenario is plausible, but so too is the one that says that the junta, deciding that the new rector would have to have strong governmental backing if he was to restore order, found an interested person with the necessary qualifications. Barros Sierra has asserted that he did not seek the rectorship at the previous election because he knew that the government wanted Chávez reelected. That he knew what the government wanted attests to the quality of his political connections. His belief that a law-and-order president wanted to continue a law-and-order rector in office is credible. It is difficult to believe that

[24] Flores Zavala, *Estudiante*, pp. 43–56, provides the best account of these events, but they can also be followed through the daily newspapers.

Díaz Ordaz would create such chaos in UNAM and run the risk of a massive student strike; so little could be gained. Other politicians may have fostered the anti-Chávez move to embarrass the government, to establish a base within UNAM, or to accomplish some equally unknown purpose. On the other hand, the strike might have been the result of the personalities of student activists and the selection of Barros Sierra the result of his personal ambitions.[25]

The students exerted more influence inside the university as a result of the 1966 strike, but they got little from Barros Sierra. He promised to work on the problem of training too many professionals for a limited labor market (an underlying concern of students), but more students were admitted to UNAM, thus reducing prep school tensions and also increasing the pool of potential professionals. The university police force was abolished to pacify the students. The new law director was driven from his post in August and Ernesto Flores Zavala was elected in September after he assured students that he was not an enemy. Between 1966 and 1970, the law school had no student society officers. Instead, there and in other parts of the university, fight committees took control of student politics. FUSA disappeared. The left had gained control of student politics but was powerless to make substantive changes.[26]

The rector's chief stratagem to pacify students was to uncap enrollments, a policy to which his successors would find themselves committed. No university administration or national government could afford to reverse this policy after the student upheaval of 1968 for fear of inciting another rebellion. UNAM enrolled 73,851 students in 1965, the last full year of the Chávez administration, and the ENP itself enrolled 25,383 or 34.4 percent of the total. In 1966 and 1967, however, ENP enrollments constituted 38 percent of the total; in 1968, the proportion was almost 43 percent. Total UNAM enrollment grew rapidly as well, even in the facultades and escuelas, where Barros Sierra had made a commitment to coordinate enrollment with the professional labor market. By 1970, when Barros Sierra resigned, the UNAM student population had increased 34.6 percent over 1965, the facultades and escuelas had increased 26.2 percent, and the ENP had risen 50.5 per-

[25] See Barros Sierra, 1968, p. 33, for his statement.

[26] Flores Zavala, *Estudiante*, pp. 55–67; "Student Participation," p. 388; Barros Sierra, 1968, pp. 34–37.

cent. This explosion continued through 1976; by that year, UNAM had grown 223.3 percent since 1965. Most of the growth was in the ENP, which grew 347.3 percent compared to the 158.3-percent increase for the facultades and escuelas. In spite of this easier access, the number of persons receiving professional titles increased only 91.2 percent between 1965 and 1970, and this percentage reflects the easing of standards during the 1968 upheaval. Even between 1965 and 1976, the number rose only 193.5 percent, considerably less than enrollment growth.[27]

To the extent that mass enrollments and a small graduation rate alienated university students from society, these statistics explain much of what seemed to be growing student frustration. UNAM was not the only university to experience enrollment booms in the 1960s and 1970s. The Mexican economy, expanding by an average of 6 percent a year, swelled the ranks of those who could afford to attend college preparatory schools and universities. This new prosperity tended to be concentrated in urban areas, particularly the Federal District, where most of the universities were. As a result, the IPN system grew from 42,502 students in 1965 to 55,109 in 1968, having been only 24,727 in 1960. The number of students in public and private universities rose from 279,373 in 1966–1967 to 449,464 in 1970–1971, an increase of 60.9 percent.[28]

The Mexican Miracle, as the boom has been called, also produced political frustration; the sixties became a decade of protest as an increasing number of Mexicans expressed dissatisfaction with the authoritarianism of their government. Near the beginning of the decade the government initiated the party deputy system to provide an outlet for dissidence, but almost immediately made a mockery of it by allotting federal deputy seats to friendly parties. Within PRI, Carlos Madrazo, the former student radical, tried to democratize the nomination of party candidates, only to be blocked by old-line politicians. Reformers were blocked in San Luis Potosí in 1961 when they tried to beat the PRI machine. Citizens, including university students, demonstrated in Sonora against the imposition of Félix Faustino Serna by the outgoing governor, Luis Encinas Johnson; they had only their injuries to show

[27] Nacional Financiera, *La economía mexicana en cifras*, p. 421.
[28] Nacional Financiera, *Economía*, p. 421; Thomas Noel Osborne, II, *Higher Education in Mexico*, pp. 52–53.

for it. In northern Baja California in 1968, PRI had to nullify some elections and falsify others to prevent PAN from taking municipal and state legislative seats. One indication of the growing political frustration of the decade was the gains made by PAN, heretofore a party that few took seriously. Leftists had no party or organization that gave them much hope of influencing government policy. The Mexican Communist party (PCM) was small and isolated from the mainstream, tolerated because it had some noteworthy supporters (Valentín Campa and Demetrios Vallejo were two) and because it was a convenient scapegoat when the government needed one. Lombardo Toledano and the Partido Popular Socialista were still active but less potent than PAN. The Movimiento de Liberación Nacional, created in 1961, had little effect even during the years when Cárdenas openly supported it. The leftist groups inside UNAM, the IPN, and other universities were too factionalized to present a united front. To the left in 1967, the PRI appeared invincible.[29]

Student rather than national politics had a more immediate effect on student behavior and perceptions of it. Students had little or no influence in making national policy. Since PRI controlled elections, voting was almost irrelevant. Demonstrations might signal student attitudes, but student groups were only some of the many that policymakers watched. At the university level, however, students could influence academic and disciplinary policy, drive out officials, or coerce bus companies into paying indemnities or maintaining low fares.

Students in state universities and schools were active between 1966 and 1968 in struggles over curriculum, personnel, and bus fares. Although there is some danger of misrepresentation in citing an incomplete list, its length is suggestive. In 1966, university students conducted strikes and fights in Aguascalientes, Campeche, Chihuahua, Guerrero, Jalisco, Michoacán, Puebla, and Sinaloa. The strike at the University of Michoacán (San Nicolás) in Morelia in October was particularly bloody and ominous; soldiers broke the strike when anti-gov-

[29] For background on Mexican politics in the 1960s, see Mabry, *Mexico's Acción Nacional*, including the bibliographic essay; Robert Bezdek, "Electoral Oppositions in Mexico: Emergence, Suppression, and Impact on Political Processes"; Stevens, *Protest and Response*; Kenneth Johnson, *Mexican Democracy: A Critical View*. There are many other works, almost all of which are cited in Mabry, but the Johnson work, although biased, gives the flavor of alienation. For the view that PRI was invincible, see Liebman, Walker, and Glazer, *Latin American University Students*, p. 184.

ernment overtones became too noticeable to ignore. In 1967, student strikes and alterations erupted in Chihuahua, Durango, Nuevo León, Puebla, San Luis Potosí, Sonora, Tabasco (where the army intervened), Tamaulipas, Veracruz, and Yucatán. Before the student movement began in 1968, there had been strikes or tumults in Jalisco, Puebla, San Luis Potosí, Tabasco, and Tamaulipas. Some students died in these events. Whether there was more or less turbulence than in a previous period is not clear, but that the government was willing to use soldiers in Morelia and Tabasco suggests that tolerance of this behavior was diminishing. The number of incidents also suggests that many students were unhappy with university life.[30]

Although there were few strikes in UNAM before July 1968, students and pseudo-students were creating enough turmoil to raise serious questions about continued governmental, if not general public, tolerance of students. Every instance has not been catalogued, nor were all the students from UNAM. Some were from other institutions in the Federal District; some were from gangs or porras. Bus companies suffered most from student depredations, not because an occasional bus killed a student and students held buses for ransom but because buses were such convenient targets. There were at least eleven attacks on buses in 1967 and over thirty in 1968 between January and July. Merchants complained to police about student robberies and vandalism. Prep students fought each other, secundaria students, and vocational students. Three policemen were kidnapped on March 1. Seven ENP units went on strike in mid-March to protest the arraignment of some prep students arrested during an upheaval. In April, students from many UNAM units joined prep students in sequestering buses to protest a student death.

Intermixed throughout these events were the acts of porras, which had taken control of the FEU in 1967 and continued to expand their activities inside and outside UNAM, beating, robbing, and vandalizing at will. Barros Sierra could not use the police inside UNAM for fear of provoking a mass student protest, nor could he use the university po-

[30] Flores Zavala, *Estudiante*, pp. 113–121, gives a good descriptive list of these incidents. The October 1966 Morelia strike has drawn considerable attention; it can be followed in the Mexico City daily newspapers and, in English, in "Bus Fares and Student Demonstrations in Mexico," *Minerva* 5 (1967): 301–303. Fausto Burgueno, "El movimiento estudiantil en la provincia," in Juvencio Wing, et al., *Los estudiantes, la educación y la política*, pp. 46–53, gives a good summary of state political movements.

lice because the corps had been abolished in 1966. In January 1968 he promised that university authorities would not take sides in student disputes nor would they tolerate disorder within the university. Only courageous officials tried to do something about porras, however. In May 1968, Rosalinda Núñez of the Coapa prep school led a movement to expel thirteen porristas who had been terrorizing the school, but her example was singular. Some of the porras had support from government officials, making action against them dangerous.[31]

Student and porra violence continued well into July 1968 in spite of signs that the police were planning a crackdown. Since they had been able to continue their internecine fights, vandalism, and violent protests with impunity, few groups heeded the warnings of Barros Sierra in January and of the Federal District attorney general in March or the more frequent appearances of police and granaderos at the most common sites of turmoil. In still another confrontation over a bus maiming a person, UNAM students captured sixty-four buses (some of which they destroyed) by July 10 and beat up a woman professor. The police did not intervene, however, and what remained of the buses was returned after the company paid an indemnity. A few days later, on July 22, students from the Isaac Ochoterena prep school (private but incorporated into UNAM) and vocational schools #2 and #5 of the IPN fought in the Ciudadela, a section of the central city containing a park surrounded by schools, historic buildings, businesses, and a few dwellings. Participating in the fracas were the Ciudadelos and the Arañas, porras of the area. The fight was one of many that had been occurring for months (students of Voca #2, for example, had attacked the prep school and an electricians' union school on March 14), and the immediate cause of this one is not important. In large measure, the fights resulted from class tensions exacerbated by inter-school and teenage rivalries. Tired of suffering from these altercations, which often meant vandalism, neighbors and merchants pleaded with the police to do something. On July 23, some two hundred granaderos were dispatched to the Cuidadela in response to reports that students were again fighting.[32]

[31] See Flores Zavala, *Estudiante*, pp. 121–135, and *Gaceta*, April 1, 1968, 2–3, for descriptive lists of these incidents. Guitán Berniser, "Las porras," p. 39–45, provides more detail on the porras.

[32] The police warning and the March 14 incident are detailed in Flores Zavala, *Estudiante*, p. 130. The bus incident can be followed in *Universal* and other Mexico City

The granadero variable quickly changed the political equation being worked out in the Cuidadela. Vocational students chased the prep students into their school and stoned it while the granaderos watched. After the vocas returned to their school, the granaderos took command of the plaza. The students taunted the policemen, who responded in kind, and then the students began throwing stones and other projectiles. After enduring several volleys, the granaderos attacked, firing tear gas and clubbing students. Some invaded Voca #5, the least-involved school, and beat everyone in sight. The melee became generalized for some three hours as voca and prep students squared off against granaderos, who left the field as "victors." By disobeying their orders to control the situation and by rioting instead, the granaderos had accomplished the rare feat of unifying students of the rival schools.[33]

This misuse of public force symbolized what many students, in Mexico and elsewhere, found wrong with modern government and society. The granadero corps had been controversial since its founding in 1944, for it had been used to repress dissidence as often as to suppress riots. The granaderos enjoyed a reputation for fierceness and a willingness to obey commands without question. Their enemies claimed that the existence of the corps was unconstitutional. Regardless of the legality of the corps, IPN students were particularly hostile to them, having suffered repeatedly from the corps. The first issue to arise out of

[33] Chávez G., "Torpe jornada"; Prieto, "Poder"; Universal, July 25, 1968; Ortega, "Hechos"; and González de Alba, Los días, p. 23. The Universal article contains the assertion that "students" in beige uniforms acted as provocateurs, but the truth and meaning of this assertion are unknown. These and subsequent events can be followed in the major Mexico City dailies and in Ramón Ramírez, ed., El movimiento estudiantil de México, julio-diciembre de 1968, vol. 1, which contains lengthy excerpts from the columns of such periodicals as El Universal, Excelsior, El Día, Gaceta de la UNAM, and Novedades. In addition, the Archivo Económico of the Biblioteca Miguel Lerdo de Tejada has an extensive newspaper clipping file on "Conflictos Estudiantiles." For the sake of space, I will only make specific citations when further clarification seems necessary. Zermeño, México, pp. 11–12, stresses that the granaderos provoked the students.

dailies and in Stevens, Protest and Response, pp. 192–193. The July 22 incident is variously described in Ortega, "Hechos," El Día, August 17, 1968; José Luis González de Alba, Los días y los años, p. 23; Elías Chávez G., "Torpe jornada policiana ante 3,000 agitadores estudiantes," Universal, July 24, 1968; Raúl Prieto, "El poder anticubano en México," El Día August 14, 1968. Zermeño, México, pp. 11–12, asserts that these porras led the voca students.

the July 23 incident was not the legality of the corps but the police brutality involved, the wanton disregard for the safety and rights of those who had not been confronting the granaderos. It was this arrogance of power, this belief that *anything* government forces did was legitimate, that angered students and non-students alike.

The IPN student organization, the Federación Nacional de Estudiantes Técnicos (FNET), staged a protest march on July 26, but lost control of it. The plan was to march from the Ciudadela to the Casco de Santo Tomás on the IPN campus northwest of the Alameda (a park in downtown Mexico City). The timing of the march reflected the several days necessary to organize and get police permission and the fact that vacations would start on the twenty-seventh. Independently of this march, the Central Nacional de Estudiantes Democráticos (CNED) and other Communist and pro-Communist students were marching to the Alameda for a rally to commemorate the fifteenth anniversary of Fidel Castro's attack on the Moncada army barracks. The two demonstrations were unrelated; FNET was controlled by PRI. The lines of the march never touched and the FNET march was scheduled to end before the CNED rally began. Not all of the FNET marchers, estimated as high as 50,000, reached Santo Tomás, and others left shortly after their arrival. Some defected at the Monument to the Revolution; others rode buses from the IPN campus to the Alameda. By 8:30 P.M., thousands of students had converged in the Alameda, only a few blocks from the Zócalo and the old university quarter.

Police officials were prepared for any possible trouble that might emanate from the pro-Castro rally and had stationed granaderos and other police between the Alameda and the Zócalo, but they had not expected the trouble that followed. The pro-Castro speakers called for urban guerrilla warfare and the seizure of the schools to make them centers of opposition to the regime. The oratory was loud, bombastic, and violent. Whether it was oratory or the opportunity presented by the IPN grievances or the work of provocateurs or some combination thereof is unknown, but the group in the Alameda decided to march to the Zócalo to protest in front of the National Palace. The government version of the events asserts that the group began vandalizing businesses as it marched; the student version is that they were attacked by granaderos and the property damage occurred during the melee. Regardless, the result was a major confrontation between the granaderos on the one hand and students and their allies on the other in the very heart of the city, with numerous injuries to both sides.

Had the confrontation ended there, little would have come of it, but students and granaderos fought again in the old university quarter near Prepas #2 and #3, less than ten blocks away. Accounts of the events are murky, but it appears that, as students fled from Cinco de Mayo street to the safety of the prep schools, granaderos shifted with them. Both groups joined comrades who were in the old university zone. The ensuing battle raged for hours. When the students burned a bus, more police rushed to the scene. Faced with such numbers, students turned buses into barricades to prevent the granaderos from invading the prep schools. Early in the morning of the twenty-seventh, the director of Prepa #3 arranged a truce with the granadero commandant, but the policemen stayed on guard and the students remained behind their barricades and within the schools, afraid to leave for fear of being assaulted by the granaderos. The battlefield was strewn with the charred remains of city buses and the litter of combat, the air pungent with smoke, all within shouting distance of the National Palace in the Zócalo.[34]

What makes the student-granadero conflict more puzzling was the raid on the PCM headquarters that night at 9:30, less than two hours after the street fighting started. In addition to arresting several persons, the judicial and secret police destroyed files and equipment and confiscated party propaganda. Since the government immediately began accusing the Communists of inciting the riot, the raid may have been staged when officials realized that they had to rationalize their actions to the public. Just as plausibly, however, the police may have planned (and even incited) a confrontation between granaderos and the CNED (not expecting FNET and prep students to be involved) and the raid on the PCM as part of an anti-leftist campaign. On the twenty-seventh, however, government spokesmen began asserting that Communists and foreigners (as opposed to loyal Mexicans) had provoked the Cinco de Mayo and old university quarter battles.

In fact, the events revealed the incompetence of public officials.

[34] In addition to the newspaper accounts, see also "A Conflagration of Obscure Origins," *Minerva* 7 (1968–1969): 256–263.

CNED leaders had failed to get the FNET to march to the Zócalo but emerged as heroes and prophets after the battles. They and other young Communists would play an important, but not critical, role in subsequent events. By pursuing the demonstrators into the old university quarter and by engaging in pitched battle with those previously in the area, the granaderos had again merged IPN and UNAM forces and created an anti-government redoubt within blocks of the National Palace. Even efforts to blame the Communists, foreigners, and outside agitators or to arrange public condemnations by tame unions and business groups such as the Mexico City Chamber of Commerce lacked conviction because the tactic had been used so many times before. Too many people had been involved.

Students responded to these events much as students had done for decades. Student patrols and, later, bus barricades sealed off the large area around Prepas #1, #2, and #3, thus keeping the police at bay. During a mass meeting in the ENP amphitheater, the scene of so many student meetings since 1910, the assembled students demanded the release of their peers arrested the night before and vowed not to remove the barricades until it had been done. The chief of the preventive police, for his part, asked for and got a student delegation to identify the students who were arrested and later announced that the students had been released. He warned, however, that maximum force would be used if more violence occurred, and stated that police generosity in this instance was proof that the police were not hostile to students, only to the professional agitators who were intent on undermining the Olympic Games (scheduled to begin October 12). Both the economics school of the ENP and, later, a broad-based assembly of IPN students demanded the abolition of the granadero corps and other "repressive forces." The economics group also wanted the abolition of the FNET and the expulsion from the school of FNET leaders and PRI pseudo-students who were actually government agents. The more representative group also demanded that the top two officials of the preventive police be fired, vowing to stay on strike until these two demands were met. This IPN group repudiated the FNET because it saw FNET as an arm of the government and because the chief of the preventive police had asserted that his corps had responded to the call of the FNET president when it appeared on the scene on July 26.

Although student groups solidified their demands on July 28, relations between them and the police appeared to improve. In the early morning hours, the students gave up the buses they were holding and the police released the arrested Voca and Prepa students, even though some two hundred porristas had unsuccessfully tried to remove the barricades and had penetrated Prepa #1 and vandalized it. As a result of the attack on Prepa #1, the striking students retook the three prep schools in the area, but no violence occurred. That same day, the CNED pleaded its innocence in the events of July 26 and issued demands:

1. Immediate liberty for all those arrested
2. End of the wave of repression
3. Respect for student organizations and the other democratic institutions
4. Punishment of the police chiefs responsible for the aggression and of the provocateurs
5. Firing of the chief and subchief of the preventive police
6. Punishment of the political instigators of this reactionary machinery
7. Clarification of the facts of the events

Students from the IPN, the Normal School, and the national agriculture school, meeting that same day, began preparing for a general strike if what turned out to be their original six demands were not met. These demands were:

1. Abolition of FNET, the university porra, and MURO
2. Expulsion of the student members of these groups and of PRI
3. Indemnification by the government of the injured students and the families of those who died
4. Freeing of the arrested students
5. Abolition of the granadero corps and the other repressive police
6. Abolition of Article 145 of the penal code

The Mexican Communist Party also issued demands calling for a full investigation of the firings, the abolition of the granaderos, and the freeing of those arrested. Thus, early in the demand-making stage, there was great similarity.

Several important differences existed among these three sets of demands, which indicated that the students and the Communists were acting independently. Whereas both Communist groups wanted *all* those arrested freed (thus including their colleagues), the students spoke only of students. The students wanted indemnities (a customary demand) and began to assert that deaths resulted from the fracas. The assertion that persons died as a result of street brawls was common in the history of student politics and, given traditional student animosity toward the police, likely to be believed without proof. The anti-rightist tone of the demands was not surprising, since leftist students were more likely to assume control of the movement. The anti-government, anti-PRI tone, common among both left- and right-wing students, was not particularly serious, for it did little more than claim the students' institutions as private bastions. The most striking aspect of the students' six demands was the inclusion of the Article 145 demand, since the crime of social dissolution, the vague anti-subversion law of the 1940s, had nothing to do with the events. No student had been or would be arrested under its provisions; the famous cases involving its use were those of Demetrio Vallejo and Valentín Campa, both leftists and both in prison. One might see the inclusion of that demand as symbolic of student unhappiness with arbitrary government, which it probably was, but it also suggested that leftists, now controlling the movement, took the opportunity to raise the issue of the treatment of two of their heroes.[35]

Some time during the evening of July 29 the government's attitude hardened, even though the students had done nothing unusual, and the result was a government action that changed the course of events. During much of the day, students in various schools—primarily in UNAM prep schools and the IPN system but also in the agriculture school—voted a strike or captured buses or did both. Some students in Prepa #7 kidnapped two policemen but soon let them go. Sometime around 7:10 P.M., granaderos broke up a student rally in the Zócalo, but it was not a serious incident. The government spent part of the day trying to blame foreigners (a few had been arrested) for the

[35]Zermeño, *México*, pp. 31–32, argues that the sixth demand of the general student group came from the Communists, as would the demand to release the political prisoners.

trouble or to deny that a student had been killed by the police, insisting, instead, that he had died of a "non-traumatic cerebral hemorrhage." Even when the fighting did start again in the old university quarter at nine that night, the events were not novel. More buses went up in flames and the granaderos used tear gas; each side tried to inflict as much damage as possible on the other. The battle lasted past midnight, since neither side tired easily.

Before one in the morning, soldiers attacked not only Prepas #1, #2, and #3, where the battle had been raging, but also Prepa #5 and Voca #5, in the process, they gave new life to the movement. Such massive force quickly achieved its objective—reestablishment of government control over these schools and their neighborhoods—but the army committed a serious tactical error in the process. In order to penetrate Prepa #1, the original ENP, soldiers used a bazooka to blast down the massive, historic doors. By doing so, they brought into the movement all of UNAM (most of which had remained aloof from what was considered an INP fight) and, in short order, virtually every postelementary school in the nation. The bazukazo, as the event is called, unnecessary and illogical, marks a major turning point not only in the events of 1968 but also in the history of UNAM student activism. No government efforts to pacify UNAM by claiming that the students had destroyed the door with Molotov cocktails or to blame the problems on Communists, foreigners, Castro, or the FBI/CIA could alter the effect of that single bazooka shot.

By July 30, 1968, the Díaz Ordaz government had demonstrated its hostility toward, if not contempt for, universities and their students. The ouster of Chávez in 1966, the first such ouster since 1948, signaled this hostility, for, even if Díaz Ordaz or his government had not had a hand in the affair, the lack of support guaranteed his fall. Because Chávez himself was unpopular with numerous persons, few recognized the government hostility toward the institution that the 1966 event represented. Similarly, the use of the army to quell the student movement in Michoacán later in 1966 and for a similar purpose in Tabasco in 1967 frightened activists and the thoughtful, but UNAM members assumed that it could never happen to them, forgetting that the army had been used against UNAM during Luis Garrido's student days. Although the use of granaderos on July 23, 1968, and subsequently can be explained for other reasons, the bazukazo must be interpreted as an act contemptuous of UNAM and its traditions. The bazukazo was a clear signal that *no* institution was immune from government force.

The emergence of a national student movement after the bazukazo is a complicated story, one that needs telling on its own.

9. The Great Conflict and After, July 30, 1968–June 10, 1971

SENDING the army against the students on July 29–30, 1968, was but the opening act in the drama that unfolded in the months of August and September; by the time of the final act on October 2, the tragedy of Tlatelolco, students and government officials revealed their fears, failures, and unrealistic views of life. The student movement of 1968 and the government's reaction to it make sense only when one remembers the context, the ambience in which they took place.

For Mexico, 1968 was a special year, one in which it would host the Olympics during October 5–27 to demonstrate to the world how modernized and civilized it was. The Mexican Miracle was to be displayed so the world would know that the nation had arrived. That this would be the first time the Olympics had ever been held in a Spanish-speaking country gave the nation a special claim to prominence among Latin American countries and allowed it to surpass Spain itself. The government spared no expense to provide excellent facilities for the athletes, retainers, journalists, and others who would flock to the country. Realizing that Mexico would not fare well in the medal competition and sensitive to the ancient charges that the nation was barbaric, government leaders arranged a cultural olympics that would allow Mexicans to shine and give the Mexican Olympics a special tone. Not all of the $140 million dollars spent on the Olympics was to be a one-shot affair, for many of the buildings would be used later by the general population for housing and recreation; the money was also a capital investment in the tourist business, an important source of profit and foreign exchange.

President Díaz Ordaz and other government officials believed, no doubt, that hosting the Olympics was the most important act of the year, if not of decades, and that nothing could be allowed to interfere with this great enterprise. Believing this, they assumed that all other Mexicans were equally concerned with the Olympics, that the consuming passion of the organizers and promoters was shared by students, workers, peasants, and provincials. Thus, all acts were seen through the filter of the Olympic Games; all words and events were linked to this great celebration of youth.

But Mexican officials differed little from their counterparts in the United States, France, and other nations of the Western world; they did not recognize the causes of or understand the rationale behind the youth cult flowering in the 1960s and the emergence of the iconoclastic New Left. Youthful rebellion was nothing new in Mexico, as the long history of university student strikes demonstrated and as many in the government knew from having once participated themselves. Mexico in 1968 seemed to be riding a wave of prosperity and the government was proudly proclaiming to the world that the Mexican Revolution worked, so how could the managers of the miracle understand that affluence brought guilt and rebellion, that middle- and upper-strata youngsters felt ashamed that they were doing so well while the bulk of their fellow citizens suffered from privation and despair, that they chafed under the yoke of the contradictions between what schools, the media, and government officials had told them and the reality they saw around them? Even though the rebellion of the young was evident in the United States, even at elite schools such as Columbia, or in France during the May Revolution, these seemed irrelevant to Mexico, for the latter was moving upward and onward, and Mexican chauvinism would not consider the possibility that Mexican students could be as "decadent" as those in France or the United States.

Because of these attitudes, the Mexican government almost immediately began to assert that the "student troubles" were the result of outside agitators or Communists or foreigners or some other group of devils who wanted to embarrass Mexico before the world, or get the Olympics moved to some other country, or start a revolution. Given the assumptions and experiences of those in power, nothing else made sense, for, unlike students in previous upheavals, these were not trying to get easier exams, higher grades, or the removal of an unpopular administrator. As events became more incomprehensible to those in power, the level of fear, even paranoia, rose. The cry of subversion became hysterical, and serious, tragic mistakes were made.[1]

Students erred seriously as well, for they, too, labored under delusions. They assumed that if commanded, the government would respond, that the justice of their cause meant that they would win, and that their "purity" and numbers would prevail. They refused to believe the warnings issued periodically by the secretary of defense, the secretary of the interior (gobernación, or government), and the president himself that whatever force necessary would be used, for they could not conceive of a government turning brutally on its elite youth. They thought that if they invoked the Constitution the government would have to obey it, that they could force the government to respond le-

[1]The 1968 student movement has produced voluminous pages of analysis, debate, and description. The events themselves have been reconstructed for this chapter through the use of newspapers, the Ramón Ramírez anthology, the Archivo Estudiantil of the Hemeroteca Nacional, the collection "Datos sobre los estudiantes universitarios de 1910 a 1971" of the Archivo Económico of the Biblioteca Miguel Lerdo de Tejada, videotapes in the Television Archives of Vanderbilt University, and the writings of participants, analysts, and observers. This last group includes: Raúl Alvarez Garín, et al. *Los procesos de México 68: Acusaciones y defensa*; Barros Sierra, 1968; Roberto Blanco Moheno, *Tlatelolco: Historia de una infamia*; Jorge Carrión, Sol Arguedes, and Fernando Carmona, *Tres culturas en agonía*, and "Las tendencias políticas dentro del conflicto estudiantil," ¿*Por Qué?* (September 11, 1968): 256–263; Daniel Cosío Villegas, "Como en Grecia: Los siete años de una tragedia," *Excelsior*, September 28, 1968, and *Labor periodista*; Juan Miguel de Mora, *Tlatelolco 68: ¡Por fin toda la verdad!*; Lewis H. Dinguiel, "Mexico's Night of Death," *Progressive* 32 (1968): 22–25; Roberto Escudero and Salvador Martínez Della Roca, "Mexico: Generation of '68," *NACLA Reports* 12 (1978); Estrada Rodríguez, *El movimiento estudiantil*; Victor Flores Olea, et al. *La rebelión estudiantil y la sociedad contemporánea*; Flores Zavala, *Estudiante*; Comité Coordinador de Huelga de la UNAM, *Gaceta* (various issues); Gastón García Cantú, *Política mexicana* and *Universidad y antiuniversidad*; Luis González de Alba, *Los días*; James N. Goodsell, "Mexico: Why the Students Rioted," *Current History* 56 (1969): 31–35, 53; Guitán Bernisier, "Las porras"; Judith Alder Hellman, *Mexico in Crisis*; Salvador Hernández, *El PRI y el movimiento estudiantil de 1968*; "México, 1968. Contra la represión, por la democracia," *Historia y Sociedad* 3 (1968), supplement #5; Carlos Monsiváis, *Días de guardar*; "The Movement Finds a Cause in Mexico," *Minerva* 7 (1969): 563–569; Tarsicio Ocampo V., comp. *Mexico: Conflicto estudiantil 1968*; Octavio Paz, "The Other Mexico: Critique of the Pyramid; Elena Poniatowska, *La noche de Tlatelolco: Testimonios de historia oral*; Silva Herzog, *Una historia*; Luis Spota, *La Plaza*, a novel; Stevens, *Protest and Response*; Fausto E. Vallardo Berrón, *Proceso a la Universidad y a los universitarios*; Rosalío Wences Reza, *El movimiento estudiantil y los problemas nacionales*; Zermeño, *México*. Rather than cite most of these works for each footnote, especially since there is little dispute as to what happened, I will use footnotes only for clarification.

gally by making it respond in public and under the scrutiny of international reporting of the events. The movement was a series of media events. The students saw their own violence as moral but governmental violence as immoral. They believed that they were the hope of Mexico, as so many orators had told them, but they did not realize that 50,000 or 100,000 or 300,000 persons marching through the streets of a national capital calling for revolution frightened those in power. Nor did they understand that university autonomy did not mean sovereignty, that it did not mean that the police powers of the state could not be, and had not been, used against UNAM.

In the first day after the post-midnight assault of the army, both sides struggled to cope with the events. At his 2:30 A.M. press conference on July 30, Minister of Interior Luis Echeverría and Federal District officials charged that the Communist party was responsible for the troubles and that the government had acted legally in defending the public against subversion; later in the day, the PCM denied the charges and suggested that right-wing groups were responsible. The Secretariat of Public Education canceled classes in the IPN and other schools under its control, and UNAM followed suit, thus spilling thousands of students into the streets. At noon, Barros Sierra addressed the crowd milling on the esplanade in the university city, deploring the events and vowing to defend university autonomy; the flag waved at half-mast. Across town in the Ciudadela, students were fighting granaderos and soldiers until, after three hours, paratroopers took control. Even while these events were occurring, Minister of Defense Marcelino García Barragán warned during his 2 P.M. press conference that the army was prepared to repel whatever aggression and would do so with total energy. Two and one-half hours later, the army gave up Voca #5 and Prepas #1, #2, and #3.

FNET leaders, hoping to gain control of the budding movement and divert it as their government sponsors wanted, visited Mexico City Regent Alfonso Corona del Rosal to issue seven demands:

1. The firing of the granadero and metropolitan police chiefs
2. Dismissal of all those responsible for the outrages committed against Voca #5 students
3. Indemnification for students hurt by the granaderos
4. Creation and use of regulations limiting police intervention

5. Destruction of the police records of the arrested students
6. Release of student prisoners and complete information on those who had disappeared
7. Immediate withdrawal of army and police units from the occupied schools

That night, IPN Director Guillermo Massieu offered to transmit the petition to the national authorities and then met later with the Coordinating Committee of the General Strike Movement of IPN (CCMGH in Spanish), who wanted him to make a public statement and demand the release of those arrested.

In Mexico City and in the states, some facultades/escuelas and universities began declaring stoppages. UNAM students held meetings on campus to determine what to do next. Others, including students, were chased out of the Zócalo by soldiers and policemen. Government and business leaders denounced the students and the Communist party; no one was sure who should be blamed.

Even though both UNAM and IPN had been assaulted by the army, students of the two institutions continued to act independently in these early days. During a mass protest meeting on July 31, Barros Sierra announced plans to lead a protest march through the city streets (but not into the center of the city) and called for the students to resist provocateurs (whom he accused of having begun the troubles). On the other side of town, the secretary-general of the Federal District government responded to the FNET petition by saying that Corona del Rosal would resolve points 1 and 2 within eight days, that the city government would have to know the names and details concerning those injured before indemnification could occur, that FNET should present concrete ideas on new regulations, that point 5 was granted, that point 6 was granted except in the case of crimes but these cases would receive immediate attention, and that point 7 was granted. That the FNET appeared to have gained major concessions was quickly disproven when the CCMGH repudiated the former. Students were arraigned during the course of the day and the strikes spread into other states. The army abandoned Voca 7. The government announced the arrest of five "Frenchmen" whom it accused of being participants in the May Revolution and of having come to Mexico to incite riots.

Whether they were French or May Revolutionists or involved in the Mexican events is debatable.

Two events made August 1 important in the history of the movement. President Díaz Ordaz, visiting in Guadalajara, sent a conciliatory public message to the students, calling for national unity, extending the hand of friendship, a customary tactic of the presidency, and offering to start a dialogue with the students. The use of the army, however, meant that the students would ignore a gesture other students had readily sought in the past, for the president expressed no regret that his soldiers had attacked. At 4:30 that afternoon, Barros Sierra led an estimated 100,000 persons (some from IPN and other schools besides UNAM) north from the campus toward the center and then back south toward the campus. No incidents occurred as marchers shouted, chanted, sang, and waved placards castigating the government, and soldiers and policemen watched from the sides and intersections of streets. The rain that fell before the end of the march dampened enthusiasm only a little; once back on campus, the marchers held another meeting.[2]

On the IPN campus, faculty and student representatives met to create a group to coordinate the activities of faculty from both campuses, defend the student movement, and press for six demands. The demands were essentially the same as those made earlier by the FNET, CNED, a large IPN-UNAM group, and the PCM:

1. Respect for democratic liberties
2. Release of the professors, students, and citizens arrested since July 26
3. Abolition of Articles 145 and 145 *bis* of the Penal Code
4. Dismissal of the authorities responsible for the violence
5. Abolition of the granadero corps and prohibition of the creation of similar groups
6. Indemnification of the families of the injured students

Both sides were acting out their ceremonial roles.

The movement followed a traditional pattern for the next few days

[2]González de Alba, *Los días*, pp. 53–55, correctly argues that Barros Sierra's participation was essential to the success of the march. By leading it, he made it an all-UNAM affair instead of one of a few dissident students.

until new demands altered its character. On August 2, IPN professors issued six demands identical to those of the day before, FNET continued to cry conspiracy, IPN students announced their own mass march for the fifth, and *El Día* diagnosed the movement, correctly, as a student versus government conflict. By the fourth, the ENP and the economics school of UNAM were on strike. More significant, the students had organized political brigades of five to ten students, a tactic used in 1966, to proselytize and defend their actions to the citizenry; they had no confidence in the press, which continued to attack the movement. The new six demands, drawn up by representatives from IPN, UNAM, the agricultural school, and representatives from other schools and universities in the nation, went further than the previous sets. The students called for:

1. Liberty for political prisoners
2. Dismissal of [police chiefs] Generals Luis Cueto Ramírez and Raúl Mendiolea, and Lt. Colonel Armando Frías
3. Abolition of the granadero corps, direct instrument of repression, and prohibition of the creation of similar corps
4. Abolition of Articles 145 and 145 *bis* of the Penal Code, juridical instruments of aggression
5. Indemnification of the families of the dead and injured who had been victims of the aggression since July 26
6. Clarification of the responsibility of officials for the acts of repression and vandalism committed by the police, granaderos, and army

Most of these demands were impossible for the government to grant, for it would have to admit total responsibility and would allow students and their allies to control the government. Just as Portes Gil had rejected the demand for firings made by students in 1929, so too would Díaz Ordaz. Demands 1 and 4, which had emerged previously, had little or nothing to do with what had happened to students and should be seen as evidence of the impact of the left on the movement and as a symbolic protest against arbitrary government. The claim that students were killed was inflammatory, but the students produced no evidence that any student had been killed as a result of the melees or that, if a student had been killed, he was not trying to maim or kill a member of the public forces. On the other hand, by naming the persons they wanted fired, the students offered the government a concrete act that might pacify them.

The government continued to think that it could break the movement without using more force. When, on August 5, the IPN staged a mass march of some 100,000 through the streets near the institute, FNET leaders and their government sponsors had to recognize that FNET was useless, for it had tried to stage its own march two hours earlier but almost no one had come. The next day, FNET tried to undermine the central strike committee of IPN by claiming that its members were trying to influence the choice of the 1970 presidential candidate and that Central Intelligence Agency personnel and Communists were creating the trouble. The Confederacion de Jóvenes Mexicanos attested, for its part, that MURO (an ultraconservative student group), the CIA, and the FBI were behind the movement. On the seventh, IPN director Massieu, a reluctant participant in the mass march, called for a return to classes, having failed two days earlier to persuade IPN students to act independently of the others.

The movement could not end at that point, however, for neither side could claim victory; nothing had been settled. The government had admitted no guilt, contrary to what the students wanted, and soldiers and riot police continued to patrol the streets. The students refused to follow the government's lead and place the blame on non-Mexicans or "disloyal" Mexicans. From the government's viewpoint, to concede to the student demands was to concede the right to govern; from the students' viewpoint, to quit was to concede the right of the government to abuse citizens whenever it wanted and to allow the suffering of their peers to have been in vain. Besides, the government believed it had the necessary physical force; the students believed they had the necessary moral authority. That the movement was growing rapidly as more schools adhered to it sparked euphoria.

During these first nine days of August, the Coalition of Secondary and Higher Education Professors of the Nation for Democratic Liberties (CMEMSPPLD in Spanish), purporting to represent all IPN and most UNAM professors, joined the student movement. The coalition spoke for itself but gave an aura of professorial support to the students. When the government began arresting movement leaders, coalition leaders were among those singled out.

The most important group in the strike, the Consejo Nacional de Huelga (CNH) was composed of representatives from each of the schools involved in the strikes. The original structure included a plenary assembly with sovereignty and "political power of decision," but trying to congregate a majority of the more than 200,000 students was rarely possible, futile and even foolhardy later in the movement. Recognizing this, the students created the CNH, composed of committees dealing with the provinces, brigades, propaganda, finances, information, and juridical affairs. Each committee was to have two UNAM and two IPN representatives and one each from the National Agricultural School and the Normal School, thus totaling thirty-six persons. As the strike spread, the CNH grew to over 150 persons (some estimates run as high as 210) as more schools sent representatives. Membership fluctuated as the base assemblies in the individual facultades, escuelas, and other units coped with the issues.

The CNH proved to be a critical weakness of the movement. Many of its members came from the fight committees organized in UNAM in 1966, giving the council a more leftist or activist orientation than that of students in general. These tensions and those emanating from inter-school rivalry meant that members could commit their constituents only on selected issues, having to return to the general or base assembly of their representative schools for approval. The use of consensus techniques made decisions difficult to reach or alter in the face of events. Interminable debates were one result. Those with oratorical skill, persistence, and stamina could dominate sessions but not the movement, but a single individual, timing his suggestions properly, could effect the adoption of a favored tactic. The most serious weakness, however, was that the group was too large, too fluid, and too diverse in its composition to act effectively when a crisis occurred or new tactics were necessary. Once the six-point petition or the demand for a public dialogue was adopted, the CNH could not change them, thus having to live with a fatal inflexibility. When the government decided to arrest CNH members, lines of communications were disrupted, meetings became rump sessions, and the fugitive members could rarely assemble in one place.[3]

[3] González de Alba, *Los días,* pp. 83–85, 105. Other participants have also remarked on the difficulty of effective action by the CNH.

On the other hand, the CNH's representative and national character maintained student unity and forced the government to recognize its legitimacy. The consensus method offered a strong contrast to the authoritarianism of the government it was trying to reform. The large membership and the lack of a single identifiable leader meant that government agents could not stop the movement by arresting a single leader or a small group. That the CNH was formed and survived the tribulations of several months was a significant event in Mexican history, a fact the students knew.[4]

Given the structure of the CNH and the delicate task of maintaining a united front against the government, most of the social reform demands of the movement were made through the brigades, wall signs, handbills, placards, and university radio broadcasts. Few newspapers, save *El Día*, reported what the students wanted, for they feared government reprisal and/or opposed change. *El Día* reported some CNH social goals on August 9—the need for dialogue on creating union freedom, the institution of a forty-hour work week, the creation of people's fight committees to establish wage and price controls, and support of the farmers' fight committees to control the allocation of land. Handbills and other ephemeral literature in the collections of the Hemeroteca Nacional and the Instituto Nacional de Antropología e Historia are indicative of what the students were disseminating. Many were appeals to the citizenry to join the movement and its fight for democratic government, more schools, and an equitable distribution of wealth. Workers were reminded of government repression of the labor strikes of 1958–1959, teachers of the repression of their strike in 1958, and physicians of their strike in 1965.

The handbills became more critical of the inequities both in Mexico and in the world as the movement progressed through the weeks, but, contrary to the assertions of the government and its allies, few demanded revolution. German leftist journalists, visiting the student leadership, were astonished that the Mexicans were considered revo-

[4]González de Alba, *Los días*, contends that Marcelino Perelló was a publicity hound rather than a leader and that Sócrates Campos Lemus made the unauthorized demand on August 27 that the public dialogue be held in the Zócalo on September 1 at the exact time that the president made his State of the Union address. That the leaders of the movement were difficult to identify hurt as well as helped the movement.

lutionary because they were demanding the enforcement of a democratic constitution. Some real leftist groups, such as the Leftist Revolutionary Student Movement, tried to avail themselves of the opportunity to recruit followers and proselitize its views, but this was looking to the future.

Many observers, particularly within the government, remained baffled at the ability of the students to finance the movement, to produce the numerous handbills, placards, paid advertisements, and other paraphernalia that were so commonplace. During and after the movement, some government officials would insist that money was being poured into Mexico from hostile countries (the United States, the U.S.S.R., and France were often listed) or that local leftists or antigovernment persons were financing the movement.[5] Some money may have come from one or more of these sources, but it was hardly necessary. The students had control of the printing presses, mimeograph machines, and other facilities of their schools. No one could stop them from using them, nor could they be stopped from using the university radio stations. The UNAM administration might have been able to do so but decided to aid the students. Individuals in the movement contributed money or collected donations on the street, as had been done for decades. Given the amount of free facilities and free labor, the actual peso costs were small. The drama and excitement of the mass marches, street battles, and publicity easily sustained even casual participants.[6]

The CNH clearly emerged by August 10 as the one group that controlled the movement, as much as any group actually did, but the government tried not to acknowledge the fact, preferring to work through FNET and IPN director Massieu. Corona del Rosal sent a letter on August 9 to Massieu, ostensibly answering the FNET demands by agreeing to appoint a commission, composed of students, government officials, and others, to investigate the charges and study possible reforms. Although hailed by pro-government forces as a major concil-

[5] Sócrates Campos Lemus, after his arrest, asserted that Mexican politicians and educators were financing the movement. Since he was in government hands, the validity of his assertions is dubious.

[6] Zermeño, *México*, p. 62, argues that UNAM officials aided the movement with money, equipment, and orders to employees to cooperate. To what extent this was official policy is unclear. The students could appropriate much of what they used.

iatory act, the Corona del Rosal move was an effort to discredit and divide the movement, as the students realized immediately. The regent was ignoring the CNH and the non-IPN students in the movement, for the letter was sent to the IPN director, who had no authority in the strike but was a loyal government official. The CNH quickly pointed out that only it could speak for the student movement and that Corona del Rosal was laying a trap, that the commission would get bogged down in trivia and eventually disappear without anything concrete having been done, except to kill the movement.

As early as August 9, the IPN strike coordinating committee began demanding that the dialogue with the government be public so everyone would know what was happening; six days later the CNH adopted this demand. Initially, public dialogue meant that discussion of the differences between the students and the government could be held through newspapers, but radical members of the movement, probably not wishing for discussions to take place, managed to change the demand to mean televised discussions. On August 18, the CNH arrogantly "invited" congressional deputies to appear for a public debate on August 20, but none did. Government leaders, for their part, believed that they had gone as far as necessary, that Corona del Rosal's offer of an investigatory commission and Interior Minister Echeverría's public statement on August 22 that he was willing to talk, followed by a telephone call to the CNH, were enough.[7]

Government officials underestimated the strength of the movement and the ingenuity of its leaders, however, for the students found ways to revitalize the movement while avoiding the traps laid by the government. The Corona del Rosal letter, backed by editorials and public statements by important persons as to its generosity, put the students on the defensive and demoralized many. If the CNH did not act quickly to counter its effects, the government would only have to wait for the splintering and then demise of the movement. The CNH staged a march of some 300,000 from the National Anthropology Museum in Chapultepec Park through the main boulevard of the city to the Zócalo on August 13. The CNH had managed a coup, for it had demonstrated student unity, discipline, and dedication as well as its own authority in a single maneuver. Symbolically as well, the students

[7] González de Alba, *Los días*, pp. 58, 83.

had proven that they could go to the Zócalo. Few could thereafter doubt the unity or the seriousness of the movement.[8]

During the two weeks after the march, the CNH enjoyed the peak of its influence. The UNAM University Council met on August 15 and adopted some of the student demands; the effect was to bring the council into the movement, albeit on a limited basis. The CNH became more insistent on public dialogue, tried to stage the August 20 "debate" with congress, and formed six commissions to prepare for the public dialogue it thought it had been promised by Echeverría on the twenty-second. The initiative had shifted to the students; they appeared to be winning. Government officials were telephoning to discuss the details of the dialogue. The telephone calls produced more tactical debates within the CNH, however, for some feared they might become a private dialogue, one in which individual CNH leaders might betray the movement. Similarly, leaders debated whether it was wise to stage another mass march to the Zócalo while preparations for the dialogue were under way. Some argued that it would be a provocative act unnecessary because the students had proven that they could take control of the public plaza, so rich a symbol of government power. The rapture of power was too strong; the CNH responded to the insistence of a few leaders and announced an even larger march to the Zócalo for August 27, one that would demonstrate that the "people" were supporting the movement.[9]

The march surpassed the dreams of the organizers as some 400,000 persons, many of them non-students, began the trek down Reforma Boulevard to the Zócalo, carrying signs and chanting slogans. As in the case of earlier marches, the demonstrators and their signs demanded political and economic freedom, landed Mexican national heroes and Che Guevara, and supported not only the six demands of the movement but others popular with the Mexican left. President Díaz Ordaz was personally vilified, in spite of the tradition against criticizing the president. The huge public square, bounded on one side by the National Palace, on another by municipal buildings, and on a third by the

[8] Not all observers were pleased with the march; some argued that the students were acting improperly.

[9] Comité de Lucha de la Escuela Nacional de Economía, "La posición del Comité de Lucha de la Escuela Nacional de Economía," mimeo, Caja II, Archivo Estudiantil, Hemeroteca Nacional.

National Cathedral, filled with a mass of humanity. By the time all of the demonstrators entered the Zócalo, darkness was near, for the march had started after 5 P.M. Speakers railed to the crowd while street vendors plied their trade. The cathedral was illuminated; its bells tolled. A red and black flag, the international strike symbol, was run up a flag pole. Few government demonstrations could match it. Having taken the Zócalo once before, the students agreed to the suggestion of Sócrates Campos Lemus that they keep it this time. Some five thousand persons had agreed to stay as a permanent "guard."[10]

The government had been pushed too far. Counterattacks were launched immediately. No government would allow such a group to control such a place, nor would most be willing to allow such a mass movement to grow any further. The agreement to discuss the issues, using traditional rules that favored the government, had failed; the time for tough tactics had arrived. Shortly after midnight, on the morning of August 28, police, firemen, and soldiers, supported by armored cars, entered the Zócalo. When the "guard" did not immediately leave after being ordered out for holding an illegal assembly, the public forces attacked. As the students fled, the city lights went out, adding to the panic and confusion and allowing the government forces to act with impunity. The army quickly mastered the Zócalo. Later in the day, Minister of Defense García Barragán announced that the army had no intention of occupying the campuses of UNAM and the IPN, that its duty was to restore order and defend the nation against subversion. The next day, however, the army and granadero units broke up a meeting in the Nonoalco-Tlatelolco housing project area, which was near Voca #7 and the IPN. Porras, of unknown origin but probably government-supported, shot at Voca #7 on the twenty-ninth and would be used against other schools in ensuing days. Equally ominous was the discovery of dynamite in Voca #7 on August 30.

The CNH responded with two major decisions, one sensible, one idiotic. Without fully examining the consequences, the CNH, on August 28, demanded that the public dialogue be held in the Zócalo on the morning of September 1, the date and hour that the Mexican president traditionally delivered his state of the union address. Not only

[10] See Zermeño, *México*, p. 111, for the role of Campos Lemus. Campos Lemus may have been an agent provocateur; see Zermeño, p. 139.

was the demand impossible to meet, it was a clear statement that the CNH thought that it and not the government controlled the nation, that its demands took precedence. Few verbal acts could have challenged the authority of the government more directly. On the other hand, the CNH told its followers not to oppose the military, for that would lead to disaster. The next day, August 30, the CNH declared a moratorium until after the president spoke on September 1.

The Díaz Ordaz government accepted no moratorium and worked as rapidly as possible to undermine the student movement and turn Mexican and world opinion against the students. The officially anticlerical government charged the students with desecration of the cathedral by turning on its lights and ringing its bells! The red and black flag was cited as a symbol of foreign ideology, even communism (notwithstanding its use in Mexico and elsewhere as a strike symbol). The charges of subversion by disloyal Mexicans and by foreigners were again trotted out. A counterdemonstration by government employees, staged on the twenty-eighth, backfired when the small numbers that appeared took the students' side. Most important, the government again claimed that the students and their allies were trying to stop the Olympics.

When he spoke at length on the student movement in his September 1 State of the Union address (informe) to the Congress, Díaz Ordaz made his government's position absolutely clear. It would look at the issue of Articles 145 and 145 *bis*, but it emphatically denied the existence of political prisoners in Mexico. Laced through the speech, at some points in detail, were the warnings that the government would no longer tolerate resistance, that it would use whatever force was necessary to break the movement. Implicitly, Díaz Ordaz warned that if the students wanted to continue the politics of confrontation, they would be met with the might of an irate government unwilling to tolerate any more protests this close to the Olympics. Instead, Díaz Ordaz reiterated the government's offer of a dialogue and stressed that neither he nor his advisors had received a written petition. The olive branch was extended; the students could save face by accepting it.

In the first two weeks after the speech, Díaz Ordaz's tactic appeared to be working. Although the CNH complained that the president spoke only to two of the six demands, it sent a written petition to the president on September 4 and suggested the large auditorium at the Social Security Institute Medical Center as the site for the discussion. Rector Barros Sierra on September 8 issued a call for the return to classes, as did the political and social science professors' association on the twelfth. Even though some students demonstrated against the government while Díaz Ordaz was dedicating an Olympic site on September 13, the city was reasonably quiet. Student propaganda activities went on, brigades continued their work, and various leaders of the movement issued press releases. The army and the police forces remained on guard, but few incidents occurred. Overcoming presidential prestige and apparent reason appeared impossible.[11]

To revitalize the movement, the students reached back into the history of Mexican student movements and staged another giant march to the Zócalo, but this time in silence. Perhaps as many as 250,000 persons walked without talking, the only sounds coming from footsteps and the rustle of signs and clothing. By going in silence, the demonstrators avoided any possible confrontation with government forces. More important, they demonstrated that the movement was still alive and that the CNH was still in control. Even critics of the movement had to be impressed at the discipline involved in the undertaking.[12]

The government rekindled the violence by sending the army to take over UNAM on September 18. Why the soldiers who were stationed on the edges of the campus were suddenly called into action remains something of a mystery; the official government explanation was that UNAM had become a center of subversion (which was true), controlled by non-UNAM forces (which was not true), and the government had had to act to clear out this subversion so that normal academic activities could be resumed. The rationale was lame, for numerous schools were centers of subversion (in the sense that the students and their allies were trying to alter the existing political order) and the army occupation meant the end of all academic activities. When the army moved onto the campus, soldiers arrested everyone on sight, some fifteen hundred including parents attending examinations. One goal was to arrest the CNH, but most of its members who were there

[11]González de Alba, *Los días*, pp. 109–110 says the movement was confused during the first week of September.

[12]IPN students had used the tactic in the 1950s, and physicians had used it in 1965. On the physicians, see Stevens, *Protest and Response*, p. 213. See González de Alba, *Los días*, pp. 116–124, for a participant account of the march and the strategy behind it.

escaped. Unable to meet in a single place, the CNH had to yield authority to its central coordinating committee. The government, for its part, announced the next day that the army would give up UNAM when university authorities asked for its return; public outrage had had its effect. [13]

The choice of UNAM, rather than the IPN or some other school, for the invasion revealed the importance of UNAM in the movement. Since the army had invaded the IPN in 1956, a similar invasion in 1968 would have been less controversial than that of UNAM. The IPN and some of its vocational schools, where the movement started, were also centers of radicalism and thus likely targets of government ire. UNAM, however, was *the* elite institution and a long-term foe of whatever government was in power. Díaz Ordaz apparently had a special dislike for the university. At least his government believed that UNAM was the center of the movement and that crushing the university would crush the movement.

The army invasion of UNAM sparked a wave of violence and then the military takeover of the IPN. Street battles between students and their allies on the one hand and the army and police on the other erupted on September 19, continuing intermittently for days. Voca #7 near Tlatelolco again became a major battle scene. Porras attacked Prepa #4 and El Colegio de México, a prestigious private university, early on September 20, and then hit Voca #5, Prepa #5, and Prepa #9 on the twenty-third. Tensions rose. An army lieutenant killed a granadero in the Tlatelolco housing project because the policeman assaulted his mother. Barros Sierra resigned on September 23, under pressure from Congress and the executive branch. He believed his task hopeless. More serious, however, the army and police fought students on the IPN campus the same day. That evening and during the following day, it took control of the IPN. The CNH, which had planned to meet there, moved to the Tlatelolco housing project, which became the unofficial headquarters of the movement. [14]

[13] González de Alba, *Los días*, pp. 128–129, 148; Cosío Villegas, "Como en Grecia," took the view that the army occupation was unjustified because the army was winning.

[14] Bert Quint of CBS News reported student sniper fire in his televised report, September 24, 1968, CBS News, Vanderbilt University Television Archives. See also *El Sol de México*, September 24, 1968, Roll 2, #128, Instituto Nacional de Antropología e Historia, microfilm collection on students.

This massive use of force disoriented the movement, as the government intended, but did not stop it. The UNAM junta rejected Barros Sierra's resignation, but he lost some of the moral authority he had had in the movement. Soldiers in jeeps, armored cars, and tanks guarded the main streets of the city, giving the Olympics host city a strange appearance, for the welcoming signs and banners proclaiming peace and brotherhood floated above these armed contingents. The CNH held a mass meeting on the twenty-seventh in the Plaza de Tres Culturas in Tlatelolco, but it was clear that much of the spirit of the movement was gone; the leaders present called for another to be held there on October 2, followed by a march to the IPN, one they hoped would give new life to the movement. These were tense days for the students, however, for the army and police patrols were effectively breaking the momentum of the movement, and the leaders had to move constantly and secretly to avoid arrest. The willingness to use the army against UNAM and the IPN stifled much of the vocal support of the students and encouraged critics to speak more loudly.

The government sent signals that it believed it had won. On September 28, Díaz Ordaz named two representatives, Jorge de la Vega Domínguez and Andrés Caso (son of Alfonso), to begin the dialogue with the students. The latter were making even greater efforts to convince the government and the public that they would not interfere with the Olympic Games, as some charged, and were willing to have an Olympics truce. They publicly refused to meet with the presidential representatives, however, until the troops were pulled out of UNAM. On September 30, the troops withdrew from the national university, leaving behind them broken equipment, vandalized buildings, and a record of thefts. Quietly, CNH members and the presidential representatives began meeting. On October 1, no one bothered the CNH when it held two meetings on the UNAM campus. Agustín Yáñez, public education minister, began talking of educational reform during the week before October 2. Arrests of persons accused of criminal acts and subversion continued but posed little threat to the movement. CNH representatives met with Vega Domínguez and Caso on October 2 to discuss the demands.

In the late afternoon of October 2, the crowd began to gather in the Plaza of Three Cultures to hold still another rally, to be followed by a march to the IPN campus to protest the presence of troops there; a historic event was in the making, but not the one the organizers had intended. The atmosphere was tense, for army tanks, jeeps, trucks, and soldiers were stationed near the plaza, but they had become a common sight and no efforts were made to prevent persons from assembling. By 6 P.M., a crowd of several thousand, some say five, some say ten, had gathered in the historic plaza with its mixture of Aztec, Spanish Colonial, and modern Mexican architecture. Some were residents of the adjoining Nonoalco-Tlatelolco housing project; men, women, and children had joined the students in what had become a commonplace diversion from the humdrum of everyday life. The plaza had several assets as a meeting place. The army had not taken control of it as it had the IPN or UNAM, and its open area allowed large numbers to congregate. Many residents of the housing project had demonstrated sympathy for the student cause, so the organizers knew they were in friendly territory. The plaza was easily reached from all parts of the city. More important, the Chihuahua building (the apartment buildings were named after states) had a large fourth-floor balcony from which orators could address the crowd below.

The rally was, in fact, a signal of the waning power of the student movement. Its numbers could not approach those reached earlier. The presence nearby of the army unnerved many, and rumors wormed through the crowd that government agents were present. After a few almost perfunctory speeches, leaders announced that the march to the IPN was called off, that it was too dangerous and might provoke a violent reaction from the army.

Shortly after six o'clock the rally became a nightmare as soldiers invaded the plaza, shooting into the crowd. The government contended that the troops advanced in response to sniper fire from the buildings. The reality was different. Shortly before the advance, a helicopter, circling the area, dropped two flares. Soldiers and policemen in the crowd, dressed in civilian clothes, donned white gloves on their left hands, or wrapped them in white handkerchiefs, to identify themselves from the mass. As the soldiers advanced, killing and maiming as they assaulted the fleeing, panic-stricken crowd, some of these white-gloved personnel entered the Chihuahua balcony and arrested those present, taking the opportunity to strike at will or to force them to lie where there was the greatest danger of being hit by flying bullets. Television crews from ABC and CBS, in town for the Olympics, filmed some of the action until they too had to flee to safety. The government forces were attacking everyone, and foreign newsmen were important targets. The films leave little doubt that the army initiated the violence and that innocent women and children were attacked.[15]

The massacre lasted for hours. Crowds fled in waves from one part of the plaza to another, only to turn and run again. Soldiers fired toward the center at the crowds and at each other; the crossfire was indiscriminate. Some soldiers, including those on the balcony, cried "Olympic Battalion!" to identify themselves to their fellows as members of the elite squad organized to provide protection during the games to celebrate peace and brotherhood. Tanks and other armored vehicles blocked passage, but at least their cannons were not fired into the crowds or the buildings. Students died; children died; women died; and soldiers died. No one knows how many. Certainly more than the fifty-seven the government claimed, perhaps as many as the three hundred the students claimed. Some of the dead and injured were carted away in Red Cross and Green Cross ambulances, when the army finally let them do their work, but others were taken away in military vehicles. Students and their allies claimed that bodies were burned by the government to hide the death toll. There were fires that night in Military Camp One in Chapultepec Park, from which these army units had come and to which the thousands of arrested were taken. Blood flowed that night; the Aztecs had returned to human sacrifice. The elders were devouring their young.[16]

The Tlatelolco massacre made no sense except that it stopped the movement a few days before the Olympic Games opened. Even if one accepts the government argument that snipers had begun to fire from the buildings, one is hard pressed to explain why soldiers fired again and again into a crowd. Standard procedure would have been to clear the plaza of the crowd and then use sharpshooters against snipers. The goal of the maneuver must have been different. Nor could it have been the arrest of the CNH leaders, most of whom were gathered on the balcony, for agents could have arrested them without any army assault. Certainly, some of the deaths and injuries were the result of poor leadership and panic among the soldiers, who did not know what to do in

[15]See the videotapes from ABC News and CBS News for October 3, 1968, Vanderbilt Television Archives.

[16]Octavio Paz, *The Other Mexico*, makes this argument.

the face of gunfire, but the white-gloved agents' act of grabbing leaders in the crowd so they could be shot bespoke another purpose. The government had failed to stop the movement by taking UNAM and had failed again when soldiers occupied the IPN. The Olympics were only days away. Frustrated, angry, irrational men decided to end the movement quickly, not fully realizing that unleashing the army would result in such a catastrophe. Undoubtedly, they intended that some would die and others would be hurt, but that must have seemed a small price if the result was the death of the movement and the arrest of the CNH.

Faced with the infamy of its actions, the government immediately tried to justify those actions. The rationales offered were not surprising. Student snipers fired first; machine gun fire from the Chihuahua building brought in the army to protect the crowd and the residents. Confessions of "leaders" proved that the entire student movement was a conspiracy to install a Communist regime in Mexico and to thwart the Olympics. Sócrates Campos Lemus, of the CNH and IPN, "confessed" that the goal was the abolition of existing institutions and the creation of a workers'-farmers' state, that six snipers were stationed in Tlatelolco to fire on soldiers and granaderos if they tried to break up the meeting, and that a number of distinguished intellectuals and politicians had financed the movement. The army, for its part, produced a list and 'photographs' of arms it found in buildings around the plaza; these "proved" that there was a revolutionary conspiracy.

Confessions and arrests of known leftists are easily arranged, although the validity of such confessions is dubious, but the arms list reveals the weak case of the government. Found were three submachine guns, fourteen .22-caliber rifles with telescopic sights, five shotguns, four carbines, twenty-one revolvers, ten angle irons, 425 shotgun shells of 12 and 16 gauge, nine hundred .38-caliber cartridges, 1,850 cartridges for the twenty-twos, twenty of .38 caliber, five of 7 millimeter, equipment for recharging cartridges, a radio transceiver, some dynamite, and a few other minor pieces. Since over 70,000 persons lived in the 144 buildings, the list is surprising only because so few weapons were found. More weapons would probably have been found in the same number of apartments along Lake Shore Boulevard in Chicago. As evidence that a revolution was planned or that an army was needed in Tlatelolco, the list did not vindicate the stupidity and cruelty of government officials responsible for its release.

The student movement of 1968 died in Tlatelolco on the night of October 2; the burial took place on December 1 when the strike was officially ended. Those student leaders who were not killed or arrested on October 2 went into hiding in the city, or disappeared into the states, or exiled themselves in countries around the world. Other students absented themselves as well; it was not a good time to stay in Mexico City. The horror of Tlatelolco lent credence to the widespread belief among students and their supporters that the government was killing or imprisoning students months after October 2; perhaps it was. Some prisoners were not sentenced for over a year after their arrest. The Olympics came and went, for the Olympic Committee, by a close vote, decided not to withdraw from Mexico. A rump CNH (now in the hands of diehards) made announcements to the media and held various meetings with the two presidential representatives. The six demands were never met. More political prisoners filled Mexican jails; Articles 145 and 145 *bis* were repealed in 1970, but their offensive provisions were inserted into other statutes. Students became more apathetic and suspicious; some retreated into drugs and drink, sex and cynicism.

Student efforts to revive the movement and to free their comrades failed, for Díaz Ordaz would not budge. In January 1969, Mexico City police received new weapons, including fifteen tanks. UNAM suspended classes for several days later that month because of protest rallies, but the new weapons were not needed. In mid-April, seventy students were arrested for protesting. On July 23, the anniversary of the fracas that had been so important the year before, police intervened in a prep school fight; one person died but no marches were staged. Two months later, on the anniversary of the battle for the Casco de Santo Tomás of the IPN, police used machineguns to terminate anti-government student protests; newsmen were barred from the scene. During October 1–2, granaderos patrolled Tlatelolco and important streets; the show of force prevented any trouble except for a sit-in at the National Cathedral, broken up by police. Student prisoners launched a hunger strike in Lecumberri prison in late December, fasting into January 1970, to demand bail or speedy trials, but the effort failed. After the national presidential elections in July, students at UNAM and the IPN demonstrated for the release of political prisoners, hoping that the president-elect, Echeverría, would intervene.

A more lenient policy emerged under Echeverría. From November 28 through December 3, UNAM went on strike to demand amnesty for the prisoners, but the judge sentenced sixty-eight of them. Echeverría, having taken office the preceding December, arranged to have charges dropped against seventy-two professors and students, most arrested in 1968, but others remained in jail. Nor did the leftist seizure of seven UNAM schools in April attain their release, for it was not until later that the Echeverría government began releasing the prisoners. In late 1978, the López Portillo government passed a general amnesty law and the last of those arrested in 1968 returned to civilian life.

Students received mixed signals from the Echeverría government until the June 10 (1971) incident. Since September 1969 the University of Nuevo León in the industrial city of Monterrey had been the center of disputes between the universitarios and the state government and different factions within national politics. In March 1971, Governor Eduardo Elizondo had the university's organic law, which resembled UNAM's of 1933, replaced by a new one, creating a popular assembly of thirty-six persons (of whom three were students and three were professors) to govern the university. The governor appointed the rector and the directors. The assembly included workers, farmers, and businessmen, but the left objected because PRI and the conservative establishment would, in its opinion, control the university. Elizondo revealed the purpose of the law when he appointed the ex-director of the state PRI organization, Arnulfo Treviño Garza, as rector. Student protests followed. Pablo González Casanova, UNAM rector since 1970, publicly opposed the law and was joined by other university rectors. Secretary of Public Education Víctor Bravo Ahuja, at Echeverría's behest, scurried to Monterrey and had the law changed within two days. Elizondo resigned, to be replaced by Luis M. Farías, the leader of the anti-UNAM forces in the Chamber of Deputies in 1968. The students had won a partial victory.[17]

The Coordinador de Comités de Lucha (CoCo), representing the activists in control of UNAM, the IPN, and the agricultural school,

[17]The best account of these and following events is Gerardo Medina V., *Operación 10 de junio.* Medina, a PAN press official, qualifies his statements. Other accounts used are Antonio Solís Mimendi, *Jueves de corpus sangriento (revelaciones de un halcón)*; Orlando Ortiz, ed., *Jueves de corpus;* and Manlio Tirado, et al., *El 10 de junio y la izquierda radical.*

supported the Monterrey movement and planned a mass protest demonstration for June 10, when Echeverría intervened, CoCo decided to stage the march anyway. CoCo was a leftist organization, for Tlatelolco had temporarily frightened conservative and moderate students out of university politics. Some moderate right and ultra-right students had been recruited into porras and engaged in terror tactics. CoCo decided that the students should march in support of textile workers (engaged in a dispute with employers), university autonomy, and freedom for political prisoners. The march was a major tactical error, for nothing concrete could be gained.[18]

Police officials tried to persuade the students not to march because they might be attacked by right-wing gangs, but stood passive while the attack was launched. As the marchers came down San Cosme Street, near the Normal School and PAN headquarters, gray buses and cars disgorged young men, armed with staves and rifles, who attacked the marchers, bystanders, and newsmen. Not only did the police not interfere, they apparently loaned their communications system to the attackers, Halcones (hawks). Not satisfied with the street attack, the Halcones pursued their victims into hospitals and sequestered them. The death toll is disputed, but at least eleven persons died.

Echeverría disclaimed responsibility, but the evidence points to the conclusion that members of his government trained and paid the Halcones and sent them against the students. Echeverría promised a full investigation and punishment of the guilty, but he delivered little. Alfonso Martínez Domínguez resigned as regent (presidentially appointed chief executive officer of Mexico City), as did the police chief and the attorney general. They obviously had been fired. Independent testimony and investigation linked the Halcones to right-wing government officials. Some suggested that high-ranking army officers were linked to the group. Theories abounded that the right wing of PRI was trying to embarrass the new president, who was adopting a leftist stance and who tried to woo academic leaders with larger appropriations. Regardless, Echeverría paid a price, for students increased their hostility toward him. When he went to UNAM in 1975, they booed and threw stones and bottles at him; one hit him on the head. He never went back.

[18]Roberto Escudero and Salvador Martínez Della Roca, "Mexico," pp. 14–15.

After 1971, Echeverría made unsuccessful overtures to students. He had the age qualification to hold congressional posts lowered, promised a democratic opening, supported educational reform, and took a Third World position in foreign affairs. Some students from the 1968 movement took government posts and others were released from jail. Educational reform came to mean the creation of more schools, including the Colegios de Ciencias y Humanidades by UNAM and the Colegios de Bachilleres in 1973 and the Metropolitan Autonomous University in 1974 by the government. The last has high admission standards and fees and is obviously intended as a rival to UNAM. Activist students were not impressed.[19]

The most serious strike in UNAM after 1968 involved employees, not students, in 1973. The employees demanded better pay and working conditions. Some students struck in sympathy, but not the entire student body. Rector Pablo González Casanova, a leftist who had replaced Barros Sierra in 1970, resigned in 1973. The university, in his view, was ungovernable.

Guillermo Soberón, rector from 1973 to the date of this writing, has been able to govern UNAM, but he has not tried to make major alterations in the university and has enjoyed government support. Serious professors and students rely more and more on institutes rather than the facultades and escuelas for teaching and research. Political sloganeering and meetings by students are common, but students are reluctant to be interviewed by scholars investigating student movements.

Student strikes have not ended permanently in UNAM. Local strikes in facultades and escuelas continue. Once the memory of 1968 is dim enough and a cause célèbre is discovered, UNAM students will once again shut down the university in protest. Students will continue to be concerned about grades, examination policy, and unpopular teachers and administrators, as well as social and political issues. But these strikes or movements will forever be different from what they once were. The horror of Tlatelolco will hang over UNAM for decades to come.

[19] See Yoram Shapira, "Mexico: The Impact of the 1968 Student Protest on Echeverría's Reformism," *Journal of Inter-American Studies and World Affairs* 19 (1977): 557–580, for a broad summary of the effects of the student movement.

10. Perspectives

In the early years of the National University, students played a minimal role in the development of the national political system, in spite of their efforts to create a student movement or student "class." The creation of student organizations predated the reopening of the university in 1910, but these organizations were specific to particular facultades or escuelas. Almost simultaneously with the creation of the National University of Mexico in 1910, students made an effort to create a Federal District–wide student organization. The effort died aborning, for the Mexican Revolution began that same year. Individual students joined the Revolution, but their scant numbers and lack of cohesion meant that it was not proper to speak of a student component of that Revolution. Not until 1916, when Venustiano Carranza had emerged as leader of Mexico, did students again try to create a single student organization, the Federación. This group had little effect on the university until several years after its formation. Student interest was captivated by other matters.

One of the earliest concrete interests of these students was the achievement of university autonomy. The various resolutions they passed and the bills they sent to Congress on autonomy shared a common desire: the removal of the university from political control. The autonomy advocates wanted the university to become a self-governing organization, one that selected its own leaders and decided its own internal rules. None of these proposals received the necessary congressional approval nor did any president adopt one as a goal of his administration. Instead, the idea continued to float in university circles.

The Latin American University Reform Movement, which began in 1918, also advocated autonomy, and Mexican students benefited from this larger movement. Their demands preceded the Córdoba, Argentina, student revolt of 1918, for autonomy and co-government were "old" Mexican student demands by the time of the epic Argentine upheaval. Since UNAM was born (or reborn, depending on how one counts) just before the Mexican Revolution, which occasioned the rise of many young men to power, the idea that young people could revolutionize their societies was not new in Mexico in 1918 either. What the hemispheric reform movement did was to add legitimacy and authority to the desires of Mexican students and promote networks and contacts. Events in countries such as Argentina and Peru made the Mexican demands appear less radical. Contacts kept the ideas alive. Mexican students, however, could also argue that their country, which had had a social revolution, was less progressive than other Latin American nations, thereby embarrassing Revolutionary leaders, and they could use their organizations as pressure groups in behalf of their interests.

Students expressed interest in social reform and opposition to conservative governments in the 1920s, but their essential lack of unity vitiated any claim to speak for all students. The Federación Estudiantil Universitaria, which claimed to represent all university-level students but which was controlled by National University students, elected officers, issued resolutions, split occasionally into rival groups, and then re-formed into a single federation. The other important student organization, the Confederación Nacional de Estudiantes, shared a similar history. Almost always dominated by National University students from the Federal District, it had little influence in determining national policy, educational or otherwise, in spite of its efforts to do so. Instead, the FEU and CNE advocated the goals of the Mexican Revolution, criticized governments that ignored these goals, and spent most of their efforts in intra-university struggles. As a factor in the national politics of 1910–1928, the FEU and CNE were negligible.

The importance of these early student organizations lay in their role in giving political experience to persons who would later become important state- or national-level politicians. They provided the opportunity for students to identify themselves to each other and to the governing group as persons who had the interest and aptitude for political activity. The number of FEU and CNE presidents in the 1916–1934 period who became important political figures is significant. Although no statistical techniques have been applied to these data, there is ample evidence that holding these posts was important for their later political careers.

In addition, the existence of the CNE made a difference in 1929, for it gave the strike leaders of that year an organizational base with which to pressure the government. Students had struck and demonstrated against specific components of the university before, and the government had used policemen and soldiers to control the student protests. In 1929, however, the strike leaders were able to call on their peers throughout the nation to strike in support of the National University cause. Without the experience and contacts of the CNE and the network it created, the 1929 strike would not have been as effective.

The granting of partial autonomy in 1929 was the result of a fortuitous chain of circumstances. That Emilio Portes Gil was president was important. Having attended the National University and been a student strike leader himself, and being a friend and acquaintance with many persons within the small cadre of university-trained people, he knew the university's desire for autonomy and was not antagonistic to the institution. As a former student activist he understood student behavior. Pressed on several sides in the critical year of 1929, he yielded to the students something that appeared to be of minor consequence in order to buy room to maneuver to deal with more important problems. Since a number of student leaders were active partisans of Vasconcelos, the autonomy law must have been particularly appealing, since it might dilute student support for the ex-rector and switch some of it to the government. No one could have predicted what would actually result from that decision, however.

The 1929 movement was the pivotal movement in the modern history of the National University. As the first general strike, it set both a precedent and a pattern for subsequent strikes. Partial autonomy was the critical first step toward full autonomy. The failure of the 1929 strike would have had a chilling effect on national student politics for years. Its success in achieving something, albeit not what the students had originally demanded, catapulted numerous young men into prominence and encouraged others to try the same tactics. The myth of a national student movement was given credibility. Students saw themselves as real or potential paladins against an oppressive state. Even conservative students of the 1930s advocated social reform, social justice, and anti-imperialism. It became a common argument by students that the state was corrupt but that the "pure" Mexican youth would fight to save the Mexican Revolution. The 1929 strike assumed a legendary place in Mexican history; in 1979, *Tiempo*, the weekly newsmagazine, devoted page after page to the strike and its outcome. In other places, the Generation of 1929 was feted at a banquet and hailed for its heroic deeds.

Although the 1929 strike did not achieve the complete autonomy of the university, it served several other important purposes. A number of strike leaders were also supporters of the presidential ambitions of José Vasconcelos. Even while Vasconcelos was being defeated in the 1929 presidential elections (for his defeat was a foregone conclusion), his supporters were gaining additional influence within the National University. These Vasconcelistas included not just students such as Gómez Arias but also professors such as Gómez Morín, who was the treasurer of the Vasconcelos campaign. By granting partial autonomy and by making university governance more democratic, Portes Gil was giving the losers in national politics a means of saving face and a role in influencing future national development. Whether he intended to do so or not is unclear. Portes Gil did not give control of UNAM to the Vasconcelistas, however; he insisted that his man be appointed rector. Moreover, the 1929 autonomy law guaranteed that the Mexican president would retain substantive control over the university.

The government lost control of UNAM in 1933 when it had to referee the fight between those who wanted to preserve academic freedom and those who wanted to require all teaching to be Marxist. Lombardo Toledano and others who would be strong supporters of Cárdenas decided to take control of UNAM from the traditionalists in 1933. Their move was part of a general movement toward "socialist education." UNAM was slow to change, however, for its faculty and students held traditional views of higher education. When the Lombardo Toledano group passed their pro-Marxism resolution in 1933, these traditionalists quickly organized an opposition movement that not only forced the Lombardo Toledano group from the university but also interested in socialism per se than in education that directly served society, that is, technological and scientific as opposed to humanistic education. UNAM was part of a general movement toward "socialist education" that was emerging in 1933. Socialist education, always ill-defined, was often 'misnamed, for many of its proponents were less caused interim president Abelardo Rodríguez to jettison the university. Rodríguez was not an advocate of socialist education, but he was unwilling to countenance rebellion by a government agency. Unable to seize control of the university because of the weight of tradition in favor of its independence and because of his imminent departure from office (his successor, Cárdenas, had been nominated and was campaigning), he made an independent university out of it. Few expected UNAM to survive under such circumstances. Testimony to Congress in favor of the 1933 autonomy bill made this quite clear; Secretary of Education Narciso Bassols testified that the government would have full control of the university within a short time. When UNAM reentered the government's ranks, he said, it would do the government's bidding.

The anti-UNAM forces miscalculated, however, for the UNAM forces were able to keep the university afloat without government subsidy for two years. The central figure of the 1933–1935 drama was Manuel Gómez Morín, even though he served as rector for only one year. He was one of the Siete Sabios, brilliant student leaders of what is called the Generation of 1915. With the accession of Gómez Morín to the rectorship, the Generation of 1915 and the Generation of 1929 assumed full control of the university. They filled the important posts and raised the monies necessary to fund the institution. Vasconcelistas could be rallied around UNAM; many of them were professors and administrators there. Catholic activists, particularly from UNEC, rallied as well, in part to keep Marxism out of UNAM, in part to wrest control of the university from the secularly minded. Non-governmental groups could not operate UNAM for long, however. The institution was too big, expensive, and important to remain outside the governmental budget. Survival demanded some modus vivendi.

Chico Goerne was able to create that needed modus vivendi. He was an UNAM alumnus, a distinguished academician, a man of affairs, and a clever politician in his own right. He quickly recognized that student activism was a principal cause of dissatisfaction with the university by government officials. Student activists, from both the left and the right, kept the university in sufficient turmoil to prevent normal operations. No government would want to fund such an institution. Constant student disruptions made it appear that the government was incapable of ruling, thus weakening the national government at home and abroad. Chico made deals with student leaders and hired student gangs or porras to police student politics. Student elections were rigged to guarantee officers who would support Chico. Although students were also given greater power in university governance, this was not risky, because Chico's control of student politics insured friendly students on the University Council. These measures pleased President Cárdenas, for they demonstrated that Chico knew how to govern.

Chico went beyond controlling student politics; he moved the university into supporting the Mexican Revolution. Through his friendship with Luis I. Rodríguez, personal secretary to Cárdenas, Chico was able to convince Cárdenas that UNAM was no longer a bulwark of conservatism. Cárdenas thereafter resumed the subsidy to UNAM. Although Chico was eventually thrown out by students and faculty members who accused him of making UNAM a personal fiefdom, he had fully reintegrated UNAM into the government's orbit.

This rapprochement lasted until 1968 with only one exception. Brito Foucher, an ultraconservative, tried to use UNAM as a power base from which to pursue personal political causes. In essence, he began moving UNAM into opposition to the government again. That he was overthrown through student demonstrations, riots, and violence obscured what was at stake, for many thought the problem to be ungovernable students, whereas the real cause of his overthrow was his oppositionist stance. The Caso law of 1945, which created the present governance system and prevented students from controlling or even greatly influencing the university's internal policies, was seen as the definitive answer to student politics. It did not, however, prevent the student upheavals of the late 1940s and the ouster of rectors in those years, a fact often overlooked. Peace returned to UNAM in 1948 with the advent of a politically astute rector. He and his successors would maintain cordial relations with the government. By not giving high government officials any reason to intervene in the university, rectors were able to keep student disputes at the local level. The ouster of Chávez in 1966, often seen as a move by the Díaz Ordaz administration, owed more to Chávez's tough-minded academic policies confronting "New Left" students inspired by Castroism than to any animus of the national president.

Student political activity changed after the Caso law in large part because the university was growing so fast and because it was relocated some ten miles from the National Palace. Dramatic increases in the number of students made the 1930s-style political activism difficult; personal politics can be difficult inside a mass institution. The distance between the new campus and the buildings of the national government meant that student demonstrations had less urgency and were less likely to be met by police repression, the key to generalized student strikes. Efforts in 1961 to prevent Chávez from becoming rector and his successful ouster in 1966, both important in the history of UNAM, remained localized because police repression was not used.

This restraint was not true in the 1929 and 1968 strikes, the two most important in UNAM history, and the use of and reaction to police repression made the two strikes similar even though their origins differed. In both cases, the protests and demonstrations might have been contained had governments (Mexico City and national) not used force against the students. By doing so, they unified the students, for the use of violence potentially affected *all* students. In both cases, students made an effort to solidify students into a national unit. In 1929, the university students tried to create Federal District–wide student organizations in addition to the FEU and the CNE. In 1968, the Consejo Nacional de Huelga was an effort to create a national student movement. The students failed in both instances because violence against students was the only unifying factor, one that did not last long. Neither strike began as an anti-government movement but each became one because the government mishandled the situation.

Once a strike became generalized, it became a confrontation between the university and the state. UNAM, as a state dependency, regardless of its legal status, ultimately reports to the national government, for the latter funds it. If controversy or a strike escapes the confines of the university and spills into the public arena, only the national government (the president) can deal with it. The Mexico City government has limited authority because the regent is a presidential appointee and the university is funded by the national, not the local, government. Confrontation was avoided for a number of years after the campus was moved to the southern part of the Federal District, for the distance discouraged potential strikers or, at least, made general strikes difficult. By 1966 the improvements in the transportation and communications systems facilitated general strikes by making it easier for students to assemble and by keeping everyone informed of the events through radio, television, and newspapers. The state could no longer ignore a strike, although in 1966 there was little overt state intervention.

The 1968 strike was different from its predecessors for a number of reasons. Its origins were external to the university in that they had nothing to do with exam policy, curriculum, fees, or university governance. Instead, the strike on the part of UNAM students began when the university was attacked by soldiers. The underlying causes of the strike are harder to identify. Alienation from mass society, the popularity of New Left ideology within the university, the control established in 1966 by the comités de lucha inside UNAM, the conservative and iron-fisted policies of Díaz Ordaz, and the uncertainty of future personal careers on the part of persons trained in the humanities and social sciences in a society that was increasingly technological all served as causes. The 1968 strike had a surrealistic quality to it, for it was unprecedented in Mexican history. Never before had hundreds of thousands of demonstrators marched through the streets denouncing the government, had UNAM and IPN students cooperated so closely, or had the government so blatantly used violence against its elite youth. The last of these, the extensive use of force, is the hallmark of 1968, however. Precisely why governmental officials (or which governmental officials) decided to use force and to escalate that force remains clouded. When they—or he, as the case may be—made that choice, the controversy quickly changed.

Government officials have rarely faced the choice of using force against UNAM students, however, for there have been surprisingly few general strikes in UNAM history. There were only eight, at most, in the sixty-one years covered by this study: 1929, 1933, 1934, 1938, 1944, 1945, 1948, and 1968. Little actual experience with mass UNAM strikes was actually available. Even for those who knew the course of earlier strikes, experience was not a perfect guide.

These eight general strikes resemble each other but differ in important ways from their predecessors. The 1929 and 1968 strikes were unusual because of their scale and intensity; both were national strikes. Those of 1933 and 1934 were interrelated in that both were struggles against socialist education, the first within the university, the second in the society at large. Throughout the 1933–1938 period, leftists and rightists, through students, fought for control of UNAM. Neither Gómez Morín nor Ocaranza, both conservatives, could stop leftist political activity, nor could Chico stop the constant sallies of rightists. The creation of Acción Nacional (PAN) in 1939 by Gómez Morín provided an outlet for many opponents of Cardenismo or socialism; having a pro-government rector, Baz, in office in 1938–1940 pacified others. Chico left in the 1938 strike because of accusations about his integrity, not because of ideological or academic disagreements. De la Cueva, interim rector for 1940–1942, followed Baz's lead. The next strike came in 1944 against Brito Foucher, personally ambitious and so conservative the Panistas rejected him as too conservative. The 1944 strike, which appears to have been an arranged strike, was the last of the truly ideological struggles and represents, in a sense, the last gasp of the struggles of the 1930s.

The 1945 and 1948 strikes resembled the 1929 strike in that they originated in controversies over curricula and exams, with the underlying issue of who should control university governance. In all three strikes, students protested exam policy because a change would toughen standards. In 1929 and 1948, the proposed changes in curricula, lengthening the time necessary for the completion of a degree, brought more students into the strike. In 1948, in addition, the proposal to raise fees brought even more students into the fray. The 1945 and 1948 strikes were contained within UNAM, unlike that of 1929, because police repression was not used. In all three, students wanted a larger say in university governance, something they achieved only in 1929.

Although presidents must contend with general strikes, these strikes are not inherently caused by presidential electoral politics. The strikes are not efforts to influence presidential elections. Coding each year from 1910 through 1971 as either a presidential election year (or successful coup) as Yes=1 or No=0 and for the existence of a general university strike (Yes=1, No=0), the Pearson r is -0.073 (R² = .005); not only is there little relationship between the two, but what there is turns out to be negative. Strikes did occur in the presidential election years of 1929 and 1934, and both strikes involved national politics. In 1929, many strike leaders were Vasconcelistas; in 1934, many were part of the anti-Cárdenas, anti-socialist education movement. Pre-election maneuvering during the year before the election and post-election maneuvering to test the will and policies of the new president are two other possible ways the strikes might influence presidential politics.

For both possibilities, correlation coefficients were determined; they were even lower than the one above, and that approach was abandoned as being useless. General strikes do not cycle with presidential elections or successful coups.

The issue of presidential politics remains important, nevertheless, for the president must play the key role in resolving UNAM general strikes or other strikes; he is expected to play the role of the great mediator. When he does not, events get out of hand. A comparison of the 1929 and 1968 UNAM strikes illustrates this point well. In 1929 the decision to use force was made by local officials, whereas in 1968 the national government quickly decided to send riot police and then soldiers. In 1929, Portes Gil, who was out of town when the repression started, was able to act as a mediator because he had no personal responsibility for what Federal District or National University officials had done. Díaz Ordaz could not assume the same stance successfully in 1968 because the army had been used. Once the army intervened there was no one who could offer his "good offices" as a mediator. Díaz Ordaz was a participant; Portes Gil was not. The students recognized this and demanded that the public become the mediator. That is why they demanded that negotiations take place in public. Such a demand could not be met by the government without negating its authority. From the government point of view, essentially correct, what the students were demanding was subversive and revolutionary; to accede was to invite rebellion. From the student point of view, only restoration of constitutional norms (which they believed the government had longed ignored) and total honesty could save the day. Forced to choose between its potential demise, on the one hand, and repression, on the other, the government chose the latter and won, just as it had done in the 1956 IPN strike, when it also used soldiers against students.

Rather than citing presidential politics as a cause of UNAM general strikes, some observers believe that student participation on the University Council increased the frequency of such strikes. The relationship is more complicated than it would first appear, however. Student achieved voting parity with professors in 1929 as a result of the autonomy law of that year. Yet, *the* general strike of 1929 came under the old governing rules. Similarly, during the 1929–1933 period, when students first enjoyed a large voice in the council, the only widespread strike was that of October 1933 and was the result of the attempt to make UNAM a Marxist institution. Given the opposition that would prevail against such an effort, student and faculty protests would have occurred even without student participation in governance. Likewise, continued student and faculty opposition to the socialist education amendment to Article 3 of the Constitution produced the 1934 strike, not student participation on the council. The 1934 strike and the departure of Ocaranza in 1935 were part of the struggle between UNAM and the state. Chico's departure in 1938 was not just the result of a student movement, although the charges against him did include his manipulation of student politics. The ouster of Brito Foucher in 1944 was not simply a student movement; the role of Yáñez was too important. Fernández Mac Gregor and Zubirán were driven out by students, but under the Caso law, which had shifted power to the junta, on which students were not represented. That is, students had less official power than they had had since before the 1929 strike. The Caso law itself did not stop student strikes. Instead, the combination of rectors supported by the national government and the impediments to student politics presented by the Caso law stopped the strikes. That Chávez was driven out in 1966 validates this point, for Chávez had lost government support; the Caso law could not protect him. Student participation in university governance does not cause general strikes.

Since rectors are booted from office during general strikes, a plausible explanation for the origin of such strikes is that they are staged to change the top university leadership. It is hard for a rector to stay in office if he does not have the support of the president. Between 1910 and 1929, the rector reported to the president or to the secretary of education, and his tenure was subject to that of the president. Eguía Lis, appointed by Porfirio Díaz, left after Huerta assumed control of the nation. Ezequiel A. Chávez, appointed under Huerta, left when his patron went into exile. Valentín Gama came to office under Carranza's temporary control but yielded to Macías in July 1915 when Carranza had withdrawn from Mexico City. Macías survived the shifting governments created by the struggle between Carranza and Villa, Zapata, and others. He yielded to Dávalos, appointed during the provisional presidency of Adolfo de la Huerta. Dávalos was replaced by José Vasconcelos a month later. Vasconcelos moved up the hierarchy to become secretary of education, putting Silva y Aceves and then Antonio Caso in his place. After the 1923 ENP dispute and the beginning of the presidential campaign, Caso left and Chávez returned, only to leave in December 1924 when Calles became president. Castro Leal became rector in December 1928 when Portes Gil became interim president, but was pushed out by students the next year.

New organic laws made little difference. García Téllez continued under Portes Gil, Pascual Ortiz Rubio, and Abelardo Rodríguez, the three presidents of 1928–1934. His successor, Medellín, lost the support of Rodríguez because of his defense of socialist education. With the Bassols law of 1933, the council elected two anti-government rectors, Gómez Morín and Ocaranza; they lasted about one year each. Chico, appointed in 1935, convinced President Cárdenas that UNAM supported the government. He stayed until Gustavo Baz led a movement against him. If Baz represented the forces of Manuel Ávila Camacho, who appointed Baz to a cabinet post in 1940, then the pattern of the necessity of presidential support holds true. Ávila Camacho, a conservative who pursued a national unity policy, could easily tolerate the conservatism of Cueva and the even more conservative Brito Foucher. The latter's use of porras, conservatism, and political ambitions (the obvious meaning of his statement that the rectorship was the second most important public position in the country) contributed to his ouster in 1944. The important role played by the previously apolitical veterinary medicine school and Yáñez suggest that external political forces played a major role. Brito Foucher's political capital with Ávila Camacho was low, and the death of the student gave the president the excuse he needed to step into the picture.

Presidential support appears to be important under the current Caso law. Even the origin of the Caso law was highly political. Elected by the six living ex-rectors called together by Ávila Camacho, Alfonso Caso's rise to the rectorship was a political act. Caso had no intention of staying in the job and left as soon as a successor could be named, a difficult task because the recent upheavals did not encourage applicants. The rectorships of Fernández Mac Gregor and Zubirán seem to indicate that a rector must have more than presidential support. Fernández Mac Gregor had been out of touch with the university and had naive ideas about what a rector could do; he left quickly. Zubirán might have survived the 1948 strike had President Alemán continued to support him. Why Alemán pulled the rug out from under Zubirán after reassuring junta members that he would support him remains a mystery; perhaps Alemán decided that Zubirán would never be able to keep peace in UNAM and thus had to go. The rectorships of Garrido and Carrillo demonstrate the importance of presidential support. The Ignacio Chávez case is enigmatic. A "liberal," he was elected during the presidency of the "liberal" president Adolfo López Mateos but overthrown during the presidency of the "conservative" Gustavo Díaz Ordaz. Nevertheless, Chávez resembled Díaz Ordaz in being a disciplinarian and authoritarian. These two traits may have been more important in anti-Chávez sentiment than the change in presidents. Had Chávez been willing to sacrifice law director Sepúlveda, he might have survived. Barros Sierra, a former cabinet secretary, presents an interesting case as well, for he left in 1970 when Luis Echeverría became president. Pablo González Casanova, a "leftist," under the "leftist" presidency of Echeverría, left after a major strike by employees.

Because the internal machinations of Mexico politics are so hidden, one can only suggest possible explanations rather than present definitive conclusions. It appears that rectors are dependent on presidential support to stay in office. That is, if a rector loses presidential support, the rector will soon leave. However, presidential support will not keep a rector in office if the rector does not protect his internal political front. Failing to contain a dispute within the university and thus forcing the government to resolve it almost certainly means the withdrawal of presidential support. Governors are supposed to govern; those who cannot, leave. Presumably, this withdrawal of presidential support is telegraphed to persons within the university, consciously or unconsciously inviting them to rebel against the rector.

Rectors have been pushed out by student activists, but it is the prominence of the rectorship that creates the illusion of constant and serious student rebellion in UNAM. Ousting rectors is not a constant student practice. Antonio Caso was the first rector forced out by students politics; he fell in 1923 because he was a relative and supporter of Lombardo Toledano, the force behind the student agitation, not because students were after him. Castro Leal in 1929, García Téllez in 1933, Gómez Morín in 1934, Ocaranza in 1935, Chico in 1938, Brito Foucher in 1944, Fernández Mac Gregor in 1945, Zubirán in 1948, and Chávez in 1966 left because of students. The list seems to contradict the point made, but these nine (or ten if one counts Caso) are the only ones in the seventy years between 1910 and 1980, the time of this writing. If one starts at 1929, the figure becomes nine in fifty-one years. Between 1948 and 1980, a period of thirty-two years, only one of the five rectors was booted.

That students could force *any* rector out of office, not that they have forced out some, is what gives undue significance to student activism. The UNAM rectorship is one of the most respected and visible public offices in the nation. This prestigious position carries moral authority, hence the importance of having Barros Sierra lead the first UNAM protest march in 1968 and the subsequent government-sponsored attacks on him in the Chamber of Deputies. Barros Sierra was able to count on the rector's prestige to withstand these verbal assaults; he must have known that UNAM would not accept the resignation he tendered in September 1968. Toppling a rector is serious business.

Less visible and more frequent is the ouster of a director. Students in a particular school can create enough turmoil to force a director out. The level of turmoil has only to be high enough to demonstrate to the rector that his subordinate cannot govern. The reasons for the student agitation are not important for this point. Few rectors would be willing to risk their own careers in order to protect a director. Chávez did in 1966 and was ousted. Other rectors fire directors to keep strikes localized. This turnover has a deleterious effect on the educational process but does not have the equivalent political ramifications of a rector's removal.

Numerous local strikes, combined with a few well-publicized general strikes, have given Mexican university students an undeserved reputation as radicals or revolutionaries. Some students cultivate this image by using revolutionary rhetoric. Observers sometimes assume that these students, or those engaged in a strike, or both groups, are part of an international phenomenon of university student revolution. The Mexican government made this error in 1968.

Student political activism in many countries is revolutionary, either in the sense of overthrowing governments or of trying to create a new social order. This has been true in a number of Latin American countries. Cuban students played a principal role in the overthrow of Gerardo Machado in 1933 and of Fulgencio Batista in 1958. Argentine students also have a long tradition of revolt against the government, dating back at least to the 1890s, when they were a principal component of the Unión Cívica Radical, which revolted against the government in that and subsequent decades; they have continued to revolt against dictatorial governments. Other Latin American countries have also had a tradition of student revolts against the national government. In fact, student revolts against dictatorship are common throughout the world, although one should not assume that students are always engaged in revolution.

Mexican students rarely engage in revolt against the government. A few participated in the Mexican Revolution, but the numbers were small and they did not participate as students per se. Much of what casual observers in Mexico think is student revolt is student violence. Violent acts by students against each other or against police are rarely rebellion. Rather, such acts are attempts to resolve animosities in a society in which more peaceful means are seen as ineffectual and violence itself is widespread. Few Mexican university students advocate revolution, not even those within the minority who are activists. They will rebel against police repression of students. They more commonly rebel against tuition increases, class attendance requirements, tougher admission or graduation standards, and more rigorous examination systems. That has been the history of UNAM student activism and, although UNAM is not the only university in Mexico, it sets the pace for the others.

This does not mean that there are no revolutionary students in Mexico. There are. The point that needs stressing is that their numbers are small and inconsequential. Fights with police, slogans painted on walls, and distribution of revolutionary handbills do not attract the masses, much less other students. Student radicals talk to each other and their professors, not to the common people. Student efforts in 1968 to recruit workers and peasants failed miserably.

This absence of a revolutionary student movement in Mexico has important policy consequences. Government leaders do not have to increase budgets substantially to pacify universitarios. Modest increases will do the job. These same officials do not have to expend enormous amounts of energy or other resources to keep track of internal university politics so as to stay alert to the caching of arms inside the university campus. Through ambitious student politicians or through the many politicians who also teach in the university the government can monitor the university at a nominal cost. These professors can and do serve another function; they are in a position to recruit talented students into the governing system of the nation. Although professors have traditionally done some of this since 1910, the task has become more important with the decline in importance of student organizations. Professor-politicians now occupy very strategic positions from which to recruit future politicians.

The evidence of Mabry and Camp, Camp, and Smith demonstrates the importance of an UNAM background for recruitment into the national political elite. This study clarifies the evidence by indicating a more precise relationship between this UNAM background and reaching the political heights. The data are imperfect, however, because they are incomplete for FEU and CNE presidencies. These two posts certainly were two logical points of entry into national politics for those so inclined. The data are incomplete in large part because the role of these offices changed as student politics changed.

The FEU and the CNE played important roles in political recruitment prior to the mid-1930s. Most presidents of these organizations prior to this period attained important political posts in later years. Efforts by leftists in the 1930s to replace the power of the FEU and the CNE with their own organizations (FER, Ala Izquierdista, CSM, and CESUM), of government leaders to support the Elizalde CNE, and of the PRM to create the Confederación de Jóvenes Mexicanos also attest to the importance of the traditional organizations. Conservative students had wrested control of UNAM from the government, and both the government and leftists wanted it back. They chose student politics as their means.

The fragmentation of student leadership in the mid-1930s, however, meant that the government could not use a handful of students as power brokers. It is noteworthy that the FEU and CNE ceased being rungs on the political ladder exactly at the time when UNAM was most actively in opposition to the government. Although data on post-1938 FEU and other student presidencies are fragmentary, those that exist appear to confirm this observation. Only in the case of FEU presidencies in the 1950s and 1960s (more than one FEU existed in these years) have individuals been identified who subsequently became major political figures. The break between UNAM and the state had healed by 1938, but the split in student leadership never healed. Instead, further splits developed. Given the tradition of student political opposition to the state, these splits encouraged the university-state conflict.

The 1936 split of the CNE into two rival groups definitively ended any claim to its being a national student movement. The CNE of Rodríguez Hicks would survive after a fashion until the 1950s, when Siegrist Clamont would temporarily revive some of its former dynamism. Its ultraconservatism and its own factionalism would push it back into oblivion, however. Elizalde's CNE was even more short-lived, even though it had government support. Its origin probably stemmed from the desire to deny the claim to being national to the conservatives. Once the CJM was formed, the Elizalde CNE was no longer needed. The CJM became an important training ground for future politicians; Alfonso Corona del Rosal, regent of the Federal District (1966–1970), was one of many CJM activists.

Few data were found on post-1938 CNE presidents, in part because the organization was moribund or insignificant and thus did not receive press coverage, but this was not true of earlier CNE presidents. Jorge Prieto Laurens became governor of San Luis Potosí. Rafael Corrales Ayala and Manuel Gudiño became federal deputies, Alejandro Gómez Arias a high UNAM official and vice-president of the Peoples' Socialist Party (PPS), Luis Martínez a PPS leader, Guillermo G. Ibarra oficial mayor of the Secretariat of Hydraulic Resources, Alfonso Guerrero Briones a PAN federal deputy, Armando Chávez Camacho a PAN federal deputy and then a leader of another opposition party, Benito Coquet the secretary of the presidency, and Daniel Kuri Breña a PAN founder. Of the fourteen different presidents between 1916 and 1934, only Horacio Núñez, Perfecto Gutiérrez Zamora, and José Rivera Albarrán are not known to have held high political posts; that is, 79 percent did, a large proportion. In contrast, of the six it was possible to identify for the 1938–1963 period, none held a high government post.

Much the same occurred with FEU presidents, even though the organization survived longer than the CNE. As noted above, Prieto Laurens and Gómez Arias both played important roles in Mexican politics. From what is known of other presidents between 1916 and 1936, being FEU president was one rung up the political ladder. Enrique Soto Piembert, appointed as a diplomatic attaché under Carranza, continued in politics and eventually became a federal deputy after a long diplomatic career. Miguel Palacios Macedo served as a cabinet secretary (1923–1924). Rodulfo Brito Foucher became rector of UNAM. Daniel Cosío Villegas, better known as one of Mexico's great intellectuals, became an ambassador in 1957. Manuel Yáñez Ruiz became a Supreme Court justice, Ángel Carvajal the secretary of government and a Supreme Court justice (and was seriously considered for the presidency in 1958), José M. de los Reyes a federal deputy; Ricardo García Villalobos held various government posts and then became secretary-general of UNAM in 1966; Efraín Brito Rosado became a senator, Roberto Patiño Córdoba the director of the UNAM law school, and Alfonso Guerrero Briones a federal deputy, as mentioned earlier. Francisco López Serrano became the subsecretary of agrarian affairs for 1958–1963. If anything, this list understates the number of persons who held high public office in the government or UNAM.

Between 1936 and 1956, no person identified as an FEU president rose to political prominence. Several caveats are in order here. I was unable to identify the presidents between 1938 and 1943, for 1946, for 1947, for 1952–1953, and for 1954–1955. Their names did not appear in any source I consulted, an absence that indicates the decline of the organization. On the other hand, more than one president was identified in the years of 1936–1937, 1945, 1949, and 1955–1956. Given the number who were identified, one would expect at least one to have achieved a high position if the FEU was still important in national political recruitment.

One can only speculate as to the reappearance in 1956 of FEU presidents who eventually rose to political heights. Pedro Vázquez Colmenares became oficial mayor in the Secretariat of the Presidency for 1971–1974, that his father, Genaro V. Vázquez, held two cabinet posts and became a Supreme Court justice between 1935 and 1952 probably accounts for his career. Alejandro Peraza Uribe, one of the two persons identified as an FEU president for 1957–1958, became a federal deputy. In 1979, Antonio Tenorio Adame, who was an FEU president in 1960, became a PRI official. Alfonso Olvera Reyes, an FEU president in 1961, became a PRI official in 1978. Equally noteworthy was the failure of Espiridón Payán, a 1967 FEU president and leader of the 1966 strike, to gain high political office by 1979. Since there was more than one group claiming to be the FEU and my data are incomplete, only speculation is possible. It appears that the rise of post-1955 persons was the result of their own personalities or political connections, or both, rather than the achievement of a student leadership position. They would have gotten there anyway.

Although these lists show that some student organization presidents achieved significant political prominence in later life, focusing on these positions can be misleading, for it is important to consider those who did not hold these positions. An impressive number of persons who were involved in university strikes but held no presidencies became major political figures. Of those in the 1910 strike, Luis Sánchez Pontón became secretary of public education (1940–1941), Alfonso G. Alarcón the governor of an important state, and Francisco Castillo Nájera a federal deputy. From the 1912 law strike, Emilio Portes Gil became interim president of the nation and Ezequiel Padilla secretary of public education in 1928–1930, secretary of foreign relations in 1940–1945, an opposition presidential candidate in 1946, and a senator in 1964–1970. The 1929 strike produced a number of later political leaders. José Vallejo Novelo became a federal deputy, Ramón Corona a cabinet official, Antonio González a federal deputy, Baltasar Dromundo a federal deputy, and Carlos Zapata Vela a federal deputy and ambassador to the USSR. Even the 1933 strike produced some notable figures. Andrés Iduarte became director general of the National Institute of Fine Arts, Juan Sánchez Navarro a PAN founder and leading probusiness lobbyist, Hugo Rangel Couto subsecretary of national patrimony, and Luis de Garay a PAN founder. Again, it seems significant that the identifiable student leaders of the strikes of 1938, 1944, 1945, and 1948 did not become prominent.

Most telling of all, however, is that few of the high government officials between 1935 and 1979 had been student presidents or strike leaders and that no president of Mexico had been. López Mateos participated only in the 1929 strike. Neither Luis Echeverría nor José López Portillo has been identified in the 1944 or 1945 strikes that occurred while they were students at UNAM. Agustín Yáñez, secretary of public education for 1964–1970, participated in the 1944 strike but as a faculty member. These absences strongly suggest that being president of the FEU or the CNE or leading a strike became counterproductive to a political career sometime around 1933, when conservatives gained control of UNAM.

The splintering of student politics increased in the 1960s and provided other political outlets for potential national leaders. By the early 1960s, there were hundreds of student political organizations within UNAM. Perhaps a careful study of these would reveal something significant about political socialization within the university during those years. The splintering did mean that there was no single student political organization capable of being used as a vehicle in which to launch a political career. The FUSA, Chávez's attempt to create a single student voice, failed of its purpose. The use of porras from the mid-1930s onwards hindered the rise of student leaders adept at the art of negotiation and persuasion. Muscle became important in student politics.

Nevertheless, prominent politicians continue to be UNAM alumni. Presidents Echeverría and López Portillo are the two most recent and famous examples, and represent an emerging pattern. Neither held elective public office before becoming president. Instead, their careers, and those of many others, followed a different course. While UNAM students, they earned high grades and successfully participated in a number of social, intellectual, and establishment political activities. Professor-politicians were able to identify and recruit them into the political system, where they continued to hone their organizational skills. They climbed the political ladder (or leapfrogged up it) as technicians. Party politics has become less important as a means of reaching the top, and student activism has consequently declined as a vehicle into politics. Technocrats have become important.

UNAM student political activity retains some importance, however. Even though the 1968 student movement originated in a conflict between IPN students and granaderos, UNAM assumed leadership of the movement. Had the university not been attacked with a bazooka, UNAM students might have remained aloof. Once they entered the fray, all eyes looked to Barros Sierra, as UNAM rector, for leadership, not to Massieu, the IPN director. UNAM has the prestige to influence all Mexican higher education. This influence extends beyond academic and cultural matters to politics as well. UNAM has been a center of opposition for decades to whatever government was in power. Thus, what UNAM students do reverberates throughout the nation.

The central theme of this study has been the key role played by students in the conflict between the university (in this case, the National University) and the state. As long as the state was able to control the university, open conflict was avoided. Various students, administrators, and even politicians argued that an effective university must be independent of government control, but their efforts to obtain that independence failed for years. Regardless of the government in power, no president would consciously yield control of such an expensive and valuable resource. On the contrary, the efforts of post-1910 national governments was to increase governmental authority; the state steadily and inexorably grew stronger. Presidential power, in particular, increased.

Students wrenched university autonomy from the state and have preserved it. Portes Gil granted partial autonomy in 1929 because it was a familiar demand that promised to be an easy way out of a difficult situation. Rodríguez granted full autonomy in 1933 to stop student agitation and as a prelude to what was expected to be the end of autonomy. Much to the surprise of the government, the UNAM community demonstrated that the institution had a life of its own. It survived in spite of the cutoff of funds. Realizing this institutional strength, and mollified by a change in university administration, the Cárdenas government resumed financial support, but it also followed through on an old threat and created the Instituto Politécnico Nacional. The founding of the IPN, which meant that the government had given up all hope of getting UNAM to train the scientists and technologists the government wanted, demonstrated clearly that UNAM had won. Students also prevented other changes in UNAM, such as increased tuition fees. Even though students pay almost nothing in tuition and could reasonably be expected to pay more, they refuse to do so. Although unhappy with this refusal, the state has steadily increased UNAM's funding, even after the serious upheaval of 1968. To do anything that students perceive as negative to their interests costs too much politically.

This student power came in 1933 with the Bassols law and has meant that the government cannot regain control of UNAM. It cannot do it through the rector or through the students. The former is checked by the many constituencies he must serve, and the latter resist any effort of government agents, students or non-students, to penetrate their ranks and establish control. Given the demonstrated ability of students to disrupt the national capital and the large number of UNAM alumni in high places, the state dares not destroy UNAM fiscally. The state will not grant sovereignty to UNAM, as some students demanded, in fact, in 1968, and will brutally crush student efforts to obtain it, as the state did in 1968, but the state will not use the opportunity to permanently close UNAM or remove its autonomous status, as has occurred in other countries. Instead, the state finds it necessary to pacify students. Echeverría tried to make peace with students by promising a democratic opening in politics, visiting students, going onto the UNAM campus, and adopting a "Third World" foreign policy.

In sum, the product of the long and involved conflict between the university and the state is the increased autonomy of UNAM. The government, in spite of its opposition to or unhappiness with UNAM, continues to find the university and to allow it to determine its own destiny. UNAM officials control admissions policy, academic requirements, and expenditures, subject to student acquiescence. UNAM is less regulated than most state universities in the United States and more powerful in Mexican educational and cultural circles than any university in the United States. UNAM officials operate with few external constraints. They know that they will receive increased appropriations each year to spend as they please. Certainly, they cannot allow UNAM to be an active opposition center (such as a guerrilla training base) to the government, but they can and do allow numerous opposition groups to operate within the university's confines and with its protection. Gone are the pre-1929 days when the national government could name administrators and faculty members. Whatever government intervention remains in these matters is hidden, non-existent, or difficult to achieve.

The power of the autonomy idea and of UNAM itself was demonstrated by two policies adopted by the Echeverría government. When the government created the Autonomous Metropolitan University in Mexico City (an obvious effort to create a rival to UNAM as well as to relieve enrollment pressure there), it decided to make the new university autonomous like UNAM and unlike the IPN. Such a move was a concession of defeat. The other was the decision to increase the funding of El Colegio de Mexico and give it a new campus. El Colegio had been a small, elite, "private" university that, in spite of its size, had considerable impact on national policy. The high quality of the work of its students and faculty gave it clout. Recognizing the value of such an institution, the Echeverría government substantially increased funding for El Colegio but did not assume control of it. Although not called autonomous, it is.

The López Portillo government in 1980 blocked the creation of one big union for higher education, the National Union of University Workers (SUNTU). The presidential proposal to prohibit a single union for all university employees in the nation but to provide union guarantees easily passed Congress in mid-October. SUNTU, which had no legal standing, called a national university strike for November 1, but opposition from the government and many university employees prevented it from occurring. In November elections, the Autonomous Associations of Academic Personnel (AAPA), which had not supported SUNTU, won the right to represent the academic employees of UNAM. Many faculty members feared that a single university union, as advocated by SUNTU and STUNAM, would endanger academic freedom and university autonomy. Some also objected to the leftist orientation of SUNTU and STUNAM leaders.

UNAM's escape from the controlling power of the state is significant because it is one of the few national institutions to achieve it. This is no small matter. Its enrollment and budgetary size, its influence on education and culture, and its large number of employees certainly make it worth controlling. The continued autonomy of UNAM forces scholars to reexamine hypotheses about the nature of Mexican government. The current tendency of scholars to see Mexico as a corporatist state, as a state that penetrates and controls almost every aspect of public life, is belied by the history of UNAM. Government officials cannot control UNAM.

UNAM remains autonomous because government officials cannot allow it to be otherwise. They, many of them alumni, will not destroy their alma mater. They will not run the risk of massive student protests and the consequent necessity of armed intervention; the adverse results of the use of the army in 1968 will give second thought to any president who contemplates the use of the army again. Equally important, UNAM serves a useful purpose as it is now organized. Enough persons are trained to fill the important posts in society (be they in the public or the private sector), even though most UNAM students never graduate. Some institution has to fill the central educational and cultural role played by UNAM. Finally, the sheer weight of tradition preserves university autonomy. The choice left to the state is how to fund UNAM sufficiently without giving it extra money with which to fight the state. By keeping funding at a minimal level and pouring additional funds into new or existing rival universities, the state can hope to dilute the impact of UNAM. If such a strategy exists, it will take years before its effects are fully felt. In the meantime, it is cheaper and politically more expedient to continue to fund UNAM, which occupies the time of large numbers of persons who could not be absorbed into the labor force.

In short, UNAM won.

Select Bibliography

THE items in this bibliography were selected according to their usefulness to the study. Important signed newspaper articles are included, whereas general news reportage is not, although the newspapers are listed. Participants (especially in the events of 1929 and 1968) have written extensively; no doubt some of these sources have been omitted, but, because of the high degree of repetition in what they have published, it is doubtful that any critical information was lost. Similarly, scholars have found student politics fascinating, but this bibliography makes no pretense at listing all of the works on Mexico or anywhere else but only those that contributed to this study. Given the nature of the subject, the distinction between primary and secondary sources can be vague. A journal article or a book written by a foreigner years after an event is a study; one written by a participant may or may not be, depending on one's taxonomy. The bibliography, although select, is a comprehensive guide to the documentation available.

I. Archival Materials

Archivo Estudiantil, Hemeroteca Nacional, Mexico City.

Archivo Ezequiel A. Chávez, Biblioteca Central, Universidad Nacional Autónoma de México, Mexico City.

Roderic Camp Correspondence with Mexican Leaders, Pella, Iowa.

Conflictos Estudiantiles, Archivo Económico, Biblioteca Miguel Lerdo de Tejada, Mexico City.

Peter H. Smith, Transformed Dataset on Political Elites in Mexico, 1900–1971, The University of Wisconsin-Madison.

Serie Conflicto-Estudiantil, Microfilm, Five Rolls, Department of Archivos Históricos y Bibliotecas, Instituto Nacional de Antropología e Historia, Mexico City.

Television Evening News (ABC, CBS, NBC), Vanderbilt University Television News Archives, Nashville, Tennessee.

II. Newspapers and Magazines

Acción Estudiantil
Así
Boletín de Instrucción Pública
Boletín de Secretaría de Educación Pública
Boletín de la Universidad
Boletín de la Universidad
Boletín de la Universidad Nacional de México
Diario del Sureste (Merida)
Diario de Yucatán (Mérida)
El Dictamen (Veracruz)
El Día
Excelsior
Gaceta de la Universidad
Gaceta de la Universidad Nacional Autónoma de México
Gráfico
Heraldo Estudiantil
Hispanic American Report
Hoy
La Nación
El Nacional
New York Times
Novedades
La Opinión (Los Angeles, California)
El País
La Prensa
La Prensa (San Antonio, Texas)
Reforma Universitaria
Revista de Revistas
The Times (London)
El Universal
El Universal Gráfico

III. Articles, Books, Dissertations, and Theses

Alarcón, Alfonso G. Burla, burlando: Anales epigramáticos del grupo de delegados al primer congreso nacional de estudiantes, reunido en la ciudad de México en 1910. Mexico City: "Stylo," 1952.

Alba, José de. "La generación preparatoriana 1920–24." Novedades, October 30, 1957.

Alba, Pedro de. "Escándolos y algarados estudiantiles." Novedades, October 6, 1953.

———. "Las peripecias de nuestro bachillerato." El Nacional, August 2, 1933.

Albornoz, Orlando. Estudiantes y desarrollo político. Caracas: Monte Ávila, 1968.

———. "Student Opposition in Latin America." *Government and Opposition* (November 1966): 105–118.

Alexander, Robert J. "Evolution of Student Politics in Latin America." In *The Latin American Student Movement*, edited by David Spencer. Washington, D.C.: The National Student Association, 1965.

"Aloysius." "Aniversario de la revolución de octubre." *La Nación*, October 16, 1943.

Altbach, Philip, comp. *A Select Bibliography on Students, Politics, and Higher Education*. Rev. ed. St. Louis: United Ministries in Higher Education, 1970.

Alvarado, José. "Del vasconcelismo a la farsa de los peleles." *Hoy* (March 29, 1952): 18–19, 66.

Alvarez Garín, Raúl, et al. *Los procesos de México 68: Acusaciones y defensa.* Mexico City: Editorial Estudiantes, 1970.

Arnaiz y Freg, Arturo. "Fernando Ocaranza, treinta y tres años de enseñanza médica." *Novedades*, December 18, 1949.

Arriaga Rivera, Agustín. "El movimiento juvenil." In *Mexico: Cincuenta años de revolución: La economía, la vida social, la política, la cultura.* Mexico City: Fondo de Cultura Económica, 1963, pp. 220–225.

Attolini, José. *Las finanzas de la Universidad a través del tiempo.* Mexico City: UNAM, Escuela Nacional de Economía, 1951.

"La autonomía de la Universidad." *El Universal*, September 27, 1927.

Azuela, Salvador. "XXV aniversario de la autonomía universitaria." *El Universal*, May 22, 1954.

Bakke, E. Wright. "Students on the March: The Case of Mexico and Columbia." *Sociology of Education* 37 (1964): 200–228.

Barrientos, Iván. *La formación del estudiante universitario.* Lawrence, Kansas: University of Kansas, Center for Latin American Studies, 1968.

Barragán, Juan. "La primera huelga de estudiantes." *El Universal*, May 19, 1967.

Barros Sierra, Javier. *Javier Barros Sierra, 1968: Conversaciones con García Cantu.* 2nd ed. Mexico City: Siglo XXI, 1972.

Baz, Gustavo. *Informe que rinde el Rector de la U.N.A.M. al H. Consejo Universitario, sobre las actividades desarrolladas por la Universidad hasta el 1 de febrero de 1939.* Mexico City: UNAM, 1939.

Benítez Zerteño, Raúl. "El estudiante de la Escuela Nacional de Ciencias Políticas y Sociales." *Revista Ciencias Políticas y Sociales* 7, no. 23 (January–March 1961): 43–91.

Bernal, Antonio. "Remembranzas preparatorianas." *Novedades*, January 16, 1958.

Bezdek, Robert. "Electoral Opposition in Mexico: Emergence, Suppression, and Impact on Political Processes." Ph.D. dissertation, Ohio State University, 1973.

Blanco Moheno, Roberto. *Tlatelolco: Historia de una infamia.* Mexico City: Editorial Diana, 1969.

Bonilla, Frank. "Students in Politics: Three Generations of Political Action in a Latin American University." Ph.D. dissertation, Harvard University, 1958.

———. "Student Politics in Latin America." *Political Research—Organization and Design* 3 (1959): 12–15.

———, and Myron Glazer. *Student Politics in Chile.* New York: Basic Books, 1970.

Booth, George C. *Mexico's School-Made Society.* Stanford: Stanford University Press, 1941.

Bouchet, Luis. "Bassols quiso imponer la disciplina en la Escuela de Leyes con una pistola 45." *El Nacional,* May 12, 1949.

Bremauntz, Alberto. *Autonomía universitaria y planeación educativa en México.* Mexico City: Ediciones Jurídicas Sociales, 1969.

———. *La educación socialista en México (antecedentes y fundamentos de la reforma de 1934).* Mexico City: Imprenta Rivadeneyra, 1943.

Brito Foucher, Rodulfo. *Balance de la labor realizada por el actual administración universitaria durante un año, 1943.* Mexico City: UNAM, 1943.

Brito Rosado, Efraín. "La revolución universitaria." *El Universal,* May 14, 1949.

Britton, John A. *Educación y radicalismo en México,* vol. I: *Los años de Bassols (1931–1934),* and vol. II: *Los años de Cárdenas (1934–1940).* Mexico City: SepSetentas, 1976.

———. "The Mexican Ministry of Education, 1931–1940: Radicalism and Institutional Development." Ph.D. dissertation, Tulane University, 1971.

———. "Urban Education and Social Change in the Mexican Revolution, 1931–1940." *Journal of Latin American Studies* 5 (November 1973): 233–245.

Brush, David A. "The de la Huerta Rebellion in Mexico, 1923–1924." Ph.D. dissertation, Syracuse University, 1975.

Bueno, Miguel. *Estudios sobre la universidad.* Mexico City: UNAM, 1962.

Burke, Michael E. "The University of Mexico and the Revolution, 1910–1940." *The Americas* 34 (October 1977).

"Bus Fares and Student Demonstrations in Mexico." *Minerva* 5 (Winter 1967): 301–307.

Bustamante, Octavio N. "A la carta." *El Universal Gráfico,* March 26 and April 2, 1969.

Bustillo Oro, Juan. *Germán del Campo, una vida ejemplar.* Mexico City: n.p., 1930.

Calderón Vega, Luis. *Cuba 88: Memorias de la UNEC.* Morelia: Fimax Publicistas, 1959.

———. "La U.N.E.C., un movimiento estudiantil de verdadera renovación universitaria." *La Nación,* August 4, 1945.

———. *Los Siete Sabios de México.* 2nd ed. Mexico City: Editorial Jus, 1972.

Camp, Roderic. "La campaña presidencial de 1929 y el liderazgo político en México." *Historia Mexicana* 27 (Fall 1977): 231–259.

———. "Education and Political Recruitment in Mexico: The Alemán Generation." *Journal of Inter-American Studies and World Affairs* 18 (August 1976): 295–311.

———. *Mexican Political Biographies, 1935–1975*. Tucson: University of Arizona Press, 1976.

———. *Mexico's Leaders: Their Education and Recruitment*. Tucson: University of Arizona Press, 1980.

Canibe Rosas, Manuel. "El movimiento estudiantil y la opinión pública." *Revista Mexicana de Ciencias Políticas* 16 (January-March 1970).

Capistrán Garza, René. "Calles vive aún. El caso de la Universidad Autónoma de Guadalajara." *Mañana* (May 31, 1947): 44–45.

Careaga, Gabriel. *Los jóvenes radicales*. Mexico City: UNAM, 1973.

Carlson, Harry J. "The Impact of the Cárdenas Administration on Mexican Education." Ph.D. dissertation, University of Arizona, 1964.

Carmona, Fernando, ed. *Reforma educativa y "Aperatura democrática"*. Mexico City: Editorial Nuestro Tiempo, 1972.

Carrancá, Raúl. *La universidad mexicana*. Mexico City: Fondo de Cultura Económica, 1969.

———. "La situación jurídica de la Universidad." *El Universal*, May 19, 1969.

Carreño, José. "El Plan Elizondo contra la Universidad de Nuevo León." *Siempre!* 486 (June 2, 1971): ii–iv.

"La carrera del Dr. Baz." *El Nacional*, August 12, 1944.

Carrillo, Alejandro. "El problema universitario de Mexico." *Así* (February 3, 10, 1945): 20–22, 81–82.

———, et al. *La juventud universitaria mexicana frente a su tiempo; 5 conferencias*. Toluca: Universidad Autónoma del Estado de México, 1963.

Carrión, Jorge, Sol Arguedas, and Fernando Carmona. *Tres culturas en agonía, Tlatelolco 1968*. 3rd ed. Mexico City: Editorial Nuestro Tiempo, 1971.

Casián, Francisco L. "¿Qué papel corresponde al gremio estudiantil en los movimientos políticos de la República?" *Argos* (Tehuacán), July 23, 30, and August 6, 13, 1922.

Castiello y Fernández del Valle, Jaime. *La Universidad: Estudio histórico-filosófico*. Mexico City: Ediciones Proa, 1933.

Castillo, Heberto. *Libertad bajo protesta: Historia de un proceso*. Mexico City: Federación Editorial Mexicana, 1973.

———. "Las tendencias políticas dentro del conflicto estudiantil." *¿Por Qué?* (September 11, 1968): 38–41.

Castillo Córdova, Alfonso. "La revolución estudiantil del 29." *Excelsior*, April 16, 1949.

———. "La voz de agora: La revolución universitaria del 29." *El Universal*, June 30, 1949.

Castro, Rosa. "Seis instantes estelares de la Universidad." *Hoy* (October 6, 1951): 31–33.

Castro Ruiz, Miguel. "Altibajos de la Universidad desde su reaperatura hasta el movimiento de 1929." *La Nación*, July 2, 1951.

———. "De como la Universidad tuvo dos rectores simultáneos." *La Nación*, July 30, 1951.

———. "La compleja crisis universitaria de 1944." *La Nación*, July 16, 1951.

———. "El frentepopulismo malogra en 1945 una favorable conyuntura de la Universidad." *La Nación*, July 23, 1951.

———. "La magnífica pelea universitaria contra la dictadura sectaria en 1933." *La Nación*, July 9, 1951.

———. "Mario de la Cueva, defensor de la libertad universitaria." *La Nación*, September 17, 1951.

———. "1910: La Universidad bajo el signo de la mediocridad positiva." *La Nación*, June 25, 1951.

Chávez, Ezequiel A. "Proyecto de Ley de Independencia de la Universidad Nacional de México." Archivo Histórico de la UNAM, printed in Jorge Pinto Mazal, ed., *La autonomía universitaria*, pp. 71–74.

———. *La situación actual de la Universidad Nacional de México*. Mexico City: Talleres Gráficos del Departamento Editorial de la Secretaría de Educación Pública, 1924.

Chávez, Ignacio. *La actitud de los estudiantes universitarios frente al país*. Mexico City: UNAM, 1962.

———. *Informe al Honorable Consejo Universitario*. Mexico City: UNAM, 1962.

Chávez G., Elías. "Torpe jornada policiana ante 3,000 agitadores estudiantiles." *El Universal*, July 24, 1968.

Chico Goerne, Luis. *La universidad y la inquietud de nuestro tiempo*. Mexico City: UNAM, 1937.

Colín, Mario. *Salvador Azuela, maestro emérito de la Preparatoria*. Altacomulco: n.p., 1968.

Colmenero, Sergio. "Problemas universitarios y política nacional." *Revista Mexicana de Ciencia Política* 19 (1973): 5–16.

Comité Coordinador de Huelga de la UNAM. *Gaceta* (August 13, 15, 20, 1968).

Confederación de Estudiantes Socialistas de México. *Conclusiones del Primer Congreso de Estudiantes Socialistas de México, reunido en el puerto de Álvaro Obregón, Estado de Tabasco, del 29 de julio al 2 de agosto del presente año*. Jalapa: Confederación de Estudiantes Socialistas de México, 1934.

Confederación de Estudiantes Socialistas Unificados de México. *Estatutos y conclusiones del Congreso constituyente de la Confederación de Estudiantes Socialistas Unificados de México*. Guanajuato: Confederación de Estudiantes Socialistas Unificados de México, 1937.

Confederación de Jóvenes Mexicanos. *Veinticinco años, cuadernos para la juventud*, no. 4. Mexico City: Confederación de Jóvenes Mexicanos, 1964.

Confederación Iberoamericana de Estudiantes Católicos. *Convención Iberoamericana de Estudiantes Católicos, celebrada en la ciudad de México durante los días del 12 al 22 de diciembre de 1931. Conclusiones aprobadas*. Mexico City: Ediciones Proa, 1932.

———. *Convención Ibero-Americana de Estudiantes Católicos. Convocatoria.* Mexico City: Editorial Cultura, 1931.

Confederación Iberoamericana de Estudiantes. *Segundo Congreso Iberoamericana de Estudiantes.* San José, Costa Rica: Confederación Iberoamericana de Estudiantes, 1933.

Confederación Nacional de Estudiantes. *Anteproyecto de la ley orgánica de la Universidad Nacional de México, que será presentado al Congreso de la Unión.* Mexico City: CNE, 1952.

———. *X Congreso a partir del 25 de agosto de 1933.* Veracruz: CNE [1933].

———. *El XII Congreso Nacional de Estudiantes, Monterrey, N.L. Estado y educación. Servicio social.* Mexico City: CNE, 1936.

———. *Estado y educación.* Mexico City: CNE, 1936.

———. *Estatuto orgánico . . . aprobado en el XII congreso nacional celebrado en Monterrey, N.L.* Mexico City: CNE, 1936.

———. *Homenaje a los estudiantes. XI Congreso.* San Luis Potosí: CNE, 1934.

———. *Mensaje a la juventud mexicana.* Mexico City: CNE, 1952.

———. *Primer Congreso de Universitarios Mexicanos, convocatoria.* Mexico City: CNE, 1933.

———. *XI Congreso Nacional de Estudiantes.* San Luis Potosí: CNE, 1934.

"A Conflagration of Obscure Origins in Mexico City." *Minerva 7* (Autumn–Winter 1968–1969): 256–263.

Contreras, Ariel José. *Mexico 1940: Industrialización y crisis política.* Mexico City: Siglo XXI, 1977.

Córdova, Arnaldo. *La formación del poder político en México.* Mexico City: Ediciones Era, 1972.

———. *La política de masas de Cardenismo.* Mexico City: Ediciones Era, 1974.

Cosío Villegas, Daniel. "Como en Grecia: Los siete años de una tragedia." *Excelsior,* September 28, 1968.

———. *El estilo personal de gobernar.* Mexico City: Editorial Joaquín Mortiz, 1974.

———. *Labor periodista,* Mexico City: Ediciones Era, 1972.

———. *La sucesión presidencial.* Mexico City: Editorial Joaquín Mortiz, 1975.

Cueva, Mario de la. *Informe de la rectoría, 1938–1942.* Mexico City: UNAM, 1942.

———, and Gustavo Baz. *Informe del rector de la U.N.A.M., Dr. Gustavo Baz y del secretario general Lic. Mario de la Cueva.* Mexico City: UNAM, 1940.

Dalton, Roque. "Student Youth and the Latin American Revolution." *World Marxist Review* 9 (1969): 53–61.

Damiano, Antonio. "El movimiento de mayo de 1929." *El Universal,* May 9, 1949.

———, et al. *En torno a una generación, glosa de 1929.* Mexico City: Ediciones Una Generación, 1949.

"El día del estudiante." *El Nacional*, May 23, 1933.

Diuguid, Lewis H. "Mexico's Night of Death." *Progressive* 32 (December 1968): 22–25.

Domínguez, Virgilio. *Informe de los labores desarrolladas en la Escuela Nacional de Jurisprudencia durante el trienio 1945 a 1948*. Mexico City: UNAM, 1948.

Donahue, Francis. "Students in Latin American Politics," *Antioch Review* 26 (1966): 91–106.

Drommundo, Baltasar. "Balance de la generación de 29." *Excelsior*, March 17, 1949.

———. *Crónica de la autonomía universitaria de México*. Mexico City: Editorial Jus, 1978.

———. "Elogio y defensa de mi generación." *Excelsior*, May 23, 1949.

———. "La generación de 1929. El ideal común. Respuesta a la época." *Diario del Sureste*, March 18, 1949.

———. "La generación de 1929, su formación por grupos. La Escuela Preparatoria." *Diario del Sureste*, March 17, 1949.

———. "La juventud y el XXIV aniversario de la Revolución." *Excelsior*, November 20, 1934.

Dulles, John W. F. *Yesterday in Mexico*. Austin: University of Texas Press, 1961.

Durán de Huerta, Gustavo. "Portes Gil hace un balance de lo ganado desde que él dió la autonomía a la Universidad." *Excelsior*, May 24, 1953.

Eclaire, René. "La autonomía no es buena ni mala, pero es desastrosa en la política." *El Nacional*, May 7, 1949.

———. "A Castro Leal y Bassols los sacamos de las orejas, dice Andrés Henestrosa." *El Nacional*, May 2, 1949.

———. "La libertad de cátedra, triunfo de los de 1929." *El Nacional*, May 5, 1949.

Eguía Lis, Joaquín. *Informe del rector de la Universidad Nacional de México*. Mexico City: Imprenta Escalante, 1913.

Einaudi, Luigi. "University Autonomy and Academic Freedom in Latin America." *Law and Contemporary Problems* 28 (1963): 636–646.

Emmerson, Donald K. *Students and Politics in Developing Nations*. New York: Praeger, 1968.

Escudero, Roberto, and Salvador Martínez della Roca. "Mexico: Generation of '68." *NACLA Reports* 12 (September–October 1978).

"La Escuela Nacional de Ciencias Políticas y Sociales." *Revista Ciências Políticas y Sociales* 13 (January–March 1967): 17–33.

Estrada Rodríguez, Gerardo. "El movimiento estudiantil: UNAM, 1958–1968." Thesis in Sociology, UNAM, 1969.

———. *Los movimientos estudiantiles en la UNAM, 1958–1973. Deslinde 51* (1974).

Federación Estudiantil Universitaria de México (FEU). *Anuario, 1932–1933.* Mexico City: FEU, 1933.

———. *Discursos pronunciados en la ceremonia commemorativa de la reforma universitaria.* Mexico City: Imprenta Sáinz y Herrera, 1933.

———. *Estatutos de la Federación Estudiantil Mexicana.* Mexico City: FEU, 1924.

———. *Estatutos y leyes reglamentarias de la Federación de Estudiantes de México.* Mexico City: FEU, 1922.

———. "Manifiesto de los universitarios de México." *Omega,* December 8, 1934.

Ferrer de Mendiolea, Gavriel. "El grupo 1921–1922." *El Nacional,* November 6, 1949.

Flores Olea, Victor, et al. *La rebelión estudiantil y la sociedad contemporánea.* Mexico City: UNAM, 1973.

Flores Zavala, Ernesto. *El estudiante inquieto (los movimientos estudiantiles 1966–1970).* Mexico City: UNAM, 1972.

Frente Universitario Mexicano. *¿Universidad . . . o crisis de universitarios?* Mexico City: n.p., 1973.

García Cantú, Gastón. *Política mexicana.* Mexico City: UNAM, 1974.

———. *Universidad y antiuniversidad.* Mexico City: Editorial Joaquín Mortiz, 1973.

García Naranjo, Nemesio. "La Universidad Autónoma de Guadalajara. No debe suspenderse la obra de cultura." *Novedades,* July 11, 1958.

García Téllez, Ignacio. *Informe que el abogado Ignacio García Téllez, rector de la Universidad Nacional Autónoma de Mexico, rinde al H. Consejo Universitario, acerca de las mismas labores de la Universidad durante el período de abril de 1930 a marzo de 1931.* Mexico City: UNAM, 1931.

———. "Informe de la Rectoría al H. Consejo Universitario." *Universidad de México* 2 (June 1931): 77–95.

García Villalobos, Ricardo. "La generación de 29 pidió la autonomía universitaria." *El Universal,* May 12, 1949.

Garrido Díaz, Luis. *Discursos y mensajes, 1949–1952.* Mexico City: Imprenta Universitaria, 1952.

———. *Palabras universitarias, 1951–1953.* Mexico City: Ediciones Botas, 1954.

———. *El tiempo de mi vida: Memorias.* Mexico City: Editorial Porrúa, 1974.

Gastélum, Alfonso, Jr. "El movimiento estudiantil hace 20 años." *El Demócrata Sinaloense,* May 21, 1949.

Gastélum, Bernardo J. "La universidad autónoma y sus problemas." *Excelsior,* October 13, 1955.

Gaxiola, Francisco J., Jr. *El presidente Rodríguez (1932–1934).* Mexico City: Editorial Cultura, 1938.

Gill, Clark C. *Education in a Changing Mexico.* Washington, D.C.: U.S. Government Printing office, 1969.

Glade, William P., and Stanley R. Ross, eds. *Críticas constructivas del sistema político mexicano.* Austin: Institute of Latin American Studies, University of Texas, 1973.

Gómez Morín, Manuel. *La Universidad de México. Su función social y la razón de ser de su autonomía.* Mexico City: Tipografía la Provisión, 1934.

Gómez Robleda, José. *Problemas de la Universidad Nacional Autónoma de Mexico.* Mexico City: n.p., 1949.

González A. Alpuche, Juan. *La universidad de México. Su trayectoria socio-cultural.* Mexico City: Asociación Mexicana de Sociología, 1960.

González Calzada, Manuel. *Juventud izquierdista de México. Congreso constituyente de la C.E.S.U.M., Guanajuato, México.* Mexico City: D.A.P.P., 1938.

González Cárdenas, Octavio. *Los cien años de la Escuela Nacional Preparatoria.* Mexico City: Editorial Porrúa, 1972.

González Casonova, Henrique. *La universidad: Presente y futuro.* Mexico City: UNAM, 1972.

González Casanova, Pablo. *El contexto político de la reforma universitaria: Agunas consideraciones sobre el caso de México.* Mexico City: UNAM, 1972.

González Cosío, Arturo. *Historia estadística de la Universidad, 1910–1967.* Mexico City: Instituto de Investigaciones Sociales, UNAM, 1968.

González de Alba, Luis. *Los días y los años.* Mexico City: Ediciones Era, 1971.

González Ramírez, Manuel. "Glosas al pastor." *El Nacional,* June 14, 1948; May 2, 9, 16, 1949; May 20, 1957.

Goodsell, James N. "Mexico: Why the Students Rioted." *Current History* 56 (1969): 31–35, 53.

Gortari, Eli de. "Proposiciones concretas para la Reforma Universitaria." *Historia y Sociedad* (supplement, July–December 1966): 7–9.

——, et al. "La reforma universitaria democrática." *Historia y Sociedad* (supplement, Spring 1966): entire issue.

Gottshalk, E. R. "Catholicism and Catholic Action in Mexico." Ph.D. dissertation, University of Pittsburgh, 1970.

Grompone, Antonio M. *Universidad oficial y universidad viva.* Mexico City: UNAM, 1953.

Guisa y Azevedo, Jesús. "Los del día." *El Nacional,* June 13, 1949.

Guitián Bernisier, Carmen Cira. "Las porras: Estudio de caso de un grupo de presión universitaria." Thesis, UNAM, 1975.

Gutiérrez, Alfredo F. "Veinte años después." *El Universal,* May 21, 1949.

Gutiérrez, Carlos José. "Student Participation in the Government of the University of Costa Rica." *The American Journal of Comparative Law* 17 (1969): 390–394.

Haddox, John H. *Vasconcelos of Mexico: Philosopher and Prophet.* Austin: University of Texas Press, 1967.

Harrison, John P. "Confrontation with the Political University." *The Annals of AAAPSS* 334 (1961): 74–83.

———. "Learning and Politics in Latin American Universities." *Academy of Political Science Proceedings* 27 (1964): 331–344.

———. "The Role of the Intellectual in Fomenting Change: The University." In *Explosive Forces in Latin America*, edited by John TePaske and S. Fisher. Columbus: Ohio State University Press, 1964, pp. 27–42.

Hellman, Judith Adler. *Mexico in Crisis*. New York: Holmes and Meier, 1978.

Hennessy, Alistair. "University Students in National Politics." In *The Politics of Conformity*, edited by Claudio Véliz. London: Oxford University Press, 1967, pp. 119–157.

Hernández, Salvador. *El PRI y el movimiento estudiantil de 1968*. Mexico City: Ediciones El Caballito, 1971.

Hernández Luna, Juan. "Una jornada del maestro Caso en favor de la libertad de cátedra." *Filosofía y Letras* (January–March 1947).

———. "Polémica de Caso contra Lombardo sobre la Universidad." *Historia Mexicana* 19 (July–September 1969): 87–104.

———. "Sobre la fundación de la Universidad Nacional: Antonio Caso vs. Agustín Aragón." *Historia Mexicana* 16 (January–March 1967): 368–381.

Hernández Soto, Narciso. "El Instituto Politécnico Nacional, fruta de la Revolución Mexicana." *El Legionario* (August 1954): 23–25.

Hinojosa, Roberto. *La justicia social en México. Segundo Congreso de Estudiantes Socialistas de México*. Mexico City: CESM, 1935.

Horta, Desiderio. "Quince años de autonomía universitaria." *Así* (November 11, 18, 25, 1944; December 2, 9, 16, 23, 30, 1944; January 6, 13, 1945).

Horta, José. "¡Reclama a su presa un río!" *Así* (December 30, 1944): 34.

Hurtado Márquez, Eugenio, ed. and comp. *La universidad autónoma, 1929– 1944: Documentos y textos legislativos*. Mexico City: Comisión Técnica de Estudios y Proyectos Legislativos, UNAM, 1976.

Ibarra, Alfredo, Jr. "El contenido transcendente de nuestra Revolución." *El Nacional*, November 20, 1944.

Ibarra, Guillermo. "Escuela Nacional Preparatoria." *El Nacional*, January 13, 1949.

Icaza, Xavier. *La tragedia del régimen actual*. Mexico City: Confederación de Estudiantes Socialistas de México, 1935.

"La impunidad estudiantil y la agitación clerical." *El Nacional*, October 5, 1954.

"Informe que rinde la secretaría de la Escuela Nacional de Jurisprudencia acerca de los trabajos hechos en la misma escuela en el año de 1909–1910." *Boletín de Instrucción Pública* 15 (1911): 268, 272.

Innes, John S. "The Universidad Popular Mexicana." *The Americas* (July 1973): 110–122.

"Interesante carta dirigida al señor Ezequiel A. Chávez por el Secretario de Educación Pública." *El Demócrata*, September 20, 1923, reprinted in *Boletín de la Secretaría de Educación Pública* 2 (1924): 283–285.

Islas García, Luis. "Por que deje de ser comunista." *La Nación*, June 10, 17, 1944.

Jiménez Barrios, Rodolfo. "El congreso de la C.N.E." *Diario del Sureste*, September 19, 1936.

Jiménez C., Marta R. "Alumnos irregulares de la ENCEPS." *Revista Ciencias Políticas y Sociales* 8 (July–September 1962): 445–457.

Jiménez Rueda, Julio. "La autonomía de la Universidad: La ley de 1929." *Excelsior*, July 20, 1949.

———. *Historia jurídica de la Universidad de México*. Mexico City: UNAM, 1955.

———. "Narciso Bassols y la educación." *El Nacional*, November 4, 1934.

Johnson, Kenneth. *Mexican Democracy: A Critical View*. Boston: Allyn and Bacon, 1971.

King, Richard, et al. *The Provincial Universities of Mexico*. New York: Praeger, 1971.

Kneller, George F. *The Education of the Mexican Nation*. New York: Columbia University Press, 1951.

Krauze, Enrique. *Caudillos culturales en la Revolución Mexicana*. Mexico City: Siglo XXI, 1976.

"Labores del Departamento Universitario, 1918–1919." *Boletín de la Universidad*, 2 (December 1919): 9–19.

Larroyo, Francisco. "Educación pública en México: La autonomía de la Universidad." *Excelsior*, March 5, 1950.

Ledit, Joseph. *Rise of the Downtrodden*. New York: Society of St. Paul, 1959.

Levy, Daniel C. "University Autonomy in Mexico: Implications for Regime Authoritarianism." *Latin American Research Review* 14 (1979): 129–152.

———. *University and Government in Mexico: Autonomy in an Authoritarian System*. New York: Praeger, 1980.

"Ley constitutiva de la Universidad Nacional de México." *Boletín de Instrucción Pública* 14 (1910): 638–646.

Liebman, Arthur, Kenneth Walker, and Myron Galzer. *Latin American University Students: A Six Nation Study*. Cambridge, Mass: Harvard University Press, 1972.

Lipset, Seymour Martin. "The Political Behavior of University Students in Developing Nations." *Social and Economic Studies* 14 (1965): 35–75.

———. *Students Politics*. New York: Basic Books, 1967.

Lombardo Toledano, Vicente. "¿La enseñanza es una función del Estado o un derecho de los particulares?" *Excelsior*, September 26, 1929.

Lomnitz, Larissa A. de. "Carreras de vida en la UNAM." *Plural* (March 1976): 18–22.

———. "Conflict and Mediation in a Latin American University." *Journal of Inter-American Studies and World Affairs* 19 (August 1977): 315–338.

———. "La antropología de la investigación científica en la UNAM." *In La ciencia en México*, edited by L. Estrada and L. Cañedo. Mexico City: Fondo de Cultura Económica, 1976.

López Cámara, F. *Hacia una concepción dialéctica de la autonomía universitaria.* Mexico City: UNAM, 1974.

Love, Joseph. "Sources for the Latin American Student Movement: Archive of the United States National Student Association." *The Journal of Developing Areas* 1 (1967): 216–226.

"La lucha de los estudiantes por la libertad." *La Nación,* October 3, 1942.

Luján, José M. "Adhesiones y manifestación." *El Universal,* August 17, 1945.

———. "El fin de la huelga." *El Universal,* August 24, 1945.

———. "La huelga de 29." *El Universal,* July 13 and August 3, 10, 17, 24, 1945.

Luna Arroyo, Antonio, ed. *La obra educativa de Narciso Bassols. Documentos para la historia de la educación pública en México.* Mexico City: Editorial Patria, 1934.

Mabry, Donald J. "Manuel Gómez Morín." In *Revolutionaries, Traditionalists, and Dictators in Latin America,* edited by Harold E. Davis. New York: Cooper Square, 1973, pp. 112–118.

———. *Mexico's Acción Nacional: A Catholic Alternative to Revolution.* Syracuse: Syracuse University Press, 1973.

———, and Roderic Camp. "Mexican Political Elites, 1935–1973: A Comparative Study." *The Americas* 31 (April 1975): 452–469.

Macías, José Natividad. "La supresión del Departamento Universitario." *El Universal,* July 11, 1917, reprinted in Jorge Pinto Mazal, *La autonomía universitaria,* pp. 51–54.

Maier, Joseph, and Richard W. Weatherhead, eds. *The Latin American University.* Albuquerque: University of New Mexico Press, 1979.

Martínez Nateras, Arturo, ed. *No queremos apertura, queremos revolución.* Mexico City: Ediciones de Cultura Popular, 1972.

Martínez Suárez, Rodolfo. "La fundación de la Escuela Libre de Derecho." *Excelsior,* October 7, 1955.

Mayo, Gabriel del, ed. *La reforma universitaria,* vol. 6. Buenos Aires: Federación Universitaria de Buenos Aires, 1927.

Mayo, Sebastián. *La educación socialista en México: El asalto a la Universidad Nacional.* Rosario, Argentina: Editorial Bear, 1964.

Medellín, Jorge L. "La vida ejemplar del Ing. Roberto Medellín Ostos." *El Nacional,* March 5, 1950.

Medellín, Roberto. *Reformas a la enseñanza universitaria propuestas a la academias de los profesores y alumnos de las facultades y escuelas universitarias.* Mexico City: UNAM, 1933.

Medina, Gerardo. *Operación 10 de junio.* Mexico City: Editorial Jus, 1972.

"Memorial que los profesores y estudiantes de la Universidad llevan a la H. Cámara de Diputados." *El Universal,* July 28, 1917, reprinted in Jorge Pinto Mazal, *La autonomía universitaria,* pp. 75–82.

Mendieta y Núñez, Lucio. *Ensayo sobre los problemas de la Universidad.* Mexico City: UNAM, 1948.

———. "Ensayo sociológico sobre la universidad." In *Primer Censo Nacional Universitario.* Mexico City: UNAM, 1949.

———. "Grandezas y miserias de la Universidad de México." *El Universal*, October 15, 1952.

———. *Historia de la Facultad de Derecho*. Mexico City: Editorial Porrúa, 1956.

———. *La reforma universitaria integral*. Mexico City: UNAM, 1967.

———. *La universidad creadora y otros ensayos*. Mexico City: Editorial Cultura, 1936.

Mendrichaga Cueva, Tomás. "La Universidad Socialista de Nuevo León." *Humanitás* 9 (1968): 361–388.

"México, 1968: Contra la represión, por la democracia." *Historia y Sociedad* 3, no. 12 (April–June 1968), supplement #5.

Mexico. Cámara de Diputados. *Dictamen que consulta que no es de accederse a la solicitud de la "Confederación Cívica Independiente," relativa a la supresión de la Universidad Nacional y la Escuela de Altos Estudios*. Mexico City: Imprenta de la Cámara de Diputados, 1912.

Meyer, Jean. *La Cristiada*. 3 vols. Mexico City: Siglo XXI, 1973–1974.

Meyer, Lorenzo, with Rafael Segovia and Alejandra Lajous. *Los inicios de la institucionalización. La política del Maximato*, vol. 12 of *Historia de la Revolución Mexicana*. Mexico City: El Colegio de México, 1978.

Michaels, Albert. "The Crisis of Cardenismo." *Journal of Latin American Studies* (May 1970): 51–79.

Millon, Robert P. *Mexican Marxist—Vicente Lombardo Toledano*. Chapel Hill: University of North Carolina Press, 1966.

"Minutero histórico: Se funda la Escuela Libre de Derecho." *El Universal Gráfico*, July 24, 1944.

Molina, Pastor B. *El supuesto conflicto estudiantil y el H. consejo universitario*. Mérida: Imprenta Triay Hnos., 1939.

Monsiváis, Carlos. *Días de guardar*. Mexico City: Ediciones Era, 1970.

Mora, Juan Miguel de. *Tlatelolco 68: ¡Por fin toda la verdad!* 3rd ed. Mexico City: Editores Asociados, 1973.

———. *Todo lo que Ud. siempre quiso saber sobre los conflictos en la UNAM pero se lo habían ocultado*. Mexico City: Editores Asociados, 1977.

Morales Jiménez, Alberto. "La generación del 29 ni está corrompida ni es retrógrada." *El Nacional*, May 2, 1949.

———. "Los de la generación de 1929 son unos fracasados, dijo Rubén Salazar Mallén." *El Nacional*, May 10, 1949.

———. "Los Siete Sabios de 1915 fueron unos equivocados, dice Moreno Sánchez." *El Nacional*, May 4, 1949.

———. "No han permitido actuar a la generación universitaria del año 1919, dice Reynoso." *El Nacional*, May 3, 1949.

———. "Portes Gil es el padre de la autonomía universitaria." *El Nacional*, May 11, 1949.

Moreno, Daniel A. *Presencia de la Universidad, ensayo crítico sobre la ley orgánica de la U.N.A.M., con discusión sobre la ley orgánica de 1933 y la ley orgánica de 1929.* Mexico City: Imprenta Gráficos de Guanajuato, 1948.

Moreno Sánchez, Manuel. "La Universidad de ayer y la de ahora." *Excelsior,* February 28, 1957.

Morton, Ward. *Woman Suffrage in Mexico.* Gainesville: University of Florida Press, 1962.

"The Movement Finds a Cause in Mexico." *Minerva* 7 (Spring 1969): 563–569.

Muñoz Ledo, Porfirio. "La educación superior." In *México: Cincuenta años de Revolución.* Mexico City: Fondo de Cultura Económica, 1963, pp. 406–410.

Myers, Charles N. *Education and National Development in Mexico.* Princeton: Princeton University Press, 1965.

Nacional Financiera. *La economía mexicana en cifras.* Mexico City: Nacional Financiera, 1978.

Navarro Palacios, Enrique. "La juventud de hoy día y el movimiento del 29." *El Universal,* May 16, 1949.

"Nobramiento de profesores de escuelas y facultades universitarias hechos por elección." *Boletín de la Universidad de México,* IV Epoca, Tomo I, no. 1 (August 1920): 69–74.

Noriega, Raúl. "Raúl Noriega y la generación del 29." *El Nacional,* June 10, 1949.

"Objeciones hechas al presidente de la República por el Directorio de Huelga Estudiantil, respecto de la Ley de Autonomía Universitaria." *El Universal,* June 1, 1929, reprinted in Jorge Pinto Mazal, *La autonomía universitaria,* pp. 151–161.

Ocampo V., Tarsicio, comp. *México: Conflicto estudiantil 1968.* 2 vols. Cuernavaca: Centro Intercultural de Documentación, 1968.

——, comp. *México, huelga de la UNAM, marzo-mayo, 1966: Documentos y reacciones de prensa.* Cuernavaca: Centro Intercultural de Documentación, 1967.

Ocaranza, Fernando, *La novela de un médico.* Mexico City: Talleres Gráficos de la Nación, 1940.

——. *La tragedia de un rector. Continuación de la novela de un médico.* Mexico City: Talleres Linotipográficos Numancia, 1943.

——. "Universidad." *La Nación,* April 22, 1944.

Ochoa Campos, Moisés. *Calles: El estadista.* Mexico City: Trillas, 1976.

"Oposición estudiantil al Gral. Díaz." *Excelsior,* November 28, 1937.

Ortega. "Hechos." *El Día,* August 17, 1968.

Ortiz, Orlando, ed. *Jueves de corpus.* Mexico City: Ediciones Diógenes, 1971.

Osborne, Thomas N. III. *Higher Education in Mexico.* El Paso: Texas Western Press, 1976.

Pacheco Calvo, Ciriaco. "La organización estudiantil." *El Universal,* March 20, 27, and April 4, 6, 1934.

——. *La organización estudiantil en México.* Mexico City: Publicaciones de la Conferación Nacional de Estudiantes, 1934.

Palavicini, Félix F. "Proyecto de ley para dar autonomía a la Universidad." *El Universal*, July 14, 1917, reprinted in Jorge Pinto Mazal, *La autonomía universitaria*, pp. 55–62.

Palerm, Angel. "El movimiento estudiantil: Notas sobre un caso." *Comunidad* 4 (1969): 90–102.

Pallares, Eduardo. "La huelga de estudiantes." *El Universal*, June 4, 1929.

Palma, Gabino A. "La universidad mexicana del futuro." *El Universal Gráfico*, September 9, 11, 12, 14, 15, 18, 21, 22, 1933.

Paz, Octavio. *The Other Mexico: Critique of the Pyramid*. Translated by Lysander Kemp. New York: Grove Press, 1972.

Pérez Abreu, Carlos. "La Universidad de México." *El Nacional*, September 26 and October 5, 1946.

Pérez Correa, Fernando. "La universidad: Contradicciones y perspectivas." *Foro Internacional* 14 (1974): 375–401.

Pérez Orozco, Luis. "Sí existe la generación de 1929 y es más brillante que ha producido México." *El Nacional*, May 14, 1949.

Pérez San Vicente, Guadalupe. "La Universidad Nacional Autónoma de México y su documentación histórica." *Boletín del Instituto de Investigaciones Bibliográficas* 2 (July–December 1970): 299–314.

Petersen, John H. "Student Political Activism in Guatemala." *Journal of Inter-American Studies and World Affairs* (January 1971).

Phillips, Richard B. "José Vasconcelos and the Mexican Revolution of 1910." Ph.D. dissertation, Stanford University, 1953.

Pineda, Hugo. "José Vasconcelos, Político Mexicano, 1928–1929." Ph.D. dissertation, George Washington University, 1971.

Pineda, Salvador. "Cuatrocientos años de vida de la Universidad." *Hoy* (September 26, 1951): 18–19.

Pinto Mazal, Jorge. *El Consejo Universitario*. Mexico City: UNAM, Deslinde series, 1973.

———, comp. and ed. *La autonomía universitaria: Antología*. Mexico City: UNAM, 1974.

Poniatowska, Elena. *La noche de Tlatelolco: Testimonios de historia oral*. Mexico City: Ediciones Era, 1973.

Portes Gil, Emilio. *Autobiografía de la Revolución Mexicana*. Mexico City: Instituto México de Cultura, 1964.

———. *Quince años de política mexicana*. Mexico City: Ediciones Botas, 1954.

———. "La verdad sobre la autonomía universitaria." *Así* (November 18, 1944).

"La posición del movimiento estudiantil ante el régimen." *Oposición* 2 (June 15–30, 1971), entire issue.

Prieto, Raúl. "El poder anticubano en México." *El Día*, August 14, 1968.

Prieto Laurens, Jorge. *Cincuenta años de política mexicana: Memorias polí-*

ticas. Mexico City: Editora Mexicana de Libros, Periódicos, y Revistas, 1968.

———. "El verdadero proceso historico estudiantil." *El Universal*, March 28, 1934.

"El primer congreso internacional de estudiantes." *Boletín de la Universidad*, IV Epoca, 3 (December 1921): 59–98.

Pruneda, Alfonso. *Universidad y universitarios*. Mexico City: UNAM, 1942.

Puga, Raúl. "La autonomía de la Universidad Nacional." *Revista de Revistas* (October 22, 1933): 12–14.

Ramírez, Armando. "La revolución universitaria de 1933." *La Nación*, October 10, 1942.

Ramírez, Ramón, ed. *El movimiento estudiantil de México: Julio-diciembre de 1968*. 2 vols. Mexico City: Ediciones Era, 1969.

———, and Alma Chapoy. *Estructura de la UNAM: Ensayo socio-económico*. Mexico City: Fondo de Cultura Popular, 1970.

Ramírez Gómez, Ramón. "Análisis del reciente movimiento estudiantil universitario en México." *Historia y Sociedad* (supplement, July–December 1966): 12–27.

Ramos, Samuel. "Antecedentes de la educación socialista." *Hoy* (July 22, 1939).

"Las representaciones estudiantiles." *Acción Estudiantil* 1 (April 5, 1929): 7.

Retana Méndez, Ricardo. "Calles, Cárdenas, Ávila Camacho y Alemán." *El Universal*, June 19, 1952.

Reyes, Alfonso. *Universidad, política y pueblo*. Mexico City: UNAM, 1967.

Reyes, José María de los. "El movimiento de mayo de 1929." *El Universal*, May 10, 1949.

Rius Facius, Antonio. *La juventud católica y la Revolución Mexicana, 1910–1925*. Mexico City: Editorial Jus, 1963.

Rodríguez, Valdemar. "National University of Mexico: Rebirth and Role of the Universitarios (1910–1957)." Ph.D. dissertation, University of Texas, 1958.

Rodríguez Cambas, Agustín. "La revolución universitaria de México." *El Dictamen*, April 16, 1949.

Rotblat, Miguel. "The Latin American Student Movement." *New University Thought* 2 (1961): 29–36.

Ruiz Castañeda, María Carmen. "El movimiento estudiantil de 1875." *¡Siempre!* (March 2, 1969).

Salazar Mallén, Rubén. "La generación de 1929." *El Universal*, June 15, 22, 29, 1944.

Salazar Viniegra, Leopoldo. "¿Quién empujo a la 29?" *Excelsior*, April 12, 1949.

Sánchez, George I. *The Development of Higher Education in Mexico*. New York: King's Press, 1944.

———. *Mexico: A Revolution by Education*. New York: Viking Press, 1936.

Sánchez, Luis Alberto. "La participación de los alumnos en el gobierno universitario." *Cuadernos Americanos* 47 (September–October 1949): 42–55.

Sanromán, Mario J. "Bodas de plata de la autonomía universitaria." *El Universal*, May 17, 1954.

Scott, Robert E. "Student Political Activism in Latin America." *Daedalus* 97 (1968): 70–98.

Segovia, Rafael. "Mexican Politics and the University Crisis." In *Political Power in Latin America: Seven Confrontations*, ed. Richard Fagen and Wayne A. Cornelius, Jr. Englewood Cliffs, N.J.: Prentice-Hall, 1970.

Sepúlveda, César. "Student Participation in University Affairs: The Mexican Experience." *The American Journal of Comparative Law* 17 (1969): 384–389.

Serrano Castro, Julio. "La generación del 29 y su obra." *El Universal*, May 22, 1949.

Shapira, Yoram. "Mexico: The Impact of the 1968 Student Protest on Echeverría's Reformism." *Journal of Inter-American Studies and World Affairs* 19 (November 1977): 557–580.

Siegrist Clamont, Jorge. *En defensa de la autonomía universitaria. Trayectoria histórico-jurídica de la universidad mexicana.* 2 vols. Mexico City: Editorial Jus, 1955.

————. *El sistema jurídico de la universidad mexicana.* 2 vols. Mexico City: Editorial Jus, 1954.

Sierra, Justo. "La Universidad Nacional (proyecto de creación)." *El Centinela Español*, February 10, 1881, reprinted in Jorge Pinto Mazal, *La autonomía universitaria*, pp. 23–27.

Silva Herzog, Jesús. *Una historia de la Universidad de México y sus problemas.* Mexico City: Siglo XXI, 1974.

Silva Michelena, Héctor, and Heinz Rudolf Sonntag. *Universidad, dependencia y revolución.* Mexico City: Siglo XXI, 1973.

Smith, Peter H. *The Labyrinths of Power: Political Recruitment in Twentieth-Century Mexico.* Princeton: Princeton University Press, 1979.

Soares, Glaucio. "Intellectual Identity and Political Ideology among University Students." In *Elites in Latin America*, ed. Seymour Martin Lipset and Aldo Solari. New York: Oxford University Press, 1967.

Soberón, Guillermo. "La Universidad Nacional Autónoma de México, pasado, presente y futuro." *Revista de la Universidad de México* 28 (July 1974).

Solari, Aldo. "Los movimientos estudiantiles universitarios en América Latina." *Revista Mexicana de Sociología* 29 (October–December 1967): 853–869.

Solís Mimendi, Antonio. *Jueves de corpus sangriento (revelaciones de un halcón).* Mexico City: Imprenta Argo, 1972.

Spencer, David, ed. *The Latin American Student Movement.* Washington: The National Student Association, 1965.

Spota, Luis. "Alemán fue periodista." *Mañana* (January 31, 1948): 29–32.

————. *La Plaza.* Mexico City: Grijalbo, 1977.

Stevens, Evelyn P. *Protest and Response in Mexico.* Cambridge, Mass.: M.I.T. Press, 1974.

Suchlicki, Jamie. *University Students and Revolution in Cuba, 1920–1968.* Coral Gables: University of Miami Press, 1969.

Swadesh T., Mauricio. "La huelga estudiantil a través de unas ventas." *Historia y Sociedad* (supplement, Spring 1966): 10–11.

Tardiff, Guillermo. "Policromias: Liga Nacional de Estudiantes." *El Universal,* May 11, 1962.

Ternán Olguín, Liberato. *Sinaloa: Estudiantes en lucha.* Mexico City: Ediciones de Cultura Popular, 1973.

Testimonio en la muerte de Manuel Gómez Morín. Mexico City: Editorial Jus, 1973.

Tirado, Manlio, et al. *El 10 de junio y la izquierda radical.* Mexico City: Editorial Heteradoxia, 1971.

"El 32 aniversario de la Universidad." *La Nación,* September 26, 1942.

Tomasek, Robert, ed. *Latin American Politics.* 2nd ed. New York: Doubleday, 1970.

Torner, Miguel. "Organizaciones estudiantiles." *Boletín de la Universidad 1* (December 1917): 244–245.

Torres, Angel. "Gómez Morín y Brito Foucher se apoderaron de la Universidad por culpa de García Téllez." *El Nacional,* May 5, 1949.

———. "El movimiento universitario de 1929 ayudó a la extinción del caudillaje." *El Nacional,* May 13, 1949.

———. "Sí hubo generación universitaria en el año 1929, dice Martínez Mezquida." *El Nacional,* May 11, 1949.

Traboulay, David M. "An Institutional and Intellectual History of the University of Mexico and San Marcos, Peru." Ph.D. dissertation, University of Notre Dame, 1970.

Tubio Acuña, Servio. "Discurso." *Gaceta de la Universidad* (March 14, 1960): 4.

Tulchin, Joseph S. "Origins of Student Reform in Latin America: Córdoba, 1918." *Yale Review* 61 (June 1971): 575–590.

Tuohy, William S., and Barry Ames. *Mexican University Students in Politics: Rebels without Allies?* Denver: Social Science Foundation, University of Denver, 1970.

Turner, Frederick C. *The Dynamic of Mexican Nationalism.* Chapel Hill: University of North Carolina Press, 1968.

UNAM (Universidad Nacional Autónoma de México). *Anuario, 1931–1932.* Mexico City: UNAM, 1931.

———, Dirección General De Servicios Sociales. *La población estudiantil universitaria: datos sociales y económicos.* Mexico City: UNAM, 1966.

———. *Estatuto de la Universidad Nacional Autónoma de México.* Mexico City: UNAM, 1936.

———, Facultad de Derecho. *El pensamiento de la juventud en el IV centenario de la Facultad de Derecho.* Mexico City: UNAM, 1953.

———, Facultad de Derecho. *El pensamiento de la juventud en el II concurso nacional de estudiantes de derecho.* Mexico City: UNAM, 1955.

———, Facultad de Derecho y Ciencias Sociales. *Plan de estudios, programas* y reglamentos de reconocimientos en la Facultad de Derecho y Ciencias Sociales. Mexico City: UNAM, 1929.

——. Facultad de Filosofía y Letras. Historia, constitución y guía del estudiante de la Facultad de Filosofía y Letras. Mexico City: UNAM, 1943.

——. Indice de las labores de carácter extraordinario realizados por la Universidad Nacional durante el periodo comprendido entre el 20 de junio de 1942 y el 20 de junio de 1944. Mexico City: UNAM, 1944.

——. Informe, 1910/11. Mexico City: UNAM, 1913.

——. Informe de la Rectoría, 1938–1942. Mexico City: UNAM, 1942.

——. Informe que rinde el rector de la Universidad Nacional Autónoma de México, Febrero de 1939. Mexico City: UNAM, 1939.

——. Instituto de Investigaciones Sociales. Primer censo nacional universitario. Mexico City: UNAM, 1953.

"The University Crisis in Mexico City." Minerva 4 (Summer 1966): 588–590.

Valadés, Diego. La Universidad Nacional Autónoma de México. Mexico City: UNAM, 1974.

Vallado Berrón, Fausto E. Proceso a la Universidad y a los universitarios. Mexico City: Ediciones El Caballito, 1973.

Valle, Rafael Heliodoro, et al. Añoranza del Primer Congreso de Estudiantes (1910). Mexico City: n.p., 1943.

Vasconcelos, José. "La mentira de la autonomía." Novedades, August 11, 1944.

Vásquez de Knauth, Josefina Z. "La educación socialista de los años treinta." Historia Mexicana 18 (January–March 1969): 408–423.

——. Nacionalismo y educación en Mexico. Mexico City: El Colegio de México, 1970.

Vázquez Gómez, Francisco. "Acuerdo por él que se recomienda a los profesores y alumnos de las escuelas dependientes de la Secretaría de Instrucción Pública y Bellas Artes que se abstengan de formar agrupaciones de carácter político." Boletín de Instrucción Pública 18 (1911): 177–178.

Walker, Kenneth H. "Political Socialization in Universities." In Elites in Latin America, ed. Seymour Martin Lipset and Aldo Solari. New York: Oxford University Press, 1967.

Walter, Richard J. Student Politics in Argentina. New York: Basic Books, 1968.

Wences Reza, Rosalio. El movimiento y los problemas nacionales. Mexico City: Editorial Nuestro Tiempo, 1971.

Wilkie, James W., and Edna Monzón de Wilkie, eds. México visto en el siglo XX. Mexico City: Instituto Nacional de Investigaciones Económicas, 1969.

Wing, Juvencio, et al. Los estudiantes, la educación y la política. Mexico City: Editorial Nuestro Tiempo, 1971.

Zarraga, F. "Informe correspondiente a la marcha de la Escuela Nacional de Medicina del 1 de junio de 1910 al 8 de enero de 1912." Boletín de Instrucción Pública 19 (1912): 77–78.

Zea, Leopoldo. La universidad aquí y ahora. Mexico City: UNAM, 1969.

Zermeño, Sergio. *México: Una democracia utopia. El movimiento estudiantil del 68*. Mexico City: Siglo XXI, 1978.

Zúñiga, Horacio. *La universidad, la juventud, la Revolución*. Mexico City: n.p., 1934.

Index